*More Desired than Our
Owne Salvation*

More Desired than Our Owne Salvation

The Roots of Christian Zionism

ROBERT O. SMITH

With a Foreword by Martin E. Marty

To Monica and Jason — with
appreciation for your hospitality and
continued engagement for peace with
justice in the Middle East.

10/2013

OXFORD
UNIVERSITY PRESS

OXFORD
UNIVERSITY PRESS

Oxford University Press is a department of the University of Oxford.
It furthers the University's objective of excellence in research, scholarship,
and education by publishing worldwide.

Oxford   New York
Auckland   Cape Town   Dar es Salaam   Hong Kong   Karachi
Kuala Lumpur   Madrid   Melbourne   Mexico City   Nairobi
New Delhi   Shanghai   Taipei   Toronto

With offices in
Argentina   Austria   Brazil   Chile   Czech Republic   France   Greece
Guatemala   Hungary   Italy   Japan   Poland   Portugal   Singapore
South Korea   Switzerland   Thailand   Turkey   Ukraine   Vietnam

Oxford is a registered trade mark of Oxford University Press
in the UK and certain other countries.

Published in the United States of America by
Oxford University Press
198 Madison Avenue, New York, NY 10016

Library of Congress Cataloging-in-Publication Data
Smith, Robert O. (Robert Owen), 1974–
More desired than our owne salvation : the roots of Christian zionism / Robert O. Smith.
p. cm.
Includes bibliographical references and index.
ISBN 978-0-19-999324-6 (hardcover : alk. paper) 1. Christian Zionism.
2. Apocalyptic literature—History and criticism. 3. England—Church
history—17th century. 4. Eschatology—History of doctrines.
5. Arab-Israeli conflict—Religious aspects—Christianity. I. Title.
DS150.5.S65 2013
261.2'6—dc23
2012042662

1   3   5   7   9   8   6   4   2

Printed in the United States of America
on acid-free paper

For Carrie

We cannot doubte but that the glory of God shall be
wonderfully enlarged
by the conversion of the Iewes, and therefore it may be
more desired then our owne salvation.
                    —Thomas Morton of Berwick (1596)

The sleeping giant of Christian Zionism has awakened;
there are 50 million Christians standing up and
applauding the State of Israel.
If a line has to be drawn, draw the line around
both Christians and Jews;
we are united; we are indivisible.
                    —John Hagee (2007)

Contents

Foreword

"AFFINITY," A KEY term that courses through this book, is a beautiful word that author Robert O. Smith uses frequently and always appropriately to describe a relationship between the people of one sovereign state and a different sovereign state. "Affinity" connotes a natural attraction, a feeling of kinship, a strong connection. The reader who traces the scores of times the noun shows up will find that Smith never once writes of the "popular Christian affinity for Israel" or the "popular American affinity for Israel." Christians who take the Hebrew Scriptures *and* the New Testament—hence, their Bible—seriously cannot *not* have an affinity for Israel. In New Testament usage Israel is the root from which their faith is a branch; Israel is the "elder brother" to people of Christian faith. Smith can take that concept for granted, but it is not what provides the plot of this book.

Instead, emphatically and always, he writes of popular American affinity for the *state* of Israel, an entity that did not exist until 1948, a national unit that the United States recognized from its first day. Insert the word "state" and you are talking about a political phenomenon, and that makes all the difference. The author is consistent to the end. On the last page he quotes Peter Grose in lines that summarize the whole work: "Americans and Israelis are bonded together like no two other sovereign peoples. As the Judaic heritage flowed through the minds of America's early settlers and helped to shape the new American republic, so Israel adopted the vision and the values of the American dream. Each, the United States and Israel, grafted the heritage of the other onto itself."

That is an astonishing but quite demonstrable proposition. Smith comments: "just as apocalyptic hope was realized in human history by the American Revolution, many Americans see the typological referent of American apocalyptic nationalism in the State of Israel." The main articulators of this vision are "Christian Zionists," who—as every serious American politician knows—"seek to marshal resources and influence policy to ensure the preservation of the State of Israel, the typological touchstone without which their individual and collective lives would have no meaning." I have to repeat the judgments "astonishing" and "demonstrable" to stress the importance of the conclusion.

Americans can and many do support Israel for many reasons: democratic affinities, sympathy for the heirs of the Holocaust victims, some strategic interests in Middle Eastern politics, and disdain for or fear of some nations and forces that oppose Israel and more. Yet the engines and engineers of the support for Israel are heirs and embodiments of Anglo-American "Christo-Judaic" beliefs that, as Smith shows with careful historical analysis, developed in sixteenth-century and seventeenth-century English Protestantism. They have, through movements Smith traces with care, been transmuted and survive today: "contemporary Christian Zionism is concerned less with flesh-and-blood Jews than with preserving its own Christian theopolitical hope." By no means do all supporters of the State of Israel attend to this specific theopolitical hope, but failure to see how it lives on in politically powerful modern Evangelicalism can be fatal to political careers. It can leave one unable to comprehend the fervor of millions of non-Jewish supporters of Israel. Needless to say, though this Christian apocalypticism has no home in Judaism or the State of Israel, it is easily exploited by politicians and lobbies who welcome almost anyone who will unquestioningly support Israel.

One wishes politicians and pundits had or took time to read this whole book. Many pages will, on first glance, appear to be arcane, a feast for specialists in Puritan or Fundamentalist history. Yet if they will read the early and the final pages, they will already gain valuable insight into the world of practical politics in America today. The historian in me urges: read on, because between the early and final pages are engrossing and alluring accounts of colorful, desperate, hopeful people in movements whose "isms"—for example, "dispensationalism"—are not likely to be named at precinct or caucus meetings. I have been teaching in these fields for decades, and I have to confess, indeed I happily do confess, that many characters and events that had been unfamiliar now bid for prime attention.

I have to say a word about the tone of the book. Smith could have been satirical and even cynical when dealing with some of these movements. He had a higher purpose than merely entertaining or appealing to readers

who might find it easy to be condescending toward Puritans, dispensationalists, and Christian Zionists. Instead, he mirrors Spinoza, who, when
that philosopher set out to deal with human complexities, wrote that he
came not to laugh or to cry or to denounce, but to *understand*. Smith's is an
elegant essay in understanding, well grounded in historical sources, which
shows alertness to contemporary matters of great moment.

Martin E. Marty
The University of Chicago

Acknowledgments

THIS PROJECT COULD not have been completed without the assistance and encouragement of a broad array of people. The primary source research informing these chapters would not have been possible without the diligent work of librarians at many institutions. I am particularly mindful of staff members at the Baylor University libraries and the Billy Graham Center Archives at Wheaton University. In addition to these fine librarians, the availability of electronic resources is a profound gift for researchers throughout the global north.

I am also grateful for my colleagues in the Evangelical Lutheran Church in America. Rafael Malpica Padilla and Lita Brusick Johnson, recognizing that this work could bring benefit for the Evangelical Lutheran Church in America, allowed me sufficient time to bring it to completion. I am grateful also for the support of Bishop Mark Hanson and our synodical bishops, including Floyd Schoenhals and Bruce Burnside, who have never wavered in their commitment to seeking peace with justice for Israel and Palestine.

I am indebted to Michael West, formerly of Fortress Press, who recommended I take the manuscript to Oxford University Press. Enthusiastic support for the work from Cynthia Read and Charlotte Steinhardt gave me more than one boost of confidence. The production process improved the book greatly. Barry Hankins got the project rolling when he challenged me to locate my analysis in historical research. Hospitality experienced during time with Martin Marty has been appreciated as much as his fine foreword.

Exploring the relationship between the United States and the State of Israel can be a politically risky enterprise. I am grateful for friends and colleagues committed to engaging these questions with sensitivity and nuance. I am grateful for fellow learners, including Santiago Slabodsky, Carmen Lansdowne, Jeffery Roark, and Kevin McDonald. This book has been informed by rich conversations enjoyed during conferences and consultations hosted by the World Council of Churches, thanks to the tireless work of Beatrice Merahi, Michel Nseir, and Olav Fykse Tveit. I have benefited directly from feedback provided by Shanta Premawardhana, Elizabeth Prodromou, Tony Richie, Rabbi Amy Eilberg, and Susannah Heschel. Internationally, my horizons have been expanded through collaboration with Göran Gunner and Jens Nieper, while I have been accompanied by many Arab Christian friends, including Dr. Muna Mushawar, Rev. Mitri Raheb, Fr. Jamal Khader, and Bishop Dr. Munib A. Younan, President of the Lutheran World Federation.

Finally, I express my deepest gratitude to my family. I am grateful to my parents for taking the bold step of moving to Germany in early 1990, immediately after the wall fell in Berlin. Without my experiences in Europe and the gift of attending Frankfurt International School my horizons would not have been expanded to accommodate ideas as broad as the ones I engage here. I am grateful to my spouse, Carrie, who for years has been subjected to these ideas and my resulting late-night attempts to articulate a unified theory of American religion and national identity. Finally, I recognize with gratitude the patience of our sons, Caleb and Zion, who too often lost their father not only to international travel but to the parsonage office so generously gifted by their mother.

*More Desired than Our
Owne Salvation*

Introduction

IN RECENT YEARS, a great deal of popular media and scholarly attention has been focused on politically mobilized support for the State of Israel within the United States. In February 2006, John Hagee, pastor of Cornerstone Church in San Antonio, Texas, unveiled Christians United for Israel (CUFI), an organization intended to be a Christian counterpart to the American Israel Public Affairs Committee (AIPAC), which describes itself as "America's pro-Israel lobby." CUFI's emergence signaled a renewed presence of Christian Zionism on the national stage of American politics and religion. The next month, an essay on "The Israel Lobby" by foreign policy scholars John Mearsheimer and Stephen Walt landed with a thud in the worlds of U.S.-Israel and Jewish-Christian relations.[1] Observing that "the Lobby also includes prominent Christian evangelicals like Gary Bauer, Jerry Falwell, Ralph Reed and Pat Robertson, as well as Dick Armey and Tom DeLay, former majority leaders in the House of Representatives, all of whom believe Israel's rebirth is the fulfilment of biblical prophecy and support its expansionist agenda," Mearsheimer and Walt argued that it has "managed to skew foreign policy . . . far from what the national interest would suggest," while presenting Israel's interests as "essentially identical" to America's own. Awareness of CUFI was widespread; reaction and response to Mearsheimer and Walt was serious and sustained.[2]

Later in 2006, Walter Russell Mead, the Henry A. Kissinger senior fellow for U.S. foreign policy at the Council on Foreign Relations, published an article in *Foreign Affairs* reflecting on American evangelicalism's influence on the shape of U.S. foreign policy, especially concerning the State of Israel. Noting the numerical decline of mainline Christians in the United States, Mead took aim at Mearsheimer and Walt:

Conspiracy theorists and secular scholars and journalists in the United States and abroad have looked to a Jewish conspiracy or, more euphemistically, to a "Jewish lobby" to explain how U.S. support for Israel can grow while sympathy for Israel wanes among what was once the religious and intellectual establishment. A better answer lies in the dynamics of U.S. religion. Evangelicals have been gaining social and political power, while liberal Christians and secular intellectuals have been losing it. This should not be blamed on the Jews.[3]

In response to Mead's widely cited article, James Skillen suggested that while Mead is right to see domestic forces such as evangelical commitments as an element in the formation of U.S. foreign policy, Mead spent too much time "discussing the theological and ecclesiastical beliefs of evangelicals" rather than seeking to "illuminate the religiosity of Americans *as Americans.*" Skillen wrote that the point "at which the particular connection between Americanism and evangelicals . . . becomes truly significant for foreign policy" is the Puritan heritage of Americans seeing themselves as "a city set on a hill to be a light to the nations." This heritage, he said, "is the root that still gives light to the national identity, affecting even those who are not Christians or associated with a house of worship." Evangelical support for the State of Israel "is based on the civil-religious faith that God has chosen America to be the kind of new Israel that helps shepherd the survival of the Jewish state so that Christ's return will come about as prophesied." Therefore, Skillen concludes, it is "more accurate to say that Christian Zionism is a specific kind of political theology arising from within the American civil religion."[4]

Rather than manifesting a manipulation of American interests from any external source, popular American affinity for the State of Israel draws from the taproot of Puritan apocalyptic hope embedded within American identity and national vocation from the prerevolutionary period to the present. Christian Zionism—understood in this book as political action, informed by specifically Christian commitments, to promote or preserve Jewish control over the geographic area now comprising Israel and Palestine—is therefore best understood not as an expression of nineteenth-century theological and political trends but as a political application of this same apocalyptic hope. As Walter Russell Mead wrote in a second corrective of Mearsheimer and Walt, "To understand why U.S. policy is pro-Israel rather than neutral or pro-Palestinian, one must study the sources of nonelite, non-Jewish support for the Jewish state."[5] This book seeks to better comprehend the sources of contemporary American affinity for the State of Israel by elucidating its origins in the English Protestant tradition of Judeo-centric prophecy interpretation and investigating how that tradition was adapted to the American context.

The Israeli-Palestinian conflict has been identified as one of the chief factors perpetuating global instability.[6] Identifying the sources of the conflict's intractability is an important goal for reaching its resolution. This goal, however, can cloud the outcome of the necessary historical investigations into those sources. In the 1930s, Herbert Butterfield critiqued "the whig interpretation of history" that "studies the past with too direct reference to the present day" and that approach's propensity to defeat "the elucidation of the present" by ratifying "whatever conceptions we originally had in regard to our own times." This flattening of past history relative to our own historical locatedness, he wrote, threatens our ability to perceive "those things in which we too are merely relative" as we potentially "lose a chance of discovering where, in the stream of the centuries, we ourselves, and our ideas and prejudices, stand."[7] Given the pressing needs of the current conflict, the temptation to engage in "whiggish" historiography is ever present, for this writer as well as for others.

Explanations of British Protestant support for Jewish Zionist aspirations have been dominated since the mid-1950s by Barbara Tuchman's wide-ranging history, *Bible and Sword: England and Palestine from the Bronze Age to Balfour*, which was a self-conscious effort to support the Zionist cause. A later edition of the book would mock how "Israeli settlements in occupied territory have been virtuously denounced by Americans with short memories of how Texas was settled and then annexed."[8] More recently, Eitan bar-Yosef, in his study of Victorian-era British attitudes toward Jewish restoration to Palestine, has critiqued "accounts of Christian Zionism" influenced by Tuchman's historiography, which "often read like a dot-to-dot drawing, connecting Lord Shaftesbury, George Eliot, and Laurence Oliphant . . . only to reveal, in due course, a neatly sketched draft of the Balfour Declaration."[9]

In both journalistic and scholarly literature, the theological, political, and nationalist movements of the nineteenth century are the most commonly identified sources of both popular American Christian support for the State of Israel and contemporary Christian Zionism. Although some writers—notably British authors such as Victoria Clark, Donald Lewis, and Stephen Sizer—dedicate space in their studies to Puritan thinkers who contemplated the hope of Jewish return to Palestine as a component of Christian end-times hope, these seventeenth-century foundations are often given scant attention in comparison to treatments of their nineteenth-century counterparts or the more pressing concerns of current developments.

This foreshortened historical horizon has diminished the capacity of both scholars and popular writers to comprehend the significance of both contemporary American Christian Zionism and its reception in the American context. In 1918, Shirley Jackson Case famously attempted to dismiss the enduring significance of millenarian thought by explaining its socio-historical appeal in times of political and social struggle.[10] Few studies of popular American Christian support for the State of Israel have progressed far beyond Case's method for explaining the receptivity of American culture to Christian Zionist perspectives. Adopting Case's approach invites the presumption that the popularity of Christian Zionist perspectives results from the introduction of alien concepts into American political discourse. In the same way George Marsden presented fundamentalism as part of the "authentic conservative tradition" of "conversionist evangelicalism,"[11] this book argues that the perspectives propagated by contemporary American Christian Zionism are authentic articulations of the Puritan apocalyptic hope embedded within American identity and national vocation from the prerevolutionary period to the present.

Given this project's expansive historical scope, it is important to note what the book does not seek to cover. First, it is not an attempt to trace the whole of Christian millenarian thought. Leonard Sweet has suggested, for instance, that "the millennial motif in American history must begin not with Old or New England but with Spain, not with John Winthrop aboard the *Arbella* but with Christopher Columbus aboard the *Santa Maria*."[12] As Columbus's diaries show, it was his intention that the gold he sought would finance a crusade to rescue Jerusalem from Muslim rule. While full exploration of this topic is profitable, this project is more specifically focused on Anglo-American Protestant commitments.

The aim of this book is to identify the Judeo-centric tradition of prophecy interpretation that inspired these contemporary expressions rather than provide descriptions and taxonomies of those groups themselves. This limited scope means that many important figures, especially many of the British Protestants, are not discussed. British figures such as John Milton, Isaac Newton, William Blake, William Hechler, Laurence Oliphant, Anthony Ashley Cooper, and Lord Arthur Balfour all deserve fuller treatment than can be provided here. Colleagues familiar with European contexts outside Britain will also notice this project's lack of engagement with the contributions of Pietism to Judeo-centric thought, both in Britain and the United States. This will be a fruitful area for future study. Many readers may also notice that this project does not substantively engage the topic of Jewish political Zionism. Theodor Herzl is mentioned only briefly. The relationship between early Jewish political Zionism and Anglo-American Christian Zionism, although explored by some authors, stands in need of further investigation.

Some may be uncomfortable with the project's focus on the United States. This focus is informed, in part, by the present position of the United States as the world's sole superpower. Christian Zionist political activity—even outside the United States—often closely supports U.S. foreign policy objectives, including the maintenance of military supremacy and protection of the State of Israel. These realities provide sufficient justification for focusing on the possible sources for the foreign policy ideology informing U.S. actions. Following conventional usage I refer to characteristics within the United States as "American" but without the intention of minimizing other national or cultural expressions in the Americas more broadly considered.

Given these concerns about current policy and global projections of American and Israeli power, much more can be said about the current efforts to mobilize Christians throughout the world in support of the State of Israel. The historical trajectory of this project took me away from many elements of my earlier work on the interaction of contemporary Christian Zionism with American culture, theology, and U.S. foreign policy. Indeed, the final product is quite different from what I sought initially to produce. My own understanding of contemporary Christian Zionism has been significantly altered in the process of producing this work. Although my previous research had highlighted the fact that William Blackstone's 1891 memorial had chronologically preceded the publication of Herzl's *Der Judenstaat* in 1896 and that Christian Zionism therefore developed independently from Jewish political Zionism, I had not yet sufficiently explored the tradition's lineage in English and American Protestant history. I hope the history presented here benefits all seeking to more fully comprehend the sources of American affinity for the State of Israel, whether they are critical or supportive of that relationship.

My research establishes that American affinity for the State of Israel, like the tradition of Christian Judeo-centrism itself, is a product of western

Christian motivations rather than external manipulation by Jews. At different points in Anglo-American history, Jewish leaders have come alongside Protestants who hold Judeo-centric views, even when fully aware that these Christians were seeking Christian rather than Jewish ends. In our world, power is necessary to ensure security. It makes sense for those seeking security to seek friends with access to power, especially if those powerful friends have an ideology compelling them to seek the benefit of the weaker party. When Jews have found opportunities to shape the Judeo-centric commitments of Christian friends, those opportunities have often been seized. Such efforts were undertaken by Menasseh ben-Israel in the seventeenth century and have been undertaken by David Brog and Yechiel Eckstein in the twenty-first.

The history presented here nevertheless results in a sobering view of relationships between Christians informed by Judeo-centric apocalyptic hope and Jews seeking the best for their community. The English Protestant tradition of Judeo-centric prophecy interpretation explored here constructed Jews as essentially occidental and, as eventual converts to Protestant faith who would fight the enemies of Christendom, as standing on the correct side of the divide between civilization and savagism. For the English Protestants who originated and refined this theopolitical system in the early seventeenth century, the other side of the divide was populated with the antichristian forces of Catholicism and Islam, embodied in the Pope and the Turk. Pouring Muslims, Catholics, and Jews into its apocalyptic mould and casting them in scripturally determined roles, the English Protestant tradition of Judeo-centric prophecy interpretation traced throughout this book exhorts the cultural heirs of English Puritanism to claim their status as instruments of God's redemption of the world.

I

Blessing the Jew

THE TRAITS OF CONTEMPORARY AMERICAN
CHRISTIAN ZIONISM

IN THE DAYS after the terrorist attacks of September 11, 2001, the most common question among Americans was "why"? During a speech on the floor of the U.S. Senate on December 4, 2001, Senator James Inhofe (R-OK), describing himself as a "born-again Christian," shared his belief that 9/11 was a "satanically inspired attack against America created by demonic powers through the perverted minds of terrorists." Although some analysts had been speculating that U.S. support for the State of Israel had piqued Muslim anger and sparked the attacks, Inhofe, after a detailed reflection on the American Revolution and America's place as "the beacon of hope" and "the beacon of freedom" for the world, concluded that "America was attacked because of our system of values. . . . It is not just because we are Israel's best friend." Nevertheless, Inhofe claimed that "One of the reasons God has blessed our country is because we have honored his people. Genesis 12:3 says: I will bless them who bless you. I will curse him who curses you. This is God talking about Israel."

For Senator Inhofe, the United States and the State of Israel were struggling together in the same fight against the same enemy, an enemy that attacked both of them because it hated the basic character they shared. "Israel is under attack in the Middle East because it is the only true democracy that exists in the Middle East," Inhofe continued. "It has a Western form of government based on the laws we see in the Bible. The laws of God that our country is based on are the same laws from which Israel gets its law. It represents the laws of God. That is the reason it is under attack." Inhofe then offered "seven things I consider to be indisputable and incontrovertible evidence and grounds to Israel's right to the land. You have heard this before, but it has never been in the RECORD." The seventh point is the most salient: "Because God said so." Citing Genesis 13:14–17, Inhofe shared how Abram pitched his tent near Hebron, "where God appeared to Abram and said, 'I am giving you *this* land,' the *West Bank*." For Inhofe, therefore, Arab rejection of Israel's right to the land "is not a political battle at all. It is a contest over whether or not the word of God is true."[1]

Among the several notable characteristics of Senator Inhofe's speech is his elucidation of the shared Israeli and American struggle against their common enemy of "Islamic fundamentalist terrorism" by appealing to the shared biblical origins of their governmental systems. The effect of the speech is a conception of American and Israeli interests as identical or, at least, symbiotic. For Inhofe, as expressed in this speech, defending Israel is as important as defending the United States.

Israel's right to the territory it occupied during its 1967 war was defended again in a May 2002 television interview by then-U.S. House Majority Leader Dick Armey (R-TX). In response to a bill introduced in the House concerning the Israeli-Palestinian conflict, Armey repeatedly advocated emptying the West Bank of its indigenous population, reserving the land exclusively for the State of Israel. While Armey said he was "perfectly content to have a Palestinian state," he was not "content to give up any part of Israel for that purpose of that Palestinian state." Therefore, he explained, he was "content to have Israel grab the entire West Bank" to "have Israel occupy that land that it now occupies and to have those people who have been aggressors against Israel retired to some other arena."[2] When he clarified his thoughts the next day, Armey explained his proposal as a security measure in light of ongoing terrorist threats. "Let me be clear," he wrote. "Israel is fighting the same war on terrorism that we are fighting."[3]

When Armey's successor as House Majority Leader, Tom DeLay (R-TX), spoke at the Israeli Knesset building in July 2003, he greeted his Israeli audience by saying, "I stand before you today, in solidarity, as an Israeli of the heart." Saying that "the solidarity between the United States and Israel is deeper than the various interests we share," DeLay promised Israel, "We hear your voice cry out in the desert, and we will never leave your side." DeLay then described his worldview: "Freedom and terrorism will struggle—good and evil—until the battle is resolved. These are the terms Providence has put before the United States, Israel, and the rest of the civilized world. . . . Israel's liberation from Palestinian terror is an essential component of that victory." His concluding expression of hope was that, "One day . . . free men the world over—whether of the cross, the crescent, or the Star of David—will stand with Israel in defiance of evil."[4]

American discourse concerning the Israeli-Palestinian conflict is saturated with a blend of theology and politics that serves to reinforce both American nationalism and the "special relationship" with the State of Israel that has characterized American foreign policy since Israel's founding in 1948. Although these three perspectives were voiced by Republican leaders, leaders in the Democratic Party are just as committed to these ideas. President Jimmy Carter (D-GA), whose 2006 book, *Palestine: Peace Not Apartheid*, fomented a great deal of controversy, said in 1978 that "the establishment of the nation of Israel is the fulfillment of biblical prophecy and the very essence of its fulfillment."[5] In a 2008 speech while seeking the presidency, Senator Barack Obama (D-IL) said plainly, "I have been a stalwart friend of Israel . . . their security is sacrosanct."[6] Even these Democrats seem to take their foreign policy cues from Rev. Jerry Falwell, who once said, "There's nothing that would bring the wrath of the Christian public in this country down on this government like abandoning or opposing Israel in a critical matter."[7]

As both Senator Inhofe's Bible commentary and President Carter's public comment on prophecy show, pro-Israel sentiment is a strong element in American faith and life. It is a religious impulse, both of popular evangelical faith and American civil religion or Americanism, described by one writer as the fourth great western religion.[8] Former CIA analyst Kathleen Christison has observed that, soon after the United States voiced its support for the State of Israel in 1948, the "entire Palestinian-Israeli issue . . . became something of a zero-sum equation in which support for Israel precluded support for any aspect of the Palestinian position." In a time when the horrors of the Holocaust were fully coming to light, Palestinian resistance to U.S. and Israeli policy came to be seen as not only "uncooperative" but as "immoral."[9] In American political discourse, fundamental presumptions about Israel's innocence and the collective immorality of Palestinians have been conflated with general suspicions of Islam, suspicions developed throughout western Christian history and thrown into sharp relief by the events of 9/11.[10]

Nimrod Novik, who served as foreign policy adviser to Shimon Peres, observed in 1986 that "The more unanimous the [American Jewish] community is in its support for a given Israeli position, the more likely it is to mobilize effectively its political resources in order to try and prevent American policymakers from undermining that position." From the beginnings of the Zionist movement in the nineteenth century, however, American Jewish support for Israel has never been consistently strong.[11]

Novik, advising Israeli leaders on how to maintain strong support in the United States, urged them to promote "the idea of the two-dimensional link between the US and Israel: first, the cultural-ideological-moral affinity; second, Israel's potential and actual contribution to American interests."[12] Because Americans are generally unaware of the full spectrum of strategic American interests, Israel's "actual contribution" to those interests is rarely a topic of political discourse. However, political discourse regarding the State of Israel is filled with expressions of Novik's "cultural-ideological-moral affinity." Historically, American religious impulses to support the State of Israel—whether emanating from Christian biblical interpretation or expressions of American civil religion—involve emphases of Israel's status as a natural ally of the United States against our shared threats, including Communism and, especially since 9/11, "Islamic fundamentalist terrorism."

The Enduring Witness of Contemporary American Christian Zionism

This book attempts to trace the development and political effects of the Anglo-American Protestant tradition of Judeo-centric prophecy interpretation. The above examples demonstrate the extent to which this tradition has permeated American political discourse, with the effect of reinforcing American Christian relationships with Jews, perceived through the lens of the State of Israel, while tarnishing relationships with Muslims, perceived most recently through the lenses ground by the "war on terror" announced by President George W. Bush nine days after 9/11.[13] The next chapter will explore the prevalence of pro-Israel attitudes among Americans. Special attention will be given to the ways religious conviction and sentiment informs those attitudes in ways that preserve the "cultural-ideological-moral affinity" the United States has for the State of Israel.[14] In this chapter, we will become familiar with the rhetoric and purposes of contemporary American Christian Zionism, especially in its most recently organized form, Christians United for Israel (CUFI), and its founder, Pastor John Hagee.

Events surrounding the State of Israel have been formative for many of today's evangelical leaders. John Hagee recounts how in May 1948 "my father's eyes filled with tears" when, on the kitchen radio, he heard about President Truman's recognition of the "new State of Israel." His father said, "Son, today is the most important day of the twentieth century. God's promise to bring the Jewish people back to Israel is being fulfilled before our eyes."[15] Similarly, Richard Land, president of the Ethics and Religious Liberty Commission of the Southern Baptist Convention, recalls how, during the Suez crisis of 1956, his mother, listening to a radio report,

> called me into the kitchen while she was making supper . . . and said, "God blesses those who bless the Jews, and God curses those who curse the Jews. If America blesses the Jews, God will bless America." And then she said, "If you want to know what cursing looks like, Richard, you remember you saw the film of the planes over Germany in June of 1945. That is what happens when you curse the Jews."[16]

These two kitchen-table conversations illustrate the depth to which pro-Israel sentiment permeated popular American consciousness by 1948 and 1956. It is unreasonable to think that the process that led to this consciousness began in 1948 alone or even with the advent of Jewish political Zionism in the late nineteenth century. For these young evangelicals, the State of Israel was God's own creation, protected by the diplomatic and military might of the United States.

For many American evangelicals, the prophetic significance of 1948 was augmented by Israel's expansion in 1967, culminating in its occupation of East Jerusalem, including the Old City and the Temple Mount. The next month, the editor of the evangelical magazine *Christianity Today* offered this reflection: "That for the first time in more than 2000 years Jerusalem is now completely in the hands of the Jews gives a student of the Bible a thrill and a renewed faith in the accuracy and validity of the Bible." The pages of *Christianity Today* marveled at Israel's military prowess and assured their readers that Israel's wars—defensive or offensive—were God's will.[17]

This enduring affinity for the State of Israel, mixed with Cold War fears of nuclear annihilation and profound shifts in cultural mores, propelled Hal Lindsey's 1970 book, *The Late Great Planet Earth*, to great popularity. Still in print after reported sales of over 35 million copies, the book has been translated into several languages. Essentially, the book is a popularized expression of eschatological speculation and social analysis from the perspective of premillennial dispensationalism, the interpretive system Lindsey learned as a student at Dallas Theological Seminary. Lindsey and his coauthor, Carole Carson, saw "the revival of Mystery, Babylon" in the late-1960s trends of "astrology" and "also in spiritism, a return to the supernatural, and in drugs." Suspicion of Islam and veiled references to Roman Catholicism run throughout the book, especially in the chapter "Sheik to Sheik" and their description of the "harlot, as described in Revelation" as Rome, the city of the Antichrist's religious system. By insisting that it will be "through an ingenuous settlement of the Middle East problem that the Antichrist will make good his promise to bring peace to a world terrified by war," Lindsey and Carlson sought to theologically reinforce aspersions cast both on efforts to reach a negotiated settlement to the Israeli-Palestinian conflict and on the global governance necessary for such a settlement to endure.[18] Following the tradition popularized by Lindsey, the Antichrist of the *Left Behind* novels is introduced as the General Secretary of the United Nations.[19]

The alliance between Israel and evangelical leaders in the United States has been a matter of public display since the 1980s. This representative publicness is manifested annually during the Jewish holiday of *Sukkot* (the Festival of Tabernacles):

> Since 1981 every Israeli prime minister has made an annual political pilgrimage to receive the blessings—and the often noisy prayers— of 4000 Christians apparently eager to endorse almost everything Israel does. Whether for Begin, Shamir, Peres, or Rabin, standing ovations have been given every time, a pleasant contrast to the often cacophonous greetings the leaders receive during Knesset debates.[20]

The only exception came in 1999 when Ehud Barak did not address the gathering, much to the chagrin of the event's organizers. Former and future Prime Minister Netanyahu and Jerusalem Mayor Ehud Olmert were more than willing, however, to correct the oversight.[21] Likud efforts to establish and strengthen ties with American evangelicals were inaugurated with Menachim Begin's well-documented relationship with Jerry Falwell.[22] The most conspicuous contribution evangelical politics have made to American public life is the promotion of unwavering U.S. support for the State of Israel.

The "Selfish Reason" of Christian Zionism

Political cooperation between American evangelicals and Israeli politicians builds on a shared commitment to both American and Israeli exceptionalism and the belief that any effort to limit Israel's ability to defend itself contradicts the interests of both Israel and the United States. Even modest proposals to move toward a final settlement with Palestinians and Israel's other Arab neighbors brings strong opposition. American Christian Zionists mobilized against President Bush's endorsement of the "Roadmap" for peace introduced in April 2003 by the Quartet (the United States, Russia, the European Union, and the United Nations).[23] "Because of their apocalyptic interpretation of the Bible, they view the initiative as a betrayal," evangelical scholar Randall Balmer observed in July 2003. "They've threatened to derail the whole thing."[24]

One effort at derailing the Roadmap came from Christian Zionist policy analyst Michael Evans. Evans has been a perpetual behind-the-scenes presence in the Christian Zionist movement since the 1981 publication of *Israel: America's Key to Survival*.[25] That book cover featured a scimitar engraved with Arabic held by a hand wearing a Soviet, hammer-and-sickle ring, ripping through the joined flags of the United States and the State of Israel. In his 2003 book, *Beyond Iraq*, Evans makes clear his opposition to the Roadmap for Peace along strict lines of Christian Zionist commitment. Evans accuses the "liberal" State Department of engaging in a conspiracy, under cover of the Global War on Terror, to force "tiny Israel, our most trusted ally in the region, to pay the bill of appeasement" with a land-for-peace arrangement.[26]

Although justifying the war in Iraq because "Christianity differs from Islam as day differs from night," Evans characterized the process leading to the formal release of the Roadmap as a "theater of the absurd and festival of hypocrisy." Instead of "forcing" Israel to enter into a land-for-peace settlement, Evans argues that "both the Old and New Testaments make abundantly clear that Christians must support Israel in every possible way." Additionally, Evans identifies Genesis 12:3 as a "selfish reason" Christians should support Israel: "I will bless those who bless you, and the one who curses you I will curse." The point Evans wishes to make is clear: "When we support Israel we are supporting the only nation that was created by an act of God. We are declaring that the Bible is true. . . . Yet if we touch Jerusalem, which is prophecy, America will lose the blessing of God and America will tragically lose the war on terrorism."[27]

Christian Zionist opposition to giving any control of the Holy Land to Palestinians was apparent in Pat Robertson's televised criticisms of Israeli Prime Minister Ariel Sharon. Many Christian Zionists had expressed shock and surprise when Sharon, long a champion of Israel's religiously-motivated settlers, announced Israel's unilateral "disengagement" from the Gaza Strip.[28] The removal of Israeli settlers was undertaken in August 2005. On January 4, 2006, Sharon was incapacitated by a massive stroke. On his *700 Club* television show the next day, Robertson, invoking Joel 3:2, pronounced that although Sharon was "very likeable," the prophet Joel tells us that "God has enmity against those who 'divide my land.'" Robertson added that the 1995 assassination of Prime Minister Yitzhak Rabin was "the same thing." Sharon, Robertson concluded "was dividing God's land, and I would say woe unto any prime minister of Israel who takes a similar course to appease the E.U., the United Nations or United States of America. God said, 'This land belongs to me, you better leave it alone.'" The remarks drew immediate condemnation from Israel's ambassador to the United States, from the White House, and from several American Jewish organizations. "His remarks are un-Christian and a perversion of religion," said an Anti-Defamation League (ADL) statement. "It is pure arrogance for Robertson to suggest that he has divine knowledge of God's intent and purpose based on his interpretation of scripture."[29]

Although many would view Robertson's analysis of Sharon's stroke as morally repugnant, it would never occur to him that seeking scriptural discernment of God's intent and purpose would be arrogant. Prophetically informed critiques of public life, long a feature of the American religious landscape, are central to the Judeo-centric foundations of American identity that inform Christian Zionism. Inherited from the critical nationalism of English Puritans—developed especially in Thomas Brightman's identification of England as Laodecia, as will be discussed in Chapter Four—the American Jeremiad simultaneously emphasizes both national shortcoming and exceptionalism.[30] Again on the *700 Club* program, soon after 9/11, Jerry Falwell claimed that unless Americans repented from the sins of secularism, God would continue "to lift the curtain and allow the enemies of America to give us probably what we deserve."[31]

CUFI founder John Hagee interprets human experience through the same national-covenantal lens. When in 2006 Hagee was asked about Hurricane Katrina, he explained that because of a scheduled gay pride parade "New Orleans had a level of sin that was offensive to God" and that "Hurricane Katrina was, in fact, the judgment of God against the city of New Orleans."[32] Hagee has also modeled positive applications of the Jeremiad. He promises readers of *Jerusalem Countdown* (2006) that "When you do things to bless the Jewish people and the State of Israel, God will bless you" since "the scriptural principle of personal prosperity is tied to blessing Israel and the city of Jerusalem." In addition to emphasizing this personal level of support, Hagee reifies the logic of the Jeremiad into a principle against which all countries will be judged. Citing Genesis 12:3 to emphasize that "God promises to punish the nations that come against Israel," Hagee says that "America, the Arabs, the European Union, the United Nations, Russia, China—indeed, all nations—are in the valley of decision. Every nation that presumes to interfere with God's plan for Israel, including the United States, stands not only against Israel but ultimately against God. God is rising to judge the nations of the world based on their treatment of the State of Israel."[33]

In the Deuteronomic perspective of the American Jeremiad, God's blessings on individuals and nations are determined by faithful adherence to moral codes. Most adherents of contemporary American Christian Zionism identify support for the State of Israel as the primary arbiter of faithfulness to God's will for the United States and the other countries of the globe. As Michael Evans says openly and Richard Land's mother knew well, Genesis 12:3 provides a "selfish reason" for supporting the State of Israel. It is the key to unlocking God's blessings and protection for yourself and your country.

John Hagee and "God's Foreign Policy"

Founded in 2006, Christians United for Israel (CUFI) is a highly organized and mobilized political organization. Emulating the American Israel Public Affairs Committee, CUFI envisions itself as a "Christian AIPAC."[34] CUFI's policy recommendations stand within CUFI's larger policy perspective on the Israeli-Palestinian conflict. "The stated purpose of CUFI is to support Israel in matters related to our understanding of the Bible," James Hutchens, a CUFI regional leader, has said. "The implications of that include the fact that we do not support a two-state solution; we do not support 'land for peace.'"[35]

CUFI policy recommendations reflect the views of its founder, John Hagee. While introducing CUFI to the Jewish community, Hagee made his policy preferences clear: "I would hope the United States would join Israel in a military preemptive strike to take out the nuclear capability of Iran for the salvation of Western civilization," he said. "I don't believe that the Islamofascist mentality will ever respond favorably to diplomacy. Their agenda is the destruction of Israel and death to Jews and Christians."[36] During a dinner addressed by the Israeli ambassador to the United States during Israel's 2006 bombardment of Lebanon (precipitated by Hezbollah missile attacks), Hagee said the conflict was "a battle of good and evil" and reminded his audience that American support for the State of Israel was "God's foreign policy."[37]

The 2007 AIPAC policy conference featured Hagee at center stage. To wild applause and in themes familiar to all Christian Zionists, Hagee presented the CUFI program and sought to undermine any momentum toward a land-for-peace arrangement for the establishment of a Palestinian state:

> I am concerned that in the coming months yet another attempt will be made to parcel out parts of Israel in a futile effort to appease Israel's enemies in the Middle East. I believe that misguided souls in Europe, I believe that the misguided souls in the political brothel that is now the United Nations and sadly—and sadly even our own State Department will try once again to turn Israel into crocodile food.[38]

Previously, he had written that since the early 1970s "the United Nations has been transformed into a propaganda platform for the enemies of the United States and Israel."[39] In the right context, calling support for Israel's "God's foreign policy" can sound quaint. Doing so while holding conferences addressed by sitting United States senators (including Joseph Lieberman, Rick Santorum, and Sam Brownback), addressed by Israeli political leaders like Shimon Peres and Benjamin Netanyahu, and featuring a "Middle East Briefing" presented by former CIA director James Woolsey and former Israel Defense Forces Chief of Staff Moshe Ya'alon, indicates a movement with potentially far-reaching implications for global well-being.

A "Veteran Bigot"? Hagee on Catholicism, Islam, and Arabs

John Hagee became a truly national figure in 2008 with his endorsement of Senator John McCain (R-AZ) during the Republican presidential primaries. Hagee clarified that his support for Israel was not based in any apocalyptic scenario, while McCain emphasized the endorsement's foreign policy element: "I think he's a fine leader and I appreciate his commitment to Israel." Controversy erupted in short order, with most attention being focused on Hagee's anti-Catholic statements. William Donohue, president of the Catholic League for Religious and Civil Rights, who had already described Hagee as a "veteran bigot," commented that "for the past few decades, [Hagee] has waged an unrelenting war against the Catholic Church." The League took issue with Hagee's association of the Roman Catholic Church with the "great whore" of Revelation and historical constructions like his claim in his 2006 book, *Jerusalem Countdown*, that "the sell-out of Catholicism to Hitler began not with the people but with the Vatican itself. . . . The priests obeyed the bishops and the parishioners fell in line."[40] The next year, Hagee wrote that the teachings of "the Roman church fathers . . . sponsored the Crusades, the Inquisition, and ultimately produced the Holocaust."[41]

Although Hagee unsuccessfully sought to clarify his remarks, Donohue dropped the controversy after Hagee sent a letter of apology correcting his past statements regarding Catholic complicity in the Holocaust. But the damage was done. The controversy prompted journalists to dig further into Hagee's statements and beliefs. McCain repudiated Hagee's endorsement only after video recordings showed Hagee preaching that God used the Holocaust to drive European Jews into Israel. Theology that excluded Catholics while accommodating the Holocaust did not help build a broad coalition.[42] During the race to determine the Republican presidential nominee for the 2012 election, Hagee opened a political rally for Texas Governor Rick Perry, whom he compared to Abraham Lincoln.

At the same time he rejected Hagee's endorsement, McCain declined support from Ohio televangelist Rod Parsley. Although McCain had once described Parsley as "a moral compass, a spiritual guide," he distanced himself once Parsley's description of Islam as "a conspiracy of spiritual evil" and "the greatest religious enemy of our civilization and the world" was revealed. According to Parsley, 9/11 was only one skirmish in "a war between Islam and Christian civilization . . . raging for centuries." Citing the teachings of Jonathan Edwards and early conflicts with Barbary pirates, Parsley claimed that "America has historically understood herself to be a bastion against Islam in the world . . . founded with the intention of seeing this false religion destroyed." His message for the United States is clear: "I do not believe that our nation can truly fulfill its divine purpose until we understand our historical conflict with Islam."[43]

Although McCain's rejection of Hagee had more to do with the CUFI founder's views on Catholics and the Holocaust, Hagee also has definite views on Islam and Muslims. In keeping with Parsley's narrative of civilizational opposition between Islam and the United States, Hagee's biblical extrapolation of the causes of the Israeli-Palestinian conflict understands

Muslims, especially Arabs, to be irredeemable opponents of God's will. "The conflict between Arabs and Jews goes deeper than disputes over land," he wrote in 1996. "It is theology. It is Judaism versus Islam." In a perspective that recalls nineteenth-century ethnographic arguments about the irreducibility of racial difference, Hagee recounts that since "the people of Israel are descended from Isaac" and "the people of the Arab nations descended from Ishmael," the "competition that existed in Abraham's household exists today."[44]

While many public figures have sought to distinguish between the fanaticism of terrorists and the Muslim mainstream, Hagee insisted after 9/11 that all should "recognize that the Islamic terrorists are not fanatics—but devout followers of Muhammad who are following his example and doing what their Islamic Bible teaches them to do." In a summary statement concerning the Israeli-Palestinian conflict, Hagee echoes Senator Inhofe's assessment by saying "this is a religious war that Islam cannot—and must not—win."[45] In his March 2007 speech to the AIPAC Policy Conference, Hagee located this struggle with Muslims in "radical Islam's blood—blood-thirsty embrace of a theocratic dictatorship that believes they have a mandate from God to kill Christians and Jews."[46] Thus, in his apocalyptic vision, Hagee deploys the concept of Islamo-fascism to indict Muslims with Nazi motives. Arabs will join with Russians to spark the battle of Armageddon because "they believe that the Islamic fanatical vision of exterminating the Jews can be realized with Russia's help." In Hagee's vision, however, this "evil axis of power" between "Russia and its Islamic allies is going to be the most powerful object lesson the world has seen since Pharaoh and his army were drowned in the Red Sea." The practical effect of Hagee's view that Israel/Palestine is locked in a religious conflict between the irreducible opponents of Judaism and Islam is that God has racially excluded Palestinians from any claim on the land. "God gave the title deed for the land of Israel to Abraham, Isaac, Jacob and their descendents 'forever,'" Hagee says. "Ishmael, father of Arabs, was excluded from the title deed to the land in Genesis 17:19–21. Therefore, modern-day Palestinians have no biblical mandate to own the land."[47]

In addition to negating any right Palestinians in Israel and the occupied Palestinian territories have to the land in which they now reside, Hagee is fond of using the image of a "royal land grant" and pointing out that "when Messiah comes, Israel will gain control of every square inch of the promised land given by God to Abraham and the Jewish people for an everlasting possession." These square inches include "all of present-day

Israel, including Jerusalem, Lebanon, the West Bank of Jordan, and most of Syria, Iraq, and Saudi Arabia."[48] Believing that portions of the Middle East were given to Jews as a "royal land grant" means that questioning the State of Israel's right to the land it desires—even if your family has been living there for centuries—is an immoral challenge to God's will.

Unlike Hagee's views on Catholics and the Holocaust, his perceptions of Islam and Arabs have not garnered much criticism in political circles. One exception is Rep. Betty McCollum (D-MN), who in April 2007 rejected an invitation to speak at a regional CUFI event. In her letter to the event organizer, Rep. McCollum asserted, with documentation, that several "well publicized statements by Pastor Hagee demonstrate extremism, bigotry and intolerance that is repugnant." According to Rep. McCollum, Hagee's "toxic statements pollute the environment of peaceful religious coexistence, cooperation and respect that we strive to achieve in America, and especially in Minnesota, among Christians, Jews, Muslims and people of all faiths."[49]

Hagee, Jews, and the Question of Conversion

As Christians United for Israel was unveiled, John Hagee underwent an intensive vetting process with several prominent Jewish leaders in the United States. In November 2005, Abraham Foxman, director of the Anti-Defamation League, had publicly criticized conservative Christian efforts to shape American life and culture: "Their goal is to implement their Christian worldview," he wrote. "To Christianize America. To save us!" During the same month, Rabbi Eric Yoffie, president of the Union for Reform Judaism, criticized Christian "zealots" for focusing on "anti-gay bigotry" rather than more pressing social needs. Conservative Christian reaction to this rhetoric was strong, with one leader warning that evangelicals might "get fed up with this and say, 'Well, all right then. If that's the way you feel, then we just won't support Israel anymore.'"[50] By January 2007, after almost a full year of CUFI operation, Foxman had come around. While "there are elements in the Evangelical community who would like to impose Christianity by government edict," he said in a *Time Magazine* editorial, "we welcome and encourage Evangelical support for Israel, particularly at a time when there are serious threats to the Jewish State."[51]

Evangelical support for the State of Israel has been a source of either concern or ambivalence for Jews who support Israel. As Christian Zionists prepared to participate in Sukkot festivities in Israel for 2007, news broke that Israel's chief rabbinate had ruled that Jews should shun the event because, according to Rabbi Simcha Hacohen Kook, chief rabbi of Rehovot, "there are participants in this conference who convert Jews to Christianity and perform missionary activity throughout the year."[52] Given concerns for communal continuity, Jews have long been concerned about Christian missionary activity.[53] These concerns are not enough to keep many Jews from accepting evangelical support. As former AIPAC researcher Lenny Davis once said, "Sure, these guys give me the heebie-jeebies. But until I see Jesus coming over the hill, I'm in favor of all the friends Israel can get."[54] Although Rabbi Jack Moline doesn't like "his politics or his theology," he is still able to work with Hagee. "I'll be happy to talk about the theological context after we achieve a safe and secure Israel."[55] Hagee matches Moline's political pragmatism with doctrinal malleability. Although he has been clear that CUFI does not sponsor or condone proselytizing, he has sought to thread the needle between his Jewish and evangelical audiences on the question of whether or not Jews need Jesus to be in right relationship with God.

In 2006, the *Jerusalem Post* reported that Hagee and Rabbi Aryeh Scheinberg, also of San Antonio, had convinced fundamentalist leader Jerry Falwell that Jews did not need to have faith in Jesus to enjoy salvation. Falwell, who then sat on the CUFI board, countered, calling the claim "categorically untrue."[56] Falwell had earlier criticized Hagee for holding to a "dual covenant" theology in which Jews and Christians have separate but equal paths to God. Hagee has repeatedly insisted that he does not believe that. Nevertheless, he is equally insistent that Jews ought not to be objects of Christian proselytizing. Doing so would be an expression of "replacement theology" or supersessionism, the doctrinal belief that Judaism has been superseded by Christianity and that Jews have no further mission in the world. Hagee's doctrinal pragmatism, informed by his commitments to premillennial dispensationalism, allows him to find a different way forward.

In his 2006 book, *Jerusalem Countdown*, Hagee takes a strong stand against replacement theology: "Paul makes it very clear that the root of the tree is Jewish, and many natural branches (the Jewish people) are yet attached to the olive tree. Israel has a prominent and equal place in the economy of God forever. Paul's description demolishes replacement theology." What Hagee puts in its place, however, keeps Jesus squarely at the center of Jewish suffering and redemption. Hagee highlights "the promises of redemption to be fulfilled by Messiah, who is Jesus Christ" and offers eighteen annotated comparisons between Jesus and Moses that establish them "as God's appointed vessels to the nation of Israel." In the coming global tumult known as the Tribulation, the vast majority of unbelievers, including Jews, will perish. Nevertheless, some Jews will survive: "God promises that by His sovereign grace a 'remnant' would be saved by the grace of God, a group of survivors who have the opportunity to receive Messiah, who is a rabbi known to the world as Jesus of Nazareth." Most Jews, Hagee says, cannot convert now, before the Tribulation, because "God, by His own hand," has caused "divine blindness concerning the identity of Messiah to come upon the Jewish people." Jews "have been judicially blinded to the identity of Messiah."[57]

Between *Jerusalem Countdown* and 2007's *In Defense of Israel*, written after CUFI's founding, there was a dramatic shift in Hagee's identification of the Messiah. Following his spirited argument against the medieval logic that Jews, as a people, are responsible for Jesus' crucifixion and thus are to be persecuted, Hagee sets out to prove that Jews did not reject Jesus as their messiah. This was a new doctrinal facet for Hagee, who was in the process of being embraced by a new group of Jewish friends. In contrast to his book the previous year, one of Hagee's first proofs is a distinction between Jesus and Moses: "If God intended for Jesus to be the Messiah of Israel, why didn't he authorize Jesus to use supernatural signs to prove he was God's Messiah, just as Moses had done?" Several of Hagee's concluding statements present his point well: "The Jews were not rejecting Jesus as Messiah; it was Jesus who was refusing to be the Messiah to the Jews." "He refused to be their Messiah, choosing instead to be the Savior of the world." "The Jews did not reject Jesus as Messiah; it was Jesus who rejected the Jewish desire for him to be their Messiah." The conclusion Hagee draws from all of this argumentation is that the Gospel of Jesus (not quite the Christ) was intended for Gentiles alone: "That's why the Great Commission commanded, 'Go ye [Jews] into all the world and preach the gospel to every creature . . . ' Gentiles were considered creatures. Jesus even referred to the Gentiles as dogs. The message of the gospel was from Israel, not to Israel!" Therefore, proselytizing of Jews is a fruitless endeavor: "It is time for Christians everywhere to recognize that the nation of Israel will never convert to Christianity and join the Baptist church in their town."[58]

A second edition of *In Defense of Israel* was published soon after the first, the result of a loud cry from Hagee's evangelical constituency. In the chapter addressing these topics, now titled "The Myth of Replacement Theology," Hagee completely revises his theology of Jesus' messianic vocation and reintroduces the concept of "judicial blindness" absent in the book's first edition, perhaps to the chagrin of Jewish friends, all too familiar with such traditional anti-Jewish tropes.

Hagee's theology of Jewish-Christian relationship, expressed in his attempts to find a path between dual covenant and replacement theologies, is grounded in premillennial dispensationalism, a nineteenth-century theological system most often associated with John Nelson Darby and Cyrus I. Scofield that will be discussed in more detail in Chapter Seven. In *Jerusalem Countdown*, Hagee presents a classical dispensationalist interpretation of the image used in both Genesis 22:17 and Hebrews 11:12, depicting Abraham's children as both "the sand of the sea" and "the stars of the heavens." This dual image illustrates Darby's strong distinction between the two peoples of God, Jews on one hand and Gentile true believers in Jesus on the other. According to both Darby and Hagee, all biblical interpretation must be undertaken with this distinction in mind, lest one "confuse the obvious meaning of Scripture." Thus, "Israel has been given an earthly kingdom with an earthly Jerusalem now located in Israel. The church has been given the New Jerusalem located in heaven." This distinction between God's earthly and heavenly peoples bolsters Hagee's critique of replacement theology: "One never replaces the other. The stars have their role, and the sand has its role, but they never interact." On the other hand, this distinction does not mean that Jews will not ultimately recognize Jesus as their long-awaited Messiah. Their "spiritual resurrection" will follow their reception of their "earthly kingdom" in the State of Israel. "How and when God will cause a spiritual resurrection to come to Israel is known only to God."[59] Although, for Hagee, Jews have a continuing purpose in God's plan, their salvation will be limited to earthly things until they confess that Jesus is the Messiah.

This dispensationalist penchant for constructing Jewish futures within Christian theological frameworks—a characteristic inherited, as we will see, from the English Protestant tradition of Judeo-centric prophecy interpretation—has implications for Hagee's understanding of Jews in the present. In his 1996 book, *Beginning of the End*, Hagee divided the diversity of Jewish cultures in the State of Israel as the two faces of the Roman god Janus: "one face belongs to religious Jews who believe the holy Scriptures are absolute truth, that Israel has a divine mandate to possess the land and to build on it. Yet part of the same body is the other face, the nonreligious Jews who believe political solutions only come through the peace process." This noncomprehension and resulting denigration of secular Zionist Jews is a strong echo of nineteenth-century Christian Zionist William Blackstone, discussed in Chapter Eight. According to Hagee, far from "bringing the long-sought-for peace," any peace process "will bring the Antichrist and the most horrible war the Holy Land has ever known." Writing immediately after the November 1995 assassination of Yitzhak Rabin, Hagee imagined that Israel was "uniting" and would "with a dogged determination . . . pursue peace with a passion that throws caution to the wind." "The shot that killed Yitzhak Rabin launched Bible prophecy onto the fast track," Hagee said, for "Israel will unite and peace will prevail . . . when the country accepts the false man of peace who steps out onto the world's stage."[60] According to Hagee, the rise of the Antichrist can already be blamed on the gullible, naïve trust of nonobservant Israelis in various iterations of the peace process.

Many Jews, knowing that they disagree with almost every aspect of Hagee's theology and perspectives on domestic policy, are willing to cooperate with him because they see groups like Christians United for Israel as important tools for organizing, shaping, and mobilizing American evangelical support for the State of Israel. Confident that no element of his eschatological vision will come to fruition and grateful for his disavowal of proselytizing Jews in the here-and-now, not too many other questions need to be asked before his assistance is accepted.

After CUFI was publicly unveiled in early 2006, a strong debate erupted among Jews in Israel and the United States concerning close cooperation with evangelical Christians. Jews on one side of the debate succeeded in offering Hagee center stage at the 2007 AIPAC policy conference. "It's a new day in America. The sleeping giant of Christian Zionism has awakened; there are 50 million Christians standing up and applauding the State of Israel," Hagee announced to AIPAC and to the world. "If a line has to be drawn, draw the line around both Christians and Jews; we are united; we are indivisible."[61]

While many Jews were thrilled with this strong expression of support for Israel, others viewed this language of inclusion as a potentially fatal embrace. Orthodox Israeli journalist Gershom Gorenberg offered a unique perspective that drew a strong contrast between the aims and purposes of Christian Zionism and those of Jewish political Zionism. Christian Zionists like Hagee, he said, see

Jews as actors in a Christian drama leading toward the end of days . . .
real Zionism, as a Jewish movement, is a movement aimed at taking
Jews out of the mythological realm and making them into normal
actors in history, controlling their fate and acting for pragmatic reasons connected to the here and now. So what's called Christian Zionism is actually very distant from Zionism.[62]

The remaining chapters of this book will show that Gorenberg's analytical
perspective on Christian Zionism is profoundly accurate. The tradition of
prophecy interpretation that informs contemporary American Christian
Zionism, of which John Hagee is only the most prominent representative,
is characterized primarily by its constructions of friends and enemies according to its own eschatological expectations and apocalyptic hopes.
Some Jews, from Menasseh ben-Israel in the seventeenth century to David
Brog (a Jewish political advisor working as CUFI's executive director) in
the twenty-first, have been willing to work within those constructions for
the perceived benefit of their people. Other Jews have preferred to keep a
polite distance.

Although he has risen to national prominence and notoriety, John
Hagee is neither the sum total of contemporary American Christian Zionism nor the key for deciphering popular American Christian support for
the State of Israel. Nevertheless, Hagee, along with other politicians and
theologians sketched in this chapter, exhibits many traits central to the
English Protestant tradition of Judeo-centric prophecy interpretation underlying both Christian Zionism and popular American support for Israel.

Hagee's overt political activity epitomizes the most basic characteristic
of Christian Zionism. Although many Christians agree with the basic doctrinal commitments of premillennial dispensationalism—including, for
instance, expecting the any-moment rapture of true believers and the conviction things will steadily grow worse before that moment of rescue—but
most of them would not take the step of allowing those beliefs to explicitly
shape political activity on behalf of the State of Israel. Second, Hagee is
committed to the preservation of U.S. economic and military power so the
United States can in turn continue to preserve the State of Israel.

On the theological front, Hagee reflects the Judeo-centric tradition we
will begin discussing more fully in Chapter Three by engaging history
through his interpretation of biblical prophecy. One implication of this
approach is that he interprets politics through the eschatological expectations resulting from that prophetic hermeneutic. In the same manner, his

Judeo-centric approach to prophecy interpretation exhibits very definite anti-Catholic and anti-Islamic elements. As we will see, this trajectory is in keeping with the tradition in which he stands. Identifying Hagee and most other contemporary American Christian Zionists from Hal Lindsey to Jerry Falwell to Tim LaHaye and Rod Parsley with that tradition means that these patterns of interpreting the world will also rely on theopolitical constructions of Jews. When the circle is drawn around Christian Zionists and Jews, many Jews may not recognize themselves in the picture that results.

2

Supporting the Jew

CULTURE, DOCTRINE, AND AMERICAN POPULAR OPINION ON THE STATE OF ISRAEL

THE DEFINING CHARACTERISTIC of Christian Zionism is found not in any particular set of doctrinal beliefs, but in its political activity to promote or preserve Jewish control over the geographic area now comprising Israel and Palestine. Most forms of contemporary American Christian Zionism seek to support configurations of U.S. foreign policy that further that singular goal. These efforts are largely in line with popular American attitudes toward the State of Israel.

Since 1988, major national polling organizations have measured sympathies concerning the Israeli-Palestinian conflict. Within the United States, sympathies are consistently with Israelis rather than Palestinians. Within that broader trend, a consensus has been reached that, among Christians, levels of doctrinal traditionalism are reliable predictors of whether or not individuals will actively support the State of Israel. Utilizing polling data from several sources, this chapter discusses an important exception that demonstrates how the hypothesis holds, but only among white evangelicals. Support for U.S. policy favoring Israel is predicted less by conservative adherence to doctrine than by a nexus of religious traditionalism, American nationalist exceptionalism, and whiteness. In keeping with the nature of Christian Zionism itself, American attitudes are informed more by what George Marsden has called "cultural fundamentalism"[1] than by adherence to particular doctrinal systems, including premillennial dispensationalism.

Measuring American Attitudes

Americans rarely falter in their support for the State of Israel over and against its Arab neighbors. Since before the state's founding in May 1948, almost all polls conducted of American public opinion have indicated greater American sympathy for Israel than for its neighboring states or for Palestinians. Surveys have shown "that Americans' lopsided division of support in favor of Israel has persisted through every war in the region, through the making and collapse of peace agreements and through attacks and reprisals by all sides."[2] While American sympathies fluctuate according to other world events, sympathy for the State of Israel is consistently, and most often, substantially higher than for Arab states or Palestinians.

Even before 1948, a time when most Americans had little opinion regarding the struggle between Jews, Palestinians, and other Arabs for political rights to the land, U.S. public sympathies were with Jews. A Gallup poll conducted in November 1947, for instance, showed that 24 percent of Americans sympathized with Jews in the coming war, double the percentage who said they would sympathize with Arabs. The turning-point for American awareness of the Israeli-Palestinian conflict, and for American sympathies for the State of Israel, came with the June 1967 war. As Hazel Erskine observed in 1969, "The dramatic Six-Day War of June 1967 not only focused attention on the Middle East, but turned sympathies of the western world overwhelmingly toward the victorious small nation."[3]

Since May 1988, roughly six months into the first Palestinian Intifada ("uprising" or "shaking off"), regular polling by the Gallup Organization has often included several questions on the Israeli-Palestinian conflict. Among these questions, "In the Middle East situation, are your sympathies more with the Israelis or more with the Palestinians?" has been the most consistent. Gallup senior editor Lydia Saad observed in 2007 that "Americans are more pro-Israeli in their views today than they were 10 and 20 years ago, but, they are also more polarized, more generally." In the time Gallup has been tracking responses to the question of sympathies, "Americans have moved out of the 'no preference' columns . . . disproportionately into the pro-Israeli column."[4] The highest recorded level of American sympathy for Israelis was in February 1991, during the first Persian Gulf War. With Iraqi Scud missiles aimed at Tel Aviv, fully 64 percent of Americans sympathized with Israel. Sympathies for Palestinians have generally remained flat.

Gallup polling in February 2010 also showed that Republicans' support for Israel increased from 2009 to 2010, from 77 to 85 percent. Sixty percent of independents and 48 percent of Democrats voiced sympathies for Israel over and against Palestinians. The same poll sought to measure Americans' optimism regarding a peaceful conclusion to the Arab-Israeli conflict; 67 percent doubted that "there will come a time" when "Israel and the Arab nations will be able to settle their differences and live in peace." Gallup's analysis of the polling observed that "the only time fewer Americans were optimistic about Arab-Israeli peace (27 percent) was in July 2006, during the Israeli-Hezbollah war in southern Lebanon." Evidently, President Obama's early focus on the conflict did not engender hopes for peace within the American populace.[5]

American popular support for the State of Israel is consistent even when Israeli military actions receive international scrutiny and criticism. Israel's summer 2006 invasion of Lebanon in response to Hezbollah missile attacks—noted in Chapter One as an occasion for John Hagee's pronouncement that supporting Israel is "God's foreign policy"—did not affect positive American assessments of Israel.[6] In response to Israel's twenty-two-day assault on Gaza (from December 27, 2008, until Israel's unilateral cease-fire on January 17, 2009), American opinion did not change noticeably. A Pew Research Center survey conducted in early January 2009 found that "49 percent of Americans said they sympathized more with Israel in its dispute with the Palestinians, while just 11 percent sympathized more with the Palestinians and 15 percent said they sympathized with neither side."[7]

Polls conducted during the 2008/2009 Gaza crisis show that American sympathy for Israelis over and against Palestinians results in acceptance of Israeli policy directions. On December 30, 2008, during Israel's air bombardment on Gaza but before the ground invasion commenced, a Rasmussen poll found that 44 percent of Americans supported Israel's military action while 41 percent felt that Israel should have tried to find a diplomatic solution to the situation. At the same time, just 13 percent of those polled placed blame for the situation on Israel; 55 percent blamed the Palestinians.[8] A few days later, after Israeli artillery killed more than 40 Palestinian civilians sheltered inside a school operated by the United Nations, a Gallup survey found that 33 percent of Americans felt that the administration of George W. Bush (in a transitional period prior to President Obama's inauguration) should be doing more to resolve the conflict. A combined 52 percent of Americans, however, said that Bush was either doing too much (22 percent) or just enough (30 percent), and did not wish for greater involvement.[9] Strategic noninvolvement is an important option in the exercise of foreign policy.

American Attitudes, Evenhandedness, and the Peace Process

Since the Oslo Accords were presented on the White House lawn in September 1993, Americans have been regularly exposed to the notion that peace between Israelis and Palestinians will necessarily take the form of a "two-state solution" resulting in the State of Israel existing securely and peacefully next to a Palestinian state. Although Oslo's Declaration of Principles was signed during the Clinton Administration, George W. Bush was the first U.S. president to state explicitly that the United States sought the establishment of a Palestinian state. This policy was contained in the "Roadmap" for peace introduced in April 2003 by the Quartet (the United States, Russia, the European Union, and the United Nations).[10] Despite Christian Zionist opposition, a Gallup poll conducted in late May and early June 2003 found that 58 percent of Americans favored the establishment of a Palestinian state in the West Bank and Gaza Strip; 22 percent of Americans were opposed. Support for the idea of a Palestinian state had risen over the previous four years, with those who had previously held no opinion moving generally to support the idea. American attitudes toward supporting Israel were shaped by the experiences of 9/11. In October 2001, 58 percent said that U.S. support for Israel was "about the right amount," Gallup's highest recorded measurement of American endorsement of U.S.-Israeli policy.[11]

Bolstered by this popular affinity, U.S. foreign policy is configured to favor Israeli interests. This policy advantage is manifested most clearly in the U.S. commitment to preserving Israel's "qualitative military edge."[12] Despite such structural advantages for Israel within U.S. policy, Americans desire some measure of balance in its approach to disagreements between Israelis and Palestinians. One 2003 poll, conducted after the release of the Roadmap, asked, "In the Middle East conflict, do you think the United States should take Israel's side, take the Palestinians' side, or not take either side?" Nearly three-fourths of respondents said that the United States should not take either side; 21 percent thought the U.S. should take Israel's side; only 2 percent wanted the U.S. to side with Palestinians.[13] Although they feel that the U.S. support for Israel was at "about the right amount," Americans have a strong desire for their government to approach the Israeli-Palestinian conflict with fairness and evenhandedness.

Activists wishing to preserve the long-standing U.S. policy tilt toward the State of Israel often find themselves in the position of arguing against the basic American value of fairness. A 2003 letter to President George W. Bush, signed by Gary Bauer, Richard Land, John Hagee, and several other Christian Zionist leaders, noted, for instance, that "you and the United States are being pressured to show we are 'evenhanded' and are being urged to pressure Israel to make concessions." This would be an unacceptable approach: "Mr. President, it would be morally reprehensible for the United States to be 'evenhanded' between democratic Israel, a reliable friend and ally that shares our values, and the terrorist infested Palestinian infrastructure that refuses to accept the right of Israel to exist at all."[14]

A more recent test of the American value of being evenhanded with regard to Israeli and Palestinian interests came with President Obama's January 2009 appointment of Sen. George Mitchell as Special Envoy to the Middle East. Mitchell had been involved in several high-profile reconciliation and peace-building efforts, most notably in Ireland. He was highly respected for his evenhandedness and careful mediation, precisely the "honest broker" many had previously called for in U.S. approaches to the Israeli-Palestinian conflict. Mitchell's fundamental fairness was noted even by opponents of the appointment. "Sen. Mitchell is fair. He's been meticulously even-handed," Anti-Defamation League national director Abraham Foxman said at the time. "But the fact is, American policy in the Middle East hasn't been 'even handed'—it has been supportive of Israel when it felt Israel needed critical U.S. support. So I'm concerned. I'm not sure the situation requires that kind of approach in the Middle East."[15] Gary Bauer, noting that the Mitchell Commission report had named Israeli settlement construction along with Palestinian terrorism as obstacles to peace, shared his opinion that while "Mitchell has a reputation . . . as being evenhanded between Israel and the Palestinian extremists . . . the appointment is bad because I don't believe we should be evenhanded between Israel and the Palestinians."[16]

The uniqueness of the American "special relationship" with the State of Israel has resulted in equally unique American perspectives on the Israeli-Palestinian conflict and the relative evenhandedness of U.S. policy. In 2004, the Toronto *Globe & Mail* reported that 89 percent of Canadians "believe that both Israel and the Palestinians equally share responsibility for ongoing violence" in the conflict and that 83 percent of Canadians "believe Ottawa should remain neutral in its approach to the Middle East conflict."[17] European sympathies are significantly more weighted toward the Palestinians, even among similarly arrayed ideological segments. According to findings in the 2007 Global Attitudes Project survey "from six

Western European countries, in every ideological group there was far less sympathy for Israel and far more sympathy for the Palestinians than in roughly comparable groups in the United States."[18] As might be expected, in "most Muslim nations surveyed . . . vast majorities sided with the Palestinians, including 97 percent of the public in Jordan."[19]

Just as sympathies are different, so are assessments of the fairness of U.S. policy. "In the May 2003 Global Attitudes survey, which covered 21 countries, pluralities or majorities in every country except the United States expressed the view that American policies in the Middle East favor Israel over the Palestinians too much." Perhaps the most surprising finding in that survey is that this assessment is shared by a majority of Israelis: "Nearly half (47 percent) of Israelis expressed the belief that the U.S. favors Israel too much, while 38 percent said the policy is fair and 11 percent said the U.S. favors the Palestinians too much."[20] In global perspective, then, Americans' consistently positive attitude toward the State of Israel is exceptional.

American Religion and Public Opinion

Since the mid-1990s, major polling organizations have been including religious variables in their national polls of attitudes toward politics and foreign policy. This shift in polling strategy can be traced to the efforts of political scientists James Guth, John Green, Lyman Kellstedt, and Corwin Smidt (the so-called "gang of four") and their efforts to map the American landscape of politics and religion. Understanding Christian Zionism as "embedded deeply in a powerful theological current that has had a profound impact on American evangelicalism: dispensationalism," the "gang of four" hypothesized in 1996 that if "dispensational notions predict warmth toward Israel in the mass public, we have considerable confidence that Christian Zionism is an important contributor to pro-Israel attitudes."[21]

Their primary contribution to this question was methodological. While earlier analysts were content to accept the broadest descriptions—such as Will Herberg's heuristic "Protestant, Catholic, Jew"[22]—Guth and his colleagues were concerned that simplistic distinctions between religious categories "may hide important differences within these religious categories, especially among 'Protestants.'"[23] Taking note of denominational identification and the relative liberalism or traditionalism within a respondent's beliefs, careful categorization led to definitive findings: "clergy or activists identifying as Pentecostals or charismatics are most supportive of Israel, followed by fundamentalists and self-identifying Evangelicals. Mainline, liberal, and ecumenical Christians are much less supportive." Support for Israel was highest among Protestants who favored more literalist biblical interpretation and among those whose religious beliefs influence their political decisions. One important finding was that while "evangelical clergy and laity . . . are closely matched in their felt proximity to Israel," mainline clergy are "distinctively *less* friendly to Israel . . . than mainline laity."[24]

The evangelical proclivity to sympathize with Israelis or support U.S. pro-Israel policies is affected less by political currents than by the content of evangelical commitment. Even if U.S. policy directions were to change and perspectives critical of Israeli policy gained more currency among Americans, Guth and his colleagues "expect that among a large segment of the public, prophetic cues derived from the evangelical tradition would minimize the 'cognitive dissonance' associated with this foreign policy issue and resolve it in Israel's favor."[25] As the closing chapters of this study show, this is not the only form of "cognitive dissonance" present in evangelical political activity on behalf of Israel.

Early Efforts to Measure Religion and American Sympathies for Israel

The October 1973 war between Israel and some of its Arab neighbors provided an occasion for measuring how religious commitments informed Americans' attitudes toward the State of Israel. In dialogue with hypotheses derived from the work of Rodney Stark and Charles Glock on correlations between Christian anti-Semitism and levels of religious orthodoxy, the study, limited to Laramie County, Wyoming, found that 56 percent of those polled "identified the Middle East conflict as the most important foreign policy issue then facing the United States." Moreover, the poll found "a strong positive correlation between religious orthodoxy and the belief that the present state of Israel represents fulfillment of Biblical prophecy."[26] Respondents were cautious about the possibility of committing U.S. troops to protect Israel, suggesting that these religious attitudes had not been translated or operationalized into foreign policy attitudes.

In the mid-1980s, as the Christian Right continued to make its presence known in U.S. politics, Ronald Stockton, a political scientist at the University of Michigan–Dearborn, conducted a series of surveys in the

Dearborn area to gauge the influence of the movement. Seeking to measure the prevalence of Christian Zionism, Stockton asked, "Which of these points of view seems more correct to you? Is Israel the fulfillment of Biblical prophecy or is it not?" Within his sample, Stockton found that "Protestants are 22 percentage points more likely than Catholics to accept a prophetic interpretation of the events of 1948 [the founding of the State of Israel], even though 35 percent of all Catholics are also Christian Zionists." Those he identified as Christian Zionists, "compared with the remainder of the sample, are moderately more pro-Jewish . . . and noticeably more pro-Israeli." Assessments toward Arabs in general and the Palestinian Liberation Organization in particular were uniformly low.[27]

Stockton's early effort to measure the extent to which level of religiosity contribute to affinity toward Israel demonstrates several important aspects of Christian Zionism. First, not all evangelicals are Christian Zionists, and not all Christian Zionists are evangelicals. More akin to a movement like Pentecostalism than institutional expressions like denominations, Christian Zionism has the ability to transcend traditional Christian alignments. While not sharing ecclesial identity, 94 percent of the Christian Zionists identified by Stockton's survey shared the belief that "America has a unique destiny." This correlation indicates that those persons may be bound together more by national identity than by particular Christian doctrines. Likewise, the survey found that, in contrast with the Religious Right, Christian Zionism did not appear to be a partisan political movement. Instead, "Christian Zionism is more a mainstream cultural theme linked to American self-identity and to perception of America as a moral community." It would therefore be a mistake to simplistically dismiss the movement as "the pathological perspective of an extremist fringe, as sometimes portrayed by its detractors."[28]

Taking an approach similar to Stockton's, an October 2006 Zogby poll of likely voters, conducted just before mid-term elections in the year Christians United for Israel rose to national prominence, sought to identify the percentage of the population who could be identified as Christian Zionists. The poll asked if participants believed or did not believe "in Christian Zionism, which is defined as a belief that Israel must have all of the promised land, including Jerusalem, to facilitate the second coming of the messiah?" Among respondents, 53 percent did not express belief in the supplied definition, while 31 percent did. Results were detailed by geographic section, race, and political party. Protestants were more likely to agree with this belief than Catholics (40 percent and 19 percent, respectively). While the percentages are lower, the difference is almost identical to that re-ported by Stockton in 1987 (57 percent and 35 percent, respectively).[29]

According to a June 2003 Gallup poll, 30 percent of Americans, agree-ing that Israel and the broader Middle East "is a holy land that has personal religious significance" because "events that the Bible predicted will eventu-ally occur there," view the significance of the State of Israel in prophetic terms. Nearly 50 percent of respondents, however, recognize the region's historical significance without associating it with any personal religious significance. A "majority of Republicans (61 percent) view the region in religious terms; a little more than half of independents (54 percent) and Democrats (51 percent) do not." The poll found that views on the religious significance of the land did not significantly affect "support for an inde-pendent Palestinian state."[30]

A February 2006 survey by the Gallup Organization showed that any form of religiosity seemed to correlate with increased sympathies for Israelis; this analysis was limited to white respondents alone. As Table 2.1 shows, the survey found a "similarity of attitudes toward Israelis and the Palestinians across all three groups of whites who have a religious identification . . . and, to a light degree, sympathy for the Palestinians among the group of whites who have no religion. White Catholics are no different than white Protestants and whites who identify with other non-Catholic religions." The findings also indicated that "sympathy for the Israelis is highest among those who attend church weekly, almost weekly, and monthly," whereas it drops off "among those who seldom attend and is lowest among those who never attend."

Table 2.1 Middle East Sympathies by Religious Preference
(February 6–9, 2006)

	Israelis	Palestinians	Both/Neither/ Don't Know
	%	%	%
White Protestants/ other Christians	63	14	22
White Catholics	64	13	23
White other religions	66	10	24
White no religion	45	19	36

Source: Frank Newport and Joseph Carroll, "Republicans and Religious Americans Most Sympathetic to Israel," *Gallup News Service*, March 27, 2006. Copyright © 2006 Gallup, Inc. All rights reserved.

Moreover, "Frequent churchgoers who are Republicans have the highest levels of sympathy to Israelis, and are more sympathetic to Israelis than infrequent churchgoers who are Republicans."[31] This survey, unique among national efforts, points to the possibility that a combination of whiteness and religious practice, rather than any particular doctrinal commitment, could indicate likely support for the State of Israel.[32]

Measuring Religious Complexities

National polling organizations began regularly including religious identifiers in surveys on political issues in the early twenty-first century.[33] These data confirm that "American evangelical Protestants have distinctive—and highly positive—attitudes towards the state of Israel." The Pew Forum on Religion and Public Life showed in 2003, for instance, that white evangelical Protestants (as opposed to earlier surveys reporting results for "Protestants" in general) were "significantly more sympathetic to Israel than to the Palestinians" when compared to the general sample (55 percent of white evangelicals favored Israel compared to 41 percent of the overall survey). In addition, white evangelicals were "significantly more likely to say that religious beliefs were the single biggest influence in leading them to sympathize more with Israel" (46 percent to 26 percent), "significantly more likely to believe that God gave the land of Israel to the Jews" (72 percent to 44 percent), and "significantly more likely to believe that Israel fulfills the biblical prophecy about Jesus' second coming" (63 percent to 36 percent).[34]

The Fourth National Survey of Religion and Politics was conducted by University of Akron political scientist John Green in the spring of 2004.[35] Green's apparatus and report identified respondents' religious identifications, which "were then divided in two ways: by religious beliefs/practices and by ethnicity/race." The category "Evangelical Protestants" included individual respondents belonging to "historically white" denominations and congregations. "Mainline Protestants" were understood to be members of "historically white denominations in the Mainline Protestant tradition." The survey divided both evangelical Protestants and mainline Protestants into three subgroups—traditionalists, centrists, and modernists—based on doctrinal views and religious practices. Traditionalists in both groups, for instance, were characterized by "a high level of orthodox belief (such as a high view of the authority of the Bible) and high religious engagement (such as regular worship attendance), and also a desire to preserve such traditional beliefs and practices in a changing world."[36] This complex taxonomy allows for careful investigation of the contribution of religious commitments toward the formation of attitudes toward politics and policy.

While several surveys had measured different religious groups' sympathies toward Israel, Green took the unique approach of asking respondents if they agreed or disagreed that "The U.S. should support Israel over the Palestinians in the Middle East." Green's approach revealed a different pattern than the May 2003 PIPA survey, noted above, which showed that 73 percent of Americans said that the U.S. should not take sides in the conflict, while 21 percent thought it should take Israel's side.[37] As Table 2.2 shows, 35 percent of respondents said that the U.S. should support Israel over the Palestinians, 38 percent said it should not, and 21 percent expressed no opinion. Green was aware that the question presented a "tough choice" since it "is specifically about the U.S. taking Israel's side in the dispute with the Palestinians." In other words, the question seeks to assess a respondent's willingness to endorse policies that intentionally lack balance and evenhandedness.[38]

Table 2.2 also reveals that white evangelicals were significantly more agreeable than the general population to the notion that U.S. policy should

Table 2.2 "The U.S. should support Israel over the Palestinians in the Middle East."

	Agree	No Opinion	Disagree
Entire Sample	35%	27	38
Evangelical Protestant	52	23	25
Traditionalist Evangelical	64	18	18
Centrist Evangelical	45	26	29
Modernist Evangelical	28	37	35
Mainline Protestant	33	30	37
Traditionalist Mainline	43	28	29
Centrist Mainline	34	34	32
Modernist Mainline	22	26	52
Catholic	31	26	43
Traditionalist Catholic	43	26	31
Centrist Catholic	30	24	46
Modernist Catholic	23	29	48
Jewish	75	13	12

Source: John C. Green, *The American Religious Landscape and Political Attitudes: A Baseline for 2004.*

be configured for Israel's benefit, against Palestinian interests. Among traditionalist evangelicals, 64 percent favored a U.S. tilt toward Israel; 18 percent opposed this direction. This level of support for Israel was exceeded only by Jewish respondents. These findings are consistent with the views expressed by Gary Bauer and Abraham Foxman noted previously. Green observed that general American support for favoring Israel in the configuration of U.S. policy had increased from 28 percent in 1992 to 35 percent in 2004. In that same period, however, evangelical Protestants showed both "a double digit increase in the agreement column," from 39 percent to 52 percent, "and a decline in the disagreement column," from 29 percent to 25 percent.[39]

In July 2006, the Pew organization conducted an ambitious survey that sought to measure as comprehensively as possible the intersection of religion and politics in the United States. The survey collected extensive information related to Americans' attitudes toward the State of Israel and, importantly, measured the specific doctrinal beliefs that many associate with those policy attitudes.[40] Among those views on which white evangelicals are largely agreed is that "God gave Israel to the Jewish people" (69 percent) and that "Israel is the fulfillment of biblical prophecy" (59 percent). These views were also widely held among black Protestants, but less prevalent among white mainline and Catholic Christians. These beliefs have political implications. In Table 2.2, we see that persons holding these views are markedly more sympathetic with Israel than with the Palestinians when compared to persons not holding them. The survey also found a correlation between views of the Bible and views of Israel: "Large majorities of those who view the Bible as the literal word of God say that Israel was given by God to the Jews and that Israel is the fulfillment of prophecy" (70 percent and 62 percent, respectively). This commitment to biblical literalism is constitutive of the theological traditions that underlie Christian Zionism as well as general American affinity for the State of Israel.

The July 2006 survey also measured American Christian beliefs regarding the "Second Coming" of Christ, a doctrine of Christian faith across all denominations. The survey did not specifically investigate belief in the "rapture" but did explore other components of premillennial dispensationalist commitment. Overall, 79 percent of Christians surveyed expressed belief in the Second Coming, with 95 percent of white evangelicals and 92 percent of black Protestants showing the highest rates of belief. Although the doctrine is accepted, Christ's imminent (any-moment) return, a central tenet of premillennial dispensationalism, is not expected: only 20 percent of the Christians surveyed felt this return would occur in their lifetime. Regarding the circumstances regarding Christ's return, roughly "a third (34 percent) say that this will occur after the world situation worsens and reaches a low point, a view often referred to as premillennialism."

Regarding the conditions of Jesus' return, 37 percent say they can be known, while a small number (4 percent) "say that Christ will return after the world situation improves and reaches a high point," a characteristic of postmillennial hope. Even among white evangelicals, "half (48 percent) express a pre-millennialist view, while nearly as many (40 percent) say that it is impossible to know the circumstances that will precede Christ's return." On the question of whether or not "peoples and nations of the world can affect when Jesus Christ returns to earth," 23 percent say humans can affect divine timing while more than twice that (50 percent) take the opposite view.

Interpreting the Data—Is Dispensationalism the Cause?

What can be learned from the data presented here about the factors informing American Christian affinity for the State of Israel? We can say definitively that adults in the United States overwhelmingly sympathize with Israelis over and against Palestinians and that religious identifiers strongly correlate to levels of support. This sympathy, however, does not eliminate American desire for bringing the conflict to resolution; most Americans accept a "two-state solution" as the best outcome (a solution not every supporter of Israel agrees is, in fact, pro-Israel). The data also demonstrate that seeking to measure attitudes and sympathies produces results distinct from efforts to measure support for certain policy configurations.

The complex religious identifiers included in recent national surveys show how religion informs some Americans' views on U.S. policy concerning to the Palestinian-Israeli conflict. For the most part, however, national polls have sought to measure neither rates of belief in premillennial dispensationalism, nor specific beliefs within the system. The strongest exception is the July 2006 effort from the Pew organization, which measured some discrete beliefs that may indicate adherence to the larger system of premillennial dispensationalism.

Even more basic than specific doctrinal commitments, however, is commitment to literal or "common-sense" biblical interpretation. In their

1996 study, Guth and his colleagues found that "both religious tradition and views of the Bible have substantial effects even controlling for party identification, age, and education" on the question of whether or not the U.S. should "seek closer ties with Israel" and that, "within religious categories, support for Israel declines as activists' view of the Bible falls."[41] Nevertheless, it is striking that in 2006, when Gallup polls found sympathy for Israel measuring at 59 percent (the third highest recorded level), the Pew poll found that only 35 percent of respondents claimed a literal view of the Bible.

While significant (and corroborating the 2006 Zogby poll), this 35-percent figure does not indicate resounding popularity for either literalist hermeneutics or dispensational doctrine in contemporary American society. According to John Green's reading of survey data, only about 5 million Americans are dispensationalists, comprising "about 2.5 percent of the adult population of the United States."[42] These levels of doctrinal adherence are not sufficient to explain Americans' high levels of sympathy for Israelis. If this is so, popular American support for the State of Israel cannot be dominated by Darby and draw determinedly from dispensational doctrine. It is more likely that popular support for Israel resonates with significant elements within American history and identity rather than in any particular configuration of Christian doctrine.

Interpreting the Data—The Black Protestant Test Case

Beyond the specificities of premillennial dispensationalism, a consensus has developed that levels of religious belief correlate with levels of policy support for Israel. This consensus is challenged, however, by consideration of an underreported portion of the population: black Protestants.

When polls measure the intersection of politics, religion, and race, black understandings often go unreported. As one Gallup organization survey interpretation noted in its section on how religious commitments correlate with support for Israel, "Given that blacks tend to be very religious and tend to identify themselves more with the Democratic party, this table displays data among white respondents only."[43] Utilizing the same logic, though often far less explicitly, most survey reports seeking to measure religious and political variables exclude black perspectives and detail only the views of white respondents. Beyond the likely presumption that white respondents' views are more politically relevant and, therefore, more newsworthy, the rationale for this methodology is not clear. The general lack of media attention to black perspectives on U.S. foreign policy is matched within the academy. As Brian McKenzie has observed, "This topic has escaped the focus of most analysts of both black political life and general foreign policy."[44] Whatever the reasons for this pattern of exclusion, the observations arising from the data collected here indicate that the perspectives of black Protestants on U.S. policy configurations toward the State of Israel must be considered if we are to comprehend the complexities of American approaches to these questions.

Black Protestant perspectives are apparent in the full report of the Fourth National Survey of Religion and Politics (2004). As already noted, respondents were divided by both religious group and ethnicity. The perspectives of black and Latino Protestant respondents were placed in their own categories, separate from white evangelical and mainline Protestant results. While Green recognized that some "Latino and Black Protestants belong to denominations within the Evangelical and Mainline traditions," they tend to "overwhelmingly belong to congregations that are ethnically or racially homogenous" and therefore have "distinctive religious and political perspectives." While this strategy helps emphasize "the special features of these important religious minorities, it also highlights the special characteristics of white Christians."[45]

Black Protestants, although highly conservative in their doctrinal commitments, do not echo the attitudes toward the Israeli-Palestinian conflict expressed by similarly conservative white evangelicals. This difference is brought to light by the question of whether or not "The U.S. should support Israel over the Palestinians in the Middle East." Overall, 35 percent of the respondents agreed with a policy tilt toward Israel. Of those polled, 64 percent of traditionalist white evangelicals supported this position. In sharp contrast, just 24 percent of black Protestants supported an unfair policy configuration to favor Israel over Palestinians.[46]

According to the interpretive consensus that levels of support for Israel are related to levels of religious conservativism, one might expect to find significant religious differences between these white evangelicals and black Protestants. However, as Table 2.3 shows, the groups have similar positions on several questions of religious orthodoxy, including positions on doctrinal beliefs constitutive of premillennial dispensationalism. There are only negligible differences between the two groups on approaches to the Bible and the second coming of Jesus.

The data compiled in Table 2.3 shows general agreement between white evangelicals and black Protestants on two questions related to

Table 2.3 Points of Doctrinal Agreement between White Evangelicals
and Black Protestants

Believe . . .	White Evangelical	Black Protestant
. . . that the Bible is the actual word of God and is to be taken literally, word for word	62%	64%
. . . in the second coming of Jesus Christ	95%	92%
. . . that Jesus will return to earth in their lifetime	33%	34%
. . . Israel was given to the Jewish people by God	69%	60%
. . . that the state of Israel is a fulfillment of the biblical prophecy about the second coming of Jesus	59%	56%
. . . that churches should express their views on political questions	63%	68%

Source: Pew Research Center, *Many Americans Uneasy with Mix of Religion and Politics* (August 24, 2006).

the religious importance of the modern State of Israel, questions in which these two communities are in general agreement, though black Protestant agreement is slightly lower for both. Affirmative black responses to these questions correlate with a 2006 Gallup poll result showing that 40 percent of black adults sympathized with Israelis.[47] Likewise, the October 2006 Zogby poll seeking to measure commitment to Christian Zionism found that "African Americans (40 percent) are more likely to believe in [Christian Zionism] than either Hispanics (33 percent) or whites (29 percent)." These levels of sympathy for Israel, high when compared with the 19 percent of black voters who support configurations of U.S. policy that favor Israel, highlights the qualitative difference between the "soft" category of sympathies and the "hard" category of opinions on specific policy, a distinction important for judging the likelihood of mobilization for political action.

Given these levels of agreement between white evangelicals and black Protestants on doctrine as well as on sympathies related to the Palestinian-Israeli conflict, what accounts for the parting of ways on the more difficult question of policy configuration? The distinction is not located in a black Protestant unwillingness to have their churches speak out on social and political issues. On the contrary, by a margin of 68 percent to 63 percent, black Protestants are more likely than white evangelicals to support political speech in their churches. Black Protestants do not hesitate to translate their doctrinal commitments into positions on government policy.

One other finding from the Fourth National Survey of Religion and Politics (2004) provides an important variable for illuminating the distinction between white evangelicals and black Protestants on the question of U.S. policy and the Palestinian-Israeli conflict. Among respondents who had voted in the 2004 election, 62 percent agreed with the notion that "The U.S. has a special role to play in world affairs and should behave differently than other nations." On this question, designed to measure agreement with the enduring idea of American exceptionalism, Latter-Day Saints voters expressed high agreement (84 percent) with traditionalist evangelical voters following close behind (74 percent). Among all subgroups, black Protestant voters, at 41 percent, were least convinced of this conception of the role of the United States in the world.[48]

Neoconservative commentators Robert Kagan and William Kristol, writing in early 2002 in support of what was then the "new Bush Doctrine" developed after the terrorist attacks of 9/11, noted that in his desire to "defend and advance liberal democratic principles," President Bush "is now a man with a mission. As it happens, it is America's historic mission."[49] Confidence in this version of "America's historic mission" and the conviction that the United States "should behave differently than other nations" is shaken, however, when one focuses on unsavory elements within American history, including policies against American Indians and blacks. It should not be surprising, therefore, that African Americans, including black Protestants, approach the possibility of American exceptionalism with some difficulty.

Black dissent from American nationalism was apparent following 9/11. R. Drew Smith has noted that although black Protestants joined in the patriotic reaction to the terrorist attacks, black clergy were "disposed more toward critical than pastoral responses." These perspectives, therefore, were "not publicly welcomed by those outside of the African American community or readily offered by those within." One result of this censoring climate was that "little media attention was paid to the perspectives of black denominational officials, who were viewed by the media, perhaps, as public opinion outliers, despite the significant ecclesiastical constituencies these clergy represented."[50]

If the media had been listening to the voices of prominent black Protestants, they may have heard Bishop Larry D. Trotter's keynote address
delivered on September 29, 2001, to the Congressional Black Caucus
Foundation's annual prayer breakfast. Bishop Trotter reflected on the
central question of Psalm 11: "If the foundations be destroyed, what must
the righteous do?" Although he did not wish to "make light of the present
circumstance," he said it wasn't his assignment "to talk about Osama Bin
Laden . . . or to ask anyone to light another candle." Instead, African-
American experience led him to say that the question was no longer "if
the foundations be destroyed" but what to say "since the foundations
were destroyed." As he said, "We have known terrorists for years but they
were living in the high big house, they raped our women and enslaved us.
The foundations are *still* being destroyed."[51] No message could contrast
more thoroughly with the floor speech delivered from the floor of the
U.S. Senate that December by traditionalist white evangelical, Sen. James
Inhofe.

Despite both reported sympathies for Israelis and traditionalist religious commitments, black Protestants generally do not endorse unfair
configurations of U.S. policy regarding the Palestinian-Israeli conflict.
These findings support McKenzie's observation that while "black religiosity is often 'evangelical' in style . . . black politics differs from that of their
white Evangelical Protestant counterparts. This is especially true regarding African Americans' perceptions of U.S. policies abroad and American
political leaders."[52]

The views of black Protestants challenge the established consensus
that levels of traditionalist religious belief correlate with levels of policy
support for Israel. The consensus holds, but only for white Americans. A
person's adherence to particular doctrinal commitments alone, therefore,
cannot be accepted as a reliable predictor for support for particular policy
configurations. Survey methods like those employed by Stockton in 1987
and Zogby in 2006—based on assent to a particular doctrines—are insufficient for identifying anyone as a Christian Zionist.

The routine exclusion of black responses from polling reports guarantees a poverty of perspectives and an incomplete comprehension of the
American nexus of politics, religion, and foreign policy. Including black
Protestant perspectives helps highlight what Green called "the special characteristics of white Christians." Support for configurations of U.S. policy
that favor Israel is predicted less by adherence to conservative doctrines (the
developed consensus) than by a combination of religious traditionalism,

American nationalist exceptionalism, and whiteness.[53] When considered together, these factors indicate that support for particular configurations of U.S. policy results not from particular doctrinal commitments but from configurations of culture.

Concluding Observations

Frank Newport, editor-in-chief for the Gallup Organization, said in 2006 that "I've always felt, without data to back it up . . . that perhaps some of the relationship between Evangelical Christians and Israel is even simpler than" adherence to any particular eschatological beliefs. "Israel is just a country with which they identify as the seat of their religion, too. It may be extremely uncomplicated. . . . I believe experts make these things much more complex than the average Christian does."[54]

Indeed, white evangelical support for the State of Israel is simpler and more basic than most theorists have assumed. American supporters of Israel don't need specialized knowledge of U.S. foreign policy or any comprehension of a complex, nineteenth-century system of biblical interpretation and theological reflection. As Paul Boyer and Amy Frykholm have discussed, prophetic politics function almost as a folk religion among many American Christians. The theological and nationalist presuppositions undergirding the Left Behind product line (based on the popular series of dispensationalist adventure novels) are accepted as common sense for many Americans who exhibit little doctrinal precision or religious practice. American sympathy for the State of Israel has come to be basic to white American identity.

A prerequisite for comprehending the sources of popular American affinity for the State of Israel is acceptance of Ronald Stockton's observation that Christian Zionism is "a mainstream cultural theme linked to American self-identity and to perception of America as a moral community." Too often, liberal commentators have clouded their analysis by depicting the movement as "the pathological perspective of an extremist fringe." Instead, scholars and popular commentators must understand that, just as evangelicalism has become the default expression of American Christian commitment, contemporary American Christian Zionism draws from cultural themes informing the "common sense" of many Americans to the point that reinforcing the cultural foundations of support for the State of Israel is a noncontroversial activity. By contrast, those who challenge the movement risk placing themselves on the margins of

American consensus. From this cultural foundation, Christian Zionist leaders can unabashedly support preservation of the qualitative military edge for both the United States and the State of Israel in order defend "western civilization" in the form of the "Judeo-Christian tradition"—all while beckoning a Judeo-Christian army to march against Islam, the common enemy of true Christians and faithful Jews. How all this came to be is the subject of the next chapters.

3

Mythologizing the Jew

THE REFORMATION FOUNDATIONS OF JUDEO-CENTRIC
PROPHECY INTERPRETATION (1530–1603)

HOW DID MANY Protestants come to view Jewish control of historic Palestine as a theological commitment strong enough to elicit political action? To address this question in the fullness it deserves, we must consider the foundations of the Protestant Reformation itself, especially in its English expressions. Theological commitments and methods of biblical interpretation formed in this revolutionary milieu inform the foundations of contemporary American affinity for the State of Israel. The substantial pedigree outlined in the next few chapters indicates that the commitments emphasized by contemporary Christian Zionism will not easily disappear from the American scene.

This chapter traces the foundations of the English Protestant tradition of Judeo-centric prophecy interpretation through the encounters of English exiles with the hermeneutical and historical emphases of the Lutheran and Calvinist reformations on the European continent and the transposition of those emphases to Elizabethan England. The period explored here begins with Martin Luther's 1530 commentary on Ezekiel in which he identified the Ottoman Empire as "Gog and Magog," and ends with Arthur Dent's *The Ruine of Rome*, his full-length commentary on Revelation published in 1603.

The publications framing this chapter informed Protestant perceptions of Muslims and Roman Catholics, or, in the language of the time, the Turk and the Pope. Kenneth Setton has noted that European Christians had a long history of identifying all of Islam with the Ottoman Empire, "especially after the Turks crushed the Persians (in 1514), and had thereafter overrun eastern Anatolia and Kurdistan (in 1515), Syria and Palestine (in 1516), and finally Egypt in January 1517." With this specter of

Muslim threat, embodied in the Turk, Christians found a sharpened theo-political calling: "Pious Christians must pray for the undoing of Islam."[1] Long-standing Christian conflict with Islam, a central force in the development of Christian identities in the West as well as the East, was heightened by effective Ottoman military power. Protestant discourse would soon join anxiety about Islam to vitriol against the civil and theological authority of the Roman Catholic Church.

As Lebanese scholar Nabil Matar has observed, the Reformation era was animated by a palpable "Turko-Catholic threat." This joint threat was both martial and theological. Both enemies threatened the body as well as soul. This chapter will show how Protestant responses to the Turko-Catholic threat inspired new interpretations of biblical prophecy and, in the English context, developed a place for Jews within the Protestant narrative. In this Judeo-centric approach, Jews were eventually "granted a military-theological function within the framework of Christian history," to the point that Jews became "the cornerstone of the religious military strategy against the Turk and the Catholic." These developments are particularly salient for understanding the roots of Christian Zionism, since, as Matar says, "this particular approach to Biblical hermeneutics served in the propagation of the principle of the Jews' return to Palestine." The Judeo-centric emphasis within English Protestant prophecy interpretation will become more explicit in the writings explored in the next chapter. For now, it is helpful to keep in mind both that this prophetic construction of Jewish purpose and identity led to (1) the notion that a future Jewish conquest of Palestine was integral to God's plan for the world and (2) the conviction of many English and Anglo-American Protestants that in order to prove the veracity of the Bible their purpose was to preserve the possibility of this divine plan through political activity. As Matar puts it, "The Jew . . . was the spearhead of Protestantism into the land of unbelief and heresy, and thus his conquest of Palestine was necessary for the defence of England's faith."[2]

These specific commitments, first forged in the crucible of the Protestant Reformation in opposition to both Catholicism and Islam, would contribute directly to the theological formation of Anglo-American Protestant identity and culture. Contemporary American affinity for the State of Israel and the political activity of contemporary American Christian Zionism cannot be fully comprehended apart from this history.

The Dual Antichrist of Martin Luther and John Calvin

1517 saw both the Ottoman takeover of Jerusalem and Cairo from the Mamluks and the distribution of the *Ninety-Five Theses on the Power and Efficacy of Indulgences*, written as a service to the Pope Leo X by the young monk, Martin Luther (1483–1546). These events would shape the coming Protestant Reformation. The Ottoman Empire, under the leadership of Suleiman I ("the Magnificent," ca. 1494–1566), would soon extend into Europe and lay siege to Vienna, Austria. This gathering military threat provided part of the theopolitical context for Luther's vocations—biblical commentator, professor, social analyst, and preaching minister, among others—as well as a distraction for the papal authorities bent on silencing his dissent.

For Luther and the evangelical community that formed around him and his teachings, the sixteenth century was an apocalyptic time, a revealing moment within history when the call of the Gospel was clear. The pope and the Turk were intimately bound to one another in Luther's mind. Resisting a crusade against Suleiman led by Pope Leo X, Luther called Christians to "first mend our ways and cause God to be gracious to us" instead of blindly fighting "against an angry God and against an enemy whom we have deserved. All the pope accomplishes with his crusading indulgences and his promises of heaven is to lead Christians with their lives into death and with their souls into hell. This is, of course, the proper work of the Antichrist."[3] Defending himself against Leo's charges in *Exsurge Domine* (issued June 15, 1520), Luther applied apocalyptic imagery to his circumstances, identifying the pope and the Turk as the two heads of the Antichrist, the beast of the book of Revelation.[4]

Luther's dual identification of the Antichrist with the Pope and the Turk set an important trajectory for subsequent Protestant reflection on the topic. He had an equal disdain for both of these religio-military authorities. As he said during a lecture on Genesis 9, "They know our verdict about them, namely, that we regard and condemn both the pope and the Turk as the very Antichrist." Nevertheless, Luther did not always equate these two threats to the gospel. In his more technically reflective moments, Luther allowed that "it is more in accordance with the truth to say that the Turk is the beast, because he is outside the church and openly persecutes Christ" while "strictly speaking and by logical definition, he who sits in the church is the Antichrist."[5] Nevertheless, while the Papacy was Luther's primary opponent, the Turk was always next to the Pope in his mind. In his *War Sermon Against the Turk* (1529), Luther pointed to their functional similarities, saying "The Turk fills heaven with Christians by murdering their bodies, but the pope does what he can to fill hell with Christians through his blasphemous teachings."[6] The conflation is strongest in Luther's collected Table Talk, only a portion of which has been translated into English: "The spirit of Antichrist is the pope, the body of Antichrist is the Turk. Because of this, one devastates the church spiritually, the other bodily."[7] Nevertheless, Christian hope was strong. Although "the Turkish religion and the papacy are most powerful monsters," Luther proclaimed, "the Word and the sacraments remain, faith and the church remain in spite of the pope and the Turk."[8]

Luther approached his primary vocation as a Bible scholar through a pastoral lens. These commitments merged with his identification of the Turk and Pope as antichristian threats to faithful people. During the imperial 1530 Diet of Augsburg, Luther was housed north of Nürnberg in the Coburg Castle so he might more easily be consulted by his colleagues, including Philip Melanchthon. Suleiman had commenced his siege of Vienna in September 1529, and, as the preface to the Augsburg Confession makes clear, organizing support for defensive efforts was the Diet's main purpose.[9] Luther's purpose during his time in the "wilderness" was translating portions of the Bible into the German vernacular. His first finished product was a translation and short commentary on Ezekiel 39–40, in which Luther interpreted Ezekiel's apocalyptic "Gog" and "Magog" to be the Ottoman Empire. His hope was that "all the faithful might . . . draw courage and comfort from this passage."[10]

In 1532, Luther published a complete translation of the prophets under the title, *Die Propheten alle deutsch*. The preface he wrote for that collection, included in the complete *Deutsche Bibel* (1545), extended Luther's pastoral concern. Believing that the prophets "bear witness to the kingdom of Christ in which we now live," Luther found in them "strong comfort and comforting strength":

> By them our Christian faith is greatly comforted in the confidence that before God it is the right station or stance [*stand*], over against all other wrong, false, human holiness and sects. For these all are a source of great offense and affliction [*anfechten*] to a weak heart. . . . So, in our days, the sects of the Turk, the pope, and others are great and powerful snares.

Reading the prophets provides a balm to treat this *anfechtung*. Through the prophets, believers are assured that "the great glory of Christ's kingdom is surely ours, and will come hereafter" so that individuals "shall not grow discouraged through impatience or unbelief, or despair of that future glory."[11] Luther's approach—what might be described as pastoral apocalypticism—informed his interpretations of both scripture and history, especially the eminent threats of the pope and the Turk.[12]

In addition to calming the disquiet of believers weathering difficult times, Luther employed apocalyptic literature to interpret the times themselves. His 1530 translation of Daniel included a preface and a dedicatory letter to John Frederick of Saxony indicating Luther's belief that the world would soon end.[13] The preface identified the fourth beast of Daniel with the Roman empire and the small, arrogant horn (Dan. 7:8) as Islam: this "little horn will fight the saints and blaspheme Christ, something that we are all experiencing and seeing before our very eyes. . . . Certainly we have nothing to wait for now except the Last Day." Nevertheless, the Roman Empire will remain until the end, "even though many monarchs may have risen against the German empire and the Turks may rage against it." This is so, Luther says, because "Daniel does not lie, and up until now experience . . . has borne this out."[14] The trustworthiness of prophetic scripture provides the assurance of this interpretation: although enemies are at the gates, the empire in which we live cannot fail until it is defeated by Christ himself. This vision is cold comfort for those invested in perpetuating the empire, but a salve to common people struggling in their daily lives.

In the history of Protestant hermeneutics in the apocalyptic key, Revelation strikes the tonic while other sources provide the polyphony. Luther's initial dismissal of Revelation as useful for the Christian life is therefore noteworthy. In his 1522 preface to Revelation, Luther wrote that he "can in no way detect that the Holy Spirit produced it" and did not "think highly of it" because "Christ is neither taught nor known in it."[15] By 1530, Luther's views on Revelation had changed dramatically. Although his estimation of Revelation had grown, he was aware that interpreting the book could lead to pitfalls: "Many have tried their hands at it, but until this very day they have attained no certainty. Some have even brewed it into many stupid things out of their own heads."[16]

Crafted in the crucible of 1530, Luther's second interpretation of Revelation resonates with the pastoral apocalypticism of his work with Ezekiel and Daniel. Since the apparent purpose of the book is to help discern what will happen in the future, Luther seeks to determine a method for reading its mysteries and images:

> Since it is intended as a revelation of things that are to happen in the future . . . , we consider that the first and surest step toward finding its interpretation is to take from history the events and disasters that have come upon Christendom till now, and hold them up alongside of these images, and so compare them very carefully. If, then, the two perfectly coincided and squared with one another, we could build on that as a sure, or at least an unobjectionable, interpretation.

As we will see in the next chapter, this approach strongly foreshadows the method of synchronisms systematized in the next century by English biblical scholar Joseph Mede. Luther's list of historical examples is not exhaustive. Never a fully systematic thinker, he offers a few examples and leaves the rest for others: "scholars who know history will be able to figure this out, for it would take too long to relate and prove everything [here]."[17]

Presuming his times to the future period described in Revelation, Luther found his Catholic and Muslim enemies throughout the text. He interprets the angels and woes of Revelation 10 and 11, for instance, as referring to "the shameful Mohammed with his companions, the Saracens, who inflicted great plagues on Christendom, with his doctrines and with the sword." With this angel, Luther continues, comes "the holy papacy . . . a counterfeit church of external holiness." The final plague that will afflict the church "in the East is the second woe, Mohammed and the Saracens; here in the West are papacy and empire, with the third woe. To these is added for good measure the Turk, Gog and Magog, as will follow in chapter 20." After this final spasm of wrath, Revelation is filled "almost exclusively images of comfort, telling of the end of all these woes and abominations." This comfort was derived from the final defeat of God's enemies. "With this kind of interpretation," Luther says, believers "can rest assured that neither force nor lies, neither wisdom nor holiness, neither tribulation nor suffering shall suppress Christendom, but it will gain the victory and conquer at last."[18]

Lutheran identification of the pope as the Antichrist reached a crescendo in 1537, with the publication of Luther's *Smalcald Articles*, to which was appended the *Treatise on the Power and Primacy of the Pope*, prepared by Philip Melanchthon. In the *Smalcald Articles*, Luther asserts that the pope's desire to unite all of Christendom under the authority of his head-ship "shows overwhelmingly that he is the true end-times Antichrist" since, in doing so, the pope sets himself over God. The Turks, "despite being great enemies of the Christians," compare more favorably, since they "allow whoever desires it to have faith in Christ."[19] Melanchthon as-serted that "the marks of the Antichrist clearly fit the reign of the pope and his minions." Even if there were scriptural foundations to honor the pope, "obedience is still not owed him" when the Gospel is contradicted. "Indeed, it is necessary to oppose him as the Antichrist."[20] Robin Barnes has ob-served that the "crux of all that was new in Luther's reading of biblical prophecy, and the most influential of all his prophetic discoveries, was his identification of the Antichrist with the papacy at Rome."[21] Luther's stri-dent identification of the pope as "the true end-times Antichrist" laid the foundation for bitter and often violent Protestant resistance to Roman Catholic authority.

French reformer John Calvin (1509–1564) generally followed Luther's dual identification of the Antichrist with Catholicism and Islam, both of which seek to earn God's grace rather than accepting it as a free gift:

> The Turkes can confesse well ynough that they have neede of Gods mercie, & that hath always bin an opinion through the whole world: but they have intermingled their own satisfactions with Gods grace, as if they should say, although God be pitifull towardes us, yet muste we procure favour in his sight by our owne deserv-ings. . . . And in very deede that is the flat doctrine of the Papistes woord for woord.[22]

The similarity of Catholics and Muslims (within essentialized Protestant constructions) led Calvin to echo Luther in identifying "the Pope and Ma-homet" as "Antichristes." In a commentary on John 16:14, Calvin explained that the presence of the Holy Spirit did not mean that Christ's reign and the authority of Christ's word had come to an end, so that interpreters could "thrust the spirit into his place." This presumption, Calvin says, is the source of "the sacrileges of the Pope and Mahomet. For although these Antichristes doe much differ one from another, yet they have both one principle: to witte, that we are entred into the right faith by the gospel, but yet we must sette the perfection of doctrine somwhere else." With their new and unwarranted teachings, Calvin says, both the pope and Muham-mad "depart from the plaine trueth of Christ."[23]

Toward the end of a rousing sermon on the eighteenth chapter of Deuteronomy, preached on November 27, 1555, Calvin succinctly articulated the equivalence of the pope and Muhammad: "Lyke as Mahomet saith y^t his Alcoran is ye soveraine wisdome: so saith the Pope of his owne decrees: For they be the two hornes of Antichrist. Si[nce] it is so, doe we not see that we cannot in any wise cleave to the Pope but by renouncing Iesus Christ?" In the end, Calvin's focus on the Muslim Antichrist illustrated his disdain for the papacy rather than any concern for the prophetically predicted geopolitics of his day. He was focused more on the teachings of Muhammad than on Ottoman military threat, and was less eschatologically concerned than Luther. It was Calvin's conviction that "the Popish Religion tendeth to none other end, than to put Iesus Christ to silence."[24] This uncompromising assessment led Calvinists to develop an uncompromising stance against Catholic doctrine and the appearance of Catholic practice.

Toward the Development of Protestant Historiography

Luther's use of history as a lens for interpreting scripture marked a substantial departure from medieval methods. As Jaroslav Pelikan put it, "Medieval hermeneutics was dominated by a reliance on, and a quest for, the multiple sense of Scripture": the literary, the allegorical, the moral, and the anagogical. Pelikan saw in Luther's hermeneutics a "repudiation of allegorism." In its place, Protestant exegesis emphasized the grammatical, the literal, the historical, and, in very limited cases, the allegorical senses of scripture.[25] This method of reading history and prophecy was systematized by Lutheran historiographer Matthias Flacius Illyricus (Matija Vlačić-Ilirik).[26]

This departure from medieval readings opened the door for the development of "Protestant historiography." Avihu Zakai observes that Melanchthon's revised edition of *Carion's Chronicle* "marked the creation of a Protestant ideology of history" and finds Luther's later preface to Revelation "amazing" for "the explicitness with which history is pronounced necessary for the understanding of prophecy." According to Zakai, "With its apocalyptic orientation to history and strict correlation between history and prophecy, Protestant history infused the *saeculum* (history in its secular meaning) with divine significance, thereby transforming the role which the world and secular history assumed in sacred, providential history."[27] This approach to scriptural interpretation was no mere exercise: "For

Luther, even though it is the text of history that illuminates Revelation's obscure pictures, the message that is revealed is fundamentally an evangelical one, the trials and tribulations of the 'one holy, Christian Church.'"[28] Nevertheless, it was this transformation of the meaning of history, first established through the Lutheran expression of the Reformation in Germany, that provided the foundation for the even more radical reformation of historical thought among sixteenth-century English reformers exiled to the continent. It was those reformers who would go on to lay the hermeneutical foundations of the British Protestant tradition of Judeo-centric prophecy interpretation.

Lutheran readings of history through lenses provided by apocalyptic texts had a direct influence on English Protestants exiled during the religious upheavals of the sixteenth and seventeenth centuries. In some cases, English writers included the significance of Luther himself in their interpretations of history and text.[29] There were, however, significant differences in the appropriations of scripture, especially Revelation, between Lutherans and their English guests, differences not fully explained by the English theologians' simultaneous engagement with Reformed thinkers led by Calvin and Theodore Bèza. These differences spring from the relationship of English Protestant faith to particular elements in the development of English nationalism. As it had with Luther, historicist apocalypticism provided English Protestants with a vital tool for anti-Catholic polemics. Bernard McGinn has noted that "Nowhere was Revelation more avidly studied and more vociferously debated than in Reformation England." Focused on identifying "the papacy itself (along with the dread Turk)" as "the institutional embodiment of the Antichrist," Judeo-centric prophecy interpretation informed the "close linkage established between English national identity and the cause of the Reformation."[30]

Judeo-Centrism in John Bale's Apocalyptic Hope

John Bale (1495–1563) was one of the best-known polemicists in the first generation of English Protestantism. A biblical interpreter, historian, and writer of morality plays, Bale received support from Thomas Cromwell (*ca.* 1485–1540), vice-regent and chief minister for King Henry VIII. In 1539, the Act of Six Articles forced Bale and many others into exile on the European continent. Bale's exile continued until 1548, when Edward VI took the throne. A second exile commenced in 1553, when Queen Mary I ("Bloody Mary") acceded to the throne. His final return to the isles came only after Elizabeth's accession. The most enduring product of Bale's first exile was *The Image of Both Churches* (1545), containing the first full-length, English-language commentary on the book of Revelation. While the first edition of *The Image of Both Churches* was published in Antwerp during Mary's reign, a second, expanded edition of the book was published in London in 1570.[31]

Bale's acerbic rhetoric was aimed squarely against Catholic authorities. The exile exacerbated his sense of Catholic perfidy and his identification with St. John, the author of Revelation:

> And lyke as Babylon had the Israelytes captyve under a bodylye try-bute so hath this Rome had the Christianes both in their bodyes and sowles. At the writynge of this Prophecye felt Iohan of their cruelte beynge exyled into Pathmos . . . for the faythfull testymonye of Iesu. And so ded I poore creature with my poore wyfe and chil-dren at the gatheringe of this present Commentarye fleynge into Germanye for the same. . . . No marvele though she be here called a great whore.[32]

The conditions of suffering and martyrdom clarified for Bale the righ-teousness of both the true church and his own cause: "Marke heere the condition of Iohn being in most paynefull exile, for he in misterie through all this booke representeth every godly belever. By this shall ye well knowe in this revelation the one church from the other, for the one is mayntayned by the onely preaching of Gods pure worde, the other by all kyndes of Iew-ishe ceremonyes and heathenish superstitions." Although Luther vacil-lated in his assessment of Revelation as a source for Christian faith, Bale was convinced that knowledge of St. John's Apocalypse was "highly neces-sary . . . to him that is a true member of Christes church, as of any other booke of the sacred Byble" for "in none of them all are ye faythfull diligent hearers and readers more blessed."[33]

Although, like Luther, Bale found in Revelation a message of strong comfort in the midst of his exile, this emphasis was outweighed by his desire to prove English Protestantism to be "the true christian church . . . ye meeke spouse of ye Lambe without spot" and Catholicism to be "the proud church of hypocrites, ye rose coloured whore, the paramour of An-tichrist."[34] Bale rhetorically refashioned the duality of Augustine's *City of God* into a struggle between two churches, one true and one false. The artwork that closed *The Image of Both Churches* graphically depicted

Bale's conviction that Protestants were "The poore persecuted churche of Christe/or immaculate spowse of the lambe (Apoca. 12)" while Catholics were "The proude paynted churche of the pope/or synnefull Synagoge of Sathan (Apoca. 17)."[35]

The theopolitical yoking of Islam and Catholicism, supplied by Luther and Calvin, was an important tool in Bale's rhetorical arsenal, even if that arsenal was aimed primarily at his Catholic opponents: "For manye false cristes are abrode in the worlde to seduce the peple. The pope boasteth hymself for gods owne vicar. Mahomete calleth himself the grete prophete of the lorde. And both they to subdewe the gospell hath sett up newe lawes. The pope hys detestable decrees and Mahomete his abhominable alchorane."[36] This single Antichrist is the Gog and Magog that will be destroyed in their ill-fated "battayle agaynst the lambe." Bale nevertheless did not yoke the two parts of Antichrist so closely that the Turk could not mortally wound the papacy:

> And lyke as the Iewish sinagoge did at that tyme wholly perish for rejecting Gods word, and never could recover since, so may that false counterfayte churche of Antychrist come to distruction. . . . Muche is it to be feared, yf they stoppe GODS woorde as they have begunne, least that plague fall on them that lyghted vppon the IEWES at the Siege of Hierusalem, by the TURKE nowe, or by some other worse then he.[37]

Although Bale largely echoes themes from Luther and Calvin concerning Catholicism, Islam, and Antichrist, he introduces a new field of thought concerning Jews and their place within Christian apocalyptic hope. Bale does not repeat Martin Luther's anti-Judaic diatribes or the sharp theological constructions of Jews contained in Calvin's writing. Instead, Bale looks toward a time when "all kyndes of peple/both Iewes and Gentyles/ faythfull and heythen shall seke unto the[e]/and shall faythfullye . . . acknowlegynge the[e] for their onlye lorde God."[38] In this apocalyptic vision, there is no distinction between Jews and Gentiles, if a person has true Christian faith.

The most innovative element of Bale's teaching is his apparent hope for the national conversion of Jews to Protestant faith. Commenting on the 144,000 faithful around the Lamb on Mt. Zion in Revelation 14, Bale asserts that while this vision "hath bene spoken be concernynge the whole Christen multytude and her preachers . . . it most specially touche the

Iewes or Israelytes that shall in this latter age be converted unto Christ." This so because "the mounte Syon after the fleshe was theirs." Christian recognition of a worldly inheritance for Jews remains an animating theme in contemporary Christian Zionism. Bale is particularly impressed that these Jews who will convert to Protestant faith have the benefit of not having been afflicted with Catholic error; therefore, "not defyled are they wyth unmarryed wemen/which are the whoryshe lawes and uncleane Supersticions of the Gentyles/upon non other harpe have they common-lye harped but upon the scripturs/though it hath not bene to the pleasure of God/tyll now in thys latter age/wherin they shall whollye turne unto Christ."[39]

The national conversion of Jews to this true Protestant faith was, for Bale, part of God's cosmic plan in human history:

> And that all the worlde shall receive it, rebell the hypocrits never so sore. When the Gospell appeared in Christes tyme, the Iewes were the first that received it . . . And laste of all it shall returne agayne to the Iewes, as now very apt also to receive it. That Christes prophe-cye may be founde true. The last to be the fyrst, and the fyrst the last. For he that hath dispersed Israell, shall bringe him againe to his folde. . . . Thus shal the glory of God be within few yeares séene the world over, to the comfort of many.

Reflecting on one of the most curious puzzles within Revelation, the uneven dimensions of the New Jerusalem, Bale again returns to this vision. The "unequalnesse of length in ye furlonges & cubits," he says, perhaps signifies "the gentyls, the Iewes" coming together to make "one Hierusalem, or one perfect kingdome of Christ." In this heavenly vision, Jews and Gentiles are brought together in "one faith . . . and are made one shepefolde or flocke. Christ being one shepeherde of salvation to them both."[40] Although he imagines a Jewish return to relationship with God, this return is through conversion to Protestant faith; Bale is clear that the true Protestant church has fully replaced Judaism as the chosen people of God.[41]

John Bale sought to provide a theodicy for English Protestants suffer-ing, either in conscience or in body, under the Catholic authority. Engag-ing apocalyptic literature, especially Revelation, as a source of polemic and hope, he looked for his movement's final vindication and the defeat of the Turko-Catholic Antichrist. When this defeat occurs, all God's children will be united in God's truth. In contrast to Calvin and, especially, Luther, Bale confidently asserted that Jews, uncorrupted by exposure to Catholic doctrine and practice, will, as a nation, be among the faithful band at the throne of the Lamb. In contemporary theological terms, he was a supersessionist or replacement theologian, believing that Judaism qua Judaism had no mission beyond Christian truth. Nevertheless, it was through Bale's eschatological vision—a discourse formed within an intensely anti-Catholic and anti-Islamic milieu—that Jews, quite unbeknownst to themselves, were assigned a central place in the apocalyptic hope of Protestants in England and, later, in the United States.

The Geneva Bible and the Developing Judeo-Centric Consensus

Developing trends in Judeo-centric prophecy interpretation were first codified through the highly influential English-language translation in the Geneva Bible, first published in 1560 with a dedication "To the Most Vertuous and Noble Ladie Elizabeth, Queene of England, France, and Ireland, &c."[42] Prepared with the same exilic zeal that produced John Bale's polemics, the Geneva Bible was the first to contain divisions of the text into chapter and verse. Jaroslav Pelikan identified the bible's geographically accurate maps as "another implication drawn from the Reformation's emphasis on the historical sense of the Scriptures."[43] The bible's Calvinist orientation was communicated through its extensive marginal notes, which included scriptural cross-references, textual variants, source identifications, and theological interpretations. While the incisive translation was influential in its own regard, the major influence of the Geneva Bible, like the *Scofield Reference Bible* over three centuries later, was in its glosses and notes.

The Geneva Bible's integrated commentary, especially within Paul's Letter to the Romans, proposed a theology of Jews and Judaism that would exercise great influence on English Protestant commentators. Paul's proclamation that "God hath not cast away his people who he knewe before" (11:2) was augmented in the 1557 New Testament and in subsequent editions with the variant addition, "And elected before all begynning." The middle of the chapter included a note that drew readers toward eschatological speculation. In the Geneva Bible translation, Romans 11:15 reads, "For if the castyng away of them, be the reconciling of the world: what shal the receaving of them be, but lyfe from the dead?" The accompanying note explains that "The Iewes now remaine (as it were) in death for lacke of the Gospel: but when both they & the Gentiles shall embrace Christ, the worlde shal be restored to a newe life." The note with the following verse reinforces the variant reading of 11:2 and draws readers toward a national comprehension of Jews: "Abraham was not only sanctified, but his sede also." The interpretation of Romans 11:17 is perhaps most important for this conversation. Translated "Thogh some of the brances be broken of, & thou beyng a wylde olive tree, wast grafte in for them, and made partaker of the rote, and fatnesse of the olive tree," the note inserted just after the definite article for "olive tree" interprets the original tree as "The Churche of the Israelites." This identification is a significant departure from earlier, allegorical readings and a foundation for literalist readings that would undergird several movements within Anglo-American Protestantism, including Christian Zionism. The Geneva Bible translation of Romans 11:25b–26a reads, "partely obstinacie is come to Israel, until the fulnes of the Gentiles be come in. And so all Israel shalbe saved." Given the explanations and definitions that have come before, the "all Israel" cannot refer to anything except Jews, considered nationally. The note for 11:26 makes it clear: "He [Paul] sheweth that the time shall come that the whole nation of ye Iewes, though not every one particularly, shalbe joyned to the Church of Christ."[44]

The Geneva Bible's milieu of intra-Christian polemics opened a space for Jews to be considered from positive or, at least, neutral theological perspectives. The bible explains Revelation 1:7—"they whiche pearced him through: and all kindreds of the earth shal waile before him"—as meaning "They that condemned Christ & most cruelly persecuted him & put him to death shal then acknowledge him." This vague language deliberately does not single Jews out for condemnation or persecution. On the other hand, the notes clarifying who the "Iezabel" of Revelation 2 might be are more specific. This "harlot Iezabel" who "mainteined strange religion and exercised crueltie against the servants of God," includes all "that consent to idolatrie and false doctrine," since they "commit spiritual whoredome, whereof foloweth coporal whoredome." Although they think their doctrine "conteined the most depe knowledge of heavenlie things," it "was in deed drawen out of the depe dongeon of hell: by such termes now the Anabaptists, Libertines, Papists, Arians, &c use to beautifie their monstrous errors and blasphemies." In the same way, references in Revelation 2:9 and 3:9 to those who "call themselves Iewes and are not" but who are, rather, "the synagoge of Satan," are understood to be signs of the coming vindication of persecuted communities, when God "will cause them in thy sight to humble themselves, & to give due honour to God, and to his Sonne Christe."⁴⁵ By following this line of reasoning, the Geneva Bible helped create a space for Jews to be theologically constructed as a positive actor within English Protestant apocalyptic hope.

Apocalyptic Historiography and the Foundations of English Nationalism

John Bale's Judeo-centric interpretation of the Apocalypse finds its application in the historiography of Protestant England, to which also Bale made seminal contributions. *The Image of Both Churches* elevated the status of the book of Revelation while also applying the early Lutheran approach to reading history through the illumination of prophecy:

> A prophecye is this *Apocalips* called, and is much more excellent then all the other prophecies. Lyke as the lyght is more precious then the shadowe, the veritie then the figure, the new testament then the olde, and the gospell then the lawe, so is this holy oracle more precyous then they. . . . It is a full clerenesse to all the cronicles and most notable histories which hath bene written since Christes ascension, opening the true natures of their ages, tymes, and seasons. . . . Yet is the text a lyght to the cronycles, and not the cronicles to the text.⁴⁶

In 1546, Bale applied this apocalyptic methodology to the task of proving that Protestantism was England's true heritage while Catholicism was a foreign imposition that had led the isle to ruin.

Bale's *The Actes of Englysh Votaryes*, which sought to recount the entire history of the Christian tradition, *"from the worldes begynnynge to thys present yeare,"* represents a new trajectory in telling the history of England's nation and faith.⁴⁷ Drawing from a twelfth-century idea, Bale insisted that the Church of England was founded by Joseph of Arimathea, who had given his own tomb for Jesus' burial, thus making the English church apostolic in origin. Contact with the Roman church had brought only contamination. In this history of degeneration, Pope Gregory I (ca. 540–604, often known as Gregory the Great) was a chief villain for introducing "into the church, in their most extreme forms, the twin evils of enforced chastity for priests and interference in the business of the secular state."⁴⁸ This process reached an apex when Gregory sent "into Englande . . . a Romyshe monke called Augustyne, not of the ordre of Christ as was peter, but of the superstycyouse seete of Benet, there to sprede abrode the Romyshe faythe and relygyon, for Christes faythe was there longe afore." Augustine brought with him a great number of "monkes & Italyanes." Bale's evangelical commitments are clear in his assessment of the qualities of their learning: "Wele armed were they with Aristotles artylerye, as with logyck, Phylosophye, and other craftye scyences, but of the sacred scripturs, they knewe lyttle or nothynge."[49] This well-known history is subtly subverted through Bale's observation that "Christes faythe was" in England "longe afore" he arrived.

This historical revision was essential for Bale's larger project of proving that the "proude paynted churche of the pope" was an improper imposition on England to be rejected by the "immaculate spowse of the lambe."[50] Bale thus developed a nationalist history supported by apocalyptic interpretation, his faith community imagined as "citizens in the new Hierusalem with Iesus Christ" resisting since its earliest period "the old supersticious Babylon." Catholicism, not the Reformation, was the innovation in Christ's community.

The most immediate effect of Bale's contribution to English Protestant historiography was in the writings of a fellow exile, John Foxe (1517–1587). Foxe's *Actes and Monuments* (1563, often known as the *Book of Martyrs*)[51] divided history into six portions, with the Reformation identified as history's penultimate stage. Felicity Heal has said that Foxe's project "clothed polemical writing in historical garb, rendering chronicle ideologically charged."[52] In this apocalyptic history, "England had a special place, almost to the point where English history and ecclesiastical history were inseparable."[53] Although Foxe made a decisive contribution to the formation of English nationalism, the effects were not immediate.

Bale and Foxe returned to England in 1560, after the reign of Queen Elizabeth, dedicatee of the Geneva Bible, was determined stable. In 1570, a royal crisis brought their ideas to new relevance, leading to the publication of new editions of both *The Image of Both Churches* and *Actes and Monuments*. On January 23, James Stewart, the earl of Moray, was assassinated in Scotland. On February 25, Pope Pius V issued *Regnans in Excelsis*, excommunicating Queen Elizabeth. Stewart had been an illegitimate half-brother of Mary Stuart, Queen of Scots. In 1567, following Mary's abdication, he had been appointed Regent of Scotland, where he actively resisted Mary's attempts to regain the throne from her son, James. Many Protestant leaders therefore saw Stewart as a potentially unifying king who would marry Elizabeth, thus uniting England and Scotland under Protestant rule. His assassination presented Protestants with the challenge of affirming Elizabeth's reign while denigrating Mary.

According to Anne McClaren, the tool adopted for this dual task was Bale's *The Image of Both Churches* and its "typology of female identities" to illustrate "the ceaseless battle between the True Church and Antichrist." In text and in illustration, the various editions of Bale's *Image* (1545, 1550, and 1570) depicted "a virginal Elizabeth, presented as the Woman Clothed with the Sun and wedded both to God and the male Protestant nation," who "stood submissively yet valiantly four-square against the ceaseless machinations of the arch-seductress Mary, associated through her female identity with tyranny, treason, the pope, and Antichrist." Although complicated by traditional gender dynamics, this approach promised stability, since it sought "to identify securely the homology of monarch, state, and religion as, in England, a masculine political order: one fronted, for the moment, by a queen but headed by God."[54]

Bale's study of the Apocalypse was particularly well-suited to comprehending an English future faced with two possible paths, symbolized by two possible queens. "In the wake of *Regnans in Excelsis*," McLaren writes, "John Bale's apocalyptic typology contrasting the True and False Churches thus began a new career. It came into its own as a means of persuading Englishmen that . . . the contest was not only between embodied queens (where the evidence was necessarily equivocal) but also between good and evil, God and the devil." McLaren suggests the revised iconography of *Actes and Monuments* indicates heightened apocalyptic thinking. Specifically, she interprets a caption describing "The Image of the persecuted Church/The Image of the persecuting Church" as drawing "John Bale's explication of Christian history . . . into the narrative of the *Acts and Monuments*, and hence directly into contemporary politics." The implications of this coalescing English Protestant nationalism are tremendous: "with this resort to apocalypticism, we can date the institution of the myth of England as the 'elect nation': an island fastness preserved from papal bondage by its particular reformation history."[55]

John Bale's project of constructing Protestant meaning, with its anti-Catholic, Judeo-centric and historiographic elements, shaped both the trajectory of English nationalism and the history of theopolitical prophecy interpretation. Intended to instill courage and provide a hand-hold of certainty in the midst of confusion, these interpretations would continue to place Jews at the center of Protestant projections of God's drama unfolding within God's Protestant history.

Hopes for Absent Jews

The growing centrality of Jews for English Protestant prophecy interpretation is remarkable also for the fact that England had for several centuries
officially banned Jews from the country. As Nabil Matar observed regarding seventeenth-century restorationist debates, "Treatises were composed
and debates held over the issue, ironically, by writers many of whom, if
not most, had never met a Jew in their lives."[56] While it is possible that
Bale encountered Jews during his exile on the European mainland, the
primary source of his project was the image of Jews recounted in the biblical narrative, read through English Protestant eyes.

Jews were driven from England in 1290 under authority of the Edict of
Expulsion signed by Edward I. They would not be recognized in England
until the mid-1600s under the leadership of Oliver Cromwell, in conversation with Menasseh ben-Israel, discussed in Chapter Five. The expulsion
was preceded by increasing anti-Jewish persecution; the caricatures and
accusations against Jews that led to it persisted in English society for the
350 years of expulsion and beyond.[57] In their absence, Jews, like Muslims,
were objects of much speculation. Both communities would be constructed
for English Protestant purposes.

The potential place of Jews for English Protestant hope caught the interest of John Foxe. Foxe trafficked in more anti-Jewish imagery than Bale,
to the point of including gratuitous anti-Jewish stories at several points in
Actes and Monuments and other writings.[58] Foxe's most important reflection on Jews and Judaism is found in his *Sermon Preached at the Christening of a Certaine Jew* (1578). Bolstering his anti-Catholic polemic, Foxe
extols the need to purify Protestant practice in order to simultaneously
draw more Jews to convert, further weakening the pope. Thus, "if we will
not do this for the Iewes sake, let us yet at the least have due regard to our
owne estate. We have bene plagued sufficiently enough by the Turkes and
Saracenes for our idolatrie . . . to the great delight of the Iewes." Beyond
his anti-Catholic polemic, however, Foxe provided "a refutation of the obstinate Iewes," as well as reflections on "the finall conversion of the same."
Foxe is clear that God's relationship with Jews has not been abrogated,
despite their centuries of suffering: "the promises remayning still in their
force. Even so the Iewes, although they prescribe upon a promised place
in Sion." Foxe illustrated the "blessed and joyfull returne of the Iewes" to
the family of God as "the braunches . . . recovering the naturall verdure of
their honorable stocke." Conflating Luke 21:24 with Romans 11:25, he

speculates that "the fulnes of the Gentiles" will be complete when gentiles have possessed "Gods Church w'out the Iewes" for as long as "the Iewes did first enioy their synagogue w'out ye Gentiles." According to Foxe's calculation, "the nomber of yeres wil not be farre unequal" to "this present time." Nevertheless, Foxe quickly backs away from any form of date-setting, instead declaring simple faith "that God hath decreed upon an infallible certaintie of time, wherein the Gentiles shall mount to their fulnes, and the Iewes also after that fulnes of time shall returne unto the fayth."[59]

Foxe provides an important example of how English Judeo-centric prophecy interpretation constructed Jews toward Protestant ends. In Foxe's sermon, Jews, considered as a nation, are symbols rather than persons. Jews, collectivized and mythologized by English Protestant hermeneutics, are thus instrumentalized as symbols of God's work in history in order to verify Protestant eschatological hope and, thus, a verification of Protestant truth-claims in the present. In a time when commitment to certain expressions of Christian truth was inseparable from concomitant political orders, the theopolitical utility of Judeo-centric prophecy interpretation was clear.

Some scholars have identified Francis Kett (c.1547–1589) as the likely source for later anticipations of Jewish restoration to Palestine.[60] In 1585, Kett published a pamphlet addressed to English Catholics that identified the pope as Beast and Antichrist,[61] along with a longer book, *The Glorious and Beautifull Garland of Mans Glorification*. Although Kett had reflected deeply on the Hebrew Bible's patterns of redemption and proclaims that Jesus "shall bring redemption to the captive, and restore Israel, and set up his honour in Iuda, and in Davids stoole, that all nations shall honour him: yea kings and princes shall arise and worship this holy one of Israell," his explanation that "wee are in prison and bondage to death, without we imbrace Christ, and preferre him above the law, and above all workes, as the onely doore to enter into Gods rest: for he doth open the prison" makes clear Kett's focus on Christians rather than Jews. Instead of focusing on the literal restoration of literal Jews to geographic Palestine, Kett provided a typological reading of Jewish exile and redemption as a metaphor for Christian faith in Jesus. For Kett, Jews possess the same unfaithfulness as Muslims: "Wherefore do not crucifie Christ againe in thy hart by obstinate sinne, by wilfull blindnes, and carelessenes: like a Jew and Turke, despising the humanity of Christ that was so humble: by being malicious and unkind to him that is so good."[62] His heavenly vision makes no mention of Jews, whether or not converted to Protestant faith.

By 1588, Kett had become animated by a combination of Arian doctrine, millenarian zeal, and anti-clericalism which ultimately would lead to his being burned at the stake. Although one contemporary scholar noted in the "Blasphemous Heresyes of One Kett," that "Kett was ultra-orthodox" when he wrote *The Glorious and Beautifull Garland*, his orthodoxy had dramatically diminished in the span of three years. In addition to his Arianism, Kett's alleged "heresyes" included teaching that "Christ shall come before the last daie and raigne as materiall Kynge uppon Mounte Syon at Jerusalem," and that "no man ought to be put to death for heresies." The official condemnation charged Kett with believing "That Chryste is now in his human nature gathering a church here in earth in Judea" and "That this yeare of our Lord 1588 dyvers and fewes shall be sent into dyvers countryes to publishe the new covenant."[63] Although Kett was highly committed to understanding his Christian faith through the rhythms of the Hebrew Bible, he was not Judeo-centric in the same sense developed by John Bale and John Foxe.

Although Bale and Foxe were influential, it cannot be presumed that their ideas—especially their nascent commitments to Judeo-centric prophecy interpretation—formed the majority opinion in early Protestant England. John Napier's *A Plaine Discouery of the whole Revelation of Saint Iohn* (1593) shows that addressing the Turko-Catholic threat did not require a Judeo-centric approach. Commenting on Revelation 9:1, Napier (1550–1617) sees Muhammad as "the *Star* that in the fifth trumpet fel downe from heaven, and his *Locusts* that arose." This "must needs be the *Mahomet*," Napier says, "who fell from his former Christian profession, and became an Apostate, and out of the smoke of his heresie, stirred up the Turkes to be his armie." Echoing Luther, Napier identifies "these *Mahometanes*" as "messengers sent by God, to scourge the Christians falling away." Although Islam was God's chastising instrument, both "these Papisticall and *Mahometane* kingdoms, both enemies to God," will "be destroyed by the power & force of Gods word." Indeed, he was convinced that "*Gog* is the *Roman* and Papistick Empire, and *Magog* the *Mahometicke* Empire."[64]

Although not a majority opinion, Judeo-centrism quickly took hold within English Protestant apocalyptic hermeneutics, with dramatic consequences. John Merbecke, for instance, writing in 1581 on Romans 11, saw Jewish conversion as an essential sign of Christ's imminent return: "This conversion of the Iewes I doe dissever from those tokens which began to be done a great while a goe, & do passe before the comming of the Lorde, and I doe applie it unto those signes, which shall goe nearest before it."[65]

In 1596, Thomas Morton suggested that, "we cannot doubte but that the glory of God shall be wonderfully enlarged by the conversion of the Iewes, and therefore it may be more desired then our owne salvation."[66]

Toward the Seventeenth-Century Christian Zionist Synthesis

After Elizabeth's death in 1603, James VI of Scotland became James I, king of "Great Britain." The kingdom was unified, but many Protestant leaders were not confident that James, although highly interested in matters of theology and biblical interpretation, would support their cause. Elizabeth had deftly navigated the theopolitical minefield of her time, maintaining a level of order, but angering Puritans and Catholics alike at different turns.

Protestants seeking certainty in a time of continued upheaval continued the task of interpreting scripture to better understand their place in God's apocalyptic history. The arguments developed in the sixteenth century began to influence all manner of apologetics and intra-Christian polemics. Writing in 1605, John Dove, in his tract providing a Protestant confutation of atheism, made a singular appeal to the future conversion of the Jews, "performed in that due time which God in his secret wisdome hath appointed," as a "sufficient argument to induce Infidelles to believe."[67] The early seventeenth-century expansions of Judeo-centric prophecy interpretation resulted in fully developed geopolitical and ideological commentaries on various biblical texts.

Arthur Dent published *The Ruine of Rome*, his full-length commentary on Revelation, in 1603. Dent's effort is striking for its vitriol against Islam in the persona of the Turk, the common cause it makes between Protestants and Jews, and its Anglo-centric outlook with England at the center of the renewal of the world. For Dent, Revelation was a book by which "wee might bee both fore-warned and fore-armed" against "Sathan himselfe, and his three great instruments, the Romaine Emperour, the Pope, and the Turke." Dent's word of comfort is that the pope and Turk will be defeated by Christ, "troden downe under his feete of brasse." This defeat will be accomplished by the Bible itself, a weapon unleashed by the Reformation: "although it was long shut up in the time of Poperie, and lay buried in a straunge tongue: yet now it is opened, and publikely preached unto all the servants of God."[68] For Dent, the availability of the Bible in translation is evidence of apocalyptic hope.[69]

Dent explicitly says that "the twenty-four elders who sit on their thrones before God" in Revelation 4:4 comprise "both of Iewes and Gentiles . . . which all in most suppliant manner, doo worshippe the onely everlasting God . . . because now he had received the kingdome, the power and the glory, both Pope, and Turke, and Emperor, and all his enemies, being subdued under his feete." In this apocalyptic vision, Jews and Christians rejoice together in the defeat of Catholicism and Islam. Likewise, in his explanation of how John can refer to Rome as "Babylon," Dent says that "For as the old Easterne Babylon did a long time oppresse the church of the Iewes: so Rome this Westerne Babylon, hath long oppressed the church of the Christians."[70] For Dent, Jews and Gentiles find common cause in their mutual persecution and mutual striving for faithfulness against presumably mutual oppressors.

Dent's image of common rejoicing among Gentiles and Jews in the downfall of Catholicism and Islam allows him to functionally ignore the western church's own oppression of Jews, including the expulsion of Jews from England, in effect as he wrote. This whitewashing of history, achieved through the transference of western Christian anti-Semitism onto less faithful eastern Christians, facilitates his cooptation of Jews into his interpretive system, to the end that they are to take up arms against Muslims, both theologically and geopolitically. One can compare similar moves in John Hagee's attempt to accuse Islam of having a triumphal theology that cannot countenance Jewish security except as a threat to Muslim systems of meaning, even as he claims his tradition as fully accommodating to Jews in their fullness.[71]

Although Dent frames the cosmic battle between Christ and the devil, he is focused almost exclusively on the preservation of English Protestantism. If English Protestant faith does not endure Jesuit popery, "how shal Rome fal? how shal the Iewes ever be converted? how shall fire come downe from heaven, and devour both Gog and Magog"? Since "this kingdome [England] hath happily begun to hate the whore, and to make her desolate and naked," Dent says, "so undoubtedly shee shall continue unto the end of the world," lest St. John "be found a false prophet."[72] The trustworthiness of the Bible proves the faithful endurance of England into the future. This Anglo-centric vision of apocalyptic hope—based on the sure identification of the Roman Catholic Church as the rose-colored whore—is Dent's primary contribution to the English Protestant tradition of Judeo-centric prophecy interpretation. This tradition would soon manifest explicitly militant apocalyptic visions, with Jews, theologically conceived as proto-Puritans, drafted into theopolitical efforts to vindicate western Protestant hope.[73]

4

Militarizing the Jew

JUDEO-CENTRIC PROPHECY INTERPRETATION,
THOMAS DRAXE TO JOSEPH MEDE (1608–1627)

BEFORE HER DEATH in 1603, Elizabeth declared that James IV of Scotland would be her successor. Among Puritans, there was some hope that a new king from Scotland, where the Reformation had progressed further, would, despite his lineage, propel the progress of the gospel, for England and for the world. As the new king made his way to London, he was presented with the "Millenary Petition," a moderate statement of Puritan concerns claiming to represent the views of over a thousand English subjects. In response, James called a conference to be held in January 1604 at Hampton Court. The meeting proved to be a victory for Anglicanism; no substantive Puritan demands were granted, save the request to produce an "Authorized" version of the Bible, eventually published in 1611. Although James sought to perpetuate Elizabeth's careful balance of church politics, the mere preservation of Protestant hegemony was not the ultimate end of Puritan politics. The apocalyptic hopes fueling their fervor ensured that, in the seventeenth century, the Puritan controversies "ceased to be merely theological." They instead became "a political matter and as such dominated the English scene for several fateful decades."[1]

The Puritan program developing in the early part of James's reign was informed by specific readings of the Bible, Judeo-centric prophecy interpretation dominant among them. The tradition inaugurated by John Bale and John Foxe was refined and reapplied by Thomas Brightman, Henry Finch, and Joseph Mede. This chapter explores how consensus grew among Protestants in early seventeenth-century England regarding the relative places of Catholics, Muslims, and Jews in God's purposes for the end of the age. Even as the literal restoration of literal Jews to geographic Palestine came to be imagined as a definite component of eschatological speculation, English

Puritan perspectives continued to readily identify Catholics and Muslims as eternal enemies of God while simultaneously constructing Jews (despite their absence from the English context) as eventual allies against the Turko-Catholic Antichrist. Through the English colonial enterprise, these constructions were exported to America, where they eventually shaped the foundations of independent American identity and paved the way for twentieth and twenty-first century American Christian affinity for the State of Israel.

Thomas Draxe and the Personal Assurance of Salvation

Even as the royal transition from Elizabeth to James resulted in great theo-political anxiety, the budding tradition of Judeo-centric prophecy tradition was applied in more personal ways. In contrast to interpreters like Arthur Dent, who focused on establishing the importance of both England and the Israelites for God's end-times plans, Thomas Draxe (d. 1618/1619) was more attentive to developing personal apocalyptic piety.

Draxe's first attempt to locate the importance of Jews in eschatological speculation comes in *The Generall Signs and Forerunners of Christs Coming to Judgement* (1608), a pamphlet appended to a handbook for maintaining vibrant personal faith. Dividing the prophetic witness into signs that have been fulfilled and those that soon will be, Draxe reflects on the coming "burning and utter desolation of Rome the mother of fornication and idolatrie and the proper seate of Antichrist" and the "generall calling and conversion of the nation of the Iewes (in the places and countries where they shalbe and are residing)." Among the signs already fulfilled were the 70 c.e. "destruction and desolation of Ierusalem, togither with the Iewes state and policy," which Draxe took to be "a type and patterne of the worlds destruction." Draxe allowed that the necessity of "divulging and preaching of the Gospel throughout the whole known and inhabited world" had been accomplished by the disciples in the known world of their day. Their work was necessary so the Gospel could be carried "from thence unto the most obscure, unknowne and barbarous nations (such as are *America* and the North parts of the world)."[2] This brief reflection marks one of the first appearances of America in the prophetic timetable.

In his 1608 pamphlet, Draxe mentions his larger work on Romans 11, published later that year as *The Worldes Resurrection, or The Generall Calling of the Iewes*. Dedicated to Lucy, Countess of Bedford, *The Worldes Resurrection* shows how apocalyptic constructions of Jews can function alongside quintessentially anti-Jewish perspectives. In the dedicatory letter, for instance, Draxe says of Jews that while "the conversion of the nation of them is dayly expected" and we must "be so farre from despiseing them, or scandalizing them by our ill life," magistrates should enact laws against "their vile and intolerable usuries, whereby they plague & oppresse many poore Christians" and to "punish with al sharpnesse their horrible blasphemies against Christ and his gospel." In spite of these civil recommendations against Jews (who at the time were banished from England) Draxe developed a remarkably welcoming theology of Jewish-Christian relations. Reflecting on Paul's admonition in Romans 11 for Gentile believers to not be oppressively proud, Draxe says that "we Gentiles are beholding unto the Iewes, and in many respects inferiour unto them, howsoever they (for the present) are generally cast off and plucked from the vine." He further points out that (1) the covenant of the New Testament is "derived from them into us & we are changed into their commonwealth and not they into ours," (2) Jesus "had his birth and beginning from them," (3) Jews are God's "chosen nation, the peculiar people, and a royall Priest-hood," and (4) they are recipients of "particular promises" from God. The conclusion of these observations is obvious: Christians "must therefore acknowledge our selves debters unto the Iewes" so they can be won "to the approbation and acceptance of the Gospell."[3] Draxe's theology of Christian indebtedness to Jews is consistent with perspectives promoted by some contemporary American Christian Zionists.[4]

Draxe's apocalyptic construction of Islam is less theologically sophisticated than his understanding of Jews. Commenting on Romans 11:21, Draxe counsels the countess that we must "make our election sure to our selves" by observing the "Apostacy not only of the Iewes, but also of the whole world . . . for most are revolted long agoe: the Easterne parts to the Turke and to his Alcoron, and ye Westerne parts to the Romish Antechrist and his superstition." For Draxe, Islam demarcates the eastern and western worlds. The Turk and the churches of the East function less as symbols of geopolitical prophecy than as object lessons for western Protestant morality: "Let us marke and meditate upon Gods severity against the Hungarians and the Greekes and other places of Europe, that have beene captivated and inthralled to the Godlesse and barbarous Turkes, together with Asia and Affrica."[5]

Draxe imagines that the evangelization of America will be pivotal to bringing in "the full number of the Gentiles" (Rom. 11:25). This task should soon be completed and "no nation shall be left out" even if they are as

"barbarous, as they of America, amongst whom it is to be thought, that
some of the Apostles Disciples preached or (at the least) that the same &
sound of the Gospell might easily be brought to them from other famous
and populous places." The western expansion of Christian faith was propelled when "other parts of the world have declared themselves unthank-
full for it and unworthy of it (as all the Easterne parts have done, and therefore have justly lost the Gospell)." Once every nation has been exposed to
the Gospel, Romans 11:26–27 will be fulfilled as "the whole body of the
people of Israel . . . shalbe saved." Regarding the question of whether or not
Jews will "recover the holy land . . . and dwell their," Draxe was not yet a
restorationist. Instead, in 1608, he believed that Jews "have no such promise, neither have they any possiblity of meanes to compasse it." He thought
it likely "that they shal bee converted in those countries into which they are
dispersed" since they would then better "revive the faith of ye Gentiles
beeing mixed and conversant with them."[6] As we will see, Draxe aban-
doned these practical objections after the revolution in Judeo-centric
prophecy interpretation inaugurated by Thomas Brightman.

Brightman, Covenantal Nationalism, and the English Apocalypse

Building on the tradition established by John Bale and John Foxe, but on
the other side of Elizabeth's reign, Thomas Brightman (1562–1607) provided one of the most enduring frameworks for English Protestant prophecy interpretation. As Avihu Zakai has observed, "the revolutionary solution he offered in terms of the relation between prophecy and history
singularly inspired radical Puritans, in England as well as in New England, to attempt to realize through their own actions their millennial expectations and eschatological visions."[7]

Brightman's magnum opus, *Apocalypsis Apocalypseos*, a full-length commentary on Revelation, was distributed posthumously.[8] First published in
Latin at Frankfurt am Main in 1609, the first English edition, published in
Amsterdam, appeared in 1611. The project was conceived in a climate of
heightened Puritan concern. Many Puritans considered the 1604 conference at Hampton Court to have been a failure. In 1605 authorities discovered the "Gunpowder Plot" designed by Catholics to assassinate James as
well as the Puritans then sitting in Parliament.[9] As threats against Puritan
ideals mounted, Brightman urged his fellow presbyterians to respond to
the crisis, "For now that time is begun, when Christ shall rule in all the

earth, his enemies subdued on every side."[10] Brightman's *Apocalypsis* presented a realized and realizable eschatological vision calling Puritans to involvement in manifesting their millennial hopes. It offered a "new historical consciousness" that "aroused a sense of the imminent fulfillment of prophecy within time and history."[11] In his post-Elizabethan context, Brightman's apocalyptic interpretation remained nationalist, but in a manner different from earlier, positivist perspectives. Instead, Brightman's correlation of history and prophecy led him to a critical nationalism, which in turn produced an unprecedented interpretation of England's role in God's eschatological plan.

Brightman's commentary on Revelation 2–3 identified the seven churches listed there with different ecclesiastical eras, for instance associating Sardis, Philadelphia, and Laodicea with the Reformation period. Among these, Sardis, which had begun a new thing but was on the verge of death, was linked to Germany. The Reformed churches of Scotland and the Netherlands were symbolized by Philadelphia, the church that has "kept my word" and will be "kept from the hour of trial" (Rev. 3:8, 10). Brightman identified "the third reformed Church," Laodicea, with "ours of England." Revelation describes Laodicea as a church imagining itself to have prospered and in need of nothing, not realizing it is "wretched, pitiable, poor, blind, and naked." It is "lukewarm, and neither cold nor hot" and God therefore warns "I am about to spit you out of my mouth" (Rev. 3:15–19). Brightman applied this description to England's church, since, even before Elizabeth, "Most mighty King Henry her father had expelled the Pope, but reteyned the Popish superstition." Thus, while the Church of England has "forsaken the Romish Antichrist, and . . . rysen from that cold death . . . Hotte in deede shee is not, whose outward government for the most parte, is yet still Romish." It is the "mixing of the pure doctrine and Romish regiment together" that "maketh this lukewarmnes, whereby wee stande in the middes betweene cold & hotte; betweene the Romish & Reformed Churches."[12]

For both John the Revelator and Brightman the Puritan, the warning to Laodicea is not a final judgment but an invitation to further reform. Far from declaring that England had been removed from the apocalyptic stage, Brightman was mapping the road toward God's redemptive favor, so that England might return itself to the center of the apocalyptic narrative. Brightman's critical nationalism thus promotes what might be called a negative exceptionalism; England was the special recipient of God's reproving discipline. In this deuteronomic theology of covenantal threat, the centrality of the country in question is preserved (at least rhetorically) through the threat of losing God's blessing. This negative exceptionalism—expressed in the theopolitical form of covenantal nationalism—would be further developed in the Anglo-American Puritan context and carried forward through American faith and life. This theme is especially apparent among contemporary American Christian Zionists who identify "blessing" Jews as the singular path to securing God's blessings for themselves and their country.[13]

Despite its association with Laodicea, English Protestant faith remained at the apex of apocalyptic history, which, for Brightman, was understood in millenarian terms. He equated the seventh trumpet of Revelation, signaling when "the mystery of God will be fulfilled," when "the most gratious Queene Elizabeth . . . againe gave her Kingdome to Christ, in rooting out through all her dominions the most part of the Romish superstitions." Since this seventh trumpet has blown, Brightman proclaims that "now the time has begun, when Christ shall rule in all the earth."[14]

For Brightman, Catholics and their sympathizers represented the most serious threat to both Protestant truth and English civil order. Without their complete defeat, the English Laodicea could not achieve its Evangelical vocation: "Wee have Christ angry with us, because wee are farre from a perfect reformation: but if wee returne to our vomite, how mightily shall he rage against us? Therefore they who favour the Papists secretly . . . endevour the overthrow of our Kingdome." Overall Brightman brought a positive message: "But now after the yere 1558, a much sweeter symphonie is made, by accession of the French, English, alter Helvetian, Belgian, Bohemian, and Scottish Confessions. Al these agreeably singing one tune together, doo make a most grateful song to godly ears; but drive the enemies out of their wits." The eschatological project to which he called his fellow presbyterian Christians had already been inaugurated, "For now the time has begun."[15]

Brightman and Judeo-centric Apocalyptic Hope

In addition to providing a new historical paradigm for Puritan apocalyptic hope, Brightman's *Apocalypsis* assigned a greater role for Jews in defeating the Turko-Catholic threat. Writing in nearly the same period, Arthur Dent found it probable that "the kings of Europe shal be the greatest agents" for the overthrow of Rome, although he allowed that "the Easterne Kings may happely have some stroke in this work."[16] These kings are mentioned in

Revelation 16:12: "The sixth angel poured his bowl on the great river Euphrates, and its water was dried up in order to prepare the way for the kings from the east." Although Dent did not speculate about who these kings might be, Brightman plainly identified them as Jews:

> But who be these Kings? . . . It seemeth to me, that they are here meant, for whose sake alone the scripture mentioneth the waters of old to have bin dryed up; namely the *Iewes*, unto whom the read [Red] sea yeilded passage, and Iarden [Jordan] stayed his course, til every one were gone over, journeying on foot through the deep. This miracle is proper to this people onely.

Brightman's sure identification of Jews as the kings from the east is matched by his confidence in their coming national conversion and restoration to Palestine:

> But what need there a way to be prepared for them? Shal they returne agayn to Ierusalem? There is nothing more sure: the Prophets playnly confirme it, and beat often upon it. Yet not to the end that the ceremonial worship should be restored: but that they mercy of God may shine unto al the world, in giving to a nation now scatered over al the face of the earth, & dwelling no where but by leave; their fathers habitations, wherein they shal serve Christ purely and sincerely, according to his owne ordinance onely.

For Brightman, according to Paul's teaching in Romans 11:25, "it is certain, that this nation shal earnestly flock unto the Gospel . . . in the last times . . . of the vials." In Brightman's chronology, the destruction of Rome would remove the final impediment to the national conversion of Jews to Puritan faith, "so after that Rome is utterly abolished, straightway this consort shal appear." The event will be both a morale boost for the long-suffering faithful as well as a general proof of Puritan doctrine and practice: "Wherefore after Rome is overthrown and cut off there shal be a common bruit of this new Christian people: at the hearing whereof the Gentiles shal be astonished."[17]

So that Jews might be identified as kings of any sort, Brightman, knowing that anti-Jewish logic would lead to objections, constructed Jews as Protestants *in potentia* or, more precisely, as proto-Puritans. Thus, to the question "But what, are the Iewes *Kings*?" Brightman answered "why not?

seing al Christians are *Kings*." Brightman was confident that, in the near future, "the whole East shal obey them, that not without cause ar this people called Kings, in respect of their long and large dominion & Empire." Brightman further offers the geographical tautology that the "Kings come from the *East*, because the greatest multitude of Iewes, is in those countries." Those Jews in the east will be the first to "see the truth, and embrace the study of it" to commence their "universal calling." This national conversion would follow the end of Catholicism: "as Romes Idolatry, caled for those cruel Turks: so after that Rome is utterly abolished, straightway this consort shal appear."[18]

In Brightman's Judeo-centric eschatology, proto-Puritan Jews are deployed ideologically and militarily against the twin threats of the Turko-Catholic antichrist. Echoing Luther, Brightman understood there to be "no difference between the Ministers of the Pope and of the Turk," since although "nothing is more common with them than the name of Christ . . . they hope for life and salvation by their owne merits" and so "differ nothing from heathens, which despise Christ altogither." Muslims, therefore, deserve their coming fate to be visited upon them when Jews—after converting en masse after the destruction of Rome—move against the Turk to retake Jerusalem for themselves. "The Iewes in the East and North part shal first stirre up themselves, and make hast to goe into this holy city . . . by *Euphrates dryed*. . . . [W]hen the Easterne & Northerne Iewes are raised up, the Turke shal be greatly troubled, after he hath received newes of that thing. . . . The Southerne Iewes shall follow these, our in the West shal be last."[19] In his commentary on Daniel, Brightman says that "they holy land" is "the Jewes country" and that western military force, which first encountered Islam in the guise of the Saracens in "about the yeere six hundred and thirty," will not be able to defeat the Turk.[20] His commentary on the Song of Solomon confirms Brightman's opinion regarding the Jewish role in the destruction of Islam: "after the Conversion . . . *Gog* and *Magog*, that is the Turke and the Tartar with all the wicked *Mahumetanes* shall utterly perish by the sword of the Converted and returned *Iewes*."[21]

Although Brightman expected that the national conversion of Jews would occur after the destruction of Rome, his Judeo-centric prophecy interpretation functioned in the present against the Catholic enemy. In *Apocalypsis Apocalypseos*, Brightman allegorizes the vision of the New Jerusalem in which there is "no need of sun or moon to shine on it, for the glory of God is its light," by which "the nations will walk," and to which "the kings of the earth will bring their glory" (Rev. 21:23–24), to arrive at a peculiarly anti-Catholic reading. The "ful restoring of the Iewes," he says, will result in a church "whose fervent and singular study of true godliness" will cause "the *Churches* of the Gentiles as the *Moon & Sun*" to be "abashed at [its] greater brightness." This is so because "the Iewes were the peculiar people of the high God, and of his Church which is heavenly." In another place he returns to these verses to proclaim that a "Church is most glorious . . . covered with no cloudes of ceremonies; therfor let them see in how great errour they are, whom bring in a pompous show of ceremonies."[22] Brightman's joyful belief in a national Jewish conversion provides a literary context for anti-Catholic polemics.

Brightman's meditations on the New Jerusalem took him beyond Thomas Draxe's theology of indebtedness to Jews to imagining the eschatological superiority of the church formed by converted Jews. As he says in relation to Revelation 21:26, Jews "shal bring the glory and honour of the Gentiles unto [the New Jerusalem], that is, the Iewes themselves." For Brightman, this vision of (proto-Puritan) Jewish superiority leads him to suggest pivoting away from traditional western Christian treatment of Jews:

> Before time the Iewes alwayes found the Gentiles most hatefull, who left no meanes unattempted to doo them hurt; now contrariweise ther shal be no cause to feare that they will doo them any harme; yea rather why should they not expect all good at their hands, who shal apply al their forces to the advancing of them. But these Gentiles are not al generally, but are limited with a certain kinde, which, faith he, shal be saved. . . . [T]he Gentiles shall walke to they light, which John draweth to the elect.[23]

Brightman not only endorses a nonpersecutory approach to Jews, but seems to lay out a political program by which well-meaning Gentiles will seek to advance Jewish interests. The theopolitical point is driven home in the English edition of 1616, which supplements the above passage with this sentence: "This verse containeth the second outward matter that doth argue and set forth the excellency of this glorious Church of the Iewes, namely the glory that shall come unto it from the Gentiles."[24]

The underlying goal of *Apocalypsis Apocalypseos* was to detail the apocalyptic foundations of Puritan resistance to theological compromise. In the process of drawing a theopolitical battle line between Puritans and Anglicans, Brightman's prophetic interpretation cast Jews in the eschatological drama, opposite the arch-foes of Catholicism and

Islam. Brightman's instrumentalist Judeo-centrism has nothing to do with philo-Semitism. His eschatological expectation refuses to respect Jews as Jews:

> Solomon seemeth to appoint out the territories and borders of that land, which the Jewes at length (converted to Christ, delivered from the Nations and restored to their Country seates) shall obtaine proper and their owne. But what (will ye say) dost thou turne Iew? God forbid. I dreame not of that returne, which as yet they do, That they may renew the Temple, restore the Ceremonies, and possesse the land in times past: promised and given as an earnest of the heavenly. (These things are eternally buried, not worne out by time, but utterly abolished by Christ.) But I speak of a restoring to their Country, wherin they shall worship Christ according to his Ordinances: which is not contrary to Religion every one knoweth, and all the Prophets seeme to foretell it with one consent.[25]

For Brightman, Turks were enemies to be destroyed and Jews, even if he did deign to consider them kings, were little more than literary characters functioning as means to this national-covenantal end. Nevertheless, the precision of Brightman's approach to Jews, in tandem with the negative exceptionalism of his critical nationalism, provided an essential contribution to the English Protestant tradition of Judeo-centric prophecy interpretation, thus laying the foundations of Christian Zionism in both England and America.

The Hexapla of Andrew Willet

English Protestant interest in the eschatological function of Jews grew steadily through the first part of the seventeenth century, even among scholars not invested in stirring the pots of theopolitical controversy. The commentary on Romans from historian and biblical scholar Andrew Willet (1561/2–1621), for instance, employs the word "Iewes" 810 times in 766 pages. Although a specialist in theological disagreements between Protestants and Catholics,[26] Willet was not associated with the nonconformist trends of his time. The accession of King James sparked Willet's desire to see the completion of England's reform. In his 1603 publication, *Ecclesia triumphans*, Willet compared James to Jehosephat, son of King David (2 Chron. 17:3), and exhorted him to stand with King Henry VIII,

King Edward, and Queen Elizabeth against "the Pope and his papal brood" so that "Gods worke" of England's reformation "may in good time be perfected & accomplished."[27] If James read this text, he would no doubt notice his mother's conspicuous absence from this chronicle of righteousness. As the king's commitment to Anglican episcopacy became apparent, Willet turned his energies to biblical exegesis.

Willet's commentary on Romans utilized a broad array of secondary and primary sources, including Hebrew and Greek, as well as translations from Bèza, the Great Bible, and the Geneva Bible. Although Willet favored a noncontroversial approach, he accepted John Bale's historiography regarding the aboriginal character of English Christianity. According to Willet, "obedience to the Bishop of Rome" corrupted England "with Pseudochristianisme: As Augustine was sent into England, who first brought them under the jurisdiction of Rome, but the Christian faith they had receaved long before." Among Protestants, however, he favors the concept of *adiaphora*, exhorting readers that "S. Paul would not have them to be so earnest one in judging an other concerning the use of things indifferent: which hath beene the cause of great contentions in the Church." What is not indifferent to Willet is the role of Jews in the eschatological drama.

> Thus have I shewed, what is the most probable opinion concerning the calling of the Iewes: wherein, as we expect a more frequent and generall vocation of that nation, then hitherto hath beene seene.... [I]n this question of the Universall calling of the Iewes, I resolve still ... that the Apostles propheticall prediction here can not otherwise be understood, then of their generall calling.

Belief in the future national conversion of Jews is compelling for Draxe precisely because of the benefits that "shall accrue unto the Church of God by the conversion of the Iewes": (1) the "ioyning together both of the Iewes and Gentiles, the wall of partition beeing taken away," (2) "the Church of God shall be encreased, *when the children of Iudah, and the children of Israel, shall be gathered together to the Church*," (3) the confirmation of "the faith of the Gentiles," and (4) that God will be praised when "the veritie of his promises shall be made manifest in the salvation both of Iews and Gentiles."[28]

Willet's application of Judeo-centric prophecy interpretation served to reinforce the primacy of western Christianity. Commenting on Romans 11:22—"Note then the kindness and the severity of God: severity toward those who have fallen, but God's kindness toward you, provided you

continue in his kindness; otherwise you also will be cut off."—Willet
pronounces that, although they still are saved, "many famous Churches of
the Gentiles under the Turke are now quite fallen away and cut off." Reflecting on God's "iustice and severitie," he notes that "these nations . . .
are for their unthankfulnes now deprived of the Gospel of Christ: for
where the Gospel was sometime preached and professed, now the Turkish Alcaron is taught."[29] Despite his broad openness to hermeneutical
sources developed by fellow western Protestants, Willet fully dismisses
eastern Christians, whose failure to defend their lands against Muslim
civil rule has left them deserving of their minority status. For Willet and
for other English Protestants, theopolitical hegemony was a sign of God's
favor; living as a minority, especially within an Islamicate world, could
not be understood as anything but a curse. Proto-Puritan Jews, the Kings
of the East, would glorify God by organizing militarily against Muslims
and Catholics to extend Protestant hegemony on a global scale.

A Growing Climate of Judeo-centric Interpretation

Thomas Brightman's *Apocalypsis Apocalypseos* did not garner much attention until its first English edition in 1611. The first major response, a fifteen-
page pamphlet published in 1612 by Jean de L'Écluse, criticized Brightman
for being insufficiently uncompromising. L'Écluse focuses on Brightman's
interpretation of the Church of England as Laodicea when, he says, "the
estate of the Church of England is worse then Babylon itself." That same
year, three authors collaborated to produce a forty-page book seeking to
provide "a shield of defence" against L'Écluse's "arrows of schisme."[30]

While L'Écluse and his critics engaged in open millenarian debates,
books published in London mentioned Brightman's Judeo-centric insights only sparingly. Thomas Wilson's dictionary of significant biblical
terms noted, for instance, that meanings of "Word" in Revelation range
from "The whole will of GOD, revealed in the law and the Gospell," to
"The eternall and infallible Decree of the most high GOD, concerning the
Conversion of the Iewes, unto the Faith of Christ." Regarding the distinction between the "first resurrection" and the "second resurrection," Wilson
notes that "Maister *Brightman* expounds the First resurrection, of the calling of the Iewes againe unto the faith" through "the quickening of them
by Grace." Even more significant than Wilson's Judeo-centrism or his ap-
preciative references to Brightman is that his book was published in
London, the epicenter of English Protestant development. After 1612,

Brightman would be mentioned in several other books published in London, most often as one helpful commentator among many rather than a source of controversy.[31]

Not all manifestations of the budding tradition of Judeo-centric prophecy interpretation relied explicitly on Brightman. Patrick Forbes of Corse (1564–1635), who would later become bishop of Aberdeen, published his *Exquisite Commentarie upon the Revelation of Saint Iohn* in 1613. Forbes looked confidently for the "conversion of the Iewish people, by cleare warrant of Scripture" and sentimentally for their restoration to Palestine: "Now, whether they shall be brought to inhabite againe their owne Land, albeit I dare not determine . . . yet certainely, my heart inclineth to thinke so. Because their solemne conversion must bring with it, the remooving of their reproach, and . . . a gathering from their dispersion, to brooke a state in the [eyes] of the world."[32]

In contrast to Forbes's cautious hermeneutics, Thomas Cooper (also Cowper, 1569/70–1626) eagerly declared that "the Iewes shall then have a full and glorious conversion, before the second comming of the Lord IESUS: And why not principally at Ierusalem, the old place of their worship?" For Cooper, the question was not whether or how, but "why not." For him, the promise of God's calling, conversion, and restoration of Jews to Jerusalem was cause for an ecstatic celebration of God's redemptive purposes. This conviction, which had been brewing for decades, would soon take on even greater theopolitical significance.[33]

The later writings of Thomas Draxe provide another example of how Judeo-centric interpretation became more central to English Protestant thought. Although his books in 1609 (*The Sicke-Mans Catechisme*) and 1611 (*The Christian Armorie*) did not explicate the topic, a dedicatory epistle to one of his sermons preached in 1612 noted that Jesus would come again "not bee before Rome be ruinated, and the dispersed Iewes generally converted to Christianitie."[34] Draxe's 1615 book, *An Alarum to the Last Judgement*, demonstrated sustained engagement with Judeo-centric themes.

Rehearsing several of the subjects in *The Worldes Resurrection*, Draxe leaves until its future fulfillment the question of "whether the beleeving Iewes shall towards the end of the world, be temporally restored into their owne Country, rebuild Ierusalem, and have a most reformed, and flourishing, Church and Commonwealth."[35] He is uncomfortable with the approach of "Maister *Brightman*," who referred to 1695 as "the beginning of the generall conversion and flourishing state of the Iewes, which hee holdeth shall continue divers hundred yeares afterwards." Many other interpreters through the centuries could have benefited from heeding Draxe's advice that "it is not for us . . . *to know the times and seasons, which the Father hath reserved in his owne power*; therefore let us not bee over-curious, but wise to sobrietie."[36]

Although in 1608 Draxe had asserted that Jews, once converted, "have no such promise" of being restored to Palestine, he was later open to the possibility.[37] The fourteenth and fifteenth chapters of *The Worldes Resurrection* treat "the conversion of the Iewes" and "the extreme and finall desolation of the Turke and his Monarchy," respectively, as signs of the approaching final judgment. Once "the whole Nation of the Iewes" is brought "into the Church of Christ," Draxe says, "their purpose to returne into their owne Country" will cause them to be "assaulted by the great Turke, the King of the North, who with all his forces shall endevour to extinguish them." After they are defended by "Michaell the great Prince," these converted Jews "shall bee a most famous, reformed, and Exemplary Church of all the world, and all Nations shall flow unto it, and it shall bee, as it were, a visible heaven upon earth." The fourteenth chapter concludes with the question: "Shall the Iewes bee restored into their Countrey?" Draxe's response shows the development of his position: "It is very probable. First, all the Prophets seeme to speak of this returne. Secondly, they shall no longer bee in bondage. Thirdly, God having for so many ages forsaken his people shall the more notably shew them mercy."[38]

Draxe ties his vision of Jewish restoration to the destruction of the papacy and the eventual ruin of the Ottoman Empire. The "Turkish Gog and Magog shall plant his Palace" at Armageddon, and "shall *gather the* (converted) *Iewes to battell*," only to be defeated by the power of God. Describing the "great Turke" as possessing a "(usurped) Kindome," Draxe prefigures Christian Zionists like William E. Blackstone and John Hagee by delegitimizing any Ottoman claim to Palestine, which belongs by right and by God's promise to Jews alone. In Draxe's apocalyptic interpretation, it can be no other way, for "He [the Turk] is an arch-enemy of the Lord IESVS and his Church; he beganne with the Romish Antichrist, and why then shall not he bee confounded with him, or not long after him?"[39] In 1615, when *An Alarum to the Last Judgement* was published, Draxe began serving as vicar in Dovercourt, Essex, and as chaplain in the port of Harwich, home port of the *Mayflower*. Thus, in Thomas Draxe, we see both the growing centrality of the English Protestant tradition of Judeo-centric prophecy interpretation in conjunction with interest in America.

Henry Finch and the World's Restauration

Sir Henry Finch (*c.* 1558–1625) was a legal scholar, a Member of Parliament (such as it was under James I), a committed Puritan presbyterian, and, toward the end of life, the author of a controversial treatise on the restoration of Jews to Palestine. Finch first won election to the House of Commons in 1593. He came to be known as a strong public advocate of Puritan causes; this association decreased his public profile during the first part of the seventeenth century. Two books published in 1613—one legal (*Nomotexnia*) and one theological (*The Sacred Doctrine of Divinitie*)[40]—preceded his second election to Parliament in 1614. Finch's public profile was hampered by ongoing financial difficulties, which also caused problems for his patron and colleague, Sir Francis Bacon. Finch's financial difficulties were raised in 1621 as one of the possible grounds for Bacon's impeachment. By then, however, Finch's latest book, *The Worlds Great Restauration, or, The Calling of the Iewes*,[41] was creating controversy of its own.

Although published anonymously, Finch's authorship soon came to light. Within a month of the book's release, Joseph Mede, who would later author *Clavis Apocalyptica* (1627), wrote from his study at Christ College, Cambridge, that "Sir Henry Finch was last week examined before the high commission about the book I wrote of, but wonderfully privately. He gave up his answer in writing which was sent to the king and expected from him what should be his censure." Mede was intrigued by and somewhat sympathetic to Finch's effort, saying "I have seen Sir Henry Finch's 'The World's Great Restoration, or, Calling of the Jews, and with them, of all the nations and kingdoms of the earth, to the faith of Christ.' I cannot see, but for the main of the discourse, I might assent unto him." As for the king, Mede shared that James was not convinced that, in his coming old age, he would be able to make the journey demanded by the future Jewish hegemony: "Some say, the king says he shall be a pure king, and that he is so old he cannot tell how to do his homage at Jerusalem."[42] While the king's good humor did not shield Finch from official censure, his punishment was not severe.

In his commentary on Canticles, Finch had previously explored these Judeo-centric themes, though anonymously and to different effect. Perhaps following Thomas Brightman's utilization of the Song of Solomon as a source of prophetic interpretation, Finch presented the biblical poem as a dialogue between Christ and the Church culminating in an extended proof of Jewish national conversion. The purpose of the book was to draw

"the whole Israell of God (Iewes and Gentiles) to be knit and ioined together in one holy society." It contains, therefore, three separate prophecies: "One of the *words* incarnation, an other of the calling of the Gentiles,
the third of the conversion of the Iewes and their accesse in the last daies
unto the Church of Christ." Within this "whole Israell of God," Jews become
the primary community: "when that time shal be, it is not possible to con-
taine the Church within the narrow boundes of Ierusalem, which of a particular Church of the Iewes shall then bee made the Catholicke Church of
all the world." Finch says that the realization of the millennial age depends
on the fulfillment of this central prophecy: "When the heart of the Iewes
shall turne unto the Lord, in the generall call of that whole nation, then
come the daies of peace, ioy, happinesse, and comfort, as much as can be
upon earth, through the bright beames of the glorious Gospell, shining
most cleere." In preparation for this movement, Finch teaches, Protestants
should work for Jewish conversion in the present: "The Church of the
Iewes so carefull for the calling of the Gentiles, teacheth how earnest wee
should bee to commend their conversion unto God."[43] Although Finch
here reflects deep belief in Jewish national conversion, he does not focus
on their restoration to Palestine. His focus is on the heavenly New Jerusalem rather than the earthly city. Six years later, Finch would make the vision
concrete, moving it toward geographical (and, to King James's dismay) geopolitical manifestation.

Whereas Brightman had articulated a negative English nationalism,
Finch's vision offered no nationalism at all. Instead of utilizing Judeo-
centric prophecy interpretation to reinforce England's role in redemptive
history, Finch addresses Jews directly. The book's dedicatory epistle, for
instance, does not address the king or any of Finch's patrons, but "All the
Seed of Jacob, Farre and Wide Dispersed." Although Jews have been scattered, without a national home, as a result of their recalcitrant disbelief
and crucifixion of Jesus, Finch informs them that, in these last days, God's
"purpose is to bring thee home againe, & to marry thee to himselfe by
faith for evermore" so they might become "the most noble Church that
ever eye did see." Informing Jews of their eschatological vocation, Finch
shares the good news that, with " *Gog* and *Magog* falling before thee (which
dayes are even now at hand) thou shalt sit as a Lady in the mount of come-
linesse, that hill of beautie, the true *Tsion*, and heavenly *Ierusalem*, to the
worldes admiration." In the New Jerusalem they will rule after vanquish-
ing the forces of Islam, Gentiles will be their servants and helpers: "All the
Kings of the Gentiles shall bring their glory into they citie, and fall downe

before thee. . . . Blessed shall they be that blesse thee, & cursed shall they be that curse thee." This explicit appeal to Genesis 12:3 provides Finch's motivation for this project: "my hart shal never faile to pray for thy prosperitie all my dayes."[44]

Singular in its purpose of collecting and explaining "the Prophecies of the old and the new Testament, so far as they concerne the calling of the IEWES," *The Worlds Great Restauration* leads readers through the Bible, offering interpretations of selected readings. The entirety of the Bible is given over to the primacy of Finch's Judeo-centric eschatological interest. To this end, Finch divides biblical passages into five themes, or "heads." The first "concerneth the Iewes refusall of Christ" while the second provides assurance "of the calling of the Iewes." The third "respecteth the beginnings of their conversion; of whom it shall be, and when." Here, Finch introduces his reflections on how Jews "shall repaire towards their owne country" over the dried Euphrates in order to have a "marveilous conflict . . . with Gog and Magog, that is to say, the Turke" in "the land of Iudaea" in this "last period of the *Ottoman* Empire." The fourth "head" relates to the happy existence of these converted Jews once they have defeated the Turks. Dwelling "in their owne Countrey," Jews "shall inhabite all the parts of the land . . . in safety" and "shall continue in it for ever." In addition to their land being "more fertile than it ever was" and their "countrey more populous than before," the church they establish "shall bee most glorious." The fifth "head" focuses on the effects stemming from Jews' conversion, restoration, and territorial conquest. The primary effect is that "all nations shall honour them" and "the enemies of the Church [will be] by them subdued . . . and possessed" so they "willingly or perforce come under Christs obedience."[45] Jews, therefore, will prove the truth of their newly adopted faith through victorious military conquest and the establishment of Puritan hegemony.

To guide biblical interpretation, Finch lays out "some few rules, for the better understanding of the prophesies of this kinde." The most important of these rules is his Judeo-centric principle of literal interpretation:

Where *Israel, Iudah, Tsion, Ierusalem,* &c. are named in this argument, the Holy Ghost meaneth not the spirituall Israel, or Church of God collected of the Gentiles, no nor of the Iewes and Gentiles both (for each of these have their promises severally and apart) but Israel properly descended out of *Iacobs* loynes.

The same judgement is to bee made of their returning to their land and ancient seates, the conquest of their foes, the fruitfulnes of their soile, the glorious Church they shall erect in the land it selfe of Iudah, their bearing rule farre and neere. These and such like are not Allegories, setting forth in terrene similitudes or deliverance through Christ (whereof those were types and figures) but meant really and literally of the Iewes. It was not possible to devise more expresse or evident tearmes, then the Spirit of purpose useth to cut off all such construction.[46]

One appreciates that a lawyer of Finch's stature would articulate such a clear approach to textual hermeneutics. As we have seen, literalism was an established feature of Protestant biblical hermeneutics that had informed the Judeo-centric tradition. Finch, however, makes explicit that interpreting scriptural references to Jews is the key to his worldview.

Finch's application of literalist interpretation is inconsistent. The limitations of Finch's literalism can be seen, for instance, that throughout scripture, Jews' "conversion unto Christ in the last dayes, commonly is intimated by turning from Idolatrie. Which howsoever the Iewes be not now infected with, (if you speake of bowing to stickes and stones) was then the maine sinne of the times." Utilizing Romans 11:27, Finch says that Tanakh exhortations against idolatry promote coming to faith in Jesus since "whatsoever worship looketh not to God in Christ" is seeking after a false god.[47] Although he identifies the Children of Israel as literal Jews, the allegorical nature of this Christo-centric extrapolation is apparent. Finch's principle of limited literalism is perhaps his greatest contribution to the Judeo-centric tradition, including its manifestations in premillennial dispensationalism, the fundamentalist controversies, and contemporary American Christian Zionism. Although scientific literalism would inform the commitments of evangelical Christianity from the late nineteenth century onward, the commitment to literalism was first operationalized in Judeo-centric discourse.

Finch's required apology to King James I resulted directly from his limited literalism and its theopolitical implications. Although Finch builds his interpretive system on the foundation of an explicitly nationalist tradition, Finch's discourse in *The Worlds Great Restauration* focuses solely on Jews and their benefit rather than on explicitly naming English Protestant interests. Instead of domestic or international concerns, Finch withdrew into scripture,[48] finding there warrant for interpreting Jews as the key for the future of the entire world. Along with the manifestation of Protestant zeal for the benefit of Jews alone, it is Finch's singular focus on a literal interpretation of Jews within scripture (if not concern for literal Jews) that frames his contribution to English Protestant Judeo-centric prophecy interpretation.

The Judeo-centric Content of Joseph Mede's Millenarian Conversion

Relations between Puritans and James I deteriorated throughout his reign. The publication of the king's *Book of Sports* in 1618 infuriated Puritans for its dismissal of growing sabbatarian commitments. Many Puritans, committed to the teachings contained in Nicolas Bownd's *The Doctrine of the Sabbath*, considered the book "a royal command to disobey the will of God."[49] When the Thirty Years War broke out, many English Protestants accused James of cowardice and treachery when he did not aid his ousted son-in-law, Frederick V, Elector of the Palatine (1596–1632).[50]

Above all, however, Puritans were concerned by the king's efforts to negotiate a spouse for his son and heir. The eventual agreement for Charles to marry a sister of France's King Louis XIII specified that the queen and her attendants would be free to remain Catholic. Puritans were incensed, and some compared the new queen to Jezebel. Charles I, King of England, Scotland and Ireland, and a champion of the divine right of kings, acceded to the throne on March 27, 1625. His conflicts with Parliament would lead eventually to the English Civil War and his execution.

These developments shaped the theopolitical context of Joseph Mede's millenarian thought. A widely respected biblical scholar who winsomely navigated his theopolitical context,[51] Mede (1586–1638) was not always a controversial thinker. In 1613, he was awarded a fellowship at Christ's College, Cambridge, where his students would include the Platonist Henry More and John Milton. Although famous for igniting millenarian zeal among many Puritans, Mede was not always himself a millenarian.

Based on the thousand-year reign of Christ described in Revelation, millenarian tendencies have always been a feature of Christian devotion. As Luther and Calvin saw, however, a blend of Protestant historiography and millenarian awareness could quickly lead some Christians to construct tangible signs of impending hope. Historicist readings of millennial hope located that span of time within human history by linking its progress to significant historical events. Dutch Calvinist lawyer Hugo

Grotius (1583–1645), for instance, believed that "the millennium began in 311 A.D. and continued for one thousand years after which Satan was released in the form of the Ottoman Empire and the threat of anti-Christian Islamic religion."[52] Thomas Brightman, as we have seen, linked the millennium to the advent of Protestant rule in England. For both Grotius and Brightman, Christ's second coming was to be postmillennial, that is, expected at the end of this millennial period.

In contrast, Mede's reading of scripture eventually led him to propose in his *Clavis Apocalyptica* (1627) that the millennium would not be realized within human history but would instead come *after* the end of the present age. In this premillennial eschatology, Christ's second coming would be the turning-point of human experience. Robert Clouse identifies in Mede's work a "radical break from sixteenth century millenarian writers" that "helps to make the millennium a more important aspect of seventeenth century thought." Mede's influence on this point is far-reaching: "Other expositors were to alter his approach but he reestablished and popularized the study of the literal kingdom of God in modern thought."[53]

Although Mede departed from prominent trends in Protestant thought, he did not dilute the prophetic interpretation of history. Far from distancing Protestants from worldly concern, his premillennialism established historicism as the foundation of English Protestant prophecy interpretation. Mede's method has endured. In fact, the chart Mede included in the second edition of *Clavis Apocalyptica* to show the seven seals of the Apocalypse, the millennium, and the final consummation of all things, bears a resemblance to end-times charts produced by dispensationalist thinkers today, most of whom would be more familiar with John Nelson Darby than with Mede.

Jeffrey Jue locates Mede's "initial conversion to a millenarian reading of the Apocalypse" in or near 1625. "Subsequent years until 1632," Jue adds, "saw a thorough-going programmatic application of his millenarianism to other pertinent biblical passages."[54] It is important to observe, however, that prior to this shift Mede was highly interested in apocalyptic thought and open to Judeo-centric prophecy interpretation. Although Mede was aware in 1621 of the controversy surrounding Henry Finch's *The Worlds Great Restauration*, and its effort to prove Jewish centrality to God's end-times plan, he was sympathetic to the project. The developing tradition of Judeo-centric prophecy interpretation was essential for Mede's millenarian development.

Mede's assent to the general themes of Judeo-centric prophecy interpretation was present in the collection of sermons later published under
the title *The Apostasy of the Latter Times*. Jue dates these sermons to between 1617 and 1618, prior to Finch's *Restauration*. In his commentary on
Daniel, one can read that Mede is here squarely within the developed
stream of Judeo-centric prophecy interpretation:

> For the true account therefore of times in Scripture, we must have
> recourse to that SACRED KALENDAR and GREAT ALMANACK of
> PROPHESIE, the foure kingdomes of *Daniel*, which are a *propheti-
> call chronology* of times measured by the succession of foure princi-
> pall kingdomes, from the beginning of the captivity of Israel, untill
> the mystery of God should be finished; a course of time during
> which the Church and Nation of the Jewes, together with those
> whom by occasion of their unbeleefe in Christ . . . but these times
> once finished, all the *kingdomes* of this world should become the
> *kingdome of our Lord and his Christ.*

In *The Apostasy*, Mede's attitude toward Islam is less combative than dis-
missive: "What are Turks and Tartars, and any other unbeleeving Nation
under heaven, unto thy Lord and Saviour? are they not all as strangers to
him, and he to them." His engagement with the other component of the
Turko-Catholic threat was more direct. Even before his millenarian conversion, Catholicism was God's "*unfaithfull* and *trecherous Spouse* the *Christian Jezabel.*" Indeed, "the destruction of Papall *Rome* would be" as great a
confirmation of the faith of "the reformed Christian, who hath forsaken
the Communion of that Religion," as was "the destruction of the Jewish
state and Temple" in 70 c.e. for "those Jewes, who had withdrawne themselves from that body and Religion whereof they had once beene, to embrace the new faith of the Messiah, preached by the Apostles."[55] Mede's
evangelical hope was built on nothing less than anticipation of the coming
destruction of papal power.

Mede's *Paraleipomena*, or *Remaines on some Passages in the Revelation*,
composed of a collection of personal letters, contains the beginnings of
Mede's more detailed reflections on the Apocalypse. Dating the letters to
1624 and 1625, Jue observes that Mede has begun "firmly projecting the
millennium into the future."[56] *Remaines* has a much stronger Judeo-centric
element than *The Apostasy*. Although Mede will not "dare so much as imag-
ine" that the millennial kingdom of Christ "should be a visible converse

upon earth," he is ready to grant that Christ "shall appeare and be visibly revealed from Heaven, especially for the calling and gathering of his anti- ent People, for whom in the dayes of old he did so many wonders." Indeed, "By such a miraculous apparition of *Christ* from Heaven was Saint *Paul* converted. And I hope it is no heresie to think, That the whole Nation of those Zelotes against *Christ* may be converted by as strange a meanes as that one Zelot of their Nation." Although not following Finch in providing radical privilege to Jews in the millennial kingdom, Mede is confident that Jews will be among the "priests of God and of Christ" who "will reign with him a thousand years" (Rev. 20:6). Mede saw among these elect "the Nation of the *Jewes* . . . Those who had not worshipped the Beast, neither his Image, nor had received his marke upon their foreheads, or in their hands."[57] Jewish preservation from Roman apostasy allowed them to bypass contamination by the Beast.

As in the *Apostasy*, Mede does not engage polemically against Islam or Muslims. Instead, Mede treats Turkish geopolitics as a matter-of-fact element in his understanding of end-times events: "*Gog* and *Magog* . . . after *Satan*'s loosing, and before the Last Resurrection shall gather to- gether against the Camp of the Saints and the Beloved City." Distin- guishing Muslims from Gog and Magog in the ancient world, Mede in- terprets these identities through an "Apocalypticall" lens to identify them with "the Turke" who is moving "against the Church of Gentiles now, and must before his last Ruine attempt against *Israel* at their returne. And if there ever be an Antichrist, such as the Fathers describe, now will be the most likely time for him, when the Devill is loose but for a little season."[58]

Mede provided further insight into his Judeo-centric focus by append- ing to his *Paraleipomena* a short chart detailing "The Mystery of St. Paul's Conversion: Or, The Type of the Calling of the Jewes." This small dis- course, especially in its tenth point, shows Mede's overriding concern with Catholicism. Noting that "*Paul* reproveth *Peter,* one of the chiefe Apostles, for symbolizing with Judaisme," Mede wonders if, after their mass conversion, "*May not the Jewes likewise reprove (if not more) the Church of Rome, the chiefe of Christian Churches, for symbolizing with Gen- tilisme?*" This turn of phrase is fascinating. In a time when many authors employed associations with Judaism as a polemical tool against oppo- nents, Mede instead employs a Judeo-centric rhetorical device—in his neologism, "Gentilisme"—to critique Catholicism's supposed adoption of worldly ways.[59]

Joseph Mede, Prophetic Certainty, and Divinely Sanctioned Slaughter

Mede published two versions of *Clavis Apocalyptica* before his death in 1638. The first edition in 1627 was a study of the structure of Revelation while the second edition in 1632 contained a greatly expanded commentary on the entire book, produced through Mede's distinctive synchronistical methodology. An English translation of the second edition was first published in 1643.[60] *Clavis Apocalyptica* echoed many components of the developing interpretive tradition[61] while making its own important contribution through Mede's identification of prophetic "synchronisms."

Working "from the character of the visions themselves, purposely inserted by the Holy Spirit," Mede discovered a "self-evident scheme" within Revelation and other apocalyptic prophecies that allows careful readers to "discover the true, and to refute every erroneous opinion." Mede defined a "synchronism of the prophecies" as "a concurrence of events predicted therein within the same time." Once the "order of the seals and trumpets" is accepted as "certain and indubitable," Mede was confident readers would find that "the order of the whole Apocalypse will be manifest." The resulting certainty—apparent in Mede's description of his "synchronism of the Apocalyptical Prophecies" as the "Apocalyptical Key"[62]—provided Puritan interpreters with indefatigable confidence in their scriptural interpretation. If the key had been found for unlocking the central mystery of scripture—God's purposes for the end of the age and manifestation of God's reign of peace—the fight against ecclesiastical compromise could be waged with ever greater urgency and polemical zeal.

Despite teaching that the millennium had not yet commenced, but that "the 1000 years for which Satan is bound, are brought within the seventh trumpet," which "will contemporize with the interval from the destruction of the beast," Mede did not want to be thought a radical. Rather, he felt that his interpretation reflected the plain sense of scripture as supported by ancient tradition. As he put it, his view "relies on the irrefragable chain of apocalyptical order . . . and the agreement of the other Scriptures, especially of the prophetical ones, wonderfully confirms the same." In addition to providing a chart detailing the synchronisms of Daniel 7 and Revelation 20, Mede reproduces a portion of the dialogue between Justin Martyr and Trypho, the ancientness of the text serving as a proof of its interpretation. The defeat and judgment of Christ's enemies form the bookends of the hoped-for millennium, the seventh day of the apocalyptic timetable (interpreted through 2 Peter 3:8). The millennium will constitute "that kingdom which Daniel saw, of the Son of man, when the times of the antichristian horn being completed, or 'the times of the Gentiles being fulfilled.'" This kingdom, seen "as well by John as by Daniel," will "begin from the same terminus, namely, from the extermination of the fourth, or Roman beast."[63]

Expecting a future millennium did not diminish Mede's commitment to Protestant historiography. Indeed, the confidence engendered by his authoritative exposition confirmed the commitments of the tradition. While Finch was content to produce a nonnationalistic interpretation, Mede's analysis—echoing Bale, Foxe, and Brightman—retains a special place for England's Protestant mission. In *Clavis Apocalyptica*, Mede's exposition of the seven angelic trumpets blown in Revelation 8 charts the progress of Protestantism and the downfall of Rome, from the first stirrings of evangelical truth, to when "by the labour of Luther, and other illustrious reformers of that age" made it so that "whole provinces, dioceses, kingdoms, nations, and cities . . . renounced communion with the beast" so that "the pontifical dominion became in great measure dead." Revelation 8:11 says that when the third angel blew the trumpet, "many died from the water, because it was made bitter." Mede locates this event both "when in our kingdom of England during the reign of Elizabeth of glorious memory . . . those sanguinary managers of the authority of the beast . . . expiated their administration by their blood" and in the defeat of the Spanish Armada, "the Spanish champions of the cause of the beast . . . in that memorable slaughter of the year 1588." Mede is quite sure, however, that the fifth trumpet will result in suffering "poured out on the throne or seat of the beast that is on Rome itself."[64]

Just as the papal Antichrist remains the primary internal enemy in the West, *Clavis Apocalyptica*, in contrast to Mede's earlier writings, constructs the Turk as the primary external enemy from the East. "The Turks were prepared," Mede says, "that after a prophetic day, and a month, and a year, they should kill a third part of men."[65] Following Brightman, *Clavis Apocalyptica* finds the prophetic counterbalance to the Turk in proto-Puritan Jews. Mede, however, flavors this Judeo-centric tradition with an expository opinion that places Jews even closer to the center of Revelation's narrative of universal reconciliation. For centuries, Christians have taken Revelation's "bride" of the Lamb (18:23; 19:7; 21:2, 9; 22:17) to be the Church triumphant, comprising all believers. "I do not see," Mede says, "how the preparation of the bride can be any thing else than the conversion and collection of Israel, expected for so many ages." Gentiles, on the other hand, "cannot possibly be called that bride, because they have been long ago, and for many ages, espoused to Christ. The Jews, therefore, are those who are yet expected to become the spouse of the Lamb."[66] This interpretation is striking, both for its absolute distinction of Jews and Gentiles, which Mede expects to continue through the millennium, and for its rhetorical subordination of Gentile Christianity.

Mede's hope for the national conversion of Jews to Puritan faith is inextricably tied to his hope for the ultimate extermination of God's enemies. For Mede, the hope of the Jewish national conversion and their "taking possession of the Holy Land" is primarily a point of prophetic military strategy. Indeed, all of the other signs are "subservient" to the importance of the Euphrates being dried so "these new Christians from the East" may undertake "an expedition against the beast." The Ottoman Empire, Mede says, "will be the only obstacle to those new enemies from the East and a defence on the part of the beast." Mede thus completes the process of transposing the enemies of Christendom into also being the natural enemies of Jews, who are presumed, as proto-Puritans, to be natural allies, so that the "conversion and restoration of Israel" will be synchronous with the "destruction of the Turkish empire." Reflecting on the exhortation for harvesting in Revelation 14:15, Mede communicates a dual image, "that of reaping and threshing as well as that of gathering in, . . . the latter with reference to Israel gathered together into the garner of the Church; the former to the slaughter of enemies in conjunction with that event." These enemies are proper to each component of the future composite church of Jews and Gentiles: the two parts of "the Church of Christ, as it was about to become double by the conversion of Israel . . . " appears to have, at that time, its own peculiar enemy; the former the Roman beast, with its uncircumcised origin; the latter, the Mohammedan empire, over a circumcised people, and of an Ismaelitish origin, ominous to the descendants of Isaac. Mede is certain of the coming "extermination of both . . . to be accomplished at the coming of Christ."[67]

Mede drew a line around Puritans and Jews, a line that excluded Catholics and Muslims. The line separated two Christian opponents, pairing each with a mythologized companion: Jews for virtuous Puritans, Turks for antichristian, popish Anglicans. Thus it is that Joseph Mede, the shrewd navigator of politics between academy, church and state, the scholar who sought to avoid too much public association with the Puritan faction, offers a prophetic exposition that privileges pure Protestantism, England, and the West. In Mede's vision—undergirded by the mechanical trustworthiness of the Spirit-constructed biblical witness and interpreted through the primary text of the Apocalypse—the progress of the Gospel is marked by the execution of Catholics and the extermination of Muslims. The vision would be catalyzed when the Jewish bride of Christ converted and repaired to Palestine, a Puritan army marching to reclaim God's land from the greedy grasp of the usurping Turk.

5

Admitting the Jew

PARLIAMENTARY AUTHORITY, CHRISTIAN ZIONISM, AND BRITISH IMPERIAL IDENTITY

THE ENGLISH CIVIL War brought years of brutality, confusion, and religious fervor. England was divided primarily between Royalists, who supported King Charles I (reigned March 1625–January 1649), and Parliamentarians who objected to the king's exercise of power through civil and ecclesial authority. When the professional New Model Army was founded in 1645, Lord Thomas Fairfax was appointed as Captain-General. When the Second English Civil War erupted in 1648, some of these professional soldiers began to call for the execution of Charles I. Fairfax led a major assault against royalist support that garnered a sonnet from Puritan poet and public intellectual John Milton titled "On yᵉ Lord Gen. Fairfax at yᵉ seige of Colchester."[1] Almost exactly one month after Pride's Purge, which ensured parliamentary support for the New Model Army, the War Council met under Fairfax's authority on January 5, 1649. In addition to military matters—including the looming possibility of conflict with Scotland—the Council received several petitions on civil and political matters submitted by English subjects. These petitions included an appeal from Johanna Cartenright and Ebenezer Cartwright, an English widow and her son residing in Amsterdam.

Describing the "Councel of Warre" as being "Conveaned for Gods Glory, Izraells Freedom, Peace and Safety," the Cartwrights shared how, while in the Netherlands, they became sensitized to their Jewish acquaintances' "heavy out-cryes and clamours against the intolerable cruelty of this our English Nation, exercised against them by that (and other) inhumane exceeding great Massacre of them, in the Raign of Richard the second, King of this Land, and their banishment ever since." The Cartwrights tie their sensitivity to Jewish desires for residence and commerce in England both to expectations for Jewish conversion and for England's national mission:

> by discourse with them, and serious perusall of the Prophets, both they and we find, that the time hereall draweth nigh; whereby they together with us, shall come to know the Emanuell, the Lord of life, light, and glory; even as we are now known of him, And that this Nation of ENGLAND, with the Inhabitants of the Nerther-lands, shall be the first and readiest to transport IZRAELLS Sons & Daughters in their Ships to the Land promised to their fore-Fathers, ABRAHAM, ISAAC, AND JACOB, for an everlasting Inheritance.

This major undertaking will be of immediate benefit to England, led by the War Council, which would receive God's blessing if they lifted Richard's exile: "By which act of mercy, your Petitioners are assured of the wrath of God, will be much appeased towards you, for their [Jews'] innocent bloodshed, and they thereby dayly enlightened in the saving knowledge of him, for whom they look dayly and expect as their King of eternal glory, and both their and our Lord God of salvation (Christ Jesus.)"[2] A short note at the end of the published version of the document reports that the petition was "favourably received with a promise to take it into speedy consideration, when the present more publicke affaires are dispatched."[3]

The Cartwright petition presents a precise distillation of the Judeo-centric strands of Puritan thought developed over the previous century, since John Bale. That it presses this Judeo-centric tradition into political service makes it the first example of Christian Zionism, understood as political action, informed by specifically Christian commitments, to promote or preserve Jewish control over the geographic area now comprising Israel and Palestine. Although the petition promotes a theological perspective, its theological rhetoric is notably subdued.[4] In contrast, a petition presented the same day, seeking the release of persons in debtors' prisons, argues that the "innocent blood" of those who have died in the prisons, "cryes for vengeance to the Almighty, and doubtlesse is not the least cause of our present colamities, and of Gods judgments upon us." The Cartwright petition, while acknowledging contemporary difficulties, offers a positive statement about how God's wrath may be appeased if the recommended policy is adopted. Perhaps presuming that members of the Council were quite familiar with the Judeo-centric trends on which they based their recommendation, the Cartwrights do not lay out their beliefs in full detail.

The Cartwrights' presumption of a theopolitical common ground allowed their petition to focus on their policy recommendation and its benefit to those in a position to influence national policy.

The House of Commons named 135 commissioners, including Fairfax, as a High Court of Justice to try King Charles I on January 6, 1649, the day after the Cartwright petition was accepted by the Council of War. Charles would be executed within the month. Judeo-centric discourse had played a central role in forming the Puritan, Presbyterian, and Independent factions within English Protestantism. The Puritan resistance to compromise was bolstered by an unyielding commitment to biblical literalism, itself a central component of Judeo-centric prophecy interpretation. Judeo-centric discourse would soon come to provide important metaphors and analogies within English debates regarding church and society, to the extent that one's position on whether or not England should readmit Jews and facilitate their repatriation to Palestine signified one's commitments on a variety of domestic issues.[5] This chapter will explore English theopolitical developments leading up to the Cartwright petition in 1649 and the content of Judeo-centric discourse that led Fairfax's successor, Oliver Cromwell, to allow Jews to live as Jews in England.

Judeo-centrism and the End of Parliamentary Censorship

English official life in the early seventeenth century was dominated by the physically diminutive figure of William Laud, who served as Archbishop of Canterbury from 1633 until his beheading in 1645. A noted polemicist against both Catholics and Puritans and one of the king's closest advisors, Laud wielded considerable influence even prior to his appointment as archbishop. He matched the forced taxation imposed by Charles I with efforts to enforce conformity within church practice, scriptural interpretation, and doctrinal belief. Although Judeo-centric theology had been present in some Anglican theological perspectives, Laud rejected millenarian eschatology as akin to the dangerous enthusiasm of the radical reformers on the European continent. As Christopher Hill has observed, "Already by the early seventeenth century attempts to date the end of the world were regarded as sedition: so early had the Elizabethan consensus collapsed, and so important were eschatological studies in polarizing men's attitudes."[6]

Through the first part of the seventeenth century, the established church's orthodoxy was asserted through a rigorous (though permeable) system of censorship. It was only when the censorship regime broke down during the Long Parliament of 1640 that many books proffering explicitly Judeo-centric and millenarian perspectives could be published in England. Describing this development as "sensational," Hill has written that "the ending of ecclesiastical control seems to me the most significant event in the history of seventeenth-century English literature: it is too easily taken for granted."[7] Judeo-centric and millenarian literature, earlier judged seditious and illegal, was now publicly available. Many of the scholars discussed in the previous two chapters of this study experienced posthumous revivals in the years following 1640.

The breakdown of parliamentary censorship brought post-mortem publishing booms for both Thomas Brightman (d. 1607) and Joseph Mede (d. 1638). Two similar pamphlets were published anonymously in London in 1641, each summarizing the third and fourth chapters of Brightman's *Apocalypsis Apocalypseos*, which outlined the responsibilities and callings of the Protestant churches.[8] A copy of Brightman's commentary on the Song of Solomon was published openly in London in 1644. That same year, a printer named Samuel Cartwright published an edition of Brightman's collected works, along with a stand-alone edition of *Apocalypsis Apocalypseos*.[9] While the post-censorship interest in publishing Brightman is impressive, Sarah Hutton notes that "if quantity of editions is any guide, then Joseph Mede was more popular."[10]

Brightman and Mede were not suddenly discovered by English theologians only in 1640. Their views had been circulating through learned Puritan circles for several years. Before censorship ended, however, scholars referenced their most controversial ideas in veiled terms. Religious educator Richard Bernard, for instance, had alluded to Brightman's views in his 1617 commentary on Revelation, published in London. The "Church triumphant," he said, could be understood as foreshowing "*a most happie condition . . . after the happie conversion of the Iewes*, whose embracing the Gospell, shall be as life and riches to the Christian world, Rom. 11.1215; and in comparison of which time wee are yet, but as in a kind of livelesse state and poore condition." This New Jerusalem, inhabited by Jews, "shall eat the riches of the Gentiles" and "sucke the milke of the Gentiles."[11] Bernard, careful to not take a millenarian stand, nevertheless presents Brightman's vision as a viable alternative. Just four years later, Henry Finch would be publicly disgraced for indelicately communicating an almost identitical perspective. Although the end of parliamentary censorship made such concealment unnecessary, the Judeo-centric tradition refined by Brightman and Mede had already contributed fundamentally to

English Protestant self-understanding. Parliament's promotion of these ideas in this tumultuous theopolitical season would have effects neither author could have predicted.

Judeo-centrism and Millenarian Politics

As Christopher Hill has observed, it was a "shrewd policy to authorize publication of scholarly works discussing the coming millennium, since Parliament's case against a Divine Right monarchy could be legitimated only by appealing to the higher authority of God." The result of this official reversal, he continues, was the "spread of popular millenarian doctrines in England . . . like fire along a well-laid trail of powder."[12] Although Judeo-centric thought does not depend on millenarian eschatology, the broad distribution of millenarian hermeneutics after 1640 provided vision and vocation to English Puritans working to rid Albion of papal corruption.

Neither Brightman nor Mede was as radical as the politics their writings would inspire. Sarah Hutton has convincingly demonstrated that Mede was an especially ironic source for the role Judeo-centric and millenarian rhetoric played in stoking Civil War radicalism, which eventually took Laud's head. Focusing on John Worthington's meticulously edited volume of Mede's *Works* published in 1664, which included an extensive biographical sketch[13] placing "Mede's theological preferences . . . firmly with the Laudian church," Hutton argues that not only was Mede not a radical in the vein of those who claimed his writings as inspiration for regicide but that "it is wrong . . . to classify Mede as a puritan, even in a broadly generic sense of that misleading term." Far from stoking the flames of further radicalism, Hutton says, it is probable that "the Worthington edition of 1664 was in part a bid to reintegrate millenarianism into Anglican theology." Hutton is drawn to a startling conclusion that upends many presumptions of how Judeo-centric and millenarian ideas were transferred to later iterations of Puritan faith in Britain and New England: "Thus we have the paradox that the millenarianism of Laud's political and theological opponents was fed by a faithful supporter of his church, that the radical social and political program of the Fifth Monarchists traced its millennialism back to a figure whose religious and political formulation was in every way alien to their own." In its time, Worthington's effort to associate Mede with the enforced orthodoxy of the Laudian church failed. As a result, Hutton concludes, "the content and interpretive structures of Mede's study of the Book of Revelation informs Christian radicalism to this very day."[14]

Among the radicals inspired by the outpouring of millenarian zeal was Robert Maton (1606/7, d. ca. 1646), whose perspectives became associated with a later movement known as the Fifth-Monarchy Men.[15] Maton's central argument in *Israel's Redemption*, published in London in 1642, was that, at his return, Jesus would personally establish a monarchical reign for Jews in Jerusalem. Maton's scriptural reasoning for arriving at this conclusion echoes the logic employed by Henry Finch and Joseph Mede, but also directly fore-shadows early twentieth-century dispensationalist discourse. Cautioning readers to not misapply "all those revelations which properly and naturally concerne the Redemption and Restauration of the Jewes posterity and Prin-cipality," Maton says that "even good men" may "make way the cause they hate [Catholicism], when they faile to divide the Word of God aright; when they rob the Jew, the more to enrich the Gentile." Maton was confident that Jews will be restored physically and literally to their own land as a sign of their redemption. Just as Jews' alienation from God is seen in their present dispossession, Maton says that "Gods people" will find "the redemption . . . not onely of their soules . . . by the profession of the Gospel, but consequently of their bodies too, from their general captivitie to the repossessing of their country, by a miraculous deliverance." For Maton, "the mere conversion of the Jewes in those place where now they live," is inconceivable, for "if you seriously consider the evidence of the Prophets, I am confident you will con-fesse, that a most righteous and flourishing estate of the Jewes in their owne land, must of necessity distinguish the time of their calling."[16]

Judeo-centrism, Church Confessions, and Toleration

The tumultuous theopolitical context of England during the first and second civil wars limits our ability to construct a definitive understanding of what doctrinal views were considered "orthodox" or to state, for in-stance, what views established one as a Puritan. The fluidity of Christian doctrine prior to Constantine's enforced imperial uniformity provides a helpful analogue. The English Protestant tradition of Judeo-centric proph-ecy interpretation, however, provided a generally accepted hermeneutic for reading history through the lens of scripture, resulting in a confident hope of victory over the pressing enemies of the Turk and the Pope. In the period after 1640, Judeo-centric commitments would find their way into official worship materials and confessions.

The Westminster Confession, produced by the Westminster Assembly convened by the English Parliament in 1643, was approved by the Assembly of Scotland in 1647 and accepted by the English Parliament in June 1648. Seeking to establish Protestant consensus in the crucible of war, the confession contained the Judeo-centric consensus reflected in the Cartwright petition. In the Confession's apocalyptic interpretation of the Lord's Prayer, Jews are central to future and present Christian hope:

> In the second petition, which is [They kingdome come,] . . . we pray that the Kingdom of sin and Satan may be destroyed, the Gospel propagated throughout the world, the Jewes called, the fulnesse of the Gentiles brought in . . . that Christ would rule in our hearts here, and hasten the time of his second coming, and our reigning with him for ever; and that he would be pleased to exercise the Kingdom of his power in all the world."[17]

The Savoy Declaration of 1658 would contain similar teaching. In its section "Of the Church," the Congregationalist declaration detailed its views on the papacy—"the Pope in Rome . . . is that Antichrist . . . whom the Lord shall destroy with the brightnesse of his coming"—and then placed this eschatological vision into a larger context with Judeo-centric presumptions: "we expect that in the latter days, Antichrist being destroyed, the Jews called, and the adversaries of the kingdome of his dear Son broken, the Churches of Christ being inlarged and edified through a free and plentiful communication of light and grace, shall enjoy in this world a more quiet, peaceable and glorious condition than they have enjoyed."[18]

Prior to either of these statements of faith, however, the 1644 *Directory for the publique worship of God* offered several suggested topics for public prayer, including

> To pray for the Propagation of the Gospell and the Kingdome of Christ to all Nations, for the conversion of the Jewes, the fulnesse of the Gentiles, the fall of Antichrist, and the hastening of the second comming of our Lord; For the deliverance of the distressed Churches abroad, from the tyranny of the Antichristian faction, and from the cruell oppressions and blasphemies of the Turke: For the blessing of God upon all the Reformed Churches, especially upon the Churches and Kingdomes of England, Scotland, and Ireland, now more strictly and religiously united in the solemne Nationall League and Covenant; and for our Plantations in the remote parts of the World.[19]

These prayer topics tie together a century of developing themes in English Protestantism. Prayers following this guidance would be Judeo-centric and likely millenarian, with heavy doses of anti-Catholic, anti-Islamic, nationalist, and colonial sentiment. This discourse, disseminated through government-sanctioned statements of religious faith, informed the Christian Zionism of the Cartwright petition as well as the trans-Atlantic discourse of British and Anglo-American identity formation.

Even while Judeo-centric commitments were shaping both radical politics and official confessions, the tradition was a lively topic among advocates of toleration, many of whom took up the cause of reversing England's long-standing ban on Jews. Advocating for the admission of Jews to England necessitated some sense of Jews as real persons rather than as literary abstractions. In an address to the Jewish Historical Society of England, Theodore Rabb pointed out that this process of normalizing Jews within English Protestant consciousness had begun at least during the 1590s. Rabb identifies favorable comments concerning Jews in Richard Hooker's *Laws of Ecclesiastical Politie*, first published in 1593,[20] as "the first major step in a mental revolution that engulfed not just a few rare spirits but the Establishment itself." This ecclesial foundation was supplemented by travelogues written by Hooker's student Edwyn Sandys, his younger brother George Sandys, Richard Hakluyt, and Thomas Coryate.[21] Although, as Rabb says, these writers were not "uniformly amiable towards Jews," they are "remarkable" in that "they were so positive at all." He concludes that this travel literature contains "one of the crucial origins of the readmission of the Jews to England. Here began that essential attack on irrationality without which the Shylockian caricatures would never have been overcome and the Cromwellians could never have acted as they did."[22]

Among advocates of toleration, the enforced absence of Jews from English life was sometimes mentioned not for Jews' sake but as an example within a larger discourse advocating for toleration of diverse opinions. The 1647 disputation between William Erbury, chaplain of a New Model regiment, and Francis Cheynell, a member of the Westminster assembly, provides an example. Cheynell was offended by the content of Erbury's preaching, which appealed to soldiers in Erbury's care, as well as the fact that he "brought with him a company of solders" to their initial meeting. Erbury identified "the appearance of *Antichrist and of the Divell*" with those "who have the spirit to make a man an offender for a word." Those with the spirit of Christ, by contrast, shall not hurt in all the holy mountaine, not a Jew though he curse Christ Jesus, nor a Turk that makes a scoff of the Son of God. It is a strange hypocriticall nation this; we have prayed these eighty years for the conversion of the Jews, and yet we will not suffer a Jew to live amongst us: I feare the bloud of the Jews cast out of this nation, and abominably butchered, is not yet washed away, this is a meer mockery, there must not a Papist nor a Malignant be suffered to live amongst us.[23]

Soon after this exchange with Cheynell, Gen. Sir Thomas Fairfax, to whom the Cartwright petition was addressed, had Erbury removed from Oxford. This strong notion of toleration nevertheless became increasingly common among some segments of English popular Christianity.

A more famous advocate of toleration, Roger Williams (*c.* 1604–1683), was convinced that the Judeo-centric tradition was harmful to his tolerationist vision of Christian faith. His 1644 treatise, *The Bloudy Tenent of Persecution*, related his narrative of persecution at the hands of religious authorities in the American colonies and argued in favor of toleration for all views and perspectives. In his opening epitome, Williams declares that "the will and command of *God* . . . since the comming of his Sonne the *Lord* Jesus," has granted "a *permission* of the most *Paganish, Jewish, Turkish,* or *Antichristian consciences* and *worships* . . . to *all* men in all *Nations* and *Countries.*" The implication is that no sword should be used to challenge a believer's conscience except "the *Sword* of *God's Spirit,* the *Word* of God."[24]

Williams did not believe his tolerationist vision could be realized without challenging the dominance of the English Protestant tradition of Judeo-centric prophecy interpretation. Arguing that "The *state* of the Land of *Israel,* the *Kings* and *people* thereof, in *Peace* & *War,* is . . . *figurative* and *ceremoniall,* and no *pattern* nor *precedent* for any *Kingdom* or *civill state* in the *world* to follow," Williams declared that the Judeo-centric tradition is bankrupt. If the biblical images of Jews are figurative rather than literal, they are thoroughly decoupled from civil concerns both now and "in the *world* to follow." Because there is no Fifth Monarchy to come, Williams's eighth point follows: "*God* requireth not an uniformity of *Religion* to be *inacted* and enforced in any *civill state.*" Moreover, Williams argues, "inforced *uniformity* (sooner or later) is the greatest occasion of *civill Warre, ravishing* of *conscience, persecution* of *Christ Jesus* in his servants, and of the *hypocrise* and *destruction* of *millions* of *souls.*" Williams's ninth point provides the body-blow to Judeo-centrism in its mid-sixteenth-century mode: if "inforced *uniformity* of *Religion* in a *civill state*" is rejected, "we must necessarily *disclaime* our desires and hopes of the Jewes *conversion to Christ*." With that, for Williams at least, the entire project of Judeo-centric apocalyptic hope was dismissed.[25]

Williams's understanding is a clear illustration of Nabil Matar's observation that "The more millenarian the theologian, the more he would preach the Jews' return—since their return and subsequent conversion heralded the kingdom of Christ. The less millenarian the theologian, the less he was interested in the Jews and their whereabouts, and the more he viewed the millennial kingdom as a spiritual rather than a 'carnal' reality."[26] In 1647, the Independent preacher Hugh Peters (1598–1660), in a manner more in keeping with the Judeo-centric trends of his time, published a short pamphlet advocating, in part, that "strangers, even Jewes [be] admitted to trade, and live with us, that it may not be said we pray for their conversion, with whom we will not converse, wee being all but strangers on the Earth."[27]

The Apology of Edward Nicholas and the Covenantal Logic of Christian Zionism

The English Protestant tradition of Judeo-centric prophecy interpretation permeated the theopolitical context that carried the Cartwright petition to General Fairfax and the Council of War. Affecting extremist discourse and official church confessions alike, the tradition also set the terms for tolerationist protest. The Cartwright petition's reliance on the hermeneutical grammar provided by the Judeo-centric tradition assisted the favorable reception of its policy recommendation for the readmission of Jews to English society and economy. The War Council's reception of the Cartwright petition in January 1649 was followed in February of that year by the publication in London of another notable pamphlet, *An Apology for the Honorable Nation of the Jews, and all the Sons of Israel*. Bearing the name "Edward Nicholas, Gent.," the pamphlet is a prime example of the political application of the Judeo-centric tradition.[28]

The basic argument of the *Apology* is that to properly love God and enjoy God's blessings, a nation must honor and assist Jews, God's chosen people. In agreement with the Cartwright petition, the *Apology* suggests that Jews would best be honored by readmitting them to England and, eventually, helping them regain control of Palestine. The "strict and cruel

Laws now in force against the most honourable Nation of the world, the Nation of the Jews, a people chosen by God" are a "sin." This rejection of Jews has "highly incense[d] the Majesty of Jehovah," when England should "rather to honor them whom God honoreth." The absence of Jews from England's commerce and life has deprived the country of supernatural benefits since, when Jews are present, they bring "protection of all men" since the blessings of "Gods people . . . are continually showred down on a Land for their sakes." The "good or evil usage of God's people," therefore, "is the greatest State-interest in the world." While most arguments against Jewish presence in England were intended to protect market share, it was common to appeal instead to the "great guilt that lies on the Jews for crucifying Christ." The *Apology* points out that it was only the specific leaders, "and not . . . the whole Nation [that] were guilty." Individual Jews will prove to be an unqualified blessing when they are readmitted to England.[29]

Although they have been "cast off for a time," Jews remain God's own people. The primary proof of this continued relationship with God is

> the many promises made by God by the mouthes of his Prophets, for the reduction [return] of them into their own countrey, still owning them for his own people, a countrey, I say, still lawfully theirs, by the donation of God himself, and a propriety, that no Prince under Heaven can plead the like, the promises also setting forth the restauration of the pure worship of God, the restitution of all things to their primitive Estate.

Following the literalist commitments of the Judeo-centric tradition, the *Apology* counters arguments that the promises of restoration have already been fulfilled within history (a hermeneutical option known as preterism), that the promises made to Israel now belong to the church (an option known today as "replacement theology" or supersessionism), or that the future redemption of Israel will only be spiritual. It is "plainly proved," the *Apology* argues, "that it shall be here on Earth that the Jews shall enjoy this blessing and deliverance." A special point in the argument is made about the Ten Tribes—their whereabouts unknown since the Babylonian exile and sometimes described as "lost"—who have "never yet returned into their own Land, and the great joy that is promised them in those yet future blessed times." The valley of dry bones in Ezekiel 37 shows the future "return of all the Tribes of Israel" whose "restauration and inhabitation of their countrey here on Earth, is yet to be fulfilled . . . in the time appointed by God." Although the first goal of the *Apology* is to secure Jewish presence in England, the apocalyptic hope of Jewish national return to Palestine provides the telos of the vision. Their claim to the land is based solely on God's donation recorded in Scripture, an authority stronger than any claimed by prince or king, an argument Parliament had been cultivating to establish its own legitimacy.[30]

Given the "threats and promises" of scripture, a decision to not assist Jews in their return to both England and Palestine, the *Apology* continues, would be "a strange negligence (I conceive it a madness) in us to forego so great priviledges, as by those honourable people of the Jews may accrew unto us." To continue "abandoning these people of God" may result in separating England "from God's favor and protection." In a concise articulation of the central logic of national-covenantal Christian Zionism, the *Apology* avers that to protect and assist Jews is to protect and assist England.[31]

This Christian Zionist logic is then extended to the formation of English foreign policy. While other countries persecute Jews, England's national vocation is clear: "I hope better things for our Nation, that when our troubles at home by Gods mercy are composed, there are many gallant men now in arms, and others that may be instrumental in beating down God's Enemies, and the Enemies of his people." The *Apology* then proposes that protecting Jews should be the central concern of English foreign policy once the Civil War concludes: "I am sure . . . that our weapons (when quiet here at home) may be bent against the cruel oppressors of his people in foreign parts, and those merciless Tyrants . . . towards the Jews where they are, vexing them, and spoling them of their lives and livelihood." The *Apology* insulates itself from English Protestant critique by claiming that "I know the great impugners of this Apology for the Jews will be the Pope and his Clergy, and of them the Jesuits, his principal Agents, for that this opposeth their chief principle, the political upholding of the Papacy and themselves." Those opposing this argument, in other words, may be crypto-Catholics if not closet Jesuits. More positively, a decision to receive Jews, "giving them all possible satisfaction, and restoring them to commerce in this kingdom" will benefit England since God "will avenge them on their persecutors," both Catholics and Turks.[32]

The *Apology* is an astute political application of the English Protestant tradition of Judeo-centric prophecy interpretation. Its writer, however, most likely was not a Christian. Nothing other than this pamphlet is known about its listed author, "Edward Nicholas, Gent." The content of the Apology is not consistent with the writings of Sir Edward Nicholas (1593–1669), an official in the courts of Kings Charles I and Charles II. It has been suggested that Nicholas was, in fact, a pseudonym for Menasseh ben-Israel (1604–1657), a rabbi in Amsterdam prominent among several Judeo-centric Protestant thinkers in the Netherlands, many of whom had close ties to Christians in England.[33] Ben-Israel's family had emigrated from Portugal to the tolerationist climate of the Netherlands. Given the lack of official censorship, it is unlikely that any of ben-Israel's Christian associates would have felt the need for a pseudonym. A perspective known to have been penned by a Jew, however, would have drawn greater suspicion. Signs pointing to ben-Israel's authorship of the *Apology* include the pamphlet's conspicuous lack of concern for the eventual conversion of Jews to Christian faith prior to their "reduction" to Palestine, the extended but not sensationalist discourse on the Ten Tribes, and the Spanish-language edition published in London the same year.[34] All of this, in addition to the *Apology*'s relative lack of interest in condemning Muslims while sustaining disdain for Catholics, proves a fitting combination for someone carrying the Jewish memory of persecution and expulsion from the Iberian Peninsula.

Menasseh ben-Israel, the Lost Tribes, and the Question of Conversion

Menasseh ben-Israel rose to prominence in mid-seventeenth century English Protestant circles primarily through his contribution to Judeo-centric speculation regarding the Ten Lost Tribes of Israel. As European experience of the New World grew, the indigenous populations they encountered were employed, in part, as receptacles for several theories regarding their nature, their origins, and their significance for European Christian apocalyptic hope. Spiritual conquest was a constant companion to imperial and colonial enterprise.

In 1644, Antonio Montezinos (Aharon ha-Levi) arrived in Amsterdam after traveling through Central America. Montezinos claimed to have conversed with some of the indigenes in Hebrew and testified to his belief that they were descendents of the ten lost tribes. Montezinos's testimony, included Menasseh ben-Israel's *Orígen de los Americanos* (1650), sparked great interest in England. An enlarged edition, bearing a dedication to Parliament, appeared in Latin the same year, while two editions of an English translation by Moses Wall were published in 1650, 1651 and 1652 under the title, *The Hope of Israel*.[35]

The ground had been prepared for Montezinos and Menasseh by Edward Winslow's 1649 *The Glorious Progress of the Gospel amongst the Indians in New England*. Winslow marveled at "the juncture of time wherein God hath opened their hearts to entertain the Gospel, being so nigh the very years, in which many eminent and learned Divines, have from Scripture grounds . . . foretold the conversion of the *Iewes*."[36] England's colonial expansion was divinely timed to bring about the millennium through the conversion of indigenous Americans who were, in fact, Israelites. The writings of Thomas Thorowgood were far more influential. His book, *Jewes in America* (1650),[37] promoted the success of John Eliot in bringing indigenes he encountered to Protestant faith. "For Thorowgood," says Zvi Ben-Dor Benite in his study of the idea of the Lost Tribes, "this was proof that a distant Jewish past was still present in America. If the Indians were the descendants of the ten tribes, he reasoned, that would explain why it was easy to carry out missionary work among them."[38] Thorowgood's mission was plainly eschatological: if the Lost Tribes were not found, it would not be possible for "all Israel" to be saved.

Ben-Israel intended *Hope of Israel* to be the beginning of a monumental history of Jewish life rather than a stand-alone volume. Benite describes the book as a "seventeenth-century world geography, narrated through the search for the lost tribes—a cosmo-geography of loss." The book's forty-one sections endeavor to compile every testimony from every speculation concerning the whereabouts of the tribes. "Ben-Israel is able to place the ten tribes in every place ever suggested," Benite says. "Rather than decide which of the conflicting sources is correct, Ben-Israel establishes that they *all* are."[39] Now, with the confirmed presence of Israelites in the New World, ben-Israel could conclude that they were scattered throughout the world. Daniel's prophecy of "the shattering of the power of the holy people" (Dan. 12:7) was tantalizingly close to fulfillment. England, with its policy of exclusion, was the only remaining point on the planet devoid of Jews. This problem would need to be rectified before apocalyptic hope could be fulfilled.

Just as Menessah ben-Israel's writings made a central contribution to the development of political Christian Zionism, his Christian translator, Moses Wall, stands as an important figure in his own right. The second English edition of *The Hope of Israel* included an appendix by Wall titled "Considerations upon the Point of the Conversion of the Jews." There, Wall, who had been criticized for assisting ben-Israel's project,[40] pointedly directs readers to "not think that I aime by this Translation, to propagate or commend *Judaisme* (which its no wonder if the Author doth so much favour . . .)." Instead, as a Christian, Wall says that he is committed "to remove our sinfull hatred from off that people, whose are the Promises, and who are beloved for their Fathers sakes."[41]

To this point, the English Protestant tradition of Judeo-centric prophecy interpretation had emphasized national Jewish conversion to Protestant faith. Wall, on the other hand, claims that the fact Jews have not converted in large numbers is itself one of the last signs to be fulfilled before Christ's kingdom can be established. Other signs had recently been fulfilled by God: "he hath in our days arrested the *Turks* greatnesse; abated the formidablenesse of the *German-Austrian Beast*; revealed in good measure the hypocrisie and lies of the false Prophet, who hath his seat in *Rome*." Although there was no evidence of a coming national conversion, "nothing concerning *the returning of the Shulamite*, in *Cant.* 6 . . . which Mr. *Brightman* interprets to be the Jewes turning Christian," this was no cause to join those who believe in "the hopelesnesse of their repentance." Instead, Wall says, it has become apparent to him that "their Conversion shall be the work of God" similar to their deliverance from Egypt.[42]

After these introductory remarks, Wall offers several reasons to "love the *Jewish* Nation." In addition to being humans and thus like Christians, "*Abraham* is our common Father, and therefore we should love as brethren." Wall then asserts that "Gods covenant with the *Jewes* is not nulled, or broken, but only suspended." They are "Gods first Wife" and Christians must understand themselves as "gainers by their casting away," as "Doggs" who "have got the Childrens meat before their bellies were full," as debtors for the gift of salvation. Christians should look earnestly for Jewish conversion to Christian faith since "they minded our conversion to God. . . . Now then for us to love the notion, and in what we may, help forward their returne; what is it but an honest and just retaliation?" This conversion, however, will not result from human effort. Wall is convinced that the coming national conversion will be accomplished supernaturally. "That of the ordinary way of Christianizing a person, or people," he says, "seemes to me not of use here," he says. After "many ages" of applying those methods to Jews, the goal has not been accomplished. "I then conclude, that their conversion shall be in an extraordinary way, it shall be the worke of our Lord Jesus, and of his good Spirit."[43] This conclusion, while far from despairing in "the hopelesnesse of their repentance," calls into question missionary efforts either among Jews or Israelites now scattered in far-off lands.

Wall's toleration toward present Jewish identity and disavowal of efforts to convert these "brethren of Abraham" represents a turning-point in
relations between Jews and English Protestants. Ironically, in his effort to
challenge older Judeo-centric trends, Wall distorts the purposes of Menasseh ben-Israel. As Nabil Matar has observed, Wall "restructured" ben-
Israel's work "to suit his own theological purpose." Matar's critique of
seventeenth-century English Protestant attempts to structure their realities along apocalyptic lines has relevance for our time as well: "the principle of Restoration which emerged in such a context could not but nur-
ture a distorted and 'restructured' portrait of the Jews," and, one might
add, Muslims and Catholics:

> For not only were the English writers unfamiliar with the Jews, but
> they were also unwilling to see them outside the framework of
> Christian history and theology. Although viewed as playing an
> active role in world history, the Jews still belonged to the domain of
> the esoteric and stereotypical.[44]

Contemporary Christian Zionism, even when it strives to be as philo-
Semitic as possible, relies on similar constructions and appropriations of
Jewish identity and purpose.

For his part, ben-Israel, perhaps like contemporary Jewish leaders who
cooperate closely with Judeo-centric Protestants, was quite willing to have
his ideas misappropriated and misapplied by Judeo-centric Christians,
provided those same Christians could be convinced of his primary policy
goal of having Jews readmitted to England. In this swirl of theopolitical
agendas, ben-Israel had his own. Toon suggests that, like Mede's conversion to a millenarian perspective, ben-Israel was a convert to the notion
that Israelites were to be found in the Americas. It is no surprise that ben-
Israel would work from a self-interested motive for the benefit of his
people, even if at one time he did consider Montezinos's tale to be mere
legend. The economic benefits for Jews to be openly present in London
would become apparent when, in 1651, England's offer of economic partnership with the Netherlands was rejected, the Navigation Act was passed,
and a trade war broke out between the two Protestant economic power-
houses. As Toon says, one of the Act's direct results "was to supply a
strong inducement to Jewish merchants who were trading with Jamaica
and Barbados to transfer their business to London." Beyond such trans-
parently economic agendas, Benite suggests that ben-Israel's desire for

Jewish readmission to England had "messianic overtones" and that he himself could have been operating, at least in part, from the grounds of messianic, if not eschatological hope.[45]

Cromwell, Strategic Indecision, and Jewish Recognition

The success of *The Hope of Israel* propelled Menasseh ben-Israel into the center of mid-seventeenth century English Judeo-centric debates about theology, politics, and foreign policy. He remained focused on his goal of gaining readmission for Jews. He was granted a visa to visit England in November 1652, but conflict between England and the Netherlands prevented his immediate travel. John Durie, who had corresponded with Joseph Mede, helped facilitate ben-Israel's travel; Henry Jessey, an associate of the Fifth Monarchy movement heavily engaged with the Jewish community in Amsterdam and author of *The Glory and Salvation of Jehuda and Israel* (1650), was the primary recorder of the events.[46]

When ben-Israel finally arrived in England, his person was less influential than his books. Only Oliver Cromwell, moved both by reports of Jewish persecution at the hands of Catholics and interest in potential economic benefits, is recorded as being sympathetic to the diagnosis and treatment ben-Israel sought to prescribe. Following the regicide of 1649 and Cromwell's replacement of Fairfax as Commander in Chief of the Army, he became a repository of immense hope for the future of England and the Protestant cause. Although Cromwell was interested in prophecy, it is likely his thoughts on Jewish presence in London were driven more by questions of economics and practical politics. As a result, ben-Israel's "Humble Addresses" (published in 1655 as *To His Highnesse the Lord Protector*)[47] followed a more practical line. In December 1655, Cromwell called a special conference that included many stakeholders from civic, economic, and theological spheres to discuss the legality and plausibility of allowing Jews into London's public life.

The major rift in the Whitehall Conference was between merchants and theologians: "the mercantile community voiced their fears that readmission of Jews would enrich foreigners and impoverish the English. But the theologians were in the majority and most of them were in favour of immigration as long as the activities of the Jewish community were carefully controlled."[48] Nevertheless, it was decided that the banishment ordered in 1290 by Edward I was not a standing law, but an executive order that could be rescinded without parliamentary approval. That question notwithstanding, even theologians whose apocalyptic hope was based on Jewish conversion to Protestant faith were disquieted by the thought of Jews living openly in their midst. The Whitehall Conference closed with no definite policy shift. As Ariel Hessavon says,

> it needs to be emphasized that there was no Act of Parliament, no proclamation from Cromwell, no order from the Council of State either welcoming Jews to England or changing their legal status as a community from aliens (foreigners whose allegiance was due to a foreign state) to denizens (foreigners admitted to residence and granted certain rights, notably to prosecute or defend themselves in law and to purchase or sell land, but still subject to the same customs duties on their goods and merchandise as aliens). The only evidence we have suggests that publicly Cromwell remained undecided on the issue.[49]

Although one could say that ben-Israel's mission to Cromwell failed, the Lord Protector's official indecision was key. Whitehall did not result in the opening of England's ports to all Jews who wished to settle in England. The more modest result was permission for the *marrano* community already present in London to worship in a designated space outside of private homes and to have a Jewish cemetery outside London. Although not the unfettered equality sought by some tolerationists, the maximalist approach reached a practically negotiated end. By 1660, London's Jewish community, though small, was organized and publicly visible. To the consternation of many Christians, these Jews did not convert. Instead, they lived achingly normal lives that brought about neither the Jewish hope of a messianic kingdom nor the *parousia* of the Christian millennium.

Judeo-centric Thought and the Shape of British Identity

As debates within the Whitehall Conference show, the fluidity of doctrine in mid-seventeenth century England was matched by fluidity in perceptions of English national interest and identity. Arthur Williamson's explorations of the ways English national identity was conceived during the stirrings of the Commonwealth show that apocalyptic hope—employed as a grammar to structure national identity and vocation—was central to each configuration. He traces these trends to the 1590s, when two options emerged for the English future: one with an apocalyptic vision for

Protestant "Britain" through the incorporation of Scotland, the other "emphatically ethnic and racial, resolutely anti-British and anti-apocalyptic, and eventually anti-Semitic."[50] Jews and Turks featured prominently in each of the apocalyptically informed configurations of English national purpose.

Because visions of a British commonwealth "more in keeping with King James's sensibilities" emphasized practical Christian unity, apocalyptic concern focused "not on the papal Antichrist but on the Turkish one." These theopolitical calculations were informed by Judeo-centric concerns. "During the earlier seventeenth century the more apocalyptic an Englishman's outlook," Williamson writes, "the more likely he would find a British perspective to be congenial, the more likely he would find himself interested in contemporary Jewry, possibly to the point of seeking their re-admission."[51]

The apocalyptic interests that eventually led Cromwell to allow Jews to live openly in England provide insight into the development of British identity, especially in its growing colonial and imperial expressions. This apocalyptic identity, after reaching its apex in the 1650s, would diminish as Britain's growing self-understanding as an economic empire began to take hold. Although "the apocalypse remained remarkably resilient as an organizing principle," Williamson observes that as the seventeenth century progressed, "an economic future truly began to supplant a prophetic future within the British imagination."[52] Even as apocalyptic thought was on the wane, the English Protestant tradition of Judeo-centric prophecy interpretation provided a basic medium for articulating the overriding goal of economic expansion.

Thomas Cooper's collection of sermons, published in 1615 as *The Blessing of Iapheth Proving the Gathering in of the Gentiles, and Finall conversion of the Iewes*, contained an early utilization of Judeo-centric thought for the blessing of economic expansion. Dedicated to the city leaders of London and "the worthie Commissioners, for the plantations in Ireland and Virginia," *The Blessing of Iapheth* argued that colonial profit-taking was necessary for the progress of gospel. "The rude & savadge nations farre & neer, in *Ireland* and *Virginia*," Cooper says, "have had this blessed light convayed and enlarged unto them" while "the plantations in *Ireland* & *Virginia*, are much furthered by your industrie ... that your hearts and purses are enlarged plentifully." All of this was within God's timing and plan, since the time has come when the "fulnes of the Gentiles shal be accomplished, then shall *Shem* returne againe to the true worship of God."[53] As

Christopher Hill observes of Cooper's work, "Not for the last time in English history, piety and profit went hand in hand." Cooper, he continues,
"presciently . . . links Parliamentary government, protestantism, liberty
and trade."[54] As Thorowgood beckoned in his near-hymn in the preface to
his *Jewes in America*, "*Looke Westward then yee men of Warre, thence you
may behold a rising Sunne of glory, with riches and much honour, and not
onely for your selves, but for Christ.*"[55] This call seems perfectly attuned to
Cromwell's Western Design of 1655, intended to wrest control of Jamaica
from Spain.

The millenarian sentiment that survived in Britain after 1655 was tied
less to any notion of Jews converting to Christian faith than to the place of
commerce as the pinnacle of British concern. That is not to say, however,
that debate regarding Jews and Judeo-centric theopolitical reflection did
not continue. As noted above, the Savoy Declaration (1658) confessed eschatological expectation for "the latter days" in which, "Antichrist being
destroyed" and "the Jews called," the church would enjoy peace.

Indeed, Judeo-centric prophecy interpretation would endure as an important theme in British intellectual life. Take, for instance, the deep reflections on eschatological Bible study undertaken by Sir Isaac Newton or
the intense efforts of Unitarian minister Joseph Priestley to draw Jews to
his version of faith in Jesus.[56] British Protestants were sufficiently ac-
quainted with their rich heritage of Judeo-centric prophecy interpretation
to apply those hermeneutical lenses to the French Revolution and the Napoleonic conquests. Something so basic to the formation of national identity and vocation cannot simply or quietly disappear. Thus, when interpreting the political influence of Judeo-centric thought within British
approaches to the Holy Land and, eventually, the Zionist movement, the
elements to ascertain are not the individual commitments of, say, Lord
Shaftesbury or Lord Arthur Balfour (even if those two individuals were
vital to the development and implementation of policy) but the stream of
ideas and identity in which they stood.

In his investigation of the prophetic foundations of American national
identity and vocation, Ernest Tuveson observes that American approaches
to the world oscillate between isolationism and "active messianism." Although, he says, the latter is "generally the less powerful idea . . . in the
right situation it could become dominant."[57] The United States inherited
this dual nature, this dialectical struggle for its identity, from its English
and British parentage. Along with a fundamental commitment to commerce as the engine of development and purpose, the most enduring

traits inherited through the British colonists who arrived in North America were passed through the English Protestant tradition of Judeo-centric prophecy interpretation. As nineteenth-century American Christian Zionist William E. Blackstone said of the biblical centrality of prophecies that "Israel shall be restored to Palestine and no more pulled up out of their land," the tradition we have been exploring "runs through the whole" of Anglo-American history since the sixteenth century "like the red thread in the British rigging."[58]

Having passed through the development of this tradition from John Bale and John Foxe to its millenarian expansions in Thomas Brightman and Joseph Mede to its practical political applications by the Cartwrights and Menasseh ben-Israel, we now turn to the applications and adaptations of the tradition in North America.

6

Typologizing the Jew

THE JUDEO-CENTRIC FOUNDATIONS OF AMERICA'S COVENANTAL VOCATION

WHEN ENGLISH PURITANS arrived in the New World, they carried with them the struggles, convictions, and traditions developed since the beginnings of the English Reformations. The English Protestant tradition of Judeo-centric prophecy interpretation came to play a central role in how Puritans understood themselves, both as thoroughly English and as distinctively American. These English Christians found the vocabulary to describe their unique vocation in the biblical narratives of the Children of Israel: their sufferings, their liberations, their rejection and redemption, their unique covenantal relationship with a God who was and who would continue to be active in history. As George Marsden has observed, "New England's spiritual leaders almost universally interpreted contemporary history in such apocalyptic lights, and they continued to do so through the Revolutionary era."[1] Thus, even as these English Christians did not set out to separate themselves from their sisters and brothers in England, the process of negotiating English Protestant self-understanding in the American context sowed the seeds of a particularly American mission. This chapter will explore how the Judeo-centric tradition of prophecy interpretation informed these negotiations of identity and prepared the groundwork for the theopolitical activity of contemporary American Christian Zionism.

"The eies of all people are upon us": John Winthrop and the Colonial Covenant Sailing on the *Arbella* toward his new assignment as the first governor of the Massachusetts Bay Colony, John Winthrop articulated one of the most enduring themes of American self-understanding. Written and preached during the journey between April and June 1630, Winthrop's *Model of Christian Charity* is responsible for describing the American project in the terms of Matthew 5:14, a "city built on a hill" that "cannot be hid." Although this iconic image is drawn from Jesus's Sermon on the Mount, the prevailing logic of Winthrop's essay highlights from the deuteronomic strand of covenantal theology drawn from the Torah.[2] The centrality of covenantal thinking had been a feature of English Puritan thought since the early seventeenth century. Mark Noll identifies the notion of the national covenant as "a motif at once profoundly biblical and profoundly flexible" that tied together other Puritan commitments, including "the centrality of the new birth, the assumption of a unified society, and the church as the central link between personal religion and national reform."[3] The covenant was a unified and unifying concept that animated English and therefore Anglo-American Puritan understandings of vocation and purpose on personal, communal, and national levels.

The *Model of Christian Charity* was, practically speaking, an ethic for communal living. The *Mayflower* had sailed with its Puritan cargo in 1620. Winthrop had carefully studied the hardships of the Plymouth Colony and was determined to construct a theologically grounded but practicable guide for the cooperative spirit the colony would need to be viable past a few months of existence. He presented this ethic not just as a pact among the colonists, but as a "Covenant with [God] for this worke." Drawing explicitly from Moses's exhortation in Deuteronomy 30:19—"I have set before you life and death, blessings and curses. Choose life so that you and your descendants may live"—Winthrop told his people that "if the Lord shall please to heare us, and bring us in peace to the place wee desire, then hath hee ratified this Covenant and sealed our Commission [and] will expect a strickt performance of the Articles contained in it." If, on the other hand, God ratifies the covenant through their safe arrival and they do not adhere to the articles, "the Lord will surely breake out in wrathe against us, be revenged of such a perjured people and make us knowe the price of the breache of such a Covenant." This deuteronomic context brings the famous image: if the people follow the covenant and enjoy the manifestation of God's blessings, "men shall say of succeeding plantations: the lord make it like that of New England: for wee must consider that wee shall be as a Citty upon a Hill, the eies of all people are upon us." It was natural that they, through their vocation, would be exceptional. Their faithfulness to the covenant determined whether they would prosper or would instead "surely perishe out of the good Land."[4]

Popular representations of the roots of American identity often reference the rich typologies employed by Anglo-American Puritans to describe their circumstances. Many have read in these typological locations of

Anglo-American Puritan identity an effort both to denigrate the English communities these Puritans had left behind and to displace the covenant of the original Children of Israel. In short, popular American historiography, with academic backing by the influential writings of Perry Miller and Sacvan Bercovitch,[5] has presumed a fundamental discontinuity between New England and Old England. The broad Puritan effort to provide a critique of established English faith and culture should not, however, be understood as a rejection of that faith and culture. As Robert Middlekauff has written concerning the first generation of Puritan settlers, "Richard Mather, John Cotton, Thomas Hooker . . . continued to follow English events after their removal to America. Their interest, however, was not marked by a feeling of superiority, or a belief that the truth resided in New England and nowhere else."[6] Popular American historiography neglects the fact that these Puritans carried with them not only the English language and the Authorized Version of the Bible, but also the Anglo-centric commitments of Protestant historiography in its English iteration. The interpretation of history the Puritan colonists inherited and refined for their context was intimately informed by the apocalyptic tradition of Judeo-centric prophecy interpretation, including that tradition's anti-Catholic and anti-Islamic elements. Far from expressions of superiority, the typologies employed by Anglo-American Puritans were elaborations of established patterns of English Protestant apocalyptic hope that, in their context, provided what Martin Luther called "strong comfort and comforting strength."[7]

Primitivism and Millennialism

Understanding the commitments and perspectives of pre-Revolutionary Puritan clergy is essential not only for grasping the nuances of early American theology, but for comprehending the intellectual climate that informed the Revolution and the young United States. As Mark Noll has observed, "New England, though representing only a minority of Americans . . . , exerted an influence far beyond its size on the intellectual culture of the new United States. Puritanism is the only colonial religious system that modern historians take seriously as a major religious influence on the Revolution." Eventually, a blend of political commitments and Puritan religious concepts produced what Nathan Hatch has termed "civil millennialism," a discourse that, as Noll says, "persuaded other colonists to think that the new nation in its entirety might be specially elect of God like a new ancient Israel."[8]

How one constructs the interplay of civil and religious discourse of the pre-Revolutionary era necessarily informs one's perspective on the sources of American identity. Historiography, therefore, becomes a theatre for shaping perspectives regarding contemporary American ideology and policy. Theodore Bozeman has observed that the 1970s and 1980s saw the "American Puritans' Errand into the Wilderness . . . remodeled along eschatological lines" in which it was repeatedly proposed that "the Massachusetts Bay project presented yet another chapter in Western Christianity's periodic pursuit of the millennium." Bozeman's rejoinder to this trend, which has continued to shape popular self-understanding of American origins, was to assert that "the conceptual starting point" for the early Puritan colonists was not "eschatology, but, rather, the traditional Deuteronomic patterns of the National Covenant." He points out, for instance, that "what Richard Mather retrieved from John Foxe was not . . . a notion of millennial-national mission, but a compelling legend establishing an apostolic source for Britain's first Christianity" so that the pure English Christianity brought by Joseph of Arimathea (a point developed within John Bale's historiography, as discussed in Chapter Three) could be "at last regained."[9] Although Winthrop and Mather warned of England's coming calamity, they were not forecasting certain doom but were calling their home country to live up to its glorious and ancient potential. While it is true that millenarian commitment would not be a prominent feature of Anglo-American Puritan thought until after the momentous events of 1640, Bozeman nevertheless overstates his case when he claims that "Puritan theology generally . . . stood in no necessary affiliation with eschatology." For while it was not necessarily millenarian, the primitivist impulse manifested expectations of final redemption and ultimate apocalyptic hope.

The covenantal-national mission formulated for England by John Bale and John Foxe—a self-understanding formed by blending continental Protestant historiography and English nationalism—was extended through the millenarian biblical interpretations of thinkers such as Thomas Brightman, Henry Finch, and Joseph Mede. Once Parliamentary censorship ended in 1640, millenarian concepts—which relied heavily on Judeo-centric prophecy interpretation—were integrated publicly and organically into the established covenantal-national discourse of both England and the colonies. Bozeman's insistence that the heart of early Puritan thought in America was shaped more by covenantal-national commitments than by the specifics of any millenarian theory helps us better understand New England Puritan thought and the American identity it informs. This awareness, in turn, helps us better comprehend the nature of contemporary American popular support for the State of Israel and the Christian Zionist efforts to preserve it.

Censorship, the Millennium, and the Judeo-centric Tradition

The infusion of millenarian discourse in the 1640s opened Puritans in America to robust applications of Judeo-centric prophecy interpretations through the lens of their typological identification with the Children of Israel. Among the first of the eminent immigrant theologians to adopt a millenarian perspective was John Cotton (1585–1652). In a series of lectures on the Book of Revelation between 1639 and 1641 (which were transcribed and subsequently gathered together into three books), Cotton introduced listeners to the historicist interpretations of "holy Brightman" even though Cotton did not agree with him in all details.[10] Speaking in a time of great turmoil within England, Cotton compared those who had "gone out of the Countrey" to those who wonder how they can "*sing the Lords song, the song of Zion in a strange Land.*" Even as he taught that it was appropriate "to have an eye to our brethren in our native Country," he was critical (echoing Brightman's own critical nationalism) of previous Protestant leaders who failed to fully recover "the Country out of the jaws of Antichrist" and simply substituted the authority of the King for that of the Pope. Cotton confidently told his hearers that "neither the Pope, nor King hath power to make Laws to rule the Church, but it must be by the Laws of Christ."[11]

Cotton's commentary on the Song of Solomon, produced during the same period, more explicitly shows his wholesale appropriation of the tradition of Judeo-centric prophecy interpretation, with its anti-Catholic and anti-Islamic elements. The events in England and the open availability of millenarian writings helped develop Cotton's thinking in a way similar, perhaps, to Joseph Mede's conversion. Bozeman notes that there is no evidence that Cotton held millenarian views before 1639 and that "Cotton's first treatment of Canticles had no counterpart among . . . any other notable emigrant theologian."[12] Although Brightman is not named, his influence is felt throughout Cotton's commentary, from the subtitle's emphasis that "Canticles" details the history of "the church . . . Jewish and Christian," to the exultation that "the wonderfull excellency of this Song" is found in its intention "to bee . . . an historicall prophecie or propheticall

history." Cotton's reliance on Brightman is especially apparent in his interpretation of Song of Solomon 6:13—"Return, return, O Shulamite; return,
return, that we may look upon thee." (KJV)—as referring to "the unex-
pected admirable arising of a new Church . . . that of the Jewes which we
looke for." Following Brightman's innovative etymology that God, "for difference sake he calleth her by her countrey name, of the Old Salem" and
"now turned his speech to the old Countrey breed," Cotton's justification
for this interpretation is that "Shulamite" alludes "to *Salem* the ancient
name of *Ierusalem*, the Mother City of the JEWES." At this point, Brightman's commentary lays out the Jewish role in the destruction of Islam and
Cotton follows suit: "The Armies of the Jewes shall bee terrible to the
Turkes and Tartars, and to the false Prophet then driven from Rome by
ten Christian Princes, and associating himselfe to the Turke for succour."
This sudden, future calling of the Church of the Jews presents, for Cotton,
another opportunity to prove Gentile Christian faithfulness in actively assisting their return to Palestine: "The Jewes shall appeare unexpectedly,
prepared to embrace Christs calling: . . . their soule should no sooner
desire it, but they should bee set in all readinesse; where also is intimated
the willing readinesse of a willing people among the Gentiles, to convey
the Jewes into their owne Countrie, with Charets, and horses, and Drom-
edaries."[13] Even with this highly developed Judeo-centric vision, Cotton
was not yet operating with a full millenarian eschatology. That project
would eventually occupy the thoughts of Cotton's friend and student, Increase Mather.

The Intellectual Climate of Israel's Salvation

The period between John Cotton's 1642 commentary on Canticles and the
1669 publication of Increase Mather's first collection of sermons on the
hope of Jewish conversion and restoration was filled with dramatic developments in English Protestant theological debate. There were shifts, for
instance, in the notion that the indigenous peoples of the New World were
composed, in part, of the Lost Tribes of Israel, now revealed by God and
readied for their mass conversion to Protestant faith. In 1649, a collection
of letters from John Eliot and Thomas Mayhew asserted, during an eschatologically convenient "juncture of time," and with appeal to the corroborating authority of "Rabbi-ben-Israel, a great Dr. of the Jewes," that "there
is a sprinkling at least of *Abrahams seed* in these parts."[14] Another collection of letters published in 1652, however, subtly rejected the theory that

the indigenous groups of North America had any Israelite origin: in the mission to the Indians, they said, *"the fullnes of the Gentiles draws neere to be accomplished,* that the calling of the *Jewes* may be hastned."[15] Twenty-five years later, the notion that American Indians were descendants of the Lost Tribes was seriously in doubt: "that the ten Tribes by the Streights of *Anian,* or any other imagined passage should have conveyed themselves as to their maine body into *America,* is a farfetcht Notion, embraced by *Manasseh Ben Israel, &c.* rejected by *Acosta de Laet, Hornius, &c."*[16]

English hopes in Jewish movements as the instrument for realizing end-times prophetic expectation were raised and then dashed by another Jewish leader, Sabbatai Tzvi (1626–1676), who, inspired by the rhythms of exile and return in the Lurianic Kabbalah, gained a large following of Jews throughout Asia Minor who adhered to his claim to be the messiah. These developments were eagerly watched by Christians who believed that Jewish control over the Holy Land was central to their own eschatological hopes. Those Christians were perhaps more crushed than any group when the news spread that Tzvi, while standing before the Ottoman Sultan at Topkapi Palace in Istanbul, officially converted to Islam. This conversion, viewed as apostasy by many Jews and Christians who had viewed Tzvi as a proto-Puritan, occurred in the apocalyptically significant year of 1666.[17]

In England, the claims of Judeo-centric prophecy interpretation became a litmus test within political discourse. Soon after Jews were a publicly recognized component of English society, it became apparent that they were more interested in engaging in commerce while preserving their unique identities than they were in adopting English Protestant beliefs. The rarity of Jewish conversion is accentuated by the celebrations published when some Jews crossed that threshold. The confidence some Protestants had in the possibility of their national conversion began to wane. Moreover, as Nabil Matar has pointed out, endorsement of or resistance to the idea that Jews would be restored to the Holy Land came to function, in England, more as a slogan for one's political affiliation rather than as a biblically-founded theological position:

> The theological position towards the Jews indicated a political position towards the revolution of the saints. . . . Understandably, criticism of the idea of the Restoration came from those who neither viewed Cromwell's ascendancy to power as divinely legitimized, nor identified Interregnum England with the shortly-expected kingdom

of Christ. Specifically, Presbyterians in the Assembly of Divines were hostile to Cromwell's regime and to the whole millenarian heresy on which the justification of the civil wars, Pride's Purge, the regicide and Cromwellian dictatorship rested.[18]

Though not unaffected by the political developments and affiliations in their home country, New England Puritans were far enough removed that they could continue to engage millenarian and restorationist concepts primarily as theological questions. In the meantime, more sophisticated methods of analyzing biblical texts were growing in popularity throughout Europe, methods that eschewed what their practitioners perceived as the simplistic literalism near to the heart of the Reformation. The ground was shifting yet again. Scholars such as Thomas Hobbes, Benedict de Spinoza, Hugo Grotius, and others would soon be presenting philological and historical-contextual readings that fundamentally challenged both Catholic and Protestant hermeneutical conventions.

One of the contributions made by Increase Mather (1639–1723) to this tumultuous intellectual environment was *The Mystery of Israel's Salvation*. Published in 1669, *Mystery* has been described by Carl Ehle as "the most comprehensive work on the restoration of Israel published at a time when the hope for a New English Israel was still viable."[19] Although Mather goes beyond John Cotton by incorporating millenarian expectations into the Judeo-centric prophecy interpretation, *Mystery* is primarily a conservative reiteration of received traditions. Against newer hermeneutical methods, Mather reminded his readers that "literal interpretation of Scripture ought never to be rejected for an allegorical one, except necessity compel thereunto."[20] As it had with Henry Finch, Mather's commitment to literalism was focused on the roles of Jews, Catholics, and Muslims in the realization of Christian eschatological hopes. Forty years later, in his *A Dissertation Concerning the Future Conversion of the Jewish Nation*, Increase would repeat many of the same positions, including his warning that "If Men allow themselves the Liberty of Allegorizing, we may at last Allegorize Religion into nothing but Fancy."[21]

Mather accepted as self-evident that the hope of Jesus's glorious reign would be preceded by the collective conversion of Jews to Protestant faith and their relocation to Palestine and would result eventually in the destruction of God's own theopolitical enemies—the Pope and the Turk. As Mather put it, "it is very evident that [the city of] *Rome* must be destroyed before the *Iews* can be converted" and that "mystical *Babylon* [the Catholic Church], must be destroyed before Israel's Redemption be accomplished." Quoting Joseph Mede's interpretation that "The Turk must likewise be destroyed before all *Israel* be saved," Mather's political awareness is clear: "For that Eastern Anti-Christ (as some are wont to call him) having the Land of *Israel* in his possession, we may be sure they [Jews] shall never peaceably enjoy the Land of their Fathers again, as long as he hath any power to hinder it." Mather is confident that "the *Jews*" will be "brought into their own Land again" and that "Pope and Turk . . . shall be utterly destroyed after the Jews conversion." The "consummate salvation of *Israel*" will be completed in "the great battle of *Armageddon*" in which "Turk and Pope, and House of *Austria, &c.*" will "combine together to destroy the Kingdom of Christ amongst *Jews* and *Gentiles.*"[22]

Mather was aware that many English Protestants would contest the positions he espoused. The time was not long ago, he said, when "it seemed very paradoxical to affirm, that ever there should be a general conversion of the Jewish Nation." Nonetheless, he claimed that this "truth of late hath gained ground much throughout the world." The acceptance of this position, he said, was itself a sign of the times: "Only in these late days, these things have obtained credit, much more universally than heretofore; And that's a sign that the time of the end draweth on a-pace," the time in which "the *Israelites* shall again possesse . . . the Land promised unto their *Father Abraham.*"[23] After a long section regarding the number of Israelites "scattered even throughout the world more or less," Mather offers this observation:

> In a word, it is justly believed, that if all the Israelites which be in the world were together, they would make the greatest Nation upon the whole earth. Hence the Scripture plainly intimateth (for why should we unnecessarily refuse literal interpretations?) that at the return of Israel, the Land of their Fathers will be too little for them, such will the multitude of their number be, and that therefore they must have other Countreys adjoyning for their possession.

When the New Jerusalem is established, Mather affirms, it will be a literal place, not "meerly of the new Gospel-dispensation, for that has already come" or "the state of glory in heaven." Perhaps in response to the Sabbatarian disappointment or, more generally, to the slow pace of missionary efforts, Mather avers that "there is some reason to believe that the *Jews,* many of them, will be repossessed of their own Land again before such time as they have any general Evangelical repentance," that "after the *Isra-elites* shall be returned to their own Land again, the spirit of repentance shall be poured forth upon them." The notion that Jews would return to the Holy Land prior to their expected conversion would grow over the fol-lowing decades, until finally confirmed by the advent of Jewish political Zionism (and would even then create confusion among some prominent Christian leaders). Mather, utilizing vocabulary that would come into vogue two centuries later, additionally offers some thoughts on *"the rap-ture of the Saints into the air* to meet Christ." Referencing 1 Thessalonians 4:17, he offered support for those who said the rapture was necessary so "the Saints, whom Christ shall find alive at this coming . . . might escape that conflagration whereby the wicked upon the earth shall be destroyed" even if he did not think "that it is any Heresie to believe" differently.[24]

Increase Mather's unwavering, long-term commitment to Judeo-centric prophecy interpretation—with its constitutive literalist, anti-Catholic and anti-Islamic elements—helped solidify the tradition and its millenarian applications for the American context. His legacy is far-reaching. Although, as J.F. Maclear has demonstrated, early Puritan New England was filled with various forms of apocalyptic hope, including endorsements of Fifth Monarchy violence against established orders, "beginning with Increase's *Mystery of Israel's Salvation* (1669), the Mathers led New England in literary cultivation of the new apocalypticism."[25] Mather expected that the realiza-tion of his apocalyptic hopes would have political consequences. However, he neither envisioned a heightened status of America in God's plans for the end-times nor believed that Christians had taken the place of Jews in God's economy of salvation.

The *"Antick Fancy of America's being Hell"*

The anti-Catholic and anti-Islamic elements of the English Protestant tradition of Judeo-centric prophecy interpretation helped frame the self-understanding of Anglo-American colonists in the New World. Their contexts and experiences, however, often led them to apply elements of that tradition in new ways. The presence, for instance, of Spanish and French colonists in adjoining areas of the continent provided an existen-tial referent for the Anglo-American colonists, along with evidence that the Papal Antichrist was actively seeking to dominate both the New World and the Old. They were equally aware of the continuing contest with Muslims in both spiritual and worldly spheres. Thomas Kidd has described the colonial context as one that "trafficked in an intellectual milieu ready to make use of Islamic categories," a milieu in which "internal apologetic concerns" were paramount and in which "associating an opponent with Islam became a standard rhetorical move in religious debates, as it legitimized the accuser as a defender of righteousness."[26]

Islam and Catholicism were important forces on the international stage of the time. Protestants throughout Europe and in the American colonies watched intently as these two heads of the Antichrist battled for imperial supremacy. It was not until the Treaty of Karlowitz in 1699—the result of a counter-offensive launched by the Austrian Hapsburgs after the failure of the second Ottoman siege of Vienna in 1683—that the decline of Ottoman power became apparent. As Paul Coles has written, "The Treaty of Karlowitz marked a final, decisive turning point in the military balance between Europe and the Islamic world."[27] Judge Samuel Sewall, observing the clashes between the Hapsburgs and the Ottomans, reminded his Protestant readers that while "the diminution of the *Ottoman* Empire" may be a "matter of universal Joy . . . the Pope and his followers, by warring against the *Turk*, do not dry up *Euphrates*: but do inlarge the *Papal*."[28]

Cotton Mather (1663–1728), the grandson of Richard and son of Increase, was remarkably engaged in writing about Muslims and Islamic civilization. Mather's "interest went well beyond the ordinary awareness of the East as a region of riches and the unusual," Mukhtar Isani observes. He "appears to have kept abreast of current news from the East, especially from the Turkish Empire." In this regard, "Mather's interest in the Orient is not unusual in its direction but in its extent. This sustained interest, which spans most of his adult years, shows another side of his extraordinary inquiring nature and, in part, reflects the global awareness of Puritan America."[29] For Mather, Islamic civilization provided both example and threat, bringing both knowledge for vaccinations against smallpox and the challenge of piracy along the Barbary Coast.

In 1698, Cotton Mather published *A Pastoral Letter to the English Captives in Africa*, which was widely distributed in New England. Continuing in the national-covenantal pattern set by the first generation, Mather instructed the captives (and the colonists who were the letter's primary audience) in the superiority of Christianity and in methods of using the Qur'an itself against "any *Mohametan* Tempters."[30] The next year, while writing about conflicts with Indians, Mather made note of the sailors living in Barbary captivity: "But in the midst of these Deplorable Things, God has given up several of our Sons, into the Hands of the Fierce *Monsters* of

Africa. Mahometan Turks and Moors, and Devils, are at this Day oppress-
ing many of our Sons, with a Slavery, wherein they *Wish for Death, and
cannot find it*; a *Slavery*, from whence they cry and write unto us, *It had been
Good for us, that we had never been born.*"³¹ Just as captivity narratives would
help shape American attitudes toward American Indians by providing presumably first-hand accounts and expert knowledge of the subject, narratives of captivity among Barbary pirates provided the necessary knowledge
for American condemnation of this enemy of both commerce and faith.³²
In both cases, the national-covenantal model held true: the captives and all
who suffered should more thoroughly contemplate the sins that had
brought these punishments while they waited for their redemption.

Although Cotton Mather, informed by his constructed knowledge of
Turkish and North African Muslims, could claim that "we are afar off, in a
Land, which never had (that I ever heard of) one Mahometan breathing in
it," he could not say the same of the American Indians and persons of African descent he encountered on a daily basis.³³ Anglo-American anxiety
resulted in highly structured relationships between the colonists and those
who were other from them. This anxiety is strikingly illustrated by the
Virginia legislature's October 1705 statute regarding servants and slaves:

> XI. . . . *Be it also enacted* . . . That no negros, mulattos, or Indians
> although christians, or Jews, Moors, Mahometans, or other infidels,
> shall, at any time, purchase any christian servant, nor any other,
> except of their own complexion. . . . And if any negro, mulatto, or
> Indian, Jew, Moor, Mahometan, or other infidel, or such as are de-
> clared slaves by this act, shall . . . purchase any christian white ser-
> vant, the said servant shall, *ipso facto*, become free.³⁴

Winthrop Jordan has noted that the statute's use of the word "Christian"
"sounded more like a definition of race than of religion" since it had "somehow become intimately and explicitly linked with 'complexion.'"³⁵ By 1705,
"whiteness" was emerging as a racial category. This enduring feature of
American Protestant identity was established through interaction with
American Indians. Peter Silver has detailed how, through seventeenth-
and eighteenth-century American experience, "whiteness . . . became a
building block for public discourse" so that "in the heterogeneous middle
colonies, where color-based coalitions had not struck anyone as especially
self-evident before, the word 'white' was lastingly shaded, and given an
enormous boost in power, by its use in Indian wars."³⁶ Just as interaction

with American Indians shaped the English colonial enterprises outside of North America, the blending of scientific racialism with American expansionism would fuel the presumptions of Manifest Destiny in the nineteenth century. Interactions both with competing Catholic and Islamic commercial interests and with populations of slaves and indigenous persons made fundamental contributions to Anglo-American Protestant identity and self-understanding. The dominant, homogenizing construct of "American" identity provided by the conjoined categories of White, Anglo-Saxon, and Protestant would develop over the next decades.[37]

Those colonists who understood their presence in America in religious terms were forced early on to contend with English theologians' assessment of the prophetic significance (or, rather, insignificance) of the New World. The heritage of response to Joseph Mede's commentary on the prophetic possibilities of England's colonies demonstrates the creative negotiation of nascent American identity even as it confirms both Mede's enduring influence and the tenacity with which Anglo-American Puritans held to Judeo-centric traditions.

In March 1634, Dr. William Twisse, in one of his many letters to Joseph Mede, requested Mede's "opinion . . . of our English Plantations in the New world." When the correspondence was made available in 1664 with the first edition of Mede's writings, his response reverberated through the New World. "Concerning our Plantation in the *American* world," Mede wrote, "I wish them as well as any body; though I differ from them far, both in other things, and in the grounds they go upon." Regarding the missionary prospects among the indigenous peoples, Mede saw "little hope of the general Conversion of those Natives in any considerable part of that Continent" but it may be "pleasing to Almighty God . . . to *affront* the Devil . . . in those places where he had thought to have reigned securely." Mede then conjectured that America was peopled intentionally by Satan who, not expecting industrious European Christians, sought to preserve people for the armies of Gog and Magog. As he said in a clarifying letter, "I believe it to have been first inhabited since the days of *Constantine*, when the Devil saw he could no longer reign here without control and the continual affront of the Gospel and Cross of Christ." All of this put the English colonists at great risk: both Twisse and Mede hoped that "they shall not so far degenerate (not all of them) as to come in that Army of *Gog* and *Magog* against the Kingdom of Christ; but be translated thither before the Devil be loosed, if not presently after his tying up."[38] For Mede, the Americas were little more than a holding pen for Satan's minions, the staging ground for Armageddon. American Puritans eagerly perused the volume along with their coreligionists in England. As Reiner Smolinski observes, the significance of Mede's statements about America, from the perspective at least of Puritans in America, "cannot be overemphasized, for in essence he had consigned America to outer darkness."[39]

Mede's judgment was especially irksome to Judge Samuel Sewall (1652–1730), one of the few Puritans of the second generation to assert, in response to Mede, that not only was America destined to be part of God's millennium, but that the New Jerusalem may well be located there. Sewall responded directly to Mede's charge in his *Phaenomena quaedam Apocalyptica*, first published in Massachusetts in 1697. Acknowledging Mede to be "incomparably more than my Match," Sewall, motivated by "Love to my Country," nevertheless sought to show that, since God's "Word abides for ever . . . what cometh to pass in the New World, must be referred to some Prophesie" and that "to make *America* to be the whole, and only Object of the *Curses* denounced against *Gog* and *Magog*; and to shut them out from all *Promised Blessings*; is altogether Unscriptural and Unreasonable." In contrast to Mede's unreasonable, alien opinion, for "one that has been born, or but liv'd in *America,* between thirty, and fourty years; it may be pardonable for him to ask, Why may not that be the place of New-Jerusalem?" Sewall's patriotic perspective led to even greater conjectures in his dedication to William Stoughton, the Lieutenant Governor of Massachusetts. There, Sewall proposed that the New World, which was "*so far from deserving the Nick names of* Gog *and* Magog; *that it stands fair for being made the Seat of the Divine Metropolis,*" was the likely site of the Euphrates of Revelation 16:12 and that "New-English *Planters were the Fore-runners of the Kings of the East.*"[40]

Sewall's patriotic rejoinder to Mede's conjecture regarding the prophetic status of the American colonies is notable both as a strong assertion of American identity and its confirmation of the strength of Judeocentric prophecy interpretation. Although Sewall delighted in exposing Mede's "Antick Fancy of *America*'s being Hell" and broke with tradition by allegorically severing the New Jerusalem from the geographic location of the earthly Jerusalem, he never sought to challenge the notion that "This City of God is especially made up of *Jews*, and from thence it hath its Name." Indeed, "the *Jews* upon their Return, will eminently sustain that Character."[41] "Although," Smolinski observes, "Sewall stood alone in proclaiming America the future site of the Celestial City, he was in good company when he heralded the Jews as the leaders of the millennial New Earth."[42] Even as he kicked patriotically against the goads, Sewall demonstrated Mede's enduring authority and the centrality of Judeo-centric prophecy interpretation for American Protestant thought.

Cotton Mather did not entertain with Samuel Sewall the possibility that the New Jerusalem could be located anywhere other than in the vicinity of the historical Jerusalem in Palestine. Rather, Smolinski observes, Mather "reacted against Mede's exclusionary statements not by claiming the City of God for New England alone but by extending the boundaries of Christ's sacred geography into the American hemisphere, thus safeguarding New England's membership in Christ's kingdom."[43] Contrary to the spurious presumptions of popular Americanist historiography, even the author of *Theopolis Americana* had no intention of substituting New England as the New Jerusalem or Anglo-American Puritans as God's New Israel.

Even while Mather maintained these central elements of the established tradition of Judeo-centric prophecy interpretation, toward the end of his life he significantly departed from the fullness of the tradition his father had espoused. In the early eighteenth century, the interpretive methods to which Increase had responded in *The Mystery of Israel's Salvation* (1669) and his *Dissertation Concerning the Future Conversion of the Jewish Nation* (1709) had only grown in popularity and precision. Although Cotton was equally concerned about these hermeneutical questions, he began exploring the possibility of developing a new, hybrid hermeneutic that could accommodate the emerging philological approaches to the Bible. His effort to do so, contained in the unpublished manuscript, "*Triparadisus*," led him to a startling shift in his understanding of Judeo-centric prophecy interpretation.

The threefold combination of disappointments that the End did not come in either 1697 or 1716, the lack of any compelling evidence that Jewish communities were on the cusp of collective conversion, and the death of Increase in 1723 seems to have propelled Cotton to explore radical new directions in his eschatological speculation. When, in 1724, Cotton read the anonymous pamphlet *Good Things to Come*, he immediately made it a foundation of his eschatological system: "from that Moment, I thought I might say, *I have found it.*"[44] *Good Things to Come* provided a compelling solution to debates over the timeline of the "rapture" and "conflagration" Increase had mentioned in his 1669 *Mystery*. The solution to this vexing problem opened the door to Cotton's insight, noted in his diary entry of June 21, 1724:

> And I am now satisfied, that there is nothing to hinder the immediate Coming of our Saviour, in these Flames, that shall bring an horrible Destruction on this present and wicked World, and bring on the new Heaven, and the new Earth, wherein shall dwell Righteousness. I purpose quickly to write on these things.[45]

Although Cotton had been steeped in the notion that the national conversion of Israelites to Christian faith needed to be accomplished prior to Jesus's return, this moment of insight led him to completely restructure his views on the matter. Abandoning the well-established norms of Judeocentric prophecy interpretation—especially its limited literalism concerning the distinctions between Jews and Gentiles and the future national conversion of Jews—Mather adopted the allegorical-preterist hermeneutics that his father abhorred. In this preterist mode, Smolinski explains, "Mather did not reject the Jewish nation per se but merely insisted that their conversion had already taken place in the past."[46] The ninth section of "Triparadisus" is devoted to explaining that the national conversion of Jews is not necessary for the Second Coming of Christ.

While the de-centering of Jewish national conversion had implications for Mather's eschatological system, he nevertheless maintained a Judeocentric outlook. While remaining geographically Judeo-centric in his belief that the New Jerusalem would be situated above the historic Jerusalem in Palestine, the eschatological system he developed after 1724 did not accord Jews the privileges common in the prophetic tradition he inherited. "Will our Glorious Lord fetch His People, from one Circumcised Nation only," Mather asked in his *Terra Beata* of 1726. "No, No; This Blessed People shall be fetched out of *Many Nations*. Even the *Indians* and the *Negro's*. . . . One found in the Sultry Regions of *Africa*, or, among the *Tranquebarians* in the Eastern India, or the *Massachusettsians* in the Western . . . is as much valued by GOD, as ever any *Simeon* or *Levi*, that could show their Descent from" Jacob.[47] This expansive vision squared well with Cotton's earlier response to Mede in *Theopolis Americana* that "it will be impossible, for the *Holy* People, and the *Teachers* and *Rulers* of the *Reformed World* in the other *Hemisphere*, to leave *America* unvisited." "I that am an *American*," he said, echoing Sewall's patriotic fervor, "must needs be Lothe to allow all *America* still until the *Devils* possession, when our Lord shall possess all the rest of the world."[48]

Judeo-centrism and the Work of Redemption

The American adaptation of the Protestant tradition of Judeo-centric prophecy interpretation was continued by Jonathan Edwards (1703–1758). Although his apocalyptic thought has been said to disclose "Edwards's participation in an unattractive aspect of the Protestant exegetical tradition, namely, its religiously sanctioned prejudice and anti-Catholicism,"[49] it equally demonstrates the strength of the tradition in the American context and its pervasive influence in the formation of American Protestant theology. George Marsden has pointed out that Edwards "considered this world a transient stage where a cosmic drama was being carried out" and that "The key to this drama—the key to *history*—was the mysterious writings of the Apocalypse."[50] With his theological contemporaries in both England and New England, Edwards applied this inherited Protestant historiography to his contemporary theopolitical situation. He was equally steeped in the commitments of Judeo-centric prophecy interpretation.

Edwards looked for the national conversion of Jews to Christian faith and the restoration of Jews to the land then ruled by the Ottoman Empire, whose religion, he said, "was taught them by their false prophet Mahomet."[51] Although Edwards claimed "no certainty as to . . . the various conjectures concerning the time of the calling of the Jews, and fall of the kingdom of the Beast,"[52] these events were central to his future expectations. Because Edwards explicitly rejected the preterist hermeneutics adopted by Cotton Mather, he preached in the afterglow of the First Great Awakening that Christians must "be earnest and constant in praying for" the "future glorious advancement of the church and kingdom of God in this world" that will be marked by "the calling of the Jews" and the "utter abolishing of heathenism."[53]

In October 1757, Edwards informed the trustees of the College of New Jersey of his intention to write "a great work, which I call *A History of the Work of Redemption*, a body of divinity in an entire new method, being thrown into the form of an history." First articulated in a sermon series delivered in 1739, the book detailed a typological reading of the Bible that sought to show "the great work of redemption by Jesus Christ" as "the *summum* and *ultimum* of all the divine operations and degrees."[54] Central to the history of these divine operations was the past rejection and future restoration of the Israelites as God's people. As Edwards put it, "the Jews were rejected and apostatized from the visible church to prepare the way for the calling of the Jews which shall be in the latter days." As it was for others who stood within the Anglo-American Protestant tradition of Judeo-centric prophecy interpretation, the national conversion of Jews to Christian faith was the key to Edwards's prophetic expectation: "Nothing is more certainly foretold than this national conversion of the Jews." This conversion would follow the time in which "Antichrist shall be utterly overthrown" with the destruction of "the spiritual Babylon, that great city Rome" and "that other great kingdom that Satan has set up in opposition to the Christian church, viz. his Mohammedan kingdom." Once their conversion is accomplished, "then shall that ancient people that were alone God's people for so long a time be God's people again, never to be rejected more, one fold with the Gentiles; and then also shall the remains of the ten tribes wherever they are, and though they have been rejected much longer than [the Jews], be brought in with their brethren, the Jews."[55]

Edwards believed that the spiritual restoration of Jews as the people of God would be linked with their subsequent restoration to Palestine. As he wrote in his ongoing scripture commentary now published as the "Blank Bible," "the promises made to God's people when they should return from Babylon . . . will not have their fullest accomplishment till the last calling of the Jews . . . till after the destruction of Antichrist."[56] Although, Edwards wrote, "redemption and salvation of Christ respects chiefly the soul," as bodies are raised and restored "the external and literal Israel shall be restored by him" so that "not only shall the spiritual state of the Jews be hereafter restored, but their external state as a nation in their own land."[57] Since for Edwards the literary cycle of the biblical narrative was the key to interpreting the history of both the past and the future, he could not doubt that Jews "will return to their own land; because when their unbelief ceases, their dispersion, the dreadful and signal punishment of their unbelief, will cease too." Moreover, "it is the more evident, that the Jews will return to their own land again, because they never have yet possessed one quarter of that land, which was so often promised them, from the Red Sea to the river Euphrates."[58] In the gradual process of cosmic redemption that took hold of Edwards's imagination, "the advancement of religion and the kingdom of Christ shall be accomplished after the calling of the Jews . . . may be called a reviving of the world from the dead. And this last event must doubtless be before the millennium begins."[59]

The animating optimism of Edwards's vision of cosmic redemption was most concisely articulated in his *An Humble Attempt* (1747). In this call to unified prayer for revival, the drama of God's rejection and restoration of Israel provides the typological rhythm of national-covenantal mission. While this immensely influential essay found its "best immediate reception . . . in Scotland," Marsden observes that "as was also generally true, his views—or variations much like them—eventually became a force in nineteenth-century America. Down to the Civil War, millennial optimism became the dominant American Protestant doctrine."[60] The cosmic redemption Edwards imagined was predicated on the future conversion of Jews to Christian faith and their literal, physical restoration to Palestine. As a pivotal figure in the development of distinctively American Protestant modes of thought, Edwards carried forward the traditions inherited from England and bequeathed them to subsequent generations of American Protestants intent on discovering (and in some cases manufacturing) their place in God's cosmic drama.

In the years following the death of Jonathan Edwards, apocalyptic interpretations of history would be joined to political discourse in ways Edwards could not have imagined. Nathan Hatch has described this newly formulated amalgam as "civil millennialism." Hatch identifies in the period marked by the French and Indian wars, "a subtle but profound shift in emphasis" in which "the religious values that traditionally defined the ultimate goal of apocalyptic hope—the conversion of all nations to Christianity—became diluted with, and often subordinated to, the commitment to America as the new seat of liberty."[61] Hatch suggests that, with the fading of millenarian hopes at the close of the First Great Awakening, New England clergy found in "the Anglo-French conflicts . . . a broader basis for a millennial hope that could encompass all of society." As the colonists more closely identified with their understanding of British values and identity, Hatch says, they constructed a "moral dichotomy between themselves and the French." Thus, "Vivid perceptions of an external foe confirmed their sense of identity as God's elect people living in the end times and linked their lives to the cosmic war between good and evil." For these English colonists, civil and religious liberty became the *summum bonum* of Protestant society; "the clergy identified Great Britain as the bastion of freedom and the bulwark against Antichrist."[62]

When, however, the Stamp Act (March 1765) appeared to reveal tyranny lurking in any arbitrary use of power, New England's "civil millennialism" was easily mobilized against British impositions. In keeping with Hatch's observation that "the religious patriotism that animated the Revolution had intellectual roots far more British than American," one can recognize in Thomas Paine's *Common Sense* vestiges of the anti-Catholic

and anti-Islamic sentiment endemic to traditional British Protestant apocalyptic discourse. Asserting that "monarchy in every instance is the Popery
of government," Paine says it was once easy "to trump up some supersti-
tious tale, conveniently timed, Mahomet like, to cram hereditary right
down the throats of the vulgar."[63]

Mark Noll locates the genesis of what Hatch calls "civil millennialism"
in the efforts of Jonathan Edwards "to reattach the converted individual to
a purified church." His stringent teachings, Noll says, would eventually
"weaken the covenant as a general canopy for theology reflection." His
writings, therefore, opened American "thought to a subtle, yet powerful,
move from theology to politics, and intellectual leadership to a shift from
the clergy to men of state."[64] Following this trajectory, it would not be long
until the American project itself became identified with millennial hopes.
The "civil millennialism" that informed American self-understanding
through the Revolutionary era had far-reaching consequences for the formation of American civil religion. These far-reaching effects were apparent when, on the other side of the Revolution, Alexis de Tocqueville observed that "Americans so completely confound Christianity with liberty
that it is almost impossible to induce them to think of one without the
other. For them, moreover, this is . . . a vital article of faith."[65]

Toward the Redeemer Nation

The covenantal nationalism bequeathed to the American context through
British Puritan intellectual leadership became normative for American
self-understanding. The tradition of Judeo-centric prophecy interpretation, deeply ingrained in the British foundations of these covenantal
commitments, was highly compatible with these formulations of American identity, even as those commitments were refocused through the
Revolutionary period. Historical investigations into the foundations of
American identity rightly observe that "the history of the American civil
religion is a history of the conviction that the American people are God's
New Israel, his newly chosen people. The belief that America has been
elected by God for a special destiny in the world has been the focus of
American sacred ceremonies, the inaugural addresses of our presidents,
the sacred scriptures of the civil religion."[66] They err, however, when they
presume that these conclusions stand in continuity with the beliefs and
perspectives of the Puritan colonists. There is no doubt that the discourse

of post-Revolutionary American intellectuals, in both civil and religious spheres, often uncritically arrogated to the American republic the apocalyptic place of Israel itself. This discourse, however, signifies discontinuity rather than continuity with Puritan perspectives. Such claims are more reflective of Samuel Sewall's aberrant attempt to defend America's vocation against Joseph Mede than the writings of either John Cotton or Jonathan Edwards. Nevertheless, the new republic carried forth a great deal it inherited from the intellectual world of Puritan New England, even as it reshaped many of these traditions. These fundamental continuities are expressed in the endurance, to the present day, of American typological identification with the Children of Israel and the popular understanding of America's vocation to be a "Citty upon a Hill, the eies of all people upon us," an instrument for God's work of expanding the bounds of liberty.

The experiences of English colonists in the American context resulted in developments within Puritan thought. These developments, in concert with political and economic realities, emphasized aspects of broadly British and distinctively American identities. The tradition of Judeo-centric prophecy interpretation played a direct role in the formation of patriotic American self-understanding. Although the responses to Mede penned by Sewall and Mather demonstrate Mede's remarkable authority in the colonial context, the Judeo-centric tradition we have been discussing should not be understood as necessarily grounded in particular sets of doctrinal commitments. The first generations of Puritan colonists were not motivated by millenarian eschatologies; they were, however, steeped in an English Protestant historiography that constructed the Pope and the Turk as Antichrists and that, as we have seen, was fundamentally Judeo-centric. Although millenarian ideas more openly influenced Anglo-American discourse after 1640, those ideas served to augment rather than replace previously-held Judeo-centric commitments. Even Cotton Mather's shift from futurist literalism to preterist allegorical interpretation did not diminish his Judeo-centric vision of the New Jerusalem. Christian Judeo-centrism and the covenantal nationalism it informed is grounded less in doctrinal commitments—much less particular forms of millennialism or awareness of Jewish mysticism[67]—than in the Bible's narrative of Jewish exile and return, the basic rhythm of rejection and redemption that formed the basis of covenantal relationship. The notion that the Children of Israel, God's chosen people, occupy a central place in national-covenantal apocalyptic hope has proven as flexible and enduring in the face of American adaptations as the notion of the covenant itself.

Although Jews were present in America since the early years of colonization, Puritan intellectuals most often approached them as objects of conversion and, often, as a literary trope. The first instance was in keeping with the breadth of the Judeo-centric tradition's emphasis on national conversion; the second, especially in the mind of Jonathan Edwards, understood Jews primarily through their biblical role as harbingers of cosmic redemption. Although the colonists had long identified themselves typologically with the Children of Israel, Edwards, in his presentation of the Bible as the key to redemptive history, animated this Anglo-American national-covenantal vocation by linking it inextricably to the future hope of Jewish restoration, spiritual and geographic. For Edwards, the enduring covenantal narrative of American self-understanding is based on the rhythm of redemption; underlying this rhythm is the biblical narrative of Israel's special relationship to God. The American sense of national-covenantal vocation had a formative effect on American identity, even as the unifying intellectual concept of Puritan covenantalism disintegrated into civil millennialism and moral leadership transferred partially from the religious to the civil sphere. Just as Christian Judeo-centrism is grounded in the understanding that Jews have a central role to play in Christian apocalyptic hope, Jews (understood either literarily or literally) are central to the narrative of American identity.

Along with their various understandings of Jewish purpose, Anglo-American Puritans and, later, American Protestants continued the long-standing tradition of constructing Jews, Muslims, Catholics, eastern Christians and others according to their apocalyptic expectations. Ralph Bauer, describing Catholic and Puritan approaches to New Spain and New England, contrasts how, with some Franciscans, "Old World Redemption history could be rewritten in order to inscribe, though in a subordinate position, the Native American indigenous world," while in New England "the American Indian could enter history only as a typological referent (Canaanites), as a literal scriptural identity (the Ten Lost Tribes), or as a super- or extracanonical Gothic horror (God's rod)." Both of these processes, Bauer says, were "foundational in the 'fabrication' of colonial and (proto)nationalist identities throughout the New World to this day."[68] While Hatch observes how "vivid perceptions of an external foe confirmed" the New England colonists' "sense of identity as God's elect people living in the end times and linked their lives to the cosmic war between good and evil,"[69] the

Judeo-centric Protestant historiography through which they viewed their scriptures and their times led them to construct external allies alongside external foes.

English Protestants had long identified Jews as significant for eschatological expectation; their national conversion and restoration would confirm the truth of Puritan faith. Many Protestants in England, well versed in the tradition of Judeo-centric prophecy interpretation explored in this book, understood Jews to be an apocalyptic counterpart, an external ally in the present and future struggle against the enemies of Catholicism and Islam. Protestants in New England, on the other hand, innovatively applied the tradition into a sort of "realized typology" in which Jewish identity and purpose—literarily conceived—was brought into the core of American national identity. Jewish narrative and purpose, therefore, are not auxiliary to but constitutive of American national identity and purpose. For certain apocalyptically-conceived articulations of Americanism, therefore, Jewish and American identities are fully entwined. For Anglo-American Protestants, Jews were less an external ally than a typological referent.

In forming its identity typologically, the American national project appropriated to itself a particular Christian construction of the Jewish covenantal narrative. As we have seen, the discourse shaped by the English Protestant tradition of Judeo-centric biblical interpretation privileged Anglo-Protestant apocalyptic hope and biblically-informed constructions of Jewish roles within that hope over the needs and desires of any flesh-and-blood Jews themselves. Instead, the Judeo-centric discourse constructs flesh-and-blood Jews as signs of the literary Jew contained in its own reading of the biblical narrative. Thus, the typological referent for American Christian covenantal nationalism is the literary construction of "the Jew" rather than any particular Jewish community.

When, via civil millennialism, the Judeo-centric national covenantalism of the Puritan canopy was transferred to the American state, apocalyptic expectations had political consequences. As Ernest Tuveson has observed, their distinctive methods of biblical interpretation gave Protestants "a philosophy of history that seemed to make them partners with God in the redemption of the world." When the "age of revolution ensued . . . bestriding it was a new nation. The United States hardly needed to identify itself as the appointed agent of the Apocalypse; it seemed as if the stage manager of Providence had summoned the American people from the wings of the stage of history."[70]

When, during the nineteenth century and following, Jews would organize politically to achieve the goal of establishing a nation-state, traditionally Judeo-centric biblical interpretations and doctrines worked in tandem with American typological identification with Jewish covenantal identity to ensure that many American Christians would recognize in the State of Israel a fellow worker for the redemption of humanity.

7

Systematizing the Jew

JOHN NELSON DARBY AND THE PUTATIVE PATERNITY
OF CHRISTIAN ZIONISM

THE AGE OF revolutions was rife with apocalyptical speculation. If God was active in history through the means of governments, trade, and military conflict, these momentous events surely provided evidence that the time was drawing near when God's purposes would be realized and the curtain drawn on human history. Even if Jews were located near the center of the narrative, Christians debated heavily about the nature of their presence. Was it necessary, as English Puritans had long thought, for Jews to be restored to Palestine? If so, what seafaring power had the capacity to fulfill the 1649 vision of Johanna and Ebenezer Cartwright "to transport IZRAELLS Sons & Daughters in their Ships to the Land promised to their fore-Fathers, ABRAHAM, ISAAC, AND JACOB, for an everlasting Inheritance"?[1] Others, echoing the debate noted by Increase Mather in 1669, wondered if Jews might return en masse to Palestine prior to any mass conversion.

The climate of heightened American apocalyptic expectation that marked the Revolutionary era persisted throughout the nineteenth century. After exploring how apocalyptic prophecy interpretation changed after the American Revolution, including the question of whether or not Jews needed to convert to Christian faith prior to their expected restoration to Palestine, this chapter explores two expressions of millenarian thought that took hold among American Christians in the nineteenth century. After briefly discussing the Millerite movement, attention then turns to the theology of John Nelson's Darby's Plymouth Brethren movement. Can Darby or the doctrine he promoted be identified as the foundation of contemporary Christian Zionism? Comprehending the interaction of Judeo-centric prophecy interpretation with these nineteenth-century movements is essential for understanding the nature of current popular American Christian affinity for the State of Israel.

The Dominance of the Exegetical

Ruth Bloch's *Visionary Republic* presents the most comprehensive study of Protestant apocalyptic thought in late eighteenth-century America. Disagreeing subtly with Nathan Hatch's emphasis on the French and Indian wars, Bloch identifies the revolutionary period as a moment in which "millennialism fully merged with American secular republican ideology and became an essential ingredient of national culture." No longer identified solely with Christian belief, she says, much less with any one denomination, "American millennialism . . . became a general and diffuse cultural orientation." The tradition of Judeo-centric prophetic interpretation continued to make significant contributions to apocalyptic thought throughout this period: "Patriot polemical literature resounded with exclamations about 'the great ends' of Providence in bringing about the Revolution, the "new" and "illustrious" era about to unfold when temporal things would progress toward "perfection" and God would fulfill his ancient promises to the Jews." The Revolution was infused with cosmic significance when some imagined that it portended the destruction of the tyrannical Antichrist and the establishment of the New Jerusalem. This covenantal-national narrative, however, did not simply revel in revolutionary victory: "Already in the 1770's," Bloch says, "the need to repent and reform in order to secure continuing favor had become the automatic refrains of the revolutionary clergy." Instead, American apocalypticism continued to be infused with internal critique: "The same designation of tyranny and monarchy as the Antichrist, the same belief that liberty and republican government foreshadowed the millennial age, the same sense that history was in the throes of great providential events, pervaded millennial statements of the early and middle 1790's."[2]

In this same period, the French Revolution also seemed to have apocalyptic implications. As Bloch says, "the French Revolution seemed to demonstrate beyond doubt what only the most audacious patriots in the 1770's had dared to suppose, that the liberty and republicanism established in America would immediately spread to the rest of the world." Although the identification of the Pope with political tyranny had solidified during the French and Indian War, the simultaneous effort of French republicans to "dismantle the monarchical political system and the Catholic ecclesiastical apparatus" were interpreted as extending God's American cause. The American republican experiment was further consecrated by Britain's decision to ally with Catholic forces against the French republicans. The tradition of Judeo-centric prophecy interpretation can be detected in Bloch's observation that "the French attack on the Catholic Church" was the "connecting link" between the Revolutions and the conviction among "many millennialists in the 1790's" that "the conversion of the Jews and the downfall of the Turks [would follow] ineluctably on the heels of the French Revolution."[3]

Although her research provides a vital perspective on early American theopolitical thought, Bloch downplays the importance of Catholics, Turks, and Jews in the apocalyptical tradition she encounters. In the 1790s, interest in exegetical studies of biblical prophecy grew immensely. Bloch sees these works, which "made little or no reference to contemporary politics," as having "a preoccupation with textual detail that had little if any bearing upon the interpretation of contemporary events." Bloch reads this development as a possible result of either "the increased leisure and opportunity to delve into such scholarly matters after the revolutionary crisis had passed" or "a response to the growing need to buttress millennial faith after the excitement generated by the American Revolution had begun to flag." She further identifies the "dramatic rise of interest in the conversion and restoration of the Jews" in the late 1780s and 1790s as an "example of this inclination to dwell on remote eschatological issues." Presuming this eschatological remoteness, Bloch claims that "interest in the Jews, like that in the Turks and the Pope, transferred the main events of the Last Days a great distance away" from the concerns of American politics. The "great distance" she presumes does not highlight that the anti-christian powers of France, Britain and Spain still maintained a presence in the hemisphere. Bloch then avers that exegetical "curiosity about the Jews, like the tendency to incorporate Turks and the history of ancient kingdoms into prophetic analysis," perhaps "reflected a growing interest in the world outside American national boundaries during the years of revolutionary upheaval and abroad."[4]

Awareness of the tradition of Judeo-centric prophecy interpretation attunes readers to the possibility that the presence of these topics in late eighteenth-century apocalyptic literature reflects not only the new realities of the young United States but the reapplication and adaptation of established hermeneutical methods. While the primary subject of these exegetical writings was the Bible rather than the newspaper, it is anachronistic to characterize these authors as unconcerned with contemporary politics. Instead, the prophetically focused exegetical writing of the period shows a broad effort to craft an apocalyptic grammar for the religious exposition of

American theopolitical hope. Efforts to achieve exegetical precision would continue throughout nineteenth-century America, further establishing apocalyptic hope as what Bloch correctly describes as "an essential ingredient of national culture."[5]

The Judeo-centric specificity of this "ingredient" was displayed when in 1819, John Adams, the second President of the United States, responded to Mordecai Manuel Noah's gift of his recently published *Travels in England, France, Spain and the Barbary States* by praising the book and complaining only that Noah had not continued his travels into "Syria, Judea & Jerusalem." Imagining further, Adams said "I wish you had been . . . at the head of a hundred thousand Israelites . . . making a conquest of that country & restoring your nation to the dominion of it. For I really wish the Jews again in Judea an independent nation." For Adams, this vision was tied to eventual Jewish conversion to his form of Christian faith, when "no longer persecuted they would soon wear away some of the asperities & peculiarities of their character & possibly in time become liberal Unitarian Christians."[6]

The French Revolution, Napoleon, and the Jews

Napoleon Bonaparte's 1798 invasion of the Papal States and exile of Pope Pius VI aroused Protestant apocalyptic hope that the papacy would soon end. His subsequent campaign in the Levant renewed hopes among many Anglo-American Protestants for the return of Jews to Palestine. In 1799, Napoleon (1769–1821) issued a call to Jews in Africa and Asia to join the Syrian campaign in which he promised "to give them the Holy Land," and "to restore ancient Jerusalem to its pristine splendour." Some have linked Bonaparte's quasi-Zionist thinking to a 1798 letter "addressed by a [French] Jew to his co-religionists."[7] It did not take long, however, for Bonaparte to be viewed as a prophetically ambiguous figure and then, by some, as the Antichrist himself. Napoleon's rapprochement with the Church, including the Concordat with the Holy See (July 1801), filled formerly hopeful Protestants with rage. Bloch observes, for instance, that while American deist leader Elihu Palmer sustained "an uncritical enthusiasm for France through the phases of the Terror, the Directory, and the early Napoleonic conquests," the French leader's effort "to repair relations with the Catholic Church" left Palmer feeling "suddenly, and utterly, betrayed."[8]

By 1807, when Napoleon announced the calling of a "Great Sanhedrin" in Paris,[9] he was too compromised for most British and American Protestants to understand him as an instrument of God. Many, in fact, had begun to identify him as the Antichrist. The transfer of this title from the Pope to a civil-military leader "amounted to a revolution in typological thinking."[10] As Baptist minister James Bicheno (d. 1831) opined, "it may be said if the second beast represent the French monarchy, then this power must be signified by the false prophet, and it is certain he does not perish till the battle, or war, of Armageddon; and therefore France must still retain its bestial character."[11]

Napoleon's efforts with Jews demonstrated the plausibility that Jews might return to Palestine through political efforts quite apart from any miraculous national conversion. In the late eighteenth century, many Protestants, contradicting centuries of Judeo-centric prophecy tradition, began entertaining the possibility that Jews would be restored "in unbelief." As Mel Scult describes the tenor of the time, "The conversion would certainly take place but there was no need to be concerned about it at the present. Many writers have noted the English interest in the reestablishment of Biblical Israel but it is only during the French Revolution that some Englishmen began to think of this reestablishment in purely political terms."[12] Thomas Witherby, a British loyalist who had said in 1800 that "the ideology of the Roman Church" was "not so bad as the idolatry of the great antichrist to come," reminded his readers in 1804 "that the renunciation of Judaism is in the Holy Scripture described as the greatest crime that a Jew can commit."[13] Political realities had caused a vital shift in theological expectation. Nabil Matar is even more pointed in identifying the reasons behind this momentous shift: "Clearly, the interpretation of the Restoration 'prophecy' was being examined not from the perspective of theological orthodoxy, but of imperialistic policy. . . . The Jews did not have to convert to Christianity in order to restore: it was the white man's burden to implement the colonization of Palestine for them."[14]

One of the most prolific British authors promoting the possibility of Jewish restoration without conversion was George Stanley Faber (1773–1854). In 1804, he wrote that while "a large body of the Jews will be restored in a converted state by some great maritime power," another considerable group "will be restored by land and in an unconverted state by the Antichristian faction; and that for mere political purposes."[15] He continued his thinly veiled hints that Britain will be this great maritime power and that the restoration of unconverted Jews would be tied to the political purpose of the Antichrist. Faber's ideas rose in popularity, even as their nuance was diminished. By 1815, a writer in *The Utica Christian Magazine* could say quite plainly, "It seems most likely that the restoration of the Jews to their own land, will take place before their conversion to christianity [sic]."[16] This line of reasoning was continued by Edward Bickersteth (1786–1850), an authoritative interpreter of prophecy with long-standing, popular appeal. Bickersteth's later reflections on Jewish restoration to Palestine focused on the establishment of a Jewish political entity, with or without the added benefit of Jewish conversion to Christian faith. "In accomplishing the restoration," he wrote, "many predictions lead us to expect that the Jewish nation will be restored, in part at least, in a self-righteous and unconverted state, and will pass through great troubles, from all which, however, they are finally to be extricated."[17] These ideas were influential in America as well as in Britain. In 1853, John Cumming wrote that when Elijah returns, "in some way we cannot explain, he will give the signal for the Jews to march homeward to their own land." As for the Jews, "They will be only too happy to have such a signal; and the Jews—unconverted, I believe—will follow the beckoning sign, march in converging currents to the land of their fathers, erect the temple spoken of by Ezekiel."[18]

By the mid-nineteenth century, even before wide-scale Jewish colonization efforts were underway in Palestine, it had become increasingly untenable to believe that the world's Jews would need to convert to Christianity before their restoration to Palestine. These ideas provide the current midpoint of a tradition stretching from Moses Wall, the translator of Menasseh ben-Israel's *The Hope of Israel*, and Christian Zionists such as John Hagee in the twenty-first century who, for political reasons, minimize the evangelical impulse to seek Jewish conversion.

Mormons and the American Zion

Early followers in the Church of Jesus Christ of Latter-Day Saints (LDS) read their community's mission through the biblical narrative of Jewish restoration. Although remarkably American in their outlook—Mormonism has been described as "the American religion"—early Saints, including Joseph Smith and Orson Hyde, were steeped in the English Protestant tradition of Judeo-centric prophecy interpretation. Smith and those who followed were committed to a literalist hermeneutic that emphasized the biblical theme of Jewish restoration to Zion as essential for end-times hope.

The new era of revelation inaugurated by Smith allowed early Saints to draw clear conclusions about the location of the millennial Zion and the Israelites who would be restored. "With revelation again available through Joseph Smith," Mormon historian Grant Underwood has observed, "it was learned that the Israelite race included not only Jews and the lost Ten Tribes but the American Indians as well." This awareness was supplemented with the understanding that Gentiles "could be 'adopted' into the House of Israel through conversion to God's latter-day work and thus became equal participants in the promises of the "new covenant." The corollary of this identification with Jews led some early Mormons to equate their opponents with Gentiles, those destined to be "cut off" in the last days. Additionally, early Saints believed that the American Indians they encountered were also Israelites who would be restored. This led the way for early Mormons to interpret the Indian Removal Act and other U.S. policies of the 1830s to be evidence of the "nursing fathers" of Isaiah 49:23 working to gather a portion of God's people so they could eventually be restored to Zion.[19]

In 1697, Judge Samuel Sewall defied Joseph Mede by asking of America, "Why may not that be the place of New-Jerusalem?" Joseph Smith revealed another dynamic to Sewall's American adaptation of the Anglo-American tradition of Judeo-centric prophecy interpretation by suggesting a dual Zion, with prophetic functions for both geographic Jerusalem and the Americas. Isaiah 24:23, in the Authorized Version, offers an eschatological vision "when the Lord of hosts shall reign in mount Zion, and in Jerusalem, and before his ancients gloriously." Underwood points out that "Edward Partridge, the first Bishop of the Church, was typical of Latter-Day Saints in his exegesis of this passage when he commented, 'Thus we see that the Lord is not only to reign in Jerusalem, but in mount Zion also, which shows that Jerusalem and Zion are two places.'"[20]

Orson Hyde's pilgrimage to the Holy Land in 1841 and 1842 helped solidify these emerging themes of Mormon belief. Steven Epperson has argued that Hyde's mission existed as much to open a new front in polemical battles Saints were being forced to fight in Nauvoo as it did to reaffirm the continued significance of geographic Jerusalem for Mormon hope. Delivered at dawn on the Mt. of Olives Hyde's visionary prayer to "dedicate and consecrate this land unto Thee, for the gathering together of Judah's scattered remnants, according to the predictions of the holy prophets," did not challenge his notion that a North American Zion was also part of God's plan. His prayed that the "powers of the earth" would know "that it is thy good pleasure to restore the kingdom until Israel—raise up Jerusalem as its capital and constitute her people a distinct nation and government." When Hyde wrote to Orson Pratt, describing Mt. Zion and Calvary, it was clear that this geography was insufficient for God's glory. "What were anciently called Mount Zion and Mount Calvary, are both within the present walls of the city. We should not call them mountains in America, or hardly hills; but gentle elevations or rises of land," he wrote. "As I stood upon it and contemplated what the prophets had said of Zion in the last days, I could no more bring my mind to believe that the magnet of truth in them which guided their words, pointed to this place, any more than I could believe that a camel can go through the eye of a needle," he added. "But on the land of Joseph, far in the west, where the spread eagle of America floats in the breeze and shadows the land . . . shall Zion rear her stately temples and stretch forth the curtains of her habitation."[21]

It would be a mistake, however, to interpret Hyde's rhapsodic reflections on the western Zion as any intent to replace one with the other. Instead, as Gershon Greenberg has observed, the Saints lived in a "dialectical Zion . . . with its synthesis in America." In the restoration of the millennium, "America and the Land of Israel would both be places of gathering deliverance but part of a larger unity." While "America-as-Zion would be more central than Zion-as-Land-of-Israel," Jerusalem was still necessary for the LDS vision.[22] A corollary to this vision was the conviction among early Saints like Smith and Hyde that Jews did not need to be converted to Christian faith. Just as Jerusalem had not been replaced by the American Zion, the Saints' faith did not replace Judaism. According to Underwood, Mormons therefore "saw nothing of value in contemporary efforts to missionize the Jews. Sidney Rigdon was plain in his assessment: 'we have no scruple in saying, that Israel will never embrace the gospel, nor will the Jews believe in the Messiah as a people, till the Lord sends his word to them.'" The result of this dialectical vision was the belief that "Gentile and Indian Saints would be planted in their American inheritance, Zion, while the Jews and eventually the 'lost tribes' of Israel were to be relocated in the renovated land of Canaan with Jerusalem as their capital."[23] As notions of Mormon identity articulated by the earliest Saints evolved in ways less tied to prophetic geography, Mormons developed greater interest in global proselytization, even among Jews.[24] Early Mormonism nevertheless provides insights into how the Anglo-American tradition of Judeo-centric prophecy interpretation could be adapted to early nineteenth-century American religious culture.

William Miller: Heretic of American Civil Millennialism

The teachings of William Miller (1781–1849), first leader of the Seventh-day Adventist movement, were diametrically opposed to those of the Latter-Day

Saints. Although Miller had volunteered to fight against Britain in the War of 1812, he later doubted the wisdom of putting his hope in any nationalist cause.[25] He became convinced that the civil millennialism that had animated the Revolution could never be realized. Drawing from hermeneutical methods developed by Sir Isaac Newton[26] and other scientifically minded British millenarians, Miller in 1822 produced an extensive creed that included his belief "that the second coming of Jesus Christ is near, even at the door, even within twenty-one years,—on or before 1843."[27]

Miller's expectation dismissed the popular revivalist theology of the Second Great Awakening and its apocalyptic vision that the millennium would gradually dawn through the exercise of Christian faithfulness. Miller, in a manner similar to Cotton Mather's eager expectation of a divine conflagration, expected that Christ would come to rescue a faithful remnant while subjecting the rest of the world to God's wrath. Contrary to centuries of Protestant hesitation to name particular dates for the Second Coming, Miller taught, according to a calculation from the Jewish calendar, that Jesus would return at some point in the year following March 21, 1843. After March 21, 1844, as well as a revised date, passed with no major developments, Miller wrote to his followers, saying "I confess my error, and acknowledge my disappointment; yet I still believe that the day of the Lord is near, even at the door."[28] In August 1844, Millerite teacher Samuel Snow, in his "true midnight cry," proclaimed the further revised date of October 22, 1844. This final failure of prophetic date setting resulted in the "Great Disappointment."

Although the Disappointment caused most of Miller's associates to simply abandon his unique belief structure, others continued to accompany him. They agreed that while Jesus had not returned to earth in 1844, a new era had begun in heaven; believers were invited to demonstrate their devotion by adopting new disciplines, including observing the Sabbath on Saturday rather than Sunday. These manifestations of Seventh-day Adventist commitment have led Malcolm Bull to observe that the most distinctive characteristic of the movement is not its background in unfulfilled eschatology but its opposition to mainstream American civil religion. In this shift of worship days, Adventists rejected the emphasis on Sunday that had shaped American culture since the Puritan era. Thus, Bull writes, while "they shared the Sabbatarianism of civil religion," they "counterposed the Adventist Saturday to the American Sunday" with the effect that, within the movement, "the Adventist movement and the American nation were perceived as two rival groups competing to realize their respective millennia." Early Adventist thought began to identity the United States as an agent of Antichrist with, as one Adventist writer put it in 1851, two horns representing "its Republican civil power and its Protestant ecclesiastical power." Unlike Brightman's Laodecia, this oppositional millenarian discourse brooked no hope for redemption. From its inception, Bull concludes, the Adventist movement "modified Millerite discourse to formulate a deviant conception, not only of the millennium, but also of the American nation."[29]

Oppositional Adventist approaches to American millenarian hope— which, Bull argues, makes them "heretics" vis-à-vis American civil religion— was drawn from Miller's own commitments. Miller's vision of the coming cataclysm, for instance, removed any significance from political or ecclesiastical institutions. The result was that Millerite political involvement was noticeably limited. Bull notes, for instance, that although Miller, along with his close associates, "was well known to be an abolitionist . . . Millerite papers did not take up the cause, and the question of slavery soon lost its significance."[30] This withdrawal from the political sphere severed apocalyptic hope from the civil sphere.

Miller's teaching deviated from the received orthodoxy of American civil millennialism in one other important way: against centuries of received Anglo-American tradition, he held that Christian apocalyptic hope had no place for Jews. Among Miller's early "rules of interpretation" was the conviction that "the popular views of the spiritual reign of Christ—a temporal millennium before the end of the world, and the Jews' return— are not sustained by the word of God."[31] Reflecting on his earlier hermeneutical development, Miller concluded that including "the return of the Jews" in Christian apocalyptic denied "the positive declarations of the New Testament, which assert: 'there is no distinction between the Jew and the Greek' . . . I was, therefore, obliged to discard an objection which asserts there is a difference between the Jew and Greek." He concluded that "the Jew has had his day."[32]

It was the lack of Millerite interest in Judeo-centric prophecy interpretation that occasioned conflict with polemicists in the Church of Jesus Christ of Latter-day Saints. In April 1843, Joseph Smith had said "Judah must return, Jerusalem must be rebuilt, and the temple, and water come out from under the temple, and the waters of the Dead Sea be healed. It will take some time to rebuild the walls of the city and the temple, &c.; and all this must be done before the Son of Man will make His appearance."[33] For at least one Mormon pamphleteer, this was definitive: "As this cannot be done in a year, Mr. Miller's words must fall to the ground, or else those of the holy prophets of old."[34] That the disagreement between the Millerites and the Saints centered on the relative Judeo-centrism of their respective literalist interpretations is telling. While William Miller can be described as a "heretic" of American civil religion the LDS movement produced a form of American orthodoxy, a doctrinal nationalism reflected in the polling data included in Chapter 2.

Miller's distinctive teachings regarding Jews created controversy even within Millerite circles; debates on the matter were prominent in their publications. After the Great Disappointment, a conference was called in April 1845 to discuss "In the midst of our disappointed hopes . . . *what now is our work?*" The second resolution offered for the affirmation of the conference concerned Jews: "*Resolved*, That we consider the doctrine of the restoration of the natural Jews, as a nation, either before or after the second advent of Christ, as heirs and inheritors of the land of Canaan, as subversive of the whole Gospel system, by raising up what Christ has broken down, namely, the middle wall of partition between the Jew and Gentile."[35] Miller persisted in emphasizing this tenet of his system until his death.[36]

John Nelson Darby and the Two Peoples of God

William Miller's steadfast refusal to include Jews in his eschatological speculations finds a contrast in the equally steadfast Judeo-centric thought of John Nelson Darby (1800–1882). Ordained as a minister in the Church of Ireland, Darby would soon lose faith in all institutional forms of Christianity and, in the mid-nineteenth century, develop a system of biblical interpretation that would come to be known as premillennial dispensationalism. Despite their differences—Darby publicly criticized Miller's methods, especially regarding date-setting—both were products of the heightened interest in prophetic speculation in the age of revolutions, including the industrial revolutions within England and America. In the end, Darby's ideas would become lodged in popular American religious consciousness.

The Rapture of the true saints into heaven before the time of earthly turmoil known as the tribulation is the most emblematic of Darby's doctrines. In a 2006 Pew survey, 83 percent of Christian respondents in the United States said they "believe in the Rapture of the Church, that is, that before the world comes to an end, the religiously faithful will be saved and taken up to Heaven."[37] Historicist eschatology from Brightman to Mede and beyond emphasized that Jesus' return could be expected soon because most apocalyptic signs had been fulfilled in history. Mede kept to this interpretation even while locating the millennium in the future. The singular sign awaited by historicists was the national conversion of Jews and their restoration to Palestine. Following revolutionary-era developments in eschatology, Darby developed a futurist eschatology that allowed him to look for no sign but Jesus' sudden return to human history. Just as Cotton Mather's preterist interpretation of prophecy convinced him "that there is nothing to hinder the immediate Coming of our Saviour,"[38] Darby's futurist emphasis led him to teach that "there is no event, I repeat, between us and heaven."[39] Both approaches relieved the need to observe either mass conversions of Jews or their transfer to Palestine as evidence of God's impending action. No longer waiting for more prophecies to be fulfilled and expecting the Lord at "a time when I was able to fix the day of His appearing," Darby knew the rapture "as a present thing, uncertain when it will come."[40]

David Bebbington has observed that these ideas, "elaborated at a series of conferences at Powerscourt in Ireland during the 1830s . . . added urgency to evangelism" and "created a profoundly dramatic worldview."[41] The dispensationalist system's proclamation of spiritual truths in the midst of earthly drama has secured its place in the apocalyptic imagination of American popular Christianity. For many Americans, the Gospel of dispensationalism is a source of entertainment and comfort. The dual function of dispensationalist drama is manifested, for instance, in the massive appeal of the Left Behind series of novels and related merchandise.[42]

The popularity of the rapture in American Christian discourse does not indicate, of course, that the doctrine is fully understood. Although systematic, even scientific in its commitments, premillennial dispensationalism is filled with complexities and complicating factors. Things become even more complex when one seeks to understand Darby's own commitments and teachings. Much of Darby's writing is highly speculative; even in his published work, his ideas can seem incomprehensible. As one of Darby's contemporary reviewers observed, "If Mr. Darby cannot succeed in writing more *intelligibly* and making his case more plain, he will carry none but partisans along with him."[43] One recent dissertation that has taken on the task of constructing Darby's eschatology described his writings as "a jigsaw puzzle, unorganized and in many unrelated pieces," but with "no picture to guide the assembler." Once constructed,

Darby's theology appeared as a "house of cards" in which the removal of "one unique doctrine" will cause the remainder to "collapse into a heap."[44] The popularity of dispensational doctrine among American Christians did not depend on Darby alone. His biblical interpretations and theological positions were developed from the same Judeo-centric foundation that had shaped American identity and vocation.

In stark contrast to William Miller's belief that "the Jew has had his day,"[45] Darby taught that Jews had a special role to play in God's eschatological plan. This feature of Darby's thought stands in broad continuity with the Anglo-American tradition of Judeo-centric prophecy interpretation we have been exploring. Nevertheless, Darby's emphasis on this point leads to some unique outcomes. According to Darby,

> There are two great subjects which occupy the sphere of millennial prophecy and testimony: the church and its glory in Christ; and the Jews and their glory as a redeemed nation in Christ: the heavenly people and the earthly people; the habitation and scene of the glory of the one being the heavens; of the other, the earth. Christ shall display His glory in the one according to that which is celestial; in the other, according to that which is terrestrial.

For Darby, "the church and Israel . . . each has its respective sphere, all things in the heavens being subordinate . . . in the one, the nations of the earth in the other." Israel's relationship with God is eternal. If God's word is trustworthy, "The original promises, given unconditionally, and guaranteed by the oath of God, must find a complete fulfilment in all their extent."[46]

Darby's absolute distinction between the two peoples of God had several implications within his eschatological system. Tied to the periodization of history common within Protestant historiography—which Darby defined as legal dispensations within which God deals with humans through a series of tests—the distinction resulted in Darby's notion that God can only deal with one group at a time: "we . . . fail in understanding prophecy if we forget that the Jews are the habitual object of the thoughts of God; for, although He cannot recognise them for the moment, as being under His chastening hand, they are nevertheless still His people." Although Jews are "supplanted during their judicial blindness by the church on earth (the Gentile dispensation), [they] will by and by be re-established in all their privileges."[47] Before that reestablishment can happen, however, a series of events must take place. Of these, the most significant is the Rapture of true believers prior to the Tribulation, a dispensation and experience Darby identifies as "exclusively Jewish."[48]

In his commentary on Paul's letters to the Thessalonians, Darby says that while "there will be a general tribulation on the whole earth; then, at the last moment, a more special tribulation for the Jews," the community of saints "possesses the inestimable privilege of exemption from going through these evil days."[49] Stanley Grenz observed that "the pretribulation rapture is demanded by the dispensationalist system itself. . . . If there are two peoples of God and two phases of God's program in the world, and if the Israel phase has been placed in abeyance during the church age, then the pretribulation rapture follows logically. The church phase must come to an end before the Israel phase can once again re-emerge."[50] The Rapture "is a doctrine not derived from Scripture *per se*," Peter Lee has concluded, "but from the doctrine of the two peoples of God, which requires it."[51]

Darby, Replacement Theology, and the Judeo-centric Teaching of Contempt

The reemergence of God's earthly people in the eschatological sequence involves the covenant of land. Darby believed that just as "Israel's first entry into the Land was the result of promise," the future "restoration of the Jews is founded upon the promises made to Abraham *without* condition."[52] Darby said earlier in his career that "the restoration of the Jews to their own land" was a point "scattered through all Scripture" and related to "the whole plan of God's dispensed purposes" as well as "the blessings of the church."[53] Concerning the prophet Joel's concern for Gentile presence, Darby notes that the land is "entrusted to Israel" and that "the Gentiles have no right but by their (Israel's) sin, and none as against the Lord."[54]

Darby did not, however, expect the restoration of Israel to the land prior to the rapture (which required no further fulfillment of prophecy) or even before Christ's second coming. Darby's timeline is complicated. When "the fall of the Jewish nation was complete . . . God transferred the right of government to the Gentiles" (though "the calling and promise of God" remained with Jews). "The fourth monarchy," that is, the Roman empire, "consummated its crime at the same instant that the Jews consummated theirs, in being accessory, in the person of Pontius Pilate, to the will of a rebellious nation, by killing Him who was at once the Son of God and King of Israel." The Antichrist, the "wicked one" who will rise from a revived Roman Empire, "having joined himself to the Jews" during the Tribulation, "will be destroyed by the coming of the Lord of lords and King of kings; and Christ will anew occupy this chief seat of government." Since some rebellious souls will still remain after Christ's reign is established, "the Saviour must clear the land in order that its inhabitants may enjoy the blessings of His reign without interruption or hindrance, and that joy and glory may be established in this world, so long subjected to the enemy." Thus, the "first thing . . . the Lord will do will be to purify His land (the land which belongs to the Jews) . . . of all the wicked, in short, from the Nile to the Euphrates. It will be done by the power of Christ in favour of His people re-established by His goodness." After this divine ethnic cleansing operation is complete and (an unidentified) Gog has been defeated, "the land of the Jews" will be "at peace." Once this earthly victory is secure, Gentiles "who shall have seen the glory manifested in Jerusalem" will "confess the Jews to be the people blessed of their Anointed" and will "bring the rest of them [Jews] back into their land."[55]

Darby's teachings on the two peoples of God have led some commentators to identify him as a theologian opposed to classical Augustinian "replacement theology" or "supersessionism," the belief that Christians have displaced Jews in the divine economy of salvation. According to Stephen Spector, the standard view of contemporary Christian Zionists is that "Darby rejected the long-standing belief that God is finished with the Jewish people, that all of His promises of good to Israel have been transferred to the Church. . . . They believe that God's plan for the Jewish people is eternally valid and that to say otherwise is to assert that the Lord reneges on His promises."[56]

In collaboration with John Hagee, David Brog, executive director of Christians United for Israel, who is Jewish, observes that "the rejection of replacement theology is not incidental to Darby's dispensationalism" but "is the bedrock belief upon which the entire structure rests." Dispensationalism, Brog says, "created a solid basis for the continued election of the Jews and restored to the Jews a central role in God's continuing plan for humanity." This "dispensational clarity," he says, "prevents backsliding toward replacement theology."[57] Brog fortifies his assessment of dispensationalism by identifying Darbyite commitments among some French rescuers in the Holocaust. While this history should not be denied, this phenomenon cannot be attributed to dispensationalism alone. Huguenot culture, for instance, contributed to these acts of resistance against Nazi genocide.[58] Nevertheless, the blend of history and theology leads Brog to imply, through each system's rejection of replacement theology, a level of moral equivalence between dispensational teaching and the new paradigm of Jewish-Christian relations inaugurated in *Nostra Aetate*, the Second Vatican Council's declaration on Christian relationship with non-Christian religions, including Judaism. Accepting the definition that "supersessionism is the belief that Christianity replaced Judaism as heir of the promise of God to Israel," Peter Lee concludes that "Darby was therefore a strong anti-supersessionist."[59]

For French Jewish historian and Auschwitz survivor Jules Isaac, the Christian "teaching of contempt" was the theological foundation of the Holocaust. He located the foundation of Christian contempt for Jews in the charge of deicide leveled against the Jewish people for their presumably national rejection of and crucifixion of Jesus. "For eighteen centuries," Isaac wrote, "it has been the norm in Christianity to teach that the Jews are wholly responsible for the crucifixion and committed the inexplicable crime of deicide. There is no more deadly accusation: indeed no other accusation has led to the letting of so much innocent blood."[60] The notion of supersessionism or replacement theology is a consequence of this more basic "teaching of contempt" grounded in the charge of deicide. This concern for the charge of deicide, which had immediate influence on the formation of *Nostra Aetate*, challenges any notion that adherence to premillennial dispensationalism is a panacea for the Jewish-Christian divide.

Far from rejecting the charge of deicide most contemporary Roman Catholic and ecumenical Protestant theologians would reject as anti-Jewish, Darby made it a bedrock belief for his eschatological system. He believed that Jews, as a nation, shared with the Roman Empire responsibility for "killing Him who was at once the Son of God and King of Israel."[61] As a result, Darby identified the period following the Rapture of the saints as "the final and terrible tribulation of the Jews, guilty of having rejected their Messiah, but whose deliverance will then take place in grace . . . for God has an elect people."[62] It is thus common for dispensationalist interpreters to claim that the coming tribulation will be far worse than the Holocaust, the attempted Nazi genocide of European Jews.

Darby never taught that the distinction between Israel and the Church as God's earthly and heavenly peoples meant that they were separate but equal. As Paul Wilkinson has observed, "Darby stressed time and again that the Church had inherited *better* promises than Israel by virtue of her *spiritual* status, having been seated with Christ in heavenly, not earthly, realms."[63] This inequality is most clearly expressed in Darby's understanding of the millennial order, in which the earthly is subordinate to the heavenly and in which the raptured and returned saints rule over the Jewish remnant that was left behind. "The millennium, as regards the saints on earth, will be judicial. . . . The Jewish economy was not of grace, but law. The Church cannot depart from its standing with God, and therefore cannot have to do with a judicial economy, which must have reference therefore to an earthly people."[64] For the Church, "Jesus is the Lamb, and not the King; the manifestation of the heavenly, and not of the earthly, righteousness of God."[65] In the "millennial state," the church has "the proper, special, peculiar place of the bride, the body of Christ, the fullness of Him" and "Israel . . . has its place as Israel, distinct, and in many respects in contrast." Israel will "not govern nor judge the earth. It is the heavenly saints who do this."[66]

In a view reminiscent of the Judeo-centric tradition of prophecy interpretation that preceded him, Darby taught that "the earthly Jerusalem will take vengeance . . . on God's enemies."[67] Even this subordinate, unequal, and instrumentalized redemptive state, moreover, is accomplished by Christ: "In fact, we know that Israel refused the message, and hence the blessing remains in abeyance till the fulness of the Gentiles is come in. . . . all the efficacious value for Israel then, as for us now, is in the blood of the Lamb."[68] When accused of not requiring salvation through Christ's blood for Jews, Darby retorted, "if anyone doubts, after twenty years that I have been preaching, whether I teach the necessity of redemption through the blood for all and every redeemed soul, I could hardly expect to disabuse him by telling him the contrary twenty times over."[69] All of this adds up to a rupture in Jewish-Christian relations this side of the eschaton far more serious than John Hagee's quip to his "rabbi friends" that "when we're standing in Jerusalem, and the messiah is coming down the street, one of us is going to have a very major theological adjustment to make."[70]

While it is true that John Nelson Darby's teachings and the tradition of premillennial dispensationalism that emanates from them designate a role for Israel in God's eschatological drama, Darby's subordination of Israel to the Church nevertheless promotes the anti-Jewish teaching of contempt. As such, Darby is a faithful exponent of the Anglo-American tradition of Judeo-centric prophecy interpretation and that tradition's penchant for constructing Jews and others within exclusively Christian apocalyptic visions. In these Christian systems of belief, Jews, Catholics, and Muslims do not exist with their own integrity. In a manner similar to Jonathan Edwards,

Darby viewed Jews not as real persons but as literary tropes in his world of prophecy interpretation. In that world, the text, or more precisely, one's interpretation of the text, becomes the arbiter of the real.

For Darby, Jews were not persons but a unit within his house-of-cards theological system. In David Brog's interpretation of Darby, "the Jewish rejection of Christ did not result in their permanent replacement. Having played their role in the opening acts, the Jews were temporarily placed offstage. The Jews are still the stars of the piece, and they will yet return to center stage for the grand finale."[71] What Brog seems not to realize is that while Jews are back at center stage, the raptured and returned saints are positioned throughout the theatre, ruling with Christ, while Jews continue to perform their roles. This entire analogy is troubling to Israeli journalist Gershom Gorenberg, who dislikes the dispensationalist tendency to see "Jews as actors in a Christian drama leading toward the end of days."[72] Commitment to the eschatological system rather than to the persons—a disregard for Jews and contempt for humanity—is the hallmark of Darby's dispensationalism. Darby and others who perpetuate his theology can be thought of as anti-supersessionist only if one employs a disembodied definition of the term unrelated to contemporary understandings of Jewish-Christian relations in the post-Holocaust era. It is a fiction to equate these teachings with the compassionate approach of *Nostra Aetate* and the myriad expressions of interreligious relationship fostered by that declaration. But it is a fiction useful for the current political climate.

"We do not vote": Darby and Political Involvement

Darby's focus on the enduring relationship between God and Jews had strong implications for his theopolitical outlook. Properly distinguishing between "the Jewish and Gentile dispensations" was for Darby "the hinge upon which the . . . understanding of Scripture turns."[73] Even the literalism characteristic of premillennial dispensationalism is shaped in important ways by the system's absolute distinction between Israel and the church. As Darby says concerning the interpretation of prophecy,

> when the address is directly to the Jews, there we may look for a plain and direct testimony, because earthly things were for the Jews' proper portion. And, on the contrary . . . when the Gentiles are concerned in it, there we may look for a symbol, because earthly things

were not their portion, and the system of revelation must to them be symbolical. When therefore facts are addressed to the Jewish church . . . I look for a plain, common sense, literal statement.[74]

In a manner strongly reminiscent of Henry Finch's hermeneutic, Darby's Judeo-centric commitments mitigated his literalism.

While Finch was engaged in the political systems of his day, Darby, like William Miller, steadfastly avoided political engagement. Darby's political apathy was supported by his distinction between "the heavenly people and the earthly people" of God. The growth of the Brethren movement in France prompted Darby to write two letters detailing his Christian political philosophy. In March 1848, he wrote with concern about the involvement of some "brethren with . . . elections which are about to take place":

It seems to me so simple that the Christian, not being at all of this world . . . has no business to mix himself up with the most declared activity of the world, by an act which affirms his existence as belonging to the world, and his identification with the entire system which the Lord is about to judge. . . . But is it not true that this voting, as an act of identification with the world (in the very forms which it assumes in the last days), ought to be avoided as a snare by all Christians who understood the will of God and their position in Christ?[75]

Darby offered a similar perspective thirty years later: "I believe that the christian [sic] calling is a heavenly one," he wrote, "that the Christian is not of the world as his Master is not of it, and that he is placed down here as an epistle of Christ to manifest the life of Jesus amongst men, whilst waiting for the Lord to come to take him to be with Himself in the glory." The political implication of this perspective was consistent and clear: "We do not mix in politics; we are not of the world: we do not vote."[76] Darby believed that active engagement in politics, even through voting, risked confusing the Christian's heavenly vocation with that of God's earthly people. This risk was unacceptable: "The calling of God for the earth is never transferred to the nations; it remains with the Jews. If I want an earthly religion, I ought to be a Jew. From the instant that the church loses sight of its heavenly calling, it loses, humanly speaking, all."[77]

Darby's anti-political (as opposed to merely apolitical) stance raises doubts about the common presumption that he is the progenitor of contemporary

American Christian Zionism, a movement that is political by definition. Darby's paternity, presumed by almost all popular writers on the subject, on all sides of the debate,[78] is even more doubtful when combined with his lack of expectation for the establishment of a Jewish political entity in Palestine prior to the millennial age. Modifying traditional historicist expectations for a Jewish national conversion to Protestant faith, Darby adopted a futurist eschatology in which nothing hindered the imminent rapture of the saints. He was no restorationist, save in a radically futurist sense. Far from being a proud father, Darby would deny any connection to contemporary American Christian Zionism.

Contemporary Christian efforts to promote or preserve Jewish hegemony over the Holy Land find little foundation in Darby's writings. Even if Darby had indicated some anticipation of a Jewish political entity in Palestine prior to the millennium, such ideas would not have originated with him. As Peter Lee has helpfully observed, "very little of Darby's eschatology was unique to him." Darby's method was to take "older concepts and put them together in new ways to create a new system, which made him in reality an adapter, not an originator."[79] Given these caveats, the most elegant approach is to recognize that premillennial dispensationalism alone is not a sufficient cause to explain Christian political activity on behalf of Jews or the State of Israel. One must rather ask how Darby's ideas were themselves adapted to apocalyptic American self-understanding.

The survey data included in chapter two showed that popular American Christian support for the State of Israel is not grounded in popular adherence to dispensational doctrine. In the same way, the political involvement constitutive to contemporary Christian Zionism contradicts Darby's political philosophy. While it is true that many Christian Zionist activists also espouse elements of Darbyite doctrine, their political activity cannot be seen as an outgrowth of their adherence to premillennial dispensationalism. As Timothy Weber observed in the 1980s, "Hal Lindsey and Jerry Falwell, while obviously believing deeply in premillennialist doctrine, have not been able to show how their eschatology and political ideology fit together."[80]

Any attempt to explain the impetus for contemporary evangelical political activity through the lens of Darby's political philosophy raises more questions than answers. Angela Lahr, in her study of Cold War-era millennialism in the United States, suggests that these "inconsistencies within evangelical thought" can be resolved by recognizing that, through the twentieth century, "the focus of evangelicalism remained personal salvation" and evangelicals' belief "that God had blessed people like themselves with the power to enact his will."[81] Weber has pointed out an important passage from James M. Gray, long-time president of Moody Bible Institute in Chicago. Responding to some reasons for "Christians standing aloof from the ballot," Gray wrote that while "no Christian believes civic righteousness is a substitute for divine righteousness," Christians should not "let the rogues in some city hall steal our money, or the rum-seller or the procurer debauch our youth. It is admitted that we are not undoing the works of Satan very fast, but we are giving him all the trouble we can till Jesus comes and that is something."[82] Gray's advice is a far cry from Darby's pronouncing "We do not vote."

As we have seen, the English Protestant tradition of Judeo-centric prophecy interpretation was from its inception as political and cultural as it was biblical or theological. When judged against the breadth of this long tradition rather than its Darbyite iteration alone, involvement by evangelicals, even those who espouse elements of dispensational belief, does not present a categorical problem. As Weber has said, "premillennialists are highly adaptable people" who "can combine their view of the end times with long-standing notions of America's millennial role."[83] How this enduring combination came to be is the subject of our next chapter.

8

Politicizing the Jew

WILLIAM E. BLACKSTONE AND THE MOBILIZATION
OF CULTURAL FUNDAMENTALISM

JOHN NELSON DARBY's ideas alone are not sufficient to produce the sort
of Christian Zionist political activity one sees manifested in Anthony
Ashley Cooper or William Hechler, both of whom were men of government. Just as the mainstream of Victorian British evangelicalism, influenced by Romanticism,[1] sought to establish Britain as the primitivist
"Protestant Israel," the United States through the nineteenth century developed a self-understanding based on its "manifest destiny," a continuation of its millennial role unveiled in its revolutionary era. While the Civil
War put to rest notions of gradual, steady progress toward the establishment of the Millennium, American optimism remained. Political involvement was the *raison d'être* of the American republic, an impulse that simultaneously informed revivalist, mission-oriented Christianity and confirmed
a new form of civil millennialism. These strands of American Christian
identity and purpose were united with explicitly Judeo-centric prophecy
interpretation in the person of William E. Blackstone, the first quintessential American Christian Zionist.[2]

The Transatlantic Movement of Victorian-Era Eschatology

Early nineteenth-century British evangelicalism underwent massive shifts,
exemplified by the growing rift between "moderate" and "extreme" factions.[3] In his studies of Victorian-era British thought about Jewish restoration to Palestine, Eitan Bar-Yosef has sought to show that these perspectives formed, at best, a "marginal cultural phenomenon" within British
society. He seeks to show that "projects concerning the Jewish restoration
to Palestine were continuously associated with charges of enthusiasm,

eccentricity, sometimes even madness," labels that located Christian Zionism beyond the "cultural consensus." Curiously, Bar-Yosef does not consider the possibility that when "the ruling class élite" equated evangelical
"enthusiasm with 'delusion, obsession, madness'" they were seeking not
only to express "their aversion to the pious emotionalism" but to protect
their class interests.[4]

In contrast, Donald Lewis's recent study of philosemitism and Christian Zionism within nineteenth-century British evangelicalism provides
a helpful corrective to Bar-Yosef's minimizing of restorationist themes.
Lewis observes that "evangelical identity construction took a decisive turn
in the early nineteenth century." Judeo-centric thought, revived by eschatological speculation during and after the French Revolution, was central
to this renewed identity, so that "by the 1830s, philosemitism and anti-
Catholicism were becoming flipsides of the same coin." In a contemporary
elaboration of the British Protestant tradition of Judeo-centric prophecy
interpretation, "new layers of British identity" were refined in which "Britain as 'Protestant Israel'" was to protect and defend "Israel according to the
flesh" from its ancient persecuting enemy, Roman Catholicism." This context formed the perspectives of Edward Irving, John Nelson Darby, and
Anthony Ashley Cooper, the seventh Earl of Shaftesbury (1801–1885), the
main figure in Lewis's study. In addition to being "Victorian Britain's most
prominent social reformer as well as its quintessential evangelical lay
leader," Lord Ashley was also the most effective politically active British
Christian Zionist through the nineteenth century. Credited with popular-
izing the notion that Palestine was "a country without a people" suited for
colonization by Jews, "a people without a country,"[5] Shaftesbury, through
his parliamentary leadership but also in his quiet influence with Lord
Palmerston, the stepfather of his wife, Countess Emily Shaftesbury, and
Whig prime minister (1855–1858 and 1859–1865), managed to exercise
leadership on a number of issues related to Palestine, including the establishment of a British consulate in Jerusalem in 1838 and the establishment
of a joint bishopric with the Prussian Union Church in 1841. These ac-
complishments, which were both diplomatic and diaconal, continue to
make strong contributions to the fabric of Jerusalem.

The joint bishopric links the story of British evangelical restorationism
and Christian Zionism to the same impulses present, for different reasons, within German Pietism, a subject under-studied in North American
considerations of this topic. It also links these British themes to Rev. William Hechler (1848–1931), whose English and German backgrounds and

familial links to apocalyptically oriented missions to Jews situated him as a bridge between these traditions and whose service as chaplain to the British embassy in Vienna brought him into direct contact with Theodor Herzl. Hechler arranged for Herzl to meet with the Grand Duke of Baden, who subsequently supported the pair's meeting with Kaiser Wilhelm II. Herzl invited Hechler to be a non-voting participant in the first World Zionist Congress in Basel, Switzerland (August 1897), thus establishing Hechler as the first Christian Zionist fully involved with the aspirations of Jewish political Zionism.[6]

Judeo-centric thought in the United States, originating from the same historical foundations in Puritan thought but developing through distinct revolutionary lenses, followed similar trajectories. John Nelson Darby's seven journeys to North America between 1862 and 1877 helped propagate ideas from one end of the British evangelical spectrum. These ideas remained in relative obscurity until Darby won over popular revivalist preachers, Dwight L. Moody (1837–1899) most prominent among them. In the process of being woven into the consciousness of popular American Christianity, Darby's ideas were adapted to the American context. Just as Darby adapted them from earlier Judeo-centric thought and refined his ideas in the Albury and Powerscourt prophetic conferences, his teachings were taken up by American evangelicals at their own prophetic conferences and molded toward American ends.

Although he developed affection for the United States and the Christians there, Darby was confused by how his teachings were received. In 1862, Darby observed that "in the U.S. the church and the world are more mixed than even in England."[7] During his 1866 visit, he described the United States "a country full of worldliness" in which he labored to teach that "Christianity is quite another thing from this world."[8] In 1874, he said that "the state of the churches is scandalous indeed" but rejoiced that "God has raised up a few, several ministers even have left their systems." He was incensed, however, with one minister who was encouraging others to read Brethren books while "doing everything he could to prevent souls leaving their various . . . churches. It is a new wile of the enemy."[9] Although Moody had become associated with Plymouth Brethren teaching during his first travels to Edinburgh in 1872, Darby expressed concern regarding Moody's "soul winning" methods, concerned that it could "foster worldliness in saints" and that "the effect on the church of God will be mischievous."[10]

The separationist tendencies of the Plymouth Brethren and Darby's denigrations of fellow preachers caused their teachings to be met with ambivalence in both Britain and the United States. Ernest Sandeen notes that "the Brethren's own efforts to spread [Darby's] eschatology were always connected with other aspects of his thought—his doctrine of the church and his disdain of ordained clergy, particularly." This tendency did not win them many friends among professional church leaders. Elements of the eschatology, however, were separated out from these ecclesiastical assertions: "millenarians who vehemently protested Darby's attacks upon the church . . . still accepted and taught an eschatology almost indistinguishable from" Darby's own. Through his helpful survey of the Scottish *Quarterly Journal of Prophecy*, which enjoyed circulation in North America, Sandeen demonstrates how "historicism . . . did not retain its appeal" and "futurism became dominant." More importantly, Sandeen documents that while "the Plymouth Brethren and John Nelson Darby were anathematized" by late nineteenth-century millenarians, "the hermeneutical use of the concept of dispensations and some of the critical distinctions of Darbyite theology—the church as a divine parenthesis and the secret rapture—were discussed and advocated." The result of this functional separation of Darbyite doctrine from Darby was that his "particular set of millenarian doctrines . . . seemed to exist as free elements in the religious atmosphere."[11]

The "free elements" of dispensational doctrine were rapidly absorbed into late nineteenth-century American Christian thought. George Marsden observes that "those who turned to the new dispensational premillennialism responded to the crisis of the post-Civil-War era by shoring up the places in the foundation of Christian belief they considered most in danger of erosion." The dispensational emphasis on "a more literal interpretation of Scripture" appeared to take the Bible more seriously than the developing modernist approaches and their tendency to be "less hopeful concerning progress" seemed to fit the reality of the times. The expository method of dispensational interpretation, later featured in the *Scofield Reference Bible*,[12] promoted closely textual Bible study that seemed to make sense of scriptural mysteries. This literalist approach was the foundation of "the intellectual predispositions associated with dispensationalism" that "gave fundamentalism its characteristic hue."[13]

American denominationalism and its individualistic emphasis on free association made Americans less inclined to follow Darby's call to leave their church institutions. More important than Darbyite anti-institutionalism was "the question of how an individual was to live a spiritually . . . victorious life . . . separated from sin and worldliness." Nevertheless, when the denominational model broke down in the midst of the fundamentalist-modernist controversy of the early twentieth century, "the dispensationalist view of the church was available to account for the phenomenon and to provide a rationale for new structures." These American adaptations of Darbyite doctrine do not indicate a complete split between American and British millenarian perspectives. As Marsden observes, "From the time of the Puritans until Dwight L. Moody, British and American evangelicalism was, to some extent, part of a single transatlantic movement." Vestiges of Darby's anti-institutional teachings lived on in the separatist elements of the fundamentalist movement, made up of believers who "were almost all strict dispensational premillennialists" standing in opposition to the socially engaged evangelicalism envisioned by Carl F.H. Henry, founding editor of *Christianity Today* and father-in-law to evangelist Billy Graham.[14] Even with objections to certain elements within traditional dispensationalism, the revivalist movement that inspired both fundamentalism and evangelicalism seized upon the any-moment rapture as a compelling device for promoting morality, as an impetus for global mission, and as a grand theodicy that explained the deterioration of the human condition while assuring believers of the ultimate victory of God over the forces of evil.

Blackstone's Politically Active Premillennialism

The benefits of dispensational doctrine were joined with the commitments of American civil millennialism through the intellectual and practical efforts of William E. Blackstone (1830–1897), a successful businessman and Episcopal Methodist layperson in the Chicago area. In conjunction with publishing the first edition of *Jesus Is Coming* in 1878,[15] Blackstone decided to withdraw from the business world and devote himself to evangelistic work among North American Jews. Blackstone accepted Darby's eschatological timeline, including the probability "that the restoration of Israel (except partially in unbelief . . .), will take place . . . after the Rapture."[16] Exemplifying the American adaptation of dispensationalist doctrines to American ends, Blackstone made his singular contribution to American Christian Zionism in 1891 with his delivery of a petition to President Benjamin Harrison.

With this petition, often known as the "Blackstone Memorial," Blackstone led the way from politically passive eschatological speculation to active political participation. Motivated, in part, by a wave of pogroms in imperial Russia between 1881 and 1884, and the resulting unease and outmigration of many Ashkenazim,[17] Blackstone's petition, titled "Palestine for the Jews," opened with the question "What shall be done for the Russian Jews?" The petition went on to request that President Harrison convene an international conference to accomplish the establishment of a Jewish-administered state in Palestine, using the model of how "Roumania, Montenegro, and Greece, were wrested from the Turks and given to their natural owners. Does not Palestine as rightfully belong to the Jews?" Indeed, "Why not give Palestine back to them again? According to God's distribution of nations it is their home—an inalienable possession from which they were expelled by force." The petition, which was signed by an impressive list of notable Americans, both Christians and Jews, was remarkably muted in its theological content.[18]

In 1916, Blackstone again offered to an American president a petition on behalf of Zionist interests. In the later years of World War I, Zionist leaders in England and the United States were eager to build support for their cause. The best way to achieve this goal was to develop Christian bases of support. After encouragement from Nathan Straus, whose brother Oscar had served briefly as U.S. Ambassador to the Ottoman Empire and was a signatory on the 1891 memorial, Louis Brandeis began corresponding with Blackstone in May 1916, in the midst of his nomination to the U.S. Supreme Court.[19] This 1916 Memorial, working from the assumption that "the civilized world seeks some feasible method of relieving the persecuted Jews," suggested that "humanity and the Golden Rule demand speedy action . . . for the permanent relief of the Jews."[20] Although the petition was ready for presentation in May, and Blackstone saw that the language of the petition was adopted as resolutions by various denominations—most notably the General Assembly of the Presbyterian Church U.S.A.—President Woodrow Wilson's support for Zionist interests was growing more apparent and "Zionist leaders . . . saw no need to embarrass him by publicly presenting the petition."[21] The substance of the 1916 Memorial was a recommendation for President Wilson to revisit and enact the 1891 Memorial.

Although Blackstone cooperated closely with eminent American Jewish leaders to present his later memorial to President Wilson, the 1891 Memorial received mixed reactions within American Jewish communities. The *Jewish Messenger* described the petition as "one of those unfortunate acts of friendship which may work a vast amount of mischief" because it first "revives the old reproach of the anti-Semites that the Jews cannot be patriots if Palestine is their national home today" and "makes the Jews again a subject of newspaper comment when such publicity and notoriety work more harm than good."[22] Wolf Schur, editor of *ha-Pisgah*, strikingly prefigures contemporary Jewish advocates for close cooperation with evangelical Christian Zionists:

> It is not their intention to bring us under the wings of Christianity in our time . . . but rather in the days to come when peace returns and each of us sits under his fig tree and vine, and after the battle of Gog and Magog. Let the Christians do whatever they can do to help us in the resettlement in Palestine. As to the question of our faith, let that rest until Elijah returns and then we shall see whether or not their dream materializes.[23]

Schur clearly rejected the veracity of any Christian claims, including Blackstone's specific eschatological vision. He would have agreed, in principle, with Lenny Davis, a former researcher for the American Israel Public Affairs Committee, who said "Sure, these guys give me the heebie-jeebies. But until I see Jesus coming over the hill, I'm in favor of all the friends Israel can get."[24] As Yaakov Ariel observed about American Jewish cooperation with Blackstone, "Zionists dismissed Blackstone's doctrine but were nonetheless prepared to work with him, perhaps without realizing the scope of his involvement in actual missionary work among the Jews."[25] One wonders if the knowledge-base of Jewish cooperation with today's Christian Zionists is similarly informed. The more fundamental debate among Jews in the United States was whether or not Zionist aspirations of return to Jerusalem were constitutive of Jewish faithfulness or self-interest. Questions surrounding the necessity and character of a state intended to be a Jewish homeland remain hotly contested subjects of intra-Jewish debate.[26] The 1890s were pivotal: Blackstone's Memorial was presented in 1891; Theodor Herzl's pamphlet, *Der Judenstaat*, would be published in 1896.

Blackstone matched Jewish ambivalence toward his efforts with his own ambivalence toward Jews and Judaism. Although, as Ariel notes, "Blackstone sincerely considered himself a friend of the Jews" and his "activity in favor of the restoration of Palestine to the Jews was beneficial to the Zionist cause," Blackstone was motivated "primarily [by] his premillennial convictions." This led him to treat "the Jewish people" as "a means to an end."[27] In his 1900 book, *Satan, His Kingdom, and Its Overthrow*, Blackstone rejected secular Zionism as "Satan's counterfeit," a movement whose leaders were "for the most part Reformed Jews who have thrown away all the messianic hopes of their anecestors."[28]

The 1908 edition of Blackstone's *Jesus Is Coming*, written after the rise of Jewish political Zionism, shows Blackstone's continuing reflection on Jews, Judaism, and Zionism. A committed premillennial dispensationalist, Blackstone carefully avoids "confusing Israel with the Church." The church is the "heavenly Bride of Christ" while "Israel was an earthly bride, comforted with temporal blessings, and to these she shall be restored." The time in which he lived, however, forced Blackstone to assess the Zionist movement through his theological lenses. While, on the one hand, Blackstone claims for Jews that Zionist hopes for return to the land "are the very core of their intensely religious life, and are embedded in the most solemn devotions of their prayer-book," he complains that "The Reformed Jews . . . have rapidly thrown away their faith in the inspiration of the Scriptures" and have "flung to the wind all national and Messianic hopes." Blackstone locates this lack of messianic hope in the Reformed rabbis "joining with the most radical higher critics in the destruction of its very basis, the inspiration of the Word of God." Perhaps not knowing that his own efforts would meet with similar concerns, Blackstone was perplexed that "not all the orthodox Jews have joined the movement" since many criticized it "as an attempt to seize the prerogatives of their God." His contempt, however, was focused primarily on Jews "content to renounce all the prophesied glory of a Messianic kingdom in the land of their ancestors, preferring the palatial homes and gathered riches which they have acquired in Western Europe and the United States." "In the midst of these disputes," he observed, "the Zionists have seized the reins and eschewing the help of Abraham's God they have accepted agnostics as leaders and are plunging madly into this scheme for the erection of a Godless state."[29]

Blackstone nevertheless accepted that these secular developments could also serve to fulfill apocalyptic expectations. "What a sign is this that the end of this dispensation is near," he said. "If it stood alone we might well give heed to it. But when we find it supported by all these other signs, set forth in the Word, how can we refuse to believe it?" His final capstone of evidence related to Zionism is the significance that "this first Zionist congress assembled just 1,260 years after the capture of Jerusalem by the Mohammedans in A.D. 637. Dan. 12:7." As "the times of the Gentiles" drew to a close, and the "time of Jacob's trouble" commenced, Blackstone reminded his readers that "We are to watch and pray always that we may escape all these things that shall come to pass and stand before the Son of Man."[30]

Blackstone's interactions with governmental leaders in the United States and the prophetic significance he assigned to Jewish political Zionism afford deep insight into both the popular reception of contemporary Christian Zionism in the United States and participation in that movement by committed premillennial dispensationalists. A committed dispensationalist with ties to Darby, Moody, James H. Brookes, and Scofield,[31] Blackstone's linking of the first Zionist congress in 1897 with the Muslim capture of Jerusalem in 637 provides a clear example of how he blended *historicist* and *futurist* methods of prophecy interpretation. Darby taught that no prophecy would be fulfilled until the Rapture ended this dispensation and the prophetic clock began again with the focus of God's attention on God's earthly people after the Rapture. As he wrote in 1848, "the church cannot be the subject of prophecy." All prophecy to be fulfilled will occur in the future, after the Rapture, since the prophetic timeline does not involve the church "save in the extraordinary suspension of prophetic testimony, or period, which comes in between the sixty-ninth and seventieth week of Daniel."[32] Nevertheless, Blackstone perceived that prophecy—not just movements toward prophecy—was being fulfilled in his own time.

Historicism, Futurism, and Blackstone's Blend

In an 1893 article, "The Number of the Years," Blackstone provides his assessment of both historicist and futurist hermeneutics. Recognizing shortcomings in each approach, he proffered a compromise that "reconciles into one harmonious system the two schools of interpretation."[33] Having crafted a "mediating position" that "combined aspects of the futurist and historicist methods of interpreting prophetic texts," Jonathan Moorhead observes, "Blackstone was satisfied that he had unlocked the key to discerning the end-times."[34] This theoretical solution found its practical application in Blackstone's immediate assessment of the 1897 Zionist congress as prophetically significant.[35] He would remain convinced that prophecy was being fulfilled in his own time. Of the seven "evidences" Blackstone offered in the 1908 edition of *Jesus Is Coming* for "believing that His coming, the Rapture, is near," the seventh was "Israel," with special reference to "Zionism," for "if Israel is beginning to show signs of national life and is actually returning to Palestine, then surely the end of this dispensation 'is nigh, even at the doors.'"[36] Just as Karl Barth recommended that Christians "take your Bible and take your newspaper, and read both . . . but interpret newspapers from your Bible," Blackstone remarked in 1931 that "We can well read our Bibles with our newspapers to observe the fulfillment of Bible prophecy."[37]

Blackstone's blend of historicist and futurist expectations shaped his reading of Islam's place within God's eschatological plan, even beyond his identification of A.D. 637 as a significant corollary to 1897. Anti-Islamic sentiment is a prominent feature of the tradition of Judeo-centric tradition of prophecy interpretation. These anti-Islamic themes were heightened in the Puritan era by the threat of Barbary Pirates, especially in the writing of Cotton Mather. Thomas Kidd has observed that although "Anglo-American conservative theologians always identified a clear place for the rise of Islam in Bible prophecy," the later shift "from historicist to dispensational eschatology" caused Islam to lose "much of its natural place in American prophetic thought."[38] In *Jesus Is Coming*, Blackstone, adopting a futurist position, noted that "many think that he [the Antichrist] has already been manifested in Antiochus Epiphanes—or the Popes of Rome—or Moham-med and his successors, all of which we regard as erroneous." Each of these, he says, "is in some sense a type" of Antichrist, "but that is all" since "antichrist is still in the future, and he will not be manifested until the true Church has been taken away, at the rapture ... leaving the apostate church, adulterous Israel and the ungodly world, to believe a lie." Blackstone's compromise between historicist and futurist hermeneutics suggests that "all the horrors of papal persecution, the flaming sword of Mohammedan-ism, the raging of the heathen, and the vain imagination of the people (Israel, Ps. 2) shall be headed up into a veritable literal fulfillment under the world-wide reign of antichrist."[39]

Although Blackstone folds historicist concerns about Islam into his eschatology—thus adopting futurism's identification of the Antichrist as an unknown future leader rather than any combination of Turko-Catholic threat—Muslim political power remained an obstacle to his Christian Zi-onist geopolitical proposals for the establishment of a Jewish political entity in Palestine. In the context of his country's increasing global power and Ottoman decline, Blackstone seems to have viewed Islamic political power as a cog in the gears of prophetic fulfillment, an earthly power that would soon blow away like chaff. While British Puritans were keenly aware of Ottoman military threat to the Protestant communities in Europe and Anglo-American colonists were concerned about the economic and spiri-tual threat posed by Barbary pirates, Blackstone was confident that Amer-ican strength could achieve the goal of a Jewish state through diplomacy alone, backed with economic and military superiority. In keeping with longstanding views of Islam as a religion of imposture, Blackstone was confident that only Jews could claim "natural" rights to the land. As he said, "The title deed to Palestine is recorded, not in the Mohammedan Serai of Jerusalem nor the Serglio [sic] of Constantinople, but in hundreds of millions of Bibles now extant in more than three hundred languages of the earth."[40] Far from being an existential threat, Islam for Blackstone was an object of derision and disregard, a proving ground for American Protestant superiority. "So long as the deed to Palestine did not rest in the hands of its rulers or its indigenous people," Hilton Obenzinger observes, "Europe and America could take the attitude of advocates of reform, of righting ancient wrongs, through the vehicle of a progressive, sanctified colonialism." In the same way, Blackstone engages Roman Catholicism as an object lesson for evangelicals who must resist the temptations that lead to apostasy and corruption.[41]

Blackstone adapted Darby by blending "free elements" of futurist dispensational doctrine with historicist explanations. These historicist impulses were drawn from the long tradition of Judeo-centric prophecy interpretation upon the shoulders of which nineteenth-century forms of Anglo-American eschatology stood. Let me be clear: I am not suggesting that Blackstone rejected futurism by reverting to historicism. Until he died, he longed for prophecy to be fulfilled. It cannot be denied, however, that Blackstone adapted Darby by blending "free elements" of futurist dispensational doctrine with historicist explanations. With the resulting solution, Blackstone reintroduced an emphasis on the developments of human history and, with that emphasis, the expectation of political activity as a proper outcome of prophetic expectation.[42] After the founding of the State of Israel in 1948 and its "miraculous" expansion in 1967, very few evangelicals in the United States would accept that prophecy could not unfold in their Christian age. Blackstone's blend of futurist and historicist understandings paved the way for the belief in popular dispensationalism "that before any of the prophesied end-times events could take place, Jews would have to reestablish their own state in the Holy Land. Without a restored Jewish state, there could be no Antichrist, no great tribulation, no battle of Armageddon, and no second coming. In short, everything was riding on the Jews."[43]

Blackstone and America's Apocalyptic Mission

Far from Darby's injunction that faithful Christians should eschew worldliness and refrain from political activity, Blackstone not only engaged in the dogged work of preparing petitions to send to two U.S. presidents but also engaged in a stream of correspondence with national political leaders and lobbied for various international causes. In his capacity as a member of the World's Columbian Commission for the 1893 World's Fair in Chicago, Blackstone presented President Grover Cleveland and Secretary of State Walter Q. Gresham a memorial encouraging "Governments . . . to submit for settlement by arbitration all . . . international questions and differences."[44] Ironically, the International Court of Justice established in the same spirit as this Memorial is today derided by many contemporary American Christian Zionists as an internationalist tool of the Antichrist's coming "one world government."

More in keeping with contemporary Christian Zionist commitments is Blackstone's conviction that the United States, despite its shortcomings, was destined to be central to God's plans for Jews and for the world. In Blackstone's letter to President Harrison and Secretary of State James Blaine, accompanying the 1891 Memorial, he claimed that "not for twenty-four centuries, since the days of Cyrus, King of Persia, has there been offered to any mortal such a privileged opportunity to further the purposes of God concerning His ancient people." This possibility was available both for the country and for them as individuals who could enjoy "the high privilege" to "secure through the Conference, a home for these wandering millions of Israel, and thereby receive to yourselves the promise of Him, who said to Abraham, 'I will bless them that bless thee,' Gen. 12:3."[45] In an article Blackstone published in conservative Protestant journal *Our Hope* promoting the 1891 Memorial, he claimed that political action on behalf of Jews was necessary if the United States "would continue to enjoy the blessings of Him who hath divided to the nations their inheritance and set the bounds of the people according to the number of the children of Israel." He was convinced that the United States "will have no difficulty in securing respectful attention to its peaceable diplomatic efforts for oppressed Israel" especially since "the United States has no covetous aspirations" and "her efforts for Israel would be recognized as entirely unselfish and purely philanthropic."[46]

Blackstone's confidence in the prophetic role of the United States grew during World War I. When he wrote to President Wilson in July 1915, sharing his conviction that the U.S. should maintain its neutrality, Blackstone suggested "that God has raised up our country, for great and beneficent purposes, as foretold in HIS prophetic Word." Although admitting that "our nation is admittedly imperfect . . . the desire for peace and the manifestation of good will toward all men permeates our national spirit and life."[47] Writing in November 1916 to congratulate Wilson on his narrow reelection, under letterhead proclaiming "The Land and the People" and quoting Genesis 12:3, Blackstone opined that "there is no surer way of your being unerringly led in the difficult task, which is still upon you, at the helm of our Nation, in the maelstrom of difficulties which are arising, than to evidence determinedly your sympathy for suffering Israel" through the "kind interest of our Nation in God's ancient people, and the recovery of their predestined Palestinian home." Blackstone further shared his view of "our Nation as God's chosen instrument in these last days. Just as surely as God raised up Cyrus to befriend His ancient people . . . so I believe, has he raised up you . . . to bring blessing, not only to Israel, but to the whole world."[48] In 1920, after being elected to the presidency, Senator Warren Harding received a telegram from Blackstone informing him that "God has reserved our nation for special service in the impending crux of human history" and that "The restoration of Israel to their homeland in Palestine which has begun is very significant for it betokens the approaching end of the times of the Gentiles."[49] Blackstone's commitment to share his prophetic insights with these American presidents is extraordinary. Moorhead remarks that "it is almost as if Blackstone understood himself as fulfilling the role of a prophet with the presidents, forewarning them as the prophets of Israel had warned kings of old."[50] This legacy did not end with Blackstone. As Yaakov Ariel notes, Blackstone's "vision of America . . . enabled American evangelicals to combine their messianic belief and understanding of the course of human history with their sense of American patriotism."[51]

Along with expressions of what Paul Merkley has called "patriotic conservatism" within contemporary American Christian Zionism,[52] Blackstone's expressions of America's prophetic significance contain elements of what historian Stuart Miller described as "America's exaggerated sense of innocence" that has characterized "the question of American imperialism . . . ever since the United States acquired a formal empire at the end of the nineteenth century."[53] In his discussion of Manifest Destiny—the ideology that fueled American continental expansion through the nineteenth century—Ernest Tuveson reminds us that the "most neglected" element "is the conception of the 'chosen people' with a millennial mission." It is important to recognize that theopolitical expressions of American mission and purpose do not merely "look rather like those of apocalyptic prophecies" but that "they are literally apocalyptic, that they were regarded as the continuation of the biblical prophecies themselves."[54] Along with his identification of America itself as the messianic Cyrus, ordained by God to deliver God's ancient people from their bondage, one recognizes in Herman Melville's thoughts on American exceptionalism the pride Blackstone took in America's presumably altruistic motivations:

> We Americans are the peculiar, chosen people—the Israel of our time; we bear the ark of the liberties of the world. . . . We are the pioneers of the world. . . . Long enough have we been sceptics [sic] with regard to ourselves, and doubted whether, indeed, the political Messiah had come. But he has come in us, if we would but give utterance to his promptings. And let us always remember, that with ourselves—almost for the first time in the history of the earth— national selfishness is unbounded philanthropy; for we cannot do a good to America but we give alms to the world.[55]

As Tuveson further observes, "Two extremes have alternated in our history," both of which, along with historicist and futurist prophetic interpretation, exercise themselves in Blackstone. The first is "isolationist withdrawal," seen in Blackstone's appeals to the Monroe Doctrine and desire for the U.S. to remain uninvolved in World War I, his call to exploit weaknesses in the faltering Ottoman Empire notwithstanding. "The generally less powerful idea," Tuveson continues, "was that of active messianism; yet, like a recessive gene, in the right situation it could become dominant."[56] Noting that the height of Blackstone's activity occurred precisely during the period of America's imperial expansion and that the 1891 petition used the presumed "natural" right of Jews to Palestine as a pretext to ignore the land's existing population, Hilton Obenzinger says that "Blackstone's remarkable accomplishment" was the transformation of "already existing currents of colonialism, nationalism, and philo-Semitism into a modern ideology that exercised, if nothing else, an already well-established American ability to rationalize expansion through the narrative of Christian mission."[57]

Indians, Arabs and Expansionism: Toward a Cold War Cultural Affinity

The 1893 World's Columbian Exposition in Chicago, for which Blackstone served as a commissioner, celebrated the four hundredth anniversary of

Christopher Columbus's voyage to what would come to be known as the Americas. During the festivities, Frederick Jackson Turner presented his seminal lecture, "The Significance of the Frontier in American History," in which he claimed that "the existence of an area of free land, its continuous recession, and the advance of American settlement westward, explain American development."[58] By 1893, however, the American frontier had been closed: the ocean reached, borders decided with Mexico and Canada, and the indigenous population defeated, removed as a threat, though all the more noble in their defeat.[59] Turner argued that continued expansion and frontier experience was central to American vitality and that new frontiers must be sought. His vision was soon to be realized.

In addition to the continued westward expansion of American military power to Hawaii and the Philippines under President William McKinley, Americans had, by 1893, been quite busy laying claim to Palestine itself. Inspired by missionaries sent by the American Board of Commissioners for Foreign Missions (ABCFM) to Palestine and surrounding areas of the Ottoman Empire, tourists were traveling frequently to the area. The United States had had economic and security interests in the Holy Land since independence; now, through private citizens and missionary groups, it had colonies.[60] Most Americans were not transformed by their experience in the Holy Land; instead, tourists, missionaries, and colonists alike brought with them their own preconceptions and associations as they sought to leave their imprint on that exotic land.[61] Their desire for the land and its subjective significance was matched by their disregard for its indigenous population, a disregard fostered by experiences at home.

The British occupation of Jerusalem in December 1917 thrilled many evangelicals around the world, seemingly confirming the long-standing prophetic belief that England would be instrumental to Jewish restoration to Palestine. This sense was reinforced by the Balfour Declaration, issued on November 2 of that year, indicating that "His Majesty's government view with favour the establishment in Palestine of a national home for the Jewish people, and will use their best endeavours to facilitate the achievement of this object, it being clearly understood that nothing shall be done which may prejudice the civil and religious rights of existing non-Jewish communities in Palestine, or the rights and political status enjoyed by Jews in any other country." Several prophecy conferences were called in response to these historic events. "The capture of Jerusalem is one of those events to which the students of prophecy have been looking forward for many years," declared A.E. Thompson, pastor of the American Church in Jerusalem. "Even before Great Britain took possession of Egypt, there were keen sighted seers who foresaw a day when God would use the Anglo-Saxon peoples to restore Jerusalem. When the war broke out, there were some of us who were convinced that it would never end until Turkish tyranny was forever a thing of the past in the Holy City."[62]

The Balfour Declaration and its intention to accomplish the Anglo-Saxon defeat of Islamic tyranny sought its American counterpart through the U.S. Congress. In 1922, the House of Representatives held several days of hearings on the "Establishment of a National Home in Palestine," regarding H. Con. Res. 52, "Expressing Satisfaction at the Re-Creation of Palestine as the National Home of the Jewish Race."

American rationale for this idea was expressed differently than by British leaders. David Lloyd George made reference to religious commitment in his explanation of the Balfour Declaration: "It was undoubtedly inspired by natural sympathy, admiration, and also by the fact that, as you must remember, we had been trained even more in Hebrew history than in the history of our own country."[63] Comments from Rep. Albert B. Rossdale of New York early in the congressional hearings provide an important example of how American statesmen, by contrast, made explicit and telling references to American self-understanding, including the expansionist desire to establish and reinforce "civilization," as a primary lens for comprehending the Zionist project. "The land we now know as Palestine was peopled by the Jews from the dawn of history until the Roman era. Ancient Jewish history in this corner of old Asia gave to the world the highest and noblest inspiration for civilization," Rep. Rossdale said. "Although various alien people succeeded them at different periods, the Jews left an indelible impress upon the land. Even unto the present it is yet a Jewish country. Every landmark every monument every name and every trace of whatever civilization is there is still Jewish."

The presence of Palestinians in the land is, for Rep. Rossdale, comprehended through the American experience of the frontier, closed just three decades earlier. "The resettling of Palestine has created a situation somewhat akin to that of the American colonist in his struggle with the American Indian. For like the early American settler on this continent, the Jewish colonist frequently has to till the soil with a rifle in one hand and a hoe in the other. The Nomadic Arab raiders, on a smaller scale, are fighting the civilization of the Jewish settler as the Indian fought the American settler on this continent in the early days."[64] The inescapable conclusion of these statements is that Palestinians, yet another alien people, must inevitably give way to the advancement of civilization in its Zionist form, just as American Indians had done for his own, that the savages will be subdued as the desert is made to bloom by the rightful owners of the land. These Anglo-Saxon leaders sat in judgment of inferior cultures, determining who should be empowered and who would decline in the face of civilizational progress. "In regard to Palestine, the colonial powers considered neither Jews nor Arabs to be ready for the 'full responsibilities of statehood,'" Kathleen Christison has observed, "but Jews, being European, were regarded as educable, whereas Arabs—dull and inarticulate as they were thought to be—were not so perceived; they were not, in fact, considered even to want self-rule."[65] The House unanimously adopted the resolution in June 1922, while the Senate would adopt a similar resolution in June 1944.[66]

The founding of the State of Israel combined with the onset of the Cold War to create a climate conducive to prophetic speculation. As Angela Lahr has said, "prophecy commentators after World War II were able to utilize eschatological allure to make sense of an increasingly conflict-ridden world."[67] American competition with the Soviet Union had deep effects on American religion alongside American policy. President Harry Truman recognition of the State of Israel within minutes of its declaration in May 1948[68] brings these themes together. Much has been made of Truman's upbringing in the Baptist tradition and how this religious formation and his love of ancient history made him emotionally ripe for the diplomatic challenge of recognizing Israel. This sense has been reinforced by the rehearsal of Truman's apparent affront when, sometime later, an advisor introduced him to a group of Jewish scholars as "the man who helped create the State of Israel." "What do you mean, 'helped create'?" Truman said, "I am Cyrus, I am Cyrus!"[69] Other readings, however, reveal a Truman more emotionally detached than is often portrayed. Truman's decisive recognition of Israel, against the best efforts of his State Department advisors, set the stage for the official American relationship with Israel and helped ensure that the young state would choose the way of liberal, free-market capitalism rather than intensify the collectivist commitments of the Yishuv in a relationship with the U.S.S.R.[70] In this super-heated context, popular American disdain for Russia was joined with what Paul Boyer has described as "an anti-Arab bias" that "colored much post-1948 prophecy writing." One writer plainly declared that "The Arab world is an Antichrist-world."[71] Angela Lahr describes a peculiar conflation of traditional Antichrists when, in the Cold War period, anti-Catholic and anti-Muslim stereotypes were "united . . . with suspicions that the Arab nations were allies of the Soviet Union."[72]

In the United States following World War II, German scholars led the charge of developing new theologies of Jewish-Christian relationship. Reinhold Niebuhr, who by 1944 had formulated a realist foreign policy perspective in *The Children of Light and the Children of Darkness*,[73] recognized already in 1933, likely through his relationship with his student, Dietrich Bonhoeffer, the ultimate goal of Nazi activity concerning Jews: "They are bent upon the extermination of the Jews."[74] Niebuhr used his public standing to champion the Zionist cause until his death in 1971. His essays "Jews After the War" (1942), "Our Stake in the State of Israel" (1957), and "The Unresolved Religious Problems in Christian-Jewish Relations" (1966) have been described as being "among his most important—though usually neglected—shorter writings."[75] Paul Tillich, a refugee scholar in the United States who had participated directly in theological efforts to bring down the Nazi regime,[76] sought after the war to forge a new identity based on his understanding of the potentially fruitful relationship between Jews and Christians. In a 1952 issue of the journal *Judaism*, Tillich posed the question, "Is There a Judeo-Christian Tradition?" Tillich's affirmative answer was met in the journal's next issue by a Jewish community still reeling from the horror of the Holocaust. Most responses were decidedly negative, though some saw the potential benefits of joining a recognized relationship with western Christian power.[77] In 1955, Jewish writer Will Herberg published his seminal book, *Protestant, Catholic, Jew: An Essay in American Religious Sociology*.[78] By the mid-1950s, the United States was commonly comprehended as a manifestation of Judeo-Christian rather than simply Christian values.

The establishment of the State of Israel in 1948 confirmed evangelical hopes that Jesus would soon return. But there was a major problem. Many evangelicals (not to mention many Jews) were concerned that the new country had not claimed the entirety of biblical Israel. The 1967 war alleviated these concerns. *Life Magazine*, which had a reporter embedded with the Israeli mechanized infantry killed in Gaza, and which described the glowing faces of "conquering Israelis . . . again inside Old Jerusalem," described the Israeli victory as "astounding": "Tiny Israel stood in the role of victor over the surrounding Arab nations that had vowed to eliminate her. Middle Eastern alliances, balances of power, even political boundaries, were of a new shape, as though mutated by a Biblical cataclysm."[79]

Beyond winning general American respect through military prowess, the war bolstered evangelical confidence in Israel as a theological datum; with their conquest of "Judea and Samaria," especially the Temple Mount,

Jews had finally reclaimed their birthright. In June 1967, the highly influential evangelical magazine, *Christianity Today*, marveling at Israel's cunning, assured its readers that Israel's wars—which were always conceived as defensive—were manifestations of God's will. The next month, the magazine's editor mused that the reality that "for the first time in more than 2,000 years Jerusalem is now completely in the hands of the Jews gives a student of the Bible a thrill and a renewed faith in the accuracy and validity of the Bible."[80] By redeeming the land from the hands of its savage usurpers, the expansionist State of Israel—a country formed in the same Judeo-Christian tradition of the expansionist United States—was claiming its manifest destiny. In 1891, Blackstone had presumed the "natural" Jewish right to the land of Palestine. By 1967, the American populace generally agreed.

Fundamentalism and Political Mobilization

American evangelicals were essential participants in forging this American cultural consensus. This is due, in no small part, to premillennial attitudes, including belief in the imminent Rapture, being woven into the fabric of American popular Christianity. This weaving was accomplished through dispensationalist involvement in the movement that would become known as fundamentalism.

Several characteristic elements of dispensationalism were familiar to American Christian culture. Judeo-centric prophecy interpretation and biblical literalism were features of American (and British) Protestantism since the pre-revolutionary period. Underlying both Dwight L. Moody's revivalist preaching and William E. Blackstone's political activity, reverence for the Bible made dispensationalism attractive to fundamentalism and, in turn, eased that movement's reception in many sectors of American Christianity.

When the twelve-volume series of books titled *The Fundamentals* was published between 1910 and 1915, "it was meant to be a great 'Testimony to the Truth' and even something of a scholarly *tour de force*"[81] Several volumes included articles from well-known dispensationalists. The eleventh volume, for instance, included articles from Cyrus Scofield and Arno Gaebelein. Although Scofield did not focus on hermeneutical methods, Gaebelein argued "Fulfilled Prophecy a Potent Argument for the Bible."[82] The subsequent fundamentalist movement, defined primarily by its opposition to modernist biblical interpretation and its implications, did not retain the scholarly character of these small books.

The initial exchange of ideas concerning developments in Darwinist science and modernist biblical interpretation in May 1922 became a battle between two clearly defined sides when Harry Emerson Fosdick (1878–1969), a Baptist minister then serving First Presbyterian Church in New York City, preached "Shall the Fundamentalists Win?" While Fosdick directed his bombshell toward the Baptist situation, the resulting shrapnel ignited a fire among Presbyterians. A gifted New Testament scholar at Princeton, J. Gresham Machen (1881–1937), emerged as the leading conservative Presbyterian voice. Although he was no fan of dispensational hermeneutics, Machen recognized its adherents as valuable allies in the struggle against modernist approaches. Arguing in *Christianity and Liberalism* (1923) that "it is perfectly possible for Christian fellowship to be maintained despite differences of opinion" and rejecting the notion "that the prophecies of the Bible permit so definite a mapping-out of future events," Machen nevertheless welcomed dispensationalists. Although they have "a false method of interpreting Scripture which in the long run will be productive of harm . . . they share to the full our reverence for the authority of the Bible."[83]

Although for Machen the fundamentalist struggle was primarily for traditionalist forms of biblical interpretation (especially based on vestiges of Scottish Common Sense Realism and Baconian science), Marsden notes that "in the minds of most fundamentalists the theological crisis came to be inextricably wedded to the very survival of Christian civilization—by which they meant a Bible-based civilization. One cannot comprehend the character of the movement without recognizing this social and political dimension."[84] Laying the foundation for what Richard Hofstadter termed the "paranoid style in American politics,"[85] many fundamentalists after World War I tended to interpret American culture as a battleground between God and Satan.

This perspective, prevalent among contemporary Christian Zionists, is conducive to the acceptance of what Irving Kristol called neoconservative "attitudes" or political theory, including that "patriotism . . . should be encouraged by both private and public institutions," that "world government is a terrible idea since it can lead to world tyranny," and that "statesmen should, above all, have the ability to distinguish friends from enemies." In our own time, the blend of lament for the "steady decline in our democratic culture," the celebration of America's military strength and support for Israel as an embattled democracy has made for an easy alliance between neoconservatives and "religious traditionalists."[86] One of the most prominent neoconservative manifestoes following the terrorist attacks on

9/11, including rationales for rejecting the United Nations and attacking Iran, was titled *An End to Evil: How to Win the War on Terror*.[87] The alliance between Christian Zionists and some elements within the Jewish community was built on a well-established foundation. Marsden observes that the early fundamentalist tendency "to divide *all* reality into neat antitheses" may "shed some light on the paradox of super-patriotic millennialism." If one concludes "that Satan's hosts would appear in clearly identifiable political manifestations . . . the political battle to defend God's kingdom could not be entirely postponed until a coming era." Marsden further notes that the "fundamentalist proneness to military solutions is consonant with their end-time scenarios in which they emphasize cataclysmic warfare led by Christ himself that will destroy history's most insidious and potent coalition of the forces of darkness."[88] To the extent that fundamentalist Christians are influenced by dispensationalist commitments, these approaches to faith and political life could not be possible without a complex blend of historicist and futurist perspectives, the substantive legacy of William Blackstone.

Marsden has recently reflected on how "a soul-saving revivalistic movement that mostly steered clear of direct political involvement" could "emerge at the end of the twentieth century as known especially for its political stances and influences." Noting that "the most dedicated core" of the fundamentalist movement in the 1920s was composed of dispensationalists, the "new evangelicals" that emerged in the 1940s and later, including Carl F.H. Henry, worked against separatist tendencies, "fostering a larger social, political, and intellectual agenda."[89] Henry said that his own views "while broadly premillennial, are not partial to the dispensational postponement theory of the kingdom; this is no necessary adjunct to the premillennial view." Saying that the movement is "distorted" when viewed "in terms of eschatology only," Henry urged that "the time has come now for Fundamentalism to speak with an ecumenical outlook and voice . . . rather than in the name of secondary accretions or of eschatological biases on which evangelicals divide."[90]

For the contemporary era, Marsden uses the word "fundamentalist" to denote "an evangelical who is angry about something" so that distinctions between evangelicals and fundamentalists are "their relative degrees of militancy in support of conservative doctrinal, ecclesiastical and/or cultural issues." By this broad definition, any evangelical who is a Christian Zionist is also a fundamentalist. One can conclude that Christian Zionist leaders such as John Hagee are trying to draw evangelicals like Bill Hybels into (neo-)conservative political activism and, thus, fundamentalism. Marsden has identified a trend since the 1960s in which "culturally marginal" forms of "American Christianity have been mobilized into [a] significant mainstream national political force by adding a very 'this-worldly' or 'public' agenda." Although contemporary American Christian Zionism is certainly a part of this trend, it has always been "this-worldly" and "public." The external threat of Communism blended in the 1970s with concerns about changes in social mores to effect what Marsden calls an intentional and "dramatic transformation of cultural fundamentalism . . . into a major national political power," mostly as the initiative of "non-evangelicals who were building the new conservative coalition that reshaped the Republican Party in the late twentieth century." In addition to adopting "an ideal of cultural transformation" as their domestic goal, Marsden says that the practical result of this trend "was that American fundamentalists and most evangelicals were among the most ardent promoters of U.S. policies of support for Israel. Even though most prophetic interpreters could not find the United States directly in biblical prophecy, they could offer hope for America . . . so long as the United States made the defense of Israel a cornerstone of its foreign policy."[91]

These developments continue the authentically American tradition of adapting apocalyptic hope to challenge, renew, and recreate its identity. Contemporary American Christian Zionism is an organic outgrowth both of America's typological identification with the Children of Israel and its prophetic vocation to secure and preserve Israel's homeland. The legacy of William Blackstone lives on in the patterns of Judeo-centric prophecy interpretation still prevalent in American religion and American culture.

Conclusion

CHRISTIAN ZIONISM FROM THE CARTWRIGHT
PETITION TO AMERICAN EMPIRE

THIS BOOK HAS sought to show that popular American affinity for the State of Israel draws from the taproot of apocalyptic hope informing American identity and national vocation from the revolutionary era to the present. The English Protestant tradition of Judeo-centric prophecy interpretation informing these American adaptations of apocalyptic hope was first developed in the early Elizabethan period and refined through the first half of the seventeenth century. Brought to North America by English colonists with Puritan commitments, the tradition provided a foundational framework for American self-understanding. Given this Judeo-centric tradition's direct contribution to American popular Christianity and civil religion—through varying degrees of national-covenantalism, premillennial dispensationalism and cultural fundamentalism—claims that American popular affinity for the State of Israel is generated primarily by external manipulations or lobbies strain the bounds of credulity.

Grounded, in part, in the Protestant historiography developed by Lutheran and Calvinist reformers, this English Protestant tradition of Judeo-centric prophecy interpretation was from its inception a political theology. The tradition openly constructed friends (Jews) as well as enemies (Muslims and Roman Catholics), while cultivating an occidentocentric discourse that discounted Eastern Christians. These constructions are manifested in contemporary western discourses surrounding the Israeli-Palestinian conflict that cast Jews within Christian eschatological dramas while demonizing Muslims and casting aspersions on Christians who are Palestinian or sympathetic to the Palestinian national cause. The tradition's most visible and direct impulses are manifested in Christian Zionism, understood as political action, informed by specifically Christian commitments, to promote or preserve Jewish control over the geographic area now comprising Israel and Palestine.

In the American context, Christian Zionism has been cultivated through a series of adaptations. In Samuel Sewall's rejection of what he described as Joseph Mede's "Antick Fancy of *America's* being Hell,"[1] we see one example of nascent Anglo-American patriotism—grounded in the Anglo-American colonists' penchant for understanding their condition through typological identification with the Children of Israel—contending with the nationalist Anglo-centrism inherent to English Protestant Judeo-centric apocalyptic hope. Adaptations of this Judeo-centric tradition helped prepare the seedbed for independent American nationalism. The second major adaptation occurred in the revolutionary era, when, through the development of what Nathan Hatch has called "civil millennialism," apocalyptic hope was transferred from the ecclesial sphere and invested fully in civil institutions. Through this adaptation, the emergent United States of America, the primary sign of the *Novus ordo seclorum*, was established as an agent of apocalyptic hope.

As the age of revolutions caused the order of the ages to become confused and the resulting states failed to live up to their prophetic vocations, futurist rather than historicist eschatological schemes began to hold sway. Thus, John Nelson Darby's premillennial dispensationalism, with its profoundly pessimistic view of civil and ecclesial institutions, was received by several audiences. In the United States, however, Darby's doctrine was more influential than the practices he sought to engender, including withdrawal from organized churches and civil life. The third great adaptation of the Judeo-centric tradition was accomplished in William Blackstone's blend of futurist and historicist prophecy interpretation. Situated on the cusp between the closing of the American frontier and American imperial expansion, Blackstone became convinced that the United States could manifest its destiny and become a "redeemer nation." The path to American blessing would be secured through wielding U.S. diplomatic, economic, and military power to assist poor Jews in establishing their own nation-state in the land belonging naturally to them.

The common sense nature of Blackstone's blend of futurist and historicist prophecy interpretation was highly compatible with the pragmatic blend of biblical scholarship and revivalism characteristic of emergent Protestant fundamentalism. Just as early fundamentalism preserved many elements of the Christian tradition for the present era, Blackstone's adaptation of these eschatological traditions toward political application is to be lauded as an intellectual achievement. In his quest to provide the benefits of American imperial power to Jews, Blackstone provided a biblical, apocalyptic framework for dispensationalists—despite doctrines emphasizing the doom of all human institutions—to engage political systems toward domestic and foreign policy ends. The history detailed here demonstrates that dispensationalist withdrawal from political engagement reflects the second-order discourse of doctrine rather than the first-order discourse of self-understanding. Although dispensationalists may experience degrees of cognitive dissonance, Christian Zionists are confident that it can be resolved in favor of active support for the State of Israel.

Blackstone's dispensational articulation of America's altruistic, civilizing mission has bolstered conservative American Christian support for Jewish political Zionism from the movement's inception to the present. Through 1948 and 1967, faced with existential threats from Communism on one hand but seeing their prophetic hope fulfilled on the pages of the newspaper they held in the other, American Christians would broadly and naturally recognize Israel's national purpose as an extension of their own national covenant and mission.

In Blackstone, Judeo-centric prophecy interpretation returned from the realm of academic eschatological speculation to the realm of practical politics. His life and work establish him as one of the critical links in the Anglo-American tradition of Judeo-centric prophecy interpretation that stretches from John Bale to John Hagee. With his careful inclusion of both historicist and futurist hermeneutics and his concern for the political application of his beliefs through the apocalyptic *raison d'être* of the American republic, he stood in greater continuity with the longer tradition than did John Nelson Darby. If Christian Zionism is best understood as *political action, informed by specifically Christian commitments, to promote or preserve Jewish control over the geographic area now comprising Israel and Palestine*, the history of the movement should be traced from the Cartwright petition of 1649, through the Blackstone Memorial of 1891, to Christians United for Israel (CUFI) lobbying efforts since 2006.

These three exemplars of Christian Zionism should be understood within their respective contexts. They each are dependent on Protestant intellectual trends in their respective eras. While some of those trends, including various refinements in millenarian theory, are highly specific to certain eras in Protestant history, others, such as the commitment to literalist (or common-sense) biblical interpretation, extend in various forms from Henry Finch in 1621 to the present. The points of continuity between these three expressions of Christian Zionism illuminate our understanding of this theopolitical expression and how it preserves American popular Christian support for the State of Israel.

The Cartwrights, Blackstone, and Hagee were each willing to engage in direct communication with public officials. Even if they were reasonably sure that they represented at least a sub-section of their respective societies (as opposed to sharing merely their individual views) these Christian Zionists took the step of making public proposals to bring the policies of their respective governments into greater alignment with their apocalyptic visions. Even if they were not in full agreement with the officials they encountered (Blackstone's presidential correspondence, for instance, cuts across party affiliations in a volatile time), they did not hesitate to make their proposals.

Their public communications are remarkably free of the doctrinal commitments motivating their political activity. While in the Cartwrights' time several millenarians were publishing broadsides containing their eschatological theories, their petition to Lord Fairfax concisely presented their strategic plan for cooperation with the Netherlands in terms of Britain's national interest. The theological content of their petition was a brief statement about gaining national blessings so the civil war then raging could end. Although Blackstone shared his theological speculations in private correspondence with elected and appointed officials, his memorials are almost devoid of theological rationale. Similarly, John Hagee, though well known to be a committed dispensationalist with a highly developed theology pertaining to the State of Israel, repeatedly says that CUFI is not motivated by apocalyptic expectation.

The subdued nature of theological claims in Christian Zionist public statements is tied, perhaps, to the fact that, when considered across this historical horizon, the movement does not consistently rely on any particular eschatological or millenarian theory. The baseline commitment, however, is each Christian Zionist's commitment to his or her own interpretation of national covenant (such as the civil millennialism that informed American Manifest Destiny) and the sense that the cause of Israel is also their nation's cause. The American Christian Zionist use of Genesis 12:3 as an assurance of continued national and individual blessing is emblematic of this understanding.

In all three manifestations, Christian Zionism is an imperial theology. The nature of Christian Zionism is shaped by their historical and political contexts. Just as the Cartwright petition reached Fairfax and Cromwell on the cusp of British imperial expansion, Blackstone developed his futurist/historicist formula just as America's continental expansion ended and its imperial enterprises began. Both the Cartwrights and Blackstone understood the power inherent to empire as essential for the realization of God's purposes, either for Britain to "transport IzRAELLS Sons & Daughters in their Ships to the Land promised to their fore-Fathers"[2] or for America to persuade a weakened Ottoman Empire that Palestine belongs "naturally" to another Abrahamic people. In the same way, John Hagee, now on the other side of the hoped-for restoration, sees the preservation of American military and economic superiority (what Dwight Eisenhower called the "military-industrial complex"[3]) as necessary for the preservation of the theological fact of the State of Israel. As he said in 2006, supporting Israel is "God's foreign policy."[4]

The necessity of inaugurating or maintaining the strength of empire for achieving their Judeo-centric vision was, naturally, predicated on these Christian Zionists' theopolitical construction of Jews for Christian purposes. As we have seen throughout this study, the earliest expressions of the Anglo-American tradition of Judeo-centric prophecy interpretation offered a manufactured reality in which Jews were constructed as proto-Puritan allies within the divine drama to come. The centrality of Jews is maintained in each of these three Christian Zionist visions. None of them, however, calls for Jews to convert to Christian faith in order to enjoy the benefit of restoration to Palestine (even if their eventual conversion is part of the greater Christian vision, as was the case with Blackstone and seems also to be with Hagee). Blackstone believed that Jews in Palestine after the Rapture would join in an alliance with this coming man of sin. At one time, Hagee was likewise convinced that the struggles of the State of Israel would lead an exhausted populace to accept peace on any terms: "Israel will unite and peace will prevail . . . when the country accepts the false man of peace who steps out onto the world's stage."[5]

The Cartwrights, Blackstone, and Hagee were all intimately connected to various Jewish communities and were no doubt sincerely concerned for the future of the Jews they encountered. Nevertheless, the theopolitical stream in which they stand represents a tradition that constructs Jews for explicitly Christian purposes, purposes that are inseparable from Protestant historiography, specific expressions of Judeo-centric national covenant, and the systemic interests of empire.

Mark Noll, in his survey of evangelical intellectual life through the twentieth century, has nevertheless observed that "that worst features of the nineteenth-century intellectual situation became the methodological keystones for mental activity in the twentieth century." In addition to Darby and Cyrus I. Scofield, Blackstone is indicted by Noll's charge that "Because dispensationalism was the most intellectual form of fundamentalism, it was responsible for the most disastrous effects on the mind." The movement, Noll said, is afflicted with "the ancient heresy of Manichaeism" along with "a docetism in outlook and a gnosticism in method that together constitute the central intellectual indictment against the fundamentalist past."[6]

Hagee is an example of Noll's concern for evangelicalism's intellectual apathy. Hagee displays his gnosticism in giant, stage-length charts; Manichaeism is on display in Hagee's teachings against Catholicism, for which he has offered apology, and Islam, for which he is unrepentant. This book has shown that these commitments, characteristic of contemporary American Christian Zionism, are grounded in the English Protestant tradition of Judeo-centric prophecy interpretation. This tradition was itself conceived within a Reformation worldview under constant threat from what both Luther and Calvin identified as the dual-headed Antichrist of the Turk and the Pope. Awareness of the Turko-Catholic threat permeated English Protestant consciousness and animated Puritan resistance to compromise with crypto-Catholicism within the Church of England.

Until the end of the Cold War, Soviet Communism caused greater worry for U.S. citizens and policymakers than either Catholicism or Islam. By 1948, Catholics were nearing full integration into American culture. Although the founding of the State of Israel was resisted by Palestinians and other Arabs, most of whom were Muslims, most Americans aware of international affairs were by that time more concerned with the U.S.S.R. rather than any threat from Islam. Douglas Little, in his history of twentieth-century U.S. foreign policy toward the Middle East, observes that President Truman, "deeply concerned about possible Soviet inroads into the Middle East," seems "to have regarded a Jewish state as a stronger bulwark against communism than anything the Arabs could muster." After the effects of Israel's establishment on the Palestinian population became clear, Little notes that "Although humanitarian concerns weighed heavily on U.S. policymakers, Cold War considerations were paramount in Washington's handling of the Palestinian tragedy."[7] On November 30, 1981, President Ronald Reagan and Israeli Prime Minister Menachem Begin presented a memorandum of understanding that reaffirmed "the common bonds of friendship between the United States and Israel" and expanded "the mutual security relationship that exists between the two nations" in order to "enhance Strategic Cooperation to deter all threats from the Soviet Union in the region" including "Soviet-controlled forces."[8] Most Americans, including prophecy writers such as Hal Lindsey, preoccupied by the possibility of nuclear exchange, viewed Muslims, including Arabs regardless of their religious heritage, through Cold War lenses.

Islam did not fully return to the center of American dispensationalist and Christian Zionist consciousness until after the terrorist attacks of September 11, 2001. Historian Thomas Kidd has observed that "the dramatic transition among conservatives from historicist to dispensational eschatology" had great implications "for views of Islam's role in the last days." While "before the mid-nineteenth century, Anglo-American conservative theologians always identified a clear place for the rise of Islam in Bible prophecy," he writes, "with the rise of dispensationalism and its futurist emphasis, Islam lost much of its natural place in American prophetic thought."[9] The return of Islam to the center of American consciousness after 9/11 paved the way for new expressions of Judeo-centric Christian commitments.

The Return of History, the Return of Islam

When in 1989 the United States emerged as the world's sole superpower, some theorists declared with Francis Fukuyama that the dialectic of history had reached its apex[10] while others went searching for the next great enemy the U.S. could engage in a "clash of civilizations." Although most often associated with Samuel Huntington, the phrase was first used by Middle East historian Bernard Lewis in his 1990 article, "The Roots of Muslim Rage."[11] Both Huntington and Lewis emphasized the incommensurability of "western" or "Judeo-Christian civilization" with "Islamic civilization." The Islamist terrorist attacks of 9/11 and the ensuing "War on Terror" strengthened the relationship between the United States and the State of Israel while exacerbating the perceived dichotomy between "Islam" and "the West."[12] The end of the Cold War had brought questions about Israel's strategic value to American national interests. One practical effect of this reassessment was Secretary of State James Baker's public suggestion in 1992 that U.S. loan guarantees should be linked with a freeze on Israeli settlement activity. 9/11, on the other hand, ensured that both dimensions of the special bond between Israel and the United States— the strategic and the "cultural-ideological-moral"[13]—would continue for the foreseeable future.

The spectacular violence of 9/11 reintroduced Islam to the West as a deadly, if not existential threat. Eschatology writers responded, in part, by casting Islam as the Antichrist to be battled in the last days. In 2002, for instance, Hal Lindsey published the virulently anti-Islamic *Everlasting Hatred: The Roots of Jihad*. His conclusion pointed to Armageddon as "the climax of hate."[14] In message and tone, Lindsey reflected Joseph Mede's confidence in the coming "extermination" of God's enemies. For many Americans, 9/11 reintroduced Islam to its long-held place as a central character in Judeo-centric prophecy interpretation. In the eyes of many Americans, the old enemy returned and the clash was confirmed. The order of the ages became apparent yet again.

The return of Islam to the center of eschatological speculation brought the return of historicist hermeneutics. As this book has shown, both emphases developed from the English Protestant tradition of Judeo-centric biblical interpretation. Just as many evangelicals and fundamentalists sought to deuteronomically discern the moral causes for God to lift the blessing of protection on 9/11, others, such as Sen. James Inhofe, focused on what those events had to say about Christian responsibility to strengthen the relationship between the United States and the State of Israel.

The State of Israel, the People of Israel

Although reflections on the threat of Islam had not been a prominent feature of American Protestant prophecy interpretation during the Cold War, historicism, as a hermeneutical methodology, had been confirmed for most evangelicals and fundamentalists over sixty years before September 2001. The historical/theological fact of the State of Israel caused historicism to blossom, on theological ground cultivated by Blackstone. In contrast to the tradition as it had developed since the early seventeenth century, British and American evangelicals in the nineteenth century became convinced that Jewish restoration to Palestine would occur apart from Jewish national conversion to Protestant faith. Although Blackstone had spent most of his career in Christian evangelism working specifically for Jewish conversion, his interpretive method crystallized when he discerned that, in the movement of secular Jewish Zionism, prophecy was being fulfilled not only in his time but in front of his eyes. The events of the Balfour Declaration in 1917, the founding of the State of Israel in 1948, and, especially, its expansion in 1967 validated his blend of futurism and historicism. The expectation of Jewish national restoration, which until these events was a reified theological symbol, entered historical reality.

Thus, the State of Israel validated a theological commitment centuries in the making.

The State of Israel was not only a political *fait accompli* but a theological datum. As shown by the childhood testimonies from Richard Land and John Hagee in chapter one, the significance of the founding, continued existence, and expansion of the State of Israel was broadly and deeply felt throughout American popular culture, especially among evangelical and fundamentalist Christians. As chapter two has shown, this significance is still widely accepted by white traditionalist Protestants. The founding of the State of Israel has since been celebrated by dispensationalists as a turning point in both human history and divine timing. For this book, however, it is most important to observe how, for many Americans, the founding of the State of Israel yet again revolutionized the typological identification of American self-understanding and vocation with the Israelite national covenant with God.

In the colonial and revolutionary eras, Anglo-American Protestants appropriated to themselves biblically informed constructions of Jewish identity and vocation. When, through civil millennialism, the apocalyptic hope contained within this appropriated identity was collectivized and transferred to the emerging American state, the United States came to be understood as the agent of apocalyptic redemption. Jewish covenantal identity (constructed through Anglo-American Protestant lenses) was retained as the typological referent for American national vocation. As chapter two shows, the majority of Americans who believe that "The U.S. has a special role to play in world affairs and should behave differently than other nations" have also welcomed the State of Israel as a fellow worker for the redemption of humanity.

This typology was manifested with the founding of the State of Israel in 1948. Since that event, the State of Israel has taken the place of the people of Israel as the typological referent within Judeo-centric Christian thought. In the minds of American Christian Zionists (making no claims about Jewish understandings of the State of Israel), 1948 is a functional parallel to 1776, the dates when the "two nations under God"[15] were manifested historically in order to realize their conjoined destinies. American evangelical and fundamentalist Christian recognition of the apocalyptic significance of the State of Israel echoes their recognition of the same significance in the United States. This chronological sequence, however, does not diminish Israel's typological primacy. In this polyphony of typologies, the State of Israel remains the tonic, the main note of the key. Awareness of these typological shifts clarifies the interaction of contemporary American Christian Zionism with American politics and U.S. foreign policy.

CUFI founder John Hagee provides the clearest contemporary example of this way of interpreting history. In the same way Hagee categorizes and interacts with Jews according to their compatibility with his eschatological expectations—for instance dismissing "the nonreligious Jews who believe political solutions only come through the peace process" as fodder for the coming Antichrist[16]—he interprets the United States and the State of Israel according to their apocalyptic significance. Convinced that we are living in the "terminal generation" before the rapture and all that follows,[17] Hagee, departing from the tradition of civil millennialism, places little hope in the United States as God's instrument for redeeming the world. When, in Hagee's scripturally imagined future, the Russian-Arab axis invades Israel for the battle of Armageddon, the United States "will not come to Israel's rescue. They will not send massive military forces to drive Russia and the Arabs out of Israel. Instead, the Western World is simply going to make a passive diplomatic response."[18] Despite his ultimate pessimism that the United States can or will finally "save" the State of Israel from its scripturally determined fate, Hagee is focused on preserving Israeli security and power up to the point he is snatched away with other true Christians to watch the tribulation from the ultimate skybox.[19]

Until that point, however, Hagee is committed to influencing U.S. policy to maximize Israel's ability to pursue its interests. He raises the alarm about support for Israel in the same way he decries a bevy of domestic policies he interprets as unfaithful to God's will for any nation, using the national-covenantal grammar of the American Jeremiad: "America is at the crossoads! Will we believe and obey the Word of God concerning Israel, or will we continue to equivocate and sympathize with Israel's enemies?" The difference with those other issues, however, is that the State of Israel is the singular arbiter of how God will judge faithfulness to God's purposes in history: "God is rising to judge the nations of the world based on their treatment of the State of Israel." Echoing Jerry Falwell's claim that 9/11 was caused by secularists who convinced God to lift the "curtain of protection" long encircling the United States, Hagee observes that the United States is "bogged down in an unprovoked, worldwide war with radical Islamic terrorists with no end in sight. . . . This is not a time to provoke God and defy Him to pour out His judgment on our nation for being a principal force in the division of the land of Israel."[20] In addition to recognizing that Jews have not been replaced in God's economy, humanity must accept that the State of Israel has been established as the sole criterion of righteousness.

For John Hagee, the national vocation of the United States is solely bound up with its protection of the State of Israel. The typological referent maintains its primacy. At the same time, however, one gets the impression from Hagee's writings that the State of Israel is less important for the benefits it brings to Jews (security and communal continuity, for instance) than to the verification the nation-state provides for his Judeo-centric faith. The State of Israel is the primary point of reference of his apocalyptic hope and for his theology of Jewish-Christian relationships. "On May 15, 1948, a theological earthquake leveled replacement theology when national Israel was reborn after nearly two millennia of wandering," he says. It is this state—in its founding, expansion, and preservation—that provides Hagee's prophetic foundation: "Their rebirth was living, prophetic proof that Israel has not been replaced." Since the Israelite covenant holds, so too does "God's blood covenant with Abraham for the royal land grant of Israel."[21]

Hagee is sincere in his belief: for him, the State of Israel seems as essential to his Christian faith as it is for the self-understanding of many Jews. If indeed the State of Israel were ever subjected to truly existential threat, or if it were to somehow cease to exist, Hagee's entire worldview would crumble, his system of prophecy interpretation invalidated, leveled by a theological earthquake. Dependent on the vagaries of political developments for its validation, Hagee's theological system is fundamentally tenuous. The theological datum of the State of Israel must therefore be preserved at all costs. Ernest Tuveson has said that this way of thinking "calmly assumes that ends justify means."[22] And as prominent evangelical leader Richard Mouw has observed, "Evangelicals who are Christian Zionists want to see events unfold, but they aren't so concerned about justice."[23]

Although contemporary American Christian Zionists can be counted on to earnestly seek the greatest flexibility for the State of Israel to pursue its self-interest, they pursue political engagement through a framework of Judeo-centric prophecy interpretation that constructs Jews as theological symbols for the realization of Christian apocalyptic hope. As Judeo-centric English Protestants manufactured apocalyptic roles for Jews banished from their society, contemporary Christian Zionism is concerned less with flesh-and-blood Jews than with preserving its own Christian theopolitical hope. Concern for the system outweighs concern for persons, whether they are Israeli Jews, Arab citizens of Israel, Palestinian Muslims, Palestinian Christians, or Iranians on whom Hagee has called for a preemptive nuclear strike.

American popular affinity for the State of Israel extends far beyond groups of politically active Christian Zionists. "Liking it or not," Peter Grose has observed,

> Americans and Israelis are bonded together like no two other sovereign peoples. As the Judaic heritage flowed through the minds of America's early settlers and helped to shape the new American republic, so Israel restored adopted the vision and the values of the American dream. Each, the United States and Israel, grafted the heritage of the other onto itself [24]

Just as apocalyptic hope was realized in human history with the American Revolution, many Americans see the typological referent of American apocalyptic nationalism in the State of Israel. Drawing from this well of apocalyptic hope and following trails blazed by Joanna and Ebenezer Cartwright and William Blackstone, Christian Zionists seek to marshal resources and influence policy to ensure the preservation of the State of Israel, the typological touchstone without which their individual and collective lives would have no meaning. Protecting the typological referent of the State of Israel, therefore, "may be more desired then our owne salvation."[25]

Notes

INTRODUCTION

1. John Mearsheimer and Stephen Walt, "The Israel Lobby," *London Review of Books* (March 23, 2006): 3–12.
2. For a good summary of the early controversy surrounding the essay, see "Of Israel, Harvard and David Duke," *The Washington Post*, March 26, 2006.
3. Walter Russell Mead, "God's Country?" *Foreign Affairs* 85:5 (Sept./Oct. 2006): 41.
4. James W. Skillen, "Evangelicals and American Exceptionalism," *The Review of Faith & International Affairs* 4:3 (Winter 2006): 45, 46.
5. Walter Russell Mead, "The New Israel and the Old," *Foreign Affairs* 84:4 (July/ Aug. 2008): 30.
6. Both of the major U.S. reports on global security since 9/11 have identified the central goal of resolving the Israeli-Palestinian conflict. See Thomas H. Kean, Lee H. Hamilton, co-chairs, *The 9/11 Commission Report: Final Report of the National Commission on Terrorist Attacks upon the United States* (New York: W.W. Norton, 2004); and James A. Baker and Lee H. Hamilton, co-chairs, *The Iraq Study Group Report: The Way Forward—A New Approach* (New York: Vintage Books, 2006).
7. Herbert Butterfield, *The Whig Interpretation of History* (1931; repr., New York: W.W. Norton, 1965), 11, 62, 63.
8. Barbara W. Tuchman, "Preface from the 1983–1984 Edition," *Bible and Sword: England and Palestine from the Bronze Age to Balfour* (1956; reprint, New York: Ballantine, 1984), xii.
9. Eitan Bar-Yosef, "Eccentric Zion: Victorian Culture and the Jewish Restoration to Palestine," in *The Holy Land in English Culture, 1799–1917: Palestine and the Question of Orientalism* (Oxford: Oxford University Press, 2005), 183–84.
10. Shirley Jackson Case, *The Millennial Hope: A Phase of War-Time Thinking* (Chicago: University of Chicago Press, 1918).

11. George M. Marsden, *Fundamentalism and American Culture*, second ed. (New York: Oxford University Press, 2006), 252.

12. Leonard I. Sweet, "Christopher Columbus and the Millennial Vision of the New World," *The Catholic Historical Review* 72:3 (July 1986), 370. See also Christopher Columbus, *The Journal of Christopher Columbus During His First Voyage, 1492–93*, ed. and trans. Clements R. Markham (London: Hakluyt Society, 1893), esp. 139; John Hubers, "It is a Strange Thing: The Millennial Blindness of Christopher Columbus," *Missiology* 37:3 (July 2009): 333–53; and Djelal Kadir, *Columbus and the Ends of the Earth: Europe's Prophetic Rhetoric as Conquering Ideology* (Berkeley: University of California Press, 1992). Kadir is keen to demonstrate that the goal of reconquest provided Columbus's "enterprise of the Indies" with an "ideological 'cloak' of crusade" (80).

CHAPTER I

1. James M. Inhofe, "Senate Floor Statement of Senator Inhofe: America's Stake in Israel's War on Terrorism," December 4, 2001. http://inhofe.senate.gov (accessed September 5, 2010). In March 2002, Sen. Inhofe repeated the same seven points in another Senate floor speech titled "Peace in the Middle East."

2. Transcript, "Hardball with Chris Matthews," (9:00 PM ET, CNBC), May 1, 2002. http://www.counterpunch.org/armey0502.html (accessed September 5, 2010).

3. See David Jackson, "Armey Backs off Palestinian View," *Dallas Morning News*, May 3, 2002.

4. Tom DeLay, "Be Not Afraid," July 30, 2003. In February of that year—the day the space shuttle Columbia disintegrated on reentry with Israeli astronaut Ilan Ramon aboard—DeLay expressed an even more profound self-identification with Israel, if not Judaism, by reciting, in Hebrew, the last lines of the *kaddish*, the Jewish prayer for the dead.

5. President James Carter and Prime Minister Menachim Begin, "30th Anniversary of the State of Israel Remarks at a White House Reception" (May 30, 1978). *The Jewish Virtual Library*, http://www.jewishvirtuallibrary.org/jsource/US-Israel/Carter_Begin4.html (accessed September 25, 2012).

6. "Obama: Israel's Security Sacrosanct," *The Jerusalem Post*, February 27, 2008.

7. Quoted in "Zion's Christian Soldiers: Conservative Christian Says Founder of Islam Set a Bad Example," *CBSNews: 60Minutes*, June 8, 2003. This story accompanied a rebroadcast of the original report from Bob Simon on October 6, 2002, in which Jerry Falwell declared, "I think Mohammed was a terrorist. I read enough of the history of his life, written by both Muslims and non-Muslims, that he was a violent man, a man of war."

8. David Gelernter, *Americanism: The Fourth Great Western Religion* (New York: Doubleday, 2007).

9. Kathleen Christison, *Perceptions of Palestine: Their Influence on U.S. Middle East Policy* (Berkeley: University of California Press, 1999), 92–93.

10. A good resource on this history is provided by Rollin Armour, Sr., *Islam, Christianity, and the West: A Troubled History* (Maryknoll: Orbis, 2002). See also Norman Daniel, *Islam and the West: The Making of an Image*, rev. ed. (Oxford: OneWorld, 1993); John V. Tolan, *Saracens: Islam in the Medieval European Imagination* (New York: Columbia University Press, 2002); Douglas Little, *American Orientalism: The United States and the Middle East since 1945* (Chapel Hill: University of North Carolina Press, 2002); Emran Qureshi and Michael A. Sells, eds., *The New Crusades: Constructing the Muslim Enemy* (New York: Columbia University Press, 2003).

11. In 2010, a strong debate erupted in the Jewish community regarding Zionist leadership's ability to engage American Jews, especially youth. See Peter Beinart, "The Failure of the American Jewish Establishment," *New York Review of Books*, June 10, 2010.

12. Nimrod Novik, *The United States and Israel: Domestic Determinants of a Changing US Commitment* (Boulder, CO: Westview, 1986), 71.

13. See George W. Bush, "President Bush's Address on Terrorism Before a Joint Meeting of Congress," *New York Times*, September 21, 2001. Although neither the phrase nor the concept were new with 9/11, the implications of a war on terror were never greater.

14. Notice here the unidirectional nature of this affinity. Although there certainly are reciprocations of this affinity from the State of Israel, they are not necessary for maintaining the American impulse.

15. John Hagee, *In Defense of Israel: The Bible's Mandate for Supporting the Jewish State* (Lake Mary, FL: Frontline, 2007), 10–11.

16. The Pew Forum on Religion & Public Life, "Event Transcript: God's Country? Evangelicals and U.S. Foreign Policy," Pew Research Center, Washington, D.C., September 26, 2006.

17. L. Nelson Bell, "Unfolding Destiny," *Christianity Today* 11:21 (July 21, 1967), 28. An editorial one month earlier carried this title: "War Sweeps the Bible Lands: Frantic Nations Forget that the Prophetic Vision of World Peace is Messianic," *Christianity Today* 9:19 (June 23, 1967). There, it is noted that concerns expressed by the United Nations are marginal compared to God's prophetic timetable.

18. Hal Lindsey, with Carole C. Carlson, *The Late, Great Planet Earth* (Grand Rapids: Zondervan, 1970), 124, 133, 152.

19. Nicolae Carpathia, previously a low-level staffer from Romania, suddenly ascends to power in the first novel of the series. See Tim LaHaye and Jerry Jenkins, *Left Behind: A Novel of Earth's Last Days* (Wheaton, Ill.: Tyndale, 1995). In the second novel, *Tribulation Force: The Continuing Drama of Those Left Behind* (Wheaton, Ill.: Tyndale, 1995), a U.S. militia, joined by forces from Egypt and England, attack the United Nations headquarters relocated to Babylon.

20. David Aikman, "Christians in Zion," *The American Spectator* 28 (December 1995), 64.

21. Matt Rees, "Christian Zionists Scorn Barak for Refusing to Address Gathering," (Edinburgh) *The Scotsman*, September 29, 1999, 12.

22. See Grace Halsell, *Prophecy and Politics: Militant Evangelists on the Road to Nuclear War* (Westport, CT: Lawrence Hill, 1986), esp. 74–76, 171–73, 191. Referencing Novik and Halsell, Charles Smith notes that "how Menachim Begin used his ties to Falwell to lobby Reagan foreshadows Binyamin Netanyahu's use of Falwell to lobby Congress against Bill Clinton after 1996." See *Palestine and the Arab-Israeli Conflict: A History with Documents*, 4th ed. (Boston: Bedford/St. Martin's, 2001), 387.

23. The full name of the peace plan was "A Performance-Based Roadmap to a Permanent Two-State Solution to the Israeli-Palestinian Conflict." Contemporary Christian Zionist literature suspects *each* of the non-U.S. members of the Quartet to be unabashed enemies of the State of Israel; for many, the U.S. is the only potentially righteous component of this group.

24. Quoted by Malcolm Foster, "Christian Zionists Feel the Heat for Fighting Peace: Extremists Wield Considerable Power within Republican Party," *The Daily Star* (Beirut), July 26, 2003, 3.

25. Mike Evans, *Israel: America's Key to Survival* (Mike Evans Ministries, Inc., 1983).

26. Michael D. Evans, *Beyond Iraq—The Next Move: Ancient Prophecy and Modern Day Conspiracy Collide* (Lakeland, FL: White Stone, 2003), 11.

27. Ibid., 45, 100, 120–21.

28. It was widely believed that the disengagement from Gaza was intended to consolidate Israeli control over the West Bank. See Ari Shavit, "Weisglas: Disengagement is Formaldehyde for Peace Process," *Ha'aretz*, October 8, 2004. See also Ari Shavit, Aluf Benn, and Yair Ettinger, "U.S. asks Israel to clarify comments made by top PM aide," *Ha'aretz*, October 7, 2004.

29. See "US Christian broadcaster says Sharon's stroke divine retribution," *Agence France-Presse*, January 5, 2006; and Daniela Deane, "White House Denounces Robertson's Remarks on Sharon," *Washington Post*, January 6, 2006. A transcript of the remarks was posted by Media Matters for America (www.mediamatters.org). Soon after, it was announced that Robertson's plans for a biblically-themed amusement park in northern Israel would lose Israeli backing due to the offensive nature of his comments. See Greg Myre, "Israelis' Anger at Evangelist May Delay Christian Center," *New York Times*, January 12, 2006. The business deal was soon restored.

30. For the breadth of this tradition, including its politically conservative and progressive applications, see Andrew R. Murphy, *Prodigal Nation: Moral Decline and Divine Punishment from New England to 9/11* (New York: Oxford University Press, 2009).

31. See the transcript at "PFAW President, Ralph G. Neas, Addresses Divisive Comments by Religious Right Leaders," People for the American Way, September 13, 2001. http://www.pfaw.org (accessed September 11, 2010).

32. "Pastor John Hagee on Christian Zionism," interview by Terry Gross, *Fresh Air from WHYY*, September 18, 2006. The same program featured this soundbite from a Hagee sermon: "For those of you who are in Washington, Jerusalem is not up for negotiation with anyone for any reason at any time in the future, regardless of what your Roadmap of Peace calls for. There are people in this nation who still believe the Bible takes precedent over Washington, DC." The rhetoric of official CUFI print publications are more analytical and less incendiary. See, for instance, John Hagee, "CUFI and the Peace Process," in *The Torch: Christians United for Israel Magazine* (October 2007): 6–7.

33. John Hagee, *Jerusalem Countdown: A Warning to the World* (Lake Mary, FL: Front Line, 2006), 197, 194, 201. Amy Frykholm has noted that Hagee blends support for Israel with the distinctive characteristics of the "prosperity gospel" common in Pentecostal circles: "Drawing from roots in dispensational theology and Pentecostalism, Hagee's ministry adds elements of the global prosperity gospel and combines it all with a special passion for the defense of the state of Israel. These concerns may not all fit together smoothly at all times, but for the 19,000 members of Cornerstone Church, Hagee's ministry appears to be an effective appeal to hope, desire and fear" (Amy Frykholm, "Calculated Blessings: A Visit to John Hagee's Church," *The Christian Century*, October 7, 2008, 37).

34. Ori Nir, "Christian Pro-Israel Lobby Gets a Boost," *The Forward*, April 3, 2006.

35. James D. Besser, "Growing Acceptance Seen of Fiery Pastor," *The Jewish Week* (New York), May 4, 2007.

36. David Horovitz, "Evangelicals Seeing the Error of 'Replacement Theology,'" *Jerusalem Post*, March 20, 2006.

37. David D. Kirkpatrick, "For Evangelicals, Supporting Israel Is 'God's Foreign Policy,'" *New York Times*, November 14, 2006.

38. John Hagee, "Speech at AIPAC Policy Conference 2007," delivered March 11, 2007. http://www.aipac.org/Publications/SpeechesByPolicymakers/Hagee-PC-2007.pdf (accessed September 11, 2010).

39. John Hagee, *Day of Deception: Separating Truth from Falsehood in These Last Days* (Nashville: Thomas Nelson, 1997), 43. This antipathy to the United Nations is shared by many supporters of the State of Israel. See, for instance, Dore Gold, *Tower of Babble: How the United Nations Has Fueled Global Chaos* (New York: Crown Forum, 2004). In the 1990s, Gold was Israel's ambassador to the U.N.

40. Hagee, *Jerusalem Countdown*, 80.

41. Hagee, *In Defense of Israel*, 158.

42. See "U.S. pro-Israel Evangelical Leader Hagee Endorses McCain," (Israel) *Ha'aretz*, February 28, 2008; Liz Halloran, "McCain Is Fighting to Win the Catholic Vote," *U.S. News & World Report*, March 12, 2008; Neela Banerjee and Michael Luo, "McCain Cuts Ties to Pastors Whose Talks Drew Fire," *New York Times*, May 23, 2008; and "Hagee, McCain part ways," *Jewish Telegraphic Agency*, May 22, 2008.

43. See David Corn, "McCain's Pastor Problem: The Video," *Mother Jones.com*, May 8, 2008; and Brian Ross, Avni Patel, and Rehab el-Buri, "McCain Pastor: Islam is a 'Conspiracy of Spiritual Evil,'" *ABC News*, May 22, 2008.

44. John Hagee, *Beginning of the End: The Assassination of Yitzhak Rabin and the Coming Antichrist* (Nashville: Thomas Nelson, 1996), 24, 20. This simplistic taxonomy ignores the vast complexities within Arab cultures, including the presence of Arab Christian communities in all of their diversity. See, for instance, Betty Jane Bailey and J. Martin Bailey, *Who Are the Christians in the Middle East?* (Grand Rapids: Eerdmans, 2003); Charles M. Sennott, *The Body and the Blood: The Holy Land's Christians at the Turn of a New Millennium* (New York: Public Affairs, 2001); and, on Palestinian Christians, see Mitri Raheb, *I am a Palestinian Christian* (Minneapolis: Fortress, 2005).

45. Hagee, *Jerusalem Countdown*, 33, 43. Hagee includes an abridged version of Inhofe's speech.

46. John Hagee, "Speech at AIPAC Policy Conference 2007."

47. Hagee, *Jerusalem Countdown*, 107, 196.

48. John Hagee, *Can America Survive? Ten Prophetic Signs that We Are the Terminal Generation* (New York: Howard, 2010), 109. Cf. *Beginning of the End*, 23–24 and *Defense of Israel*, 162–63.

49. The letter, along with other documents, can be found on the website of Churches for Middle East Peace. http://www.cmep.org/Legislative_Issues/McCollum_Hammond_%20Letter.pdf (accessed September 11, 2010).

50. E.J. Kessler and Marc Perelman, "Foxman Blasts Campaign to 'Christianize' American Life," *The Forward*, November 11, 2005; and Jennifer Siegel, "Christian Right Leader Warns Foxman on Israel," *The Forward*, December 23, 2005. On Hagee's vetting process, see, for instance, Ori Nir, "Christian Pro-Israel Lobby Gets a Boost," *The Forward*, April 7, 2006, which reported Hagee's meeting with member groups during the Conference of Presidents of Major American Jewish Organizations.

51. Abraham H. Foxman, "Jews and Evangelicals: Support for Israel Isn't Everything," *Time Magazine*, January 16, 2007. Foxman's article was a counterpoint to an enthusiastic acceptance of evangelical support written by Ze'ev Chafets, "Can Jews and Evangelicals Get Along?"

52. "Rabbis Told Jews to Shun Evangelicals," *Jerusalem Post*, September 24, 2007.

53. See especially Yaakov Ariel, *Evangelizing the Chosen People: Missions to the Jews in America, 1880–2000* (Chapel Hill: University of North Carolina Press, 2000); and *Philosemites or Antisemites? Evangelical Christian Attitudes toward Jews, Judaism, and the State of Israel*. Analysis of Current Trends in Antisemitism 20. Jerusalem: Vidal Sassoon International Center for the Study of Antisemitism, 2002.

54. Cited in Paul C. Merkley, *Christian Attitudes towards the State of Israel* (Montreal: McGill-Queen's University Press, 2001), 204.

55. James D. Besser, "Growing Acceptance Seen of Fiery Pastor," *The Jewish Week* (New York), May 4, 2007.

56. Ilan Chaim, "Falwell: Jews Can Get to Heaven," *Jerusalem Post*, March 1, 2006. Falwell's response was reported widely. See "Falwell Denies Report That He Believes Jews Don't Need Jesus," Associated Press (March 2, 2006).

57. Hagee, *Jerusalem Countdown*, 185, 133, 144, 158, 170, 175.

58. Hagee, *In Defense of Israel*, 137, 140, 143, 145, 134, 148.

59. Hagee, *Jerusalem Countdown*, 167–68, 181.

60. Hagee, *Beginning of the End*, 28, 130, 14, 8, 30. Luckily for Christians who share Hagee's inside track on divine knowledge of the future, "information about how to identify the Antichrist is of no practical value to the [raptured] Church since we will be watching from the balconies of heaven by the time he is revealed" (135).

61. Hagee, "Speech at AIPAC Policy Conference 2007."

62. Fresh Air from WHYY, "Gershom Gorenberg on Christian Zionism" (September 18, 2006), available at www.npr.org. See also Gershom Gorenberg, "Unorthodox Alliance: Israeli and Jewish Interests Are Better Served by Keeping a Polite Distance from the Christian Right," *Washington Post*, October 11, 2002, A37.

CHAPTER 2

1. George M. Marsden, *Fundamentalism and American Culture*, second ed. (New York: Oxford University Press, 2006), 247.

2. Robert Ruby, "A Six-Day War: Its Aftermath in American Public Opinion," Pew Forum on Religion & Public Life (May 30, 2007).

3. Hazel Erskine, "The Polls: Western Partisanship in the Middle East," *The Public Opinion Quarterly* 33:4 (Winter 1969–1970): 628, 627. Robert Ruby's interpretation of polling results through significant events in Middle Eastern and North America contexts shows that more "Americans sympathize with Israel when it is perceived to be facing acute threats, or when the United States itself appears to be threatened by part of the Arab or Muslim world." Regarding Palestinians, on the other hand, "American sympathy generally rises when relations between Israel and the Palestinians show signs of growing closer. And it falls when Americans feel threatened by the Arab or Muslim world."

4. Lydia Saad, "Palestinian-Israeli Dispute Engenders American Sympathy for Israelis: Public's Views Have Become More Polarized over Last 10 Years," *Gallup News Service*, March 5, 2007. See also Lydia Saad, "Support for Israel in U.S. at 63 percent, Near Record High: Near-record-low 30 percent optimistic about Arab-Israeli peace," *Gallup Organization*, February 24, 2010. In Feb. 2010, another Gallup poll measured Americans' opinions of several countries. In that poll, 67 percent of respondents expressed a favorable view of the State of Israel, with 25 percent sharing an unfavorable view. Attitudes toward the Palestinian Authority were almost a mirror image, with 20 percent of Americans viewing

the Palestinian Authority favorably, 70 percent unfavorably. Of the countries listed, only Afghanistan, North Korea, and Iran ranked lower than the Palestinian Authority in American esteem. See Lydia Saad, "In U.S., Canada Places First in Image Contest; Iran Last: Favorable views of Russia, Palestinian Authority up slightly; views of Iraq down," *Gallup Organization*, February 19, 2010.

5. Hillary Rodham Clinton, "Secretary Clinton with Vice President Joe Biden Announce Appointment of Special Envoy for Middle East Peace George Mitchell and Special Representative for Afghanistan and Pakistan Richard Holbrooke," U.S. Department of State, Announcement of Appointment (Washington, DC), January 22, 2009. http://www.state.gov/secretary/rm/2009a/01/115297.htm (accessed September 25, 2012).

6. See, "Americans' Support for Israel Unchanged by Recent Hostilities: Domestic Political Distemper Continues," *Pew Center for the People & the Press*, July 26, 2006.

7. "Ideological Gaps Over Israel on Both Sides of Atlantic," *Pew Research Center Publications*, January 29, 2009.

8. "Americans Closely Divided Over Israel's Gaza Attacks," *Rasmussen Reports*, December 31, 2008.

9. Lydia Saad, "Americans Not Pressing for Bigger Role in Gaza Conflict: Few Believe Obama Should Announce His Views before He's President," *Gallup Organization*, January 9, 2009.

10. The full name of the peace plan was "A Performance-Based Roadmap to a Permanent Two-State Solution to the Israeli-Palestinian Conflict." Contemporary Christian Zionist literature suspects *each* of the non-U.S. members of the Quartet to be unabashed enemies of the State of Israel; for many, the U.S. is the only potentially righteous component of this group.

11. David W. Moore, "Widespread Support for Palestinian State: But Public Skeptical about Peace Prospects," *Gallup News Service*, June 3, 2003. See also Steven Krull, "Americans on the Middle East Road Map," *The Program on International Policy Attitudes (PIPA)/Knowledge Networks Poll: The American Public on International Issues*, May 30, 2003.

12. See the discussion of QME in Jeremy M. Sharp, "U.S. Foreign Aid to Israel," Congressional Research Service Report to Congress (September 16, 2010), p. 3–4, available online at http://www.fas.org/sgp/crs/mideast/RL33222.pdf (accessed January 29, 2012). The Naval Vessel Transfer Act of 2008 defines QME as "the ability to counter and defeat any credible conventional military threat from any individual state or possible coalition of states or from non-state actors, while sustaining minimal damage and casualties, through the use of superior military means, possessed in sufficient quantity, including weapons, command, control, communication, intelligence, surveillance, and reconnaissance capabilities that in their technical characteristics are superior in capability to those of such other individual or possible coalition of states or non-state actors."

13. Krull, "Americans on the Middle East Road Map." When "asked what they thought the US 'generally does,' a clear majority (57 percent) said the US generally takes Israel's side. Only 29 percent thought the US generally does not take a side in the conflict (Palestinians' side, 3 percent)."

14. Gary L. Bauer, et al, "Letter to President Bush," American Values, May 19, 2003. http://www.ouramericanvalues.org/press_release_article.php?id=26 (accessed September 13, 2010).

15. James D. Besser, "Mitchell As Envoy Could Split Center," *The Jewish Week*, January 21, 2009.

16. Jim Brown, "Mitchell wrong for Middle East referee?" *OneNewsNow.com*, January 22, 2009.

17. Jeff Sallot, "Neutrality on Mideast favoured, polls find," (Toronto) *Globe & Mail*, November 12, 2004.

18. Pew Research Center, "Ideological Gaps Over Israel on Both Sides of Atlantic," *Pew Research Center Publications*, January 29, 2009.

19. Jodie T. Allen and Alec Tyson, "The U.S. Public's Pro-Israel History: In Mid-East Conflicts, Americans Consistently Side with Israel," *Pew Research Center*, July 19, 2006.

20. Ibid. Notably, "Israel was the only country, aside from the U.S., in which a majority said that U.S. policies lead to more stability in the region." See also the BBC World Service Poll (PIPA/GlobeScan), "Israel and Iran Share Most Negative Ratings in Global Poll," March 6, 2007.

21. James L. Guth, Cleveland R. Fraser, John C. Green, Lyman A. Kellstedt, and Corwin E. Smidt, "Religion and Foreign Policy Attitudes: The Case of Christian Zionism," in *Religion and the Culture Wars: Dispatches from the Front*, ed. John C. Green, James L. Guth, Corwin E. Smidt, and Lyman A. Kellstedt (Lanham, Md.: Rowman & Littlefield, 1996), 335, 338. The purpose of this project differs fundamentally from those of sociologists like Rodney Stark and his repeated attempts to apply economic models to religious systems. See, for instance, Roger Finke and Rodney Stark, *The Churching of America—1776–1990: Winners and Losers in Our Religious Economy* (New Brunswick: Rutgers University Press, 1992). For the theoretical underpinnings of this reading of history, see Rodney Stark, "Bringing Theory Back In," in *Rational Choice Theory and Religion: Summary and Assessment*, ed., Lawrence E. Young (New York: Routledge, 1997), 3–23.

22. Will Herberg, *Protestant-Catholic-Jew: An Essay in American Religious Sociology* (Garden City, N.Y.: Doubleday, 1955). Herberg's effort was itself an attempt to shape interreligious engagement in a post-war era.

23. Guth, et al (1996), 334.

24. Ibid., 348, 345.

25. Ibid., 354.

26. Kenyon N. Griffin, John C. Martin, and Oliver Walter, "Religious Roots and Rural Americans' Support for Israel during the October War," *Journal of Palestine*

Studies 6:1 (Autumn 1976): 104–14. Especially for their definition of religious "orthodoxy," the authors drew principally from Rodney Stark and Charles Y. Glock, *American Piety: The Nature of Religious Commitment* (Berkeley: University of California Press, 1968), and Charles Y. Glock and Rodney Stark, *Christian Beliefs and Anti-Semitism* (New York: Harper & Row, 1966).

27. Ronald R. Stockton, "Christian Zionism: Prophecy and Public Opinion," *Middle East Journal* 41:2 (Spring 1987): 245, 248. The full question read, "In 1948 Israel became a nation once again. Many people believe that that event was the fulfillment of Biblical prophecy. Others say that while Israel is a country governed by Jews, its existence has nothing to do with Biblical prophecy. Which of these points of view seems more correct to you? Is Israel the fulfillment of Biblical prophecy or is it not?" (234–35)

28. Ibid., 251.

29. Council for the National Interest, "Poll: One-third of American voters believe in Christian Zionism," October 13, 2006. The poll was commissioned by the Council for the National Interest (CNI), a lobbying group in Washington, D.C., associated with several former foreign service officers and political leaders critical of U.S. policy tilt toward Israel. These results formed the centerpiece of a CNI presentation on Capitol Hill. Stephen Spector reports that pollster John Green "considers those numbers to be suspiciously high." See Stephen Spector, *Evangelicals and Israel: The Story of American Christian Zionism* (New York: Oxford University Press, 2009), 297 n11.

30. Lydia Saad, "Holy Land, or Just Ancient?" *Gallup News Service*, July 29, 2003.

31. Frank Newport and Joseph Carroll, "Republicans and Religious Americans Most Sympathetic to Israel," *Gallup News Service*, March 27, 2006. In this poll, black respondents "just 40 percent side with the Israelis, while 24 percent side with the Palestinians. This 16 percentage-point gap among blacks is among the lowest for any identifiable subgroup in this analysis."

32. The implications of this finding may remind one of the commitments of so-called "civil religion" in President Eisenhower's reported observation that "Our government makes no sense unless it is founded in a deeply felt religious faith—and I don't care what it is." Cited in Robert N. Bellah, "Civil Religion in America," *Dædalus, Journal of the American Academy of Arts and Sciences* 96:1 (Winter 1967): 1–21. On the provenance of the tradition, see Patrick Henry, "'And I Don't Care What It Is': The Tradition-History of a Civil Religion Proof-Text," *The Journal of the American Academy of Religion* 49:1 (1981): 35–49.

33. As one Gallup report explained in 2006, "The Gallup polls in which the Middle East sympathies question has been asked over recent years not typically included a measure of a respondent's religious identification, forestalling in-depth investigation of [the] hypothesis" that conservative religious orientations inform sympathies surrounding the Middle East. (Newport and Carroll, "Republicans and Religious Americans.")

34. The Pew Forum on Religion & Public Life, "American Evangelicals and Israel," no date.

35. This report was released under two titles: *Religion and the 2004 Election: A Pre-election Analysis* (located at http://pewforum.org/newassets/misc/green-full.pdf), and *The American Religious Landscape and Political Attitudes: A Baseline for 2004*. http://www.uakron.edu/bliss/docs/Religious_Landscape_2004.pdf (accessed February 16, 2009).

36. Green (2004), 4–5. Green's apparatus and methodology allowed for measuring the views of subgroups "not usually identified in surveys, such as traditionalists (strongly orthodox belief and high level of religious engagement), centrists (moderate belief and engagement), and modernists (strongly heterodox belief and lower levels of engagement) among white Protestants and Catholics."

37. Krull, "Americans on the Middle East Road Map."

38. Green (2004), 35, 36. Since the question is about the direction of U.S. policy rather than the conflict itself, it cannot be assumed that those offering no opinion side with either Palestinians or Israelis.

39. Green (2004), 36.

40. *Many Americans Uneasy with Mix of Religion and Politics*, Pew Research Center for The People & The Press and Pew Forum on Religion & Public Life, August 24, 2006.

41. Guth, et al (1996), 349–50.

42. Spector, 188, according to e-mail correspondence with John Green.

43. Newport and Carroll (2006). It is interesting to note that this survey did, in fact, collect data on black attitudes on sympathies toward Israel, but that when religious variables were introduced into the analysis, blacks were dropped from consideration.

44. Brian D. McKenzie, "Polling Data and Black Religious Opinion on Middle East Concerns," *The Review of Faith & International Affairs* (Spring 2008): 28. Notable exceptions to this paucity of awareness of black foreign policy perspectives include Hanes Walton, *Invisible Politics: Black Political Behavior*, SUNY Series in Afro-American Society (Albany: State University of New York Press, 1985); Michael Dawson, *Behind the Mule: Race and Class in African-American Politics* (Princeton: Princeton University Press, 1994); and Robert C. Smith and Richard Seltzer, *Contemporary Controversies and the American Racial Divide* (Lanham, Maryland: Rowman and Littlefield, 2000).

45. Green (2004), 3, 5–6. No explanation is given as how respondents are categorized if they cannot simply fit into one of the offered racial categories.

46. See James L. Guth, John C. Green, Lyman A. Kellstedt, and Corwin E. Smidt, "Faith and Foreign Policy: A View from the Pews," *The Review of Faith and International Affairs* 3:2 (Fall 2005): 5.

47. Newport and Carroll (2006). "Fifty-eight percent of whites say they sympathize with the Israelis, while just 14 percent sympathize more with the Palestinians.

Among blacks, just 40 percent side with the Israelis, while 24 percent side with the Palestinians. This 16 percentage-point gap among blacks is among the lowest for any identifiable subgroup in this analysis." 26 percent of whites offered no opinion, compared to 35 percent of black respondents.

48. Stockton (1987) also measured that persons he identified as Christian Zionists are significantly committed to nationalist interpretations of American mission; 94 percent of identified Christian Zionists that "America has a unique destiny." (250–51)

49. Robert Kagan and William Kristol, "The Bush Doctrine Unfolds," *The Weekly Standard*, March 4, 2002, 11.

50. R. Drew Smith, "Black Denominational Responses to U.S.-Middle East Policy since 9/11," in *The Review of Faith & International Affairs* (Spring 2008), 8, 15.

51. A report of Trotter's speech, discussed by R. Drew Smith, is available at BlackElectorate.com (viewed March 1, 2010). Trotter is pastor of Sweet Holy Spirit Full Gospel Baptist Church in Chicago, IL.

52. McKenzie, 30.

53. By whiteness, I do not here refer to whiteness as a *condition of being*, an empirical reality, rather than a constructed ideological category. On the latter, see, for instance, Shannon Sullivan, *Revealing Whiteness: The Unconscious Habits of Racial Privilege* (Bloomington: Indiana University Press, 2006).

54. Cited in Spector, 188.

CHAPTER 3

1. Kenneth M. Setton, *Western Hostility to Islam and Prophecies of Turkish Doom* (Philadelphia: American Philosophical Association, 1992), 17. Setton provides a fascinating discussion of the prophetic tenor of the time, among both Christians and Muslims.

2. Nabil Matar, "The Idea of the Restoration of the Jews in English Protestant Thought: From the Reformation until 1660," *The Durham University Journal* 78 (Dec. 1985): 25, 26.

3. Martin Luther, "Defense and Explanation of All the Articles, 1521," trans. Charles M. Jacobs, rev. George W. Forell, in *Luther's Works*, American Edition (55 vols.; ed. Jaroslav Pelikan and Helmut T. Lehmann; Philadelphia: Muehlenberg and Fortress, and St. Louis: Concordia, 1955–86; hereafter, *LW*), *LW* 32:89–90. The evangelicals were not opposed to war against the Turk, but were opposed, instead, to the manipulation of religion (including the granting of indulgences) in support of war. See "The Augsburg Confession, Article XXI: Concerning the Cult of the Saints," in *The Book of Concord: The Confessions of the Evangelical Lutheran Church*, ed. Robert Kolb and Timothy J. Wengert (Minneapolis: Fortress, 2000), 58–59.1. (Hereafter, *BC*) *The Joint Declaration on the Doctrine of Justification*, adopted by the Lutheran World Federation (LWF) in October

1999, repudiates the identification of the pope as the Antichrist. This understanding remains the doctrinal commitment of some Lutheran churches not within the LWF.

4. On this dual identification of the Antichrist, see Robert O. Smith, "Luther, the Turks and Islam," *Currents in Theology & Mission* 34:5 (October 2007): 351–64. For a history of Lutheran engagement with Islam, see David D. Grafton, *Piety, Politics and Power: Lutherans Encountering Islam in the Middle East* (Eugene, OR: Pickwick, 2009).

5. *LW* 2:281; 3:122.

6. Martin Luther, D. Martin Luthers *Werke: Kritische Gesamtausgabe* (Weimar: H. Bohlau, 1883–). Hereafter, *WA*, with reference to *Briefe* (Br) and *Tischreden* (TR). *WA* 30:2, 195.

7. *WA* TR 3:158, 3055b: "Spiritus Antichristi est papa, caro Antichristi est Turca, quia hic ecclesiam spiritualiter, ille corporaliter devastate." The record at 3055a is even more direct: "Corpus Antichristi est simul papa et Turca, quia corpus constituitur corpore et anima. Spiritus Antichristi est papa, caro eius Turca, qui corporaliter infestat ecclesiam, ille spiritualiter. Sunt tamen ambo exuno domino, Diabolo, cum papa sit mendax et homicida Turca."

8. *LW* 3:37. See also *LW* 4:29.

9. See "The Augsburg Confession," in *BC* 30–31.1.

10. E. Theodore Bachmann, "Introduction" to Martin Luther, "On Translating: An Open Letter (1530)," *LW* 35:175. The text of the pamphlet is collected in *D. Martin Luthers Werke*, Kritische Gesamtausgabe (Weimar: 1883–) (hereafter, *WA*), at *WA* 30^{II}, (220) 223–36.

11. Martin Luther, "Preface to the Prophets" (1532/1545), in *LW* 35:265–66.

12. More recently, Lutheran biblical scholars have reemphasized pastoral apocalypticism. As Craig R. Koester says, "Revelation warns readers not to be deceived into despair." This insight can "provide a helpful alternative to reading Revelation without either dismissing its message or reducing it to a code" See *Revelation and the End of All Things* (Grand Rapids: Eerdmans, 2001), 12. A similar approach is taken by Barbara R. Rossing, *The Rapture Exposed: The Message of Hope in the Book of Revelation* (Boulder, CO: Westview, 2004).

13. See *LW* 35:294, n. 142. Luther later prepared an extensive, heavily anti-papist commentary on Daniel 12 (*WA*, DB 6, lxxxix).

14. Martin Luther, "Preface to the Prophet Daniel (1530), *LW* 35:300, 296.

15. Martin Luther, "Preface to the Revelation of St. John" (1522), *LW* 35:398, 399. This shorter preface was included in editions of Luther's New Testament translation from 1522 to 1527; it was superseded by the preface written in 1530.

16. Martin Luther, "Preface to the Revelation of St. John (1530/1546), *LW* 35:400. This new preface appeared in all following editions of the *Deutsche Bibel*. Citations are from the 1546 edition of the Bible.

17. Luther, "Preface to the Revelation of St. John," *LW* 35:401, 404.

18. Luther, "Preface to the Revelation of St. John," *LW* 35:404–405, 406–407, 408, 409, 411. On Luther's charge that both the Turk and the pope both establish "a counterfeit church of external holiness," see Sarah Henrich and James L. Boyce, "Martin Luther—Translations of Two Prefaces on Islam: Preface to the *Libellus de ritu et moribus Turcorum* (1530), and Preface to Bibliander's Edition of the Qur'ān (1543)," *Word & World* 16:2 (Spring 1996): 250–66. Luther consistently criticizes both Islam and Roman Catholicism for what he sees as their identical qualities.

19. Martin Luther, "The Smalcald Articles" (1537), *BC* 308–9.9–14. On comparisons of pope and Turk, cf. *BC* 225.18.

20. Philip Melanchthon, "Treatise on the Power and Primacy of the Pope" (1537), 337.39, 339.57.

21. Robin Bruce Barnes, *Prophecy and Gnosis: Apocalypticism in the Wake of the Lutheran Reformation* (Stanford: Stanford University Press, 1988), 42.

22. John Calvin, *Semons of M. Iohn Calvine upon the Epistle of Saincte Paule to the Galathians*, trans. Arthur Golding (London: Lucas Harison and George Bishop, 1574), 109. See also John Calvin, *Sermons of Master Iohn Calvin, upon the booke of Iob*, trans. Arthur Golding (London: Lucas Harison and George Byshop, 1574), 79–80. These citations from early editions of Calvin's work in England show the currency of his ideas in the Elizabethan context.

23. John Calvin, *A Harmonie upon the Three Euangelists, Matthew, Mark and Luke, with the Commentarie of M. Iohn Calvine*, trans. Eusebius Pagit (London: Thomas Dawson, 1584), 368.

24. John Calvin, *The Sermons of M. Iohn Calvin upon the Fifth Booke of Moses called Deuteronomie*, trans. Arthur Golding (London: Henry Middleton and George Bishop, 1583), 666.

25. Jaroslav Pelikan, *The Reformation of the Bible, The Bible of the Reformation* (New Haven: Yale University Press, 1996), 28–29.

26. See Pelikan, 29, and Avihu Zakai, *Exile and Kingdom: History and Apocalypse in the Puritan Migration to America*, Cambridge Studies in Early Modern and British History (Cambridge: Cambridge University Press, 1992), 21–22. For one insight into Luther's view of allegorical interpretation, see his excursus, "Concerning Allegories" (*LW* 2:150ff, within his lectures on Genesis).

27. Zakai, *Exile and Kingdom*, 19, 21, 24. Zakai incorrectly says that Luther's later preface to Revelation appeared in 1545 rather than 1530 and thus incorrectly implies that it was influenced by Melanchthon's work on the *Chronicle*. Further, Zakai egregiously takes Luther out of context by implying that he claimed certainty in his interpretation of Revelation. Luther may be confident in his interpretation of scripture, but he is rarely certain. Zakai assumes uniform epistemology across all Protestant hermeneutical lines.

28. Bernard McGinn, "Revelation," in *The Literary Guide to the Bible*, ed. Robert Alter and Frank Kermode (Cambridge: Belknap/Harvard, 1987), 529.

29. Benjamin A. Ehlers, "Luther and English Apocalypticism: The Role of Luther in Three Seventeenth-Century Commentaries on the Book of Revelation," *Essays in History* 34 (1992).

30. McGinn, "Revelation," 534, 535.

31. Two editions of *The Image of Both Churches* will provide the basis of this discussion. The British Library has a copy of the first edition that unfortunately lacks the first part of the book: John Bale, *The Image Of bothe churches after the moste wonderfull and heavenley Revelacion of Sainct John the Evangelist* (Antwerp: S. Mierdman, 1545). A complete copy of the 1570 edition will also be referenced: John Bale, *The Image of bothe Churches, after the most wonderfull and heavenly Revelation of sainct Iohn the Euangelist*, second ed. (London: Thomas East, 1570).

32. Bale, *Image* (1545), 122–23; also *Image* (1570), 130.

33. Bale, *Image* (1570), 453, 2.

34. Bale, *Image* (1570), 2–3.

35. Bale, *Image* (1545), 146. Given this early example, and the continuing anti-Catholicism we will see, one can forgive William Donohue's incredulity at Hagee's attempt to explain that references to the "whore of Revelation" in his preaching do not reference the Roman Catholic Church. Bale delighted in identifying the Catholic Church as the whore of Babylon introduced in Rev. 17 and condemned in Rev. 19. At different points, he described the whore as "execrable," "glittering," "stinking," and "pestiferous," while calling those who followed her "the superstycyous church of Antichrist, the filthy famelye of spiritual whoremongers, gluttons, & hypocrytes, yea, the execrable Sinnagog of Sathan in déede." Bale, *Image* (1570), 2, 377–78, 356, 339. Bale's attacks on the priesthood were especially pointed: "The filthy whoremongers . . . consecrate themselues vnto Moloch in the fyre of fleshly concupiscence. For ever have they for sworne godly marryage, to make daily sacryfyce to the divell in buggary and other carnall beastlynesse. The most highly estemed vertue of that generation, is to have no wyves" (400).

36. Bale, *Image* (1545), 6, 50. See also 53, 86, 109–110.

37. Bale, *Image* (1570), 378, 100. Bale comprehends the common error of Islam and Catholicism as primarily theological, owing to their incomplete confession of the Gospel: "Mahomete [called] Christ the worde of God, the spirite of God, and the soule of God, the most excellent Prophet and the worthiest among creaturs. But in no case wyll hée have hym taken for the sonne of GOD, no more than the Pope wyll have hym taken for a full savyour wythout hys masses and suffrages" (377).

38. Bale, *Image* (1545), 99. Cf. "For so well ys the Gentile that hath faythe/a perfyght Israelyte,/as ys the Christen Iewe" (Bale, *Image*, 1545, p. 77). And, "For so well is the gentle that hath faith, a perfecte Israeltie, as is the Christen Iew. Yea, much rather was Zachius for his faith iudged Abrahams childe, thã was Simon for fulfilling the workes of yᵉ lawe. For God is not parciall. Whatsoever he be [that]

feareth him & worketh rightuousenesse, is accepted with him. And so is it ment heare. And therefor is not the difference written here as in ye other place, but al is ioyned in one, to comprehende all under one" (Bale, *Image*, 1570, p. 241–42). And Bale, *Image* (1570), p. 241–42.

39. Bale, *Image* (1545), 81.

40. Bale, *Image* (1570), 143, 413.

41. See, for instance, Bale, *Image* (1545), 7: "Not the earthlye Hierusalem ys thys cyte/buylded of menne/and made holye by the outwarde obseruacions and ceremonies of the iewes as manye expositours hath fantasyed. For of that (like as Christ prophecied) ys not left one stone standinge vpon an other. But thys cyte ys the sure buyldinge of God/grounded vpon the stronge foundacion of the Apostles and Prophetes/euen vpon the harde rocke stone Iesus Christ."

42. *The Bible and Holy Scriptures Conteyned in the Olde and Newe Testament, Translated According to the Ebrue and Greke, and conferred With the best translations in divers langues, With moste profitable annotations vpon all the hard places, and other things of great importance as may appeare in the epistle to the reader* (Geneva: Rouland Hall, 1560). An appreciation can be found in Bruce M. Metzger, "The Geneva Bible Of 1560," *Theology Today* 17:3 (Oct. 1960): 339.

43. Pelikan, 54.

44. *The Bible and Holy Scriptures Conteyned in the Olde and Newe Testament* (1560). Cf. Theodore Bèza, ed., *The Newe Testament of Our Lorde Iesus Christ* (Geneva: Conrad Badius, 1557), 257–59. The Geneva Bible was controversial, drawing both attack and defense. See, for instance, William Fulke, *A Defense of the sincere and true Translations of the Holie Scriptures into the English tong[ue] against the manifolde cauils, friuolous quarels, and impudent slaunders of Gregorie Martin, one of the readers of popish diuinitie in the trayterous Seminarie of Rhemes* (London: Henrie Bynneman, 1583). Fulke appended his book with a brief refutation of "quarrels . . . uttered by diverse papists in their English pamphlets" against his own writings. Bèza's note for Luke 21:24—"Ierusalem shal be troden under fote of the Gentils, untyl the tyme of the Gentils be fulfilled."—was more Judeo-centric than the 1560 Geneva Bible interpretation: "This is after the tymes appointed for the salvation of the Gentils & punishment of the Iewes" (136).

45. Ibid., Cf. *The Newe Testament of Our Lord Jesus Christ* (1557), 407, 406, 408, 407, 409. Most contemporary biblical scholars agree that intra-communal polemics were the foundation of rhetoric within the book of Revelation. See, for instance, Adela Yarbro Collins, "The Apocalypse (Revelation)," in *The New Jerome Biblical Commentary*, ed. Raymond E. Brown, Joseph A. Fitzmyer, and Roland E. Murphy (Englewood Cliffs, NJ: Prentice Hall, 1990), esp. 1002, 1003.

46. Bale, *Image* (1570), 4.

47. John Bale, *The Actes of Englysh votaryes* (Antwerp: S. Mierdman, 1546).

48. F.J. Levy, *Tudor Historical Thought* (San Marino, Calif.: Huntington Library, 1967; reprint Toronto: University of Toronto Press, 2004), 90.
49. Bale, *The actes of Englysh votaryes*, 24. Cf. Levy, 91.
50. Bale, *Image* (1545), 146.
51. John Foxe, *Actes and Monuments of these latter and perillous dayes touching matters of the Church, wherein ar comprehended and decribed the great persecutions [and] horrible troubles, that haue bene wrought and practised by the Romishe prelates, speciallye in this Realme of England and Scotlande, from the yeare of our Lorde a thousande, vnto the tyme nowe present* (London: John Day, 1563). Bale and Foxe knew each other well, even living together briefly upon returning from exile.
52. Felicity Heal, "Appropriating History: Catholic and Protestant Polemics and the National Past," *The Huntington Library Quarterly* 68:1/2, The Uses of History in Early Modern England (2005), 110. Cf. Levy, 104. "At his death Foxe left an unfinished commentary on Revelation called the *Eicasmi*, which was more mathematically precise and historicizing in its attempts to correlate history and prophecy than Bale had been" (McGinn, "Revelation," 536).
53. Zakai, 33. On Foxe, see William Haller, *Foxe's Book of Martyrs and the Elect Nation* (London: J. Cape, 1963).
54. Anne McLaren, "Gender, Religion, and Early Modern Nationalism: Elizabeth I, Mary Queen of Scots, and the Genesis of English Anti-Catholicism," *The American Historical Review* 107:3 (June 2002): 746, 745, 747.
55. Ibid., 766, 763, 758–59. McLaren acutely analyzes the gender dynamics behind and beneath this polemic: "Alert readers" of the second edition of *Actes and Monuments* "could understand that the two queens themselves represented these two churches and see beyond them to their ur progenitors, Henry VIII and the pope, God and Satan" (763).
56. Matar, 23.
57. The persistence of anti-Jewish attitudes in a polity free of Jews has often been remarked on as an example of the persistence of antisemitism. See, for instance, David Glassman, *Anti-Semitic Stereotypes Without Jews: Images of the Jews in England 1290–1700* (Detroit: Wayne State University Press, 1975), and observations on the socially constructed nature of antisemitism in Daniel Jonah Goldhagen, *Hitler's Willing Executioners: Ordinary Germans and the Holocaust* (New York: Vintage, 1997), 41.
58. Sharon Achinstein, "John Foxe and the Jews," *Renaissance Quarterly* 54:1 (Spring 2001): 86–120. Achinstein offers a troubling misreading of Bale, asserting that "Bale's Protestant mission terrifyingly calls for a compulsory conversion" (105). The context of the cited passage is against Catholics, not Jews; this misreading hinges on the assumption that in this instance Bale used "Antichrist" to refer to Jews. The article also understates Foxe's interest in the place of Jews in an apocalyptic scheme.

59. John Foxe, *A Sermon preached at the Christening of a certaine Iew at London, by Iohn Foxe. Containing an exposition of the xi. Chapter of S. Paul to the Romanes*, trans. James Bell (London: n.p., 1578), 106, 2, 28, 97, 103.

60. See, for instance, Ehle, 47–48, and Clark, 32.

61. Francis Kett, *An Epistle Sent to Divers Papistes in England proving the Pope to bee the Beast in the 13 of the Reuelations* (London: Henry Marsh, 1585).

62. Francis Kett, *The Glorious and beautifull garland of mans glorification* (London: Roger Ward, 1585), ii, verso 9, verso 15.

63. Cited in "Appendix A" in Alexander Balloch Grosart, ed., *The Life and Complete Works in Prose and Verse of Robert Greene*, 15 vols. (London: Huth Library, Printed for private circulation only, 1881–86), vol. 1, 260, 262, 260, 259. In 1592, one of Kett's critics who fondly remembered witnessing Kett's burning elaborated the charges against the condemned: "he held that whosoever wilbe saved, must before he dye, go to Ierusalem: that Christ with his Apostles, are now personally in Iudea gathering of his church: that ye faithfull should miraculously be preserved at Ierusalem, with a wall of fire, & be fed with Angels foode from heaven." See William Burton, *Dauids Evidence; or, The assurance of Gods Love Declared in Seuen Sermons* (n.p., 1592), 138.

64. John Napier, *A Plaine Discouery of the whole Reuelation of Saint Iohn* (Edinburgh: Robert Walde-Grave, 1593), 5, 6, 235–36, 241, note "n"; see also 59–61, propositions 32 and 33.

65. John Merbecke, *A Booke of Notes and Common places* (London: Thomas East, 1581), 525.

66. Thomas Morton of Berwick, *A Treatise of the Threefolde state of man* (London: R. Robinson for Robert Dexter and Raph Jackeson, 1596), 336.

67. John Dove, *A Confutation of Atheisme* (London: Printed by Edward Allde for Henry Rockett, 1605), 43–44.

68. Arthur Dent, *The Ruine of Rome: or, An exposition vpon the whole Reuelation* (Essex: Arthur Dent, 1603), 10, 99, 118–20, 123.

69. See ibid., 124, 125. Dent's confidence in the power of the Bible is similar to Luther's own faith in the power of the Word (see *LW* 51:77).

70. Ibid., 151–52, 207–208.

71. See John Hagee, *Jerusalem Countdown: A Warning to the World* (Lake Mary, FL: Front Line, 2006), esp. chap. 3.

72. Dent, *Ruine of Rome*, 243, 244, 278, 245.

73. A self-published book by Henoch Clapham demonstrates the popularity of these ideas. Clapham anticipated that the "universall conversion of the Iewes, shall bring with it a mightie advantage to the Church." He noted that "many learned Romanistes" have been studying Hebrew so that when they "turne themselves from Babel to the Ghospell" they will "bring with them a mighty people." Therefore, as "the meanes of the Iewes universall calling groweth, so, the strength and glory of the Romish Babel declineth." See Henoch Clapham, *A chronological discourse. . . .* (London: n.p., 1609), 50–51.

CHAPTER 4

1. Hans J. Hillerbrand, *The Division of Christendom: Christianity in the Sixteenth Century* (Louisville, KY: Westminster John Knox, 2007), 261.

2. Thomas Draxe, "The Generall signes and forerunners of Christs comming to judgement," in *The Churches Securitie, Togither with the Antidote or preservative of ever waking faith* (London: George Eld and John Wright, 1608), 39, 40, 36–37.

3. Thomas Draxe, *The Worldes Resurrection, or The generall calling of the Iewes* (London: G. Eld and John Wright, 1608), 3, 63–64.

4. See, for instance, John Hagee, *In Defense of Israel: The Bible's Mandate for Supporting the Jewish State*, first ed. (Lake Mary, FL: Front Line, 2007), esp. chap. 8, "Our Debt to the Jewish People."

5. Draxe, *The Worldes Resurrection*, 74–75, 80.

6. Ibid., 87, 90, 88, 89.

7. Zakai, *Exile and Kingdom*, 46.

8. Thomas Brightman, *Apocalypsis apocalypseos. . . .* (Francofurti: Prostat apud viduam Levini Hulsij, 1609), first published in English as Thomas Brightman, *A Revelation of the Apocalyps, that is, The Apocalyps of S. Iohn, illustrated with an Analysis & Scolions* (Amsterdam: Iudocus Hondius & Hendrick Laurenss, 1611). Four editions were published up to 1644; all but one of the final editions, which was printed in London, were published in the Netherlands. All citations are to the first English edition.

9. See Hugh Ross Williamson, *The Gunpowder Plot* (New York: Macmillan, 1952), and Antonia Fraser, *Faith and Treason: The Story of the Gunpowder Plot* (New York: Random House, 1997).

10. Brightman, *A revelation of the Apocalyps*, 318.

11. Zakai, 46.

12. Brightman, *A revelation of the Apocalyps*, 103, 104, 108.

13. See, for instance, John Hagee's claim that "God is rising to judge the nations of the world based on their treatment of the State of Israel" in *Jerusalem Countdown: A Warning to the World* (Lake Mary, FL: Front Line, 2006), 201.

14. Brightman, *A revelation of the Apocalyps*, 318, 319, 415–16. Regarding the Queen's enemies, it is possible that Brightman is referencing the 1588 defeat of the Spanish Armada. Richard Bauckham, arguing that apocalyptic rhetoric is concerned with otherworldly rather than temporal and political matters, too simplistically locates the rise of English self-confidence only after the defeat of the Armada. As we have seen, this event, although significant, was hardly the beginning of English apocalyptic nationalism. See *Tudor Apocalypse: Sixteenth Century Apocalypticism, Millenarianism and the English Reformation: From John Bale to John Foxe and Thomas Brightman* (Oxford: Sutton Courtenay Press, 1978).

15. Ibid., 319, 415–16.

16. Dent, *The ruine of Rome*, 258–59.

17. Brightman, *A revelation of the Apocalyps*, 439, 440, 440–41, 442, 441. In most subsequent English-language editions, "rumour" is substituted for "bruit."

18. Ibid., 441, 442.

19. Ibid., 443, 687.

20. Thomas Brightman, *A Most Comfortable Exposition of The last and most difficult part of the prophecie of Daniel* (Amsterdam: G. Thorp, 1635), 36–39. See also Thomas Brightman, *The Revelation of Saint Iohn, Illustrated with Analysis and Scholions*, fifth ed. (Amsterdam: Thomas Stafford, 1644).

21. Thomas Brightman, *A commentary on the Canticles or the Song of Salomon. . . .* (London: John Field for Henry Overton, 1644), 1055. Cf. p. 1077: "I can light upon no mark or token of time that may give even the least conjecture; *Daniel* saith, after the destruction of the Turkish Empire, (which shall be destroyed by Conversion of the Iewes) a space shall be given for the rest of the Beasts to live, *even for a time, and a time appointed.*"

22. Brightman, *A revelation of the Apocalyps*, 441, 697.

23. Ibid., 700, 697.

24. Thomas Brightman, *Apocalypsis Apocalypseos*, third ed. (Leyden: John Class [J. Claesson van Dorpe], 1616), 1119. Reference copy from the Cambridge University Library.

25. Brightman, *A commentary on the Canticles or the Song of Salomon*, 1059–1060.

26. Willet's most famous book, *Synopsis Papismi*, a collection of religious disagreements between Catholics and Protestants, was first published in 1592; a fifth edition was published in 1634.

27. Andrew Willet, *Ecclesia Triumphans; that is, The Joy of the English Church* (Cambridge: John Legat, Printer to the Universitie of Cambridge, 1603), 82–87.

28. Andrew Willet, *Hexapla: that is, A Six-Fold Commentarie upon the most Divine Epistle of the holy Apostle S. Paul to the Romanes* (Cambridge: Cantrell Legge, printer to the Universitie of Cambridge, 1611), 469, 655–56, 511, 503.

29. Ibid., 508, 704.

30. Jean de L'Écluse, *An Advertisement to Everie Godly Reader of Mr. Thomas Brightman his book, namely, A revelation of the Apocalyps* (Amsterdam: G. Thorp, 1612), 10. John Fowler, et al, *A Shield of Defence against the Arrowes of Schisme Shot abroad by Iean de L'escluse in his advertisment against Mr. Brightman* (Amsterdam: Henry Laurenson, 1612).

31. Thomas Wilson, *A Christian Dictionarie Opening the signification of the chiefe words dispersed generally through Holie Scriptures of the Old and New Testament* (London: William Iaggard, 1612), 168, 160. Copy in the British Library. See also Samuel Purchas, *Purchas his Pilgrimage* (London: William Stansby and Henrie Fetherstone, 1613); Thomas Adams, *The Blacke Devill or The Apostate Together With The Wolfe Worrying the Lambes. And The Spiritual Navigator, Bound For the Holy Land. In three Sermons* (London: William Iaggard, 1615). See also John Boys, *The Autumne Part from the Twelfth Sundy after Trinitie, to the last in the*

whole yeere (London: Melchisedech Bradwood and William Aspley, 1613), which references Brightman in one explication of Revelation; *An Exposition of the Festivall Epistles and Gospels used in our English Liturgie Together with a reason why the church did chuse the same* (London: Eduuard Griffin for William Aspley, 1615); and *The Third Part from S. Iohn Baptists Nativitie to the last Holy day in the whole yeare* (London: William Aspley, 1615).

32. Patrick Forbes, *An Exquisite Commentarie upon the Revelation of Saint Iohn* (London: W. Hall and Francis Burton, 1613), 168. Forbes makes the interesting move of using the anti-allegorical literalism of Reformation hermeneutics against over-reaching restorationist interpretations (see 238, 140).

33. Thomas Cooper, *The Blessing of Japheth, Prouing The Gathering in of the Gentiles, and Finall Conuersion of the Iewes* (London: T. Creede and Richard Redmer, 1615), 53.

34. Thomas Draxe, *The Earnest of Our Inheritance Together with a Description of the New Heaven and the New earth, and a demonstration of the glorious Resurrection of the bodie in the same substance* (London: Felix Kingston and George Norton, 1613), A3. The theme does not reappear in the published text of the sermon.

35. Thomas Draxe, *An Alarum to the Last Iudgement* (London: Nicholas Okes and Matthew Law, 1615), 22. Victoria Clark, *Allies for Armageddon: The Rise of Christian Zionism* (New Haven: Yale University Press, 2007), 35, following Douglas J. Culver, *Albion and Ariel: British Puritanism and the Birth of Political Zionism* (New York: Peter Lang, 1995), incorrectly identifies this statement from Draxe as his endorsement of restorationism. The context rather indicates Draxe's ambivalence to the concept.

36. Draxe, *An Alarum to the Last Iudgement*, 107–108.

37. Draxe, *The Worldes Resurrection*, 88–89.

38. Draxe, *An Alarum to the Last Iudgement*, 74–76, 76–77, 81.

39. Draxe, *An Alarum to the last Iudgement*, 82–84.

40. For a list of Finch's other publications, see Wilfred R. Prest, "The Published Writings of Sir Henry Finch," Notes and Queries CCXXII (Dec. 1977): 501–503.

41. [Henry Finch?], *The Worlds Great Restauration, or The Calling of the Iewes, and (with them) of all the Nations and Kindomes of the earth, to the faith of Christ* (London: Edward Griffin and William Bladen, 1621).

42. Joseph Mede to Sir Martin Stuteville, March 31, 1621, in Thomas Birch and Robert Folkestone Williams, *The Court and Times of James the First: Illustrated by Authentic and Confidential Letters, from Various Public and Private Collections,* two vols. (London: Henry Colburn, 1848), 2:244, 250–51. See also, in the same volume, John Chamberlain, London, to Sir Dudley Carleton, July 21, 1621, esp. p. 270.

43. [Henry Finch?], *An Exposition of the Song of Solomon: called Canticles, Together with Profitable Observations, collected out of the same* (London: John Beale, 1615), 4–5, 71, 72, 125, 123.

44. Finch, *The Worlds great Restauration*, A1, A1–A2, A2–A3, A4, A3.

45. Ibid., 1–5, 9.
46. Ibid., 5–6, 6. See also 117: "the ports and gates. Literally and really, of Ierusalem or the land of Iudah, that they may come thicke and threefold thither from all places without check or controlment."
47. Ibid., 8.
48. Unlike Willet, Finch's appeal to the Bible is not a retreat into non-controversial safety. Legal historian Wilfrid Prest, "The Dialectical Origins of Finch's Law," *The Cambridge Law Journal* 36:2 (Nov. 1977): 326–52, notes Finch's commitment to Ramist logic. For a discussion of the function of Ramist thought within Puritan legal and theological discourse, see Brian Cummings, *The Literary Culture of the Reformation: Grammar and Grace* (Oxford: Oxford University Press, 2007), 252–64.
49. Norris, et al, *A History of the Christian Church*, 551. See Nicolas Bownd, *The Doctrine of the Sabbath, Plainely layde forth. . . .* (London: Widdow Orwin, for John Porter, and Thomas Man, 1595).
50. James's lack of contribution to the war effort is more charitably explained by the fact that the Puritan-dominated Parliament had been repeatedly dissolved and that England did not have the funds necessary for meaningful intervention.
51. As Mede wrote in a letter of April 1637, he had kept an "obstinate silence" on matters of dispute between various Christian groups at Cambridge. However, in order to avoid the charge of "too much . . . tenderness to the Puritan faction; which is a crime here, if it be once fastened upon a man," Mede thought it prudent "to declare my self . . . with that caution and tenderness, which might not give any just cause of offence to those who were contrary-minded." See Joseph Mede, "Epistle LXXI: Mr. *Mede*'s Answer to Dr. *Twisse*'s several Expostulations; together with his judgment of Mr. *Potter*'s Discourse touching the Number of the Beast, 666," in *The Works of the Pious and Profoundly-Learned Joseph Mede* (London: Roger Norton and Richard Royston, 1672), 848–89. Hereafter, *Works*.
52. Jeffrey K. Jue, *Heaven upon Earth: Joseph Mede (1586–1638) and the Legacy of Millenarianism*, Archives internationales d'histoire des idées, 194 (Dordrecht, The Netherlands: Springer, 2006), 155.
53. Robert Clouse, "The Apocalyptic Interpretation of Thomas Brightman and Joseph Mede," *Bulletin of the Evangelical Theological Society* 11:4 (Fall 1968): 190.
54. Jue, 99, 100.
55. Joseph Mede, *The Apostasy of the Latter Times* (London: Richard Bishop and Samuel Man, 1641), 69, 50, 51, 88.
56. Jue, 99, 98. Jue carefully states that *The Remaines* show that "Mede's conversion . . . was not entirely complete" (99). Mede's deep study of Revelation, culminating in the first edition of *Clavis Apocalyptica*, would complete the process.
57. Joseph Mede, *Remaines on some Passages in the Revelation*, 23, 24, 25.
58. Mede, *Remaines*, 28.
59. Mede, *Remaines*, 37–40.

60. Joseph Mede, *Clavis apocalyptica ex innatis et insitis visionum characteribus eruta et demonstrata* (Cantabrigiae [Cambridge]: T. and J. Buck, 1627); second ed. (Cantabrigiae: Thom. Buck, 1632); first English ed., *The key of the Revelation, searched and demonstrated out of the Naturall and proper Charecters of the Visions*, trans. Richard More (London: R.B. and Phil Stephens, 1643). Citations of *Clavis Apocalyptica* are from *A Translation of Mede's Clavis Apocalyptica*, trans. Robert Bransby Cooper (London: Rivington, 1833), based on the second Latin edition. The appearance of this translation in the early nineteenth century provides an interesting facet to the growth of millennial speculation in that period.

61. Bernard McGinn ("Revelation," 536) reports that John Foxe left behind "an unfinished commentary on Revelation called the *Eicasmi*, which was more mathematically precise and historicizing in its attempts to correlate history and prophecy than Bale had been." In a sense, Mede can be understood as extending that project as his interpretation of Revelation pushed on toward greater levels of coherence and verifiability.

62. Mede, *Clavis Apocalyptica*, 1, 2.

63. See Mede, *Clavis Apocalyptica*, 32, 38, 433–34, 435–36, 437, 438, 444. Mede's footnote is important: "If you except the principal articles of faith, I know not whether a similar testimony can be found to any Christian dogma. It is a great previous argument in its favour, that all the orthodox thought the same in the age next to the apostles. Justin became a Christian about thirty years after the death of St. John, in which time it is very probable many were alive who had heard the apostles teach" (444 n).

64. Mede, *Clavis Apocalyptica*, 421, 422, 423, 427.

65. Mede, *Clavis Apocalyptica*, 195, 197. Mede's historical calculation concerning the prophetic place of the Turks is difficult and precise: "that is, in the year of Christ 1453, they [the Turks] should utterly destroy the remnant of the Roman empire in the East, by the capture of the royal city of Constantinople. For the interval from 1057 to the year 1453, when Constantinople was taken, is precisely 396 years, of which a day forms one, a month thirty, and a year three hundred and sixty five. Such is here the accuracy of the calculation" (197).

66. Mede, *Clavis Apocalyptica*, 395, 396.

67. Mede, *Clavis Apocalyptica*, 430, 431, 429, 396, 397–98, 396–97.

CHAPTER 5

1. On how the sonnet and its structure allowed Milton to communicate his analysis of the political realities, see Janel Mueller, "The Mastery of Decorum: Politics as Poetry in Milton's Sonnets," *Critical Inquiry* 13:3, Politics and Poetic Value (Spring 1987): 475–508.

2. Johanna and Ebenezer Cartwright, *The Petition of the Jewes For the Repealing of the Act of Parliament for their banishment out of England, Presented to his Excellency*

and the generall Councell of Officers on Fryday January 5, 1648, With their favour-able acceptance thereof (London: George Roberts, 1649). Dating the petition is complicated by the "old style" and "new style" dating. Until 1752, England's civic year began on March 25. Thus, the petition, presented on January 5, fell within the year 1648 (Old Style) but would be understood in contemporary terms as 1649 (New Style). Nahum Sokolow includes the petition as a foundational docu-ment for proto-Zionist thought (*History of Zionism, 1600–1918*).

3. H. Henriques notes that although the Cartwright petition was favorably received by the War Council, it was, in effect "completely overlooked; at least nothing was done upon it nor was the law altered or relaxed in their favour." Nevertheless, there were many rumors that a change in policy had occurred. Henriques cites one circular published by "the disappointed and defeated Presbyterians entitled 'the last damnable Designe of Cromwell and Ireton and their Junto or Caball,' in which it is stated that 'their real designe is to plunder and disarme the City of London and all the country round about . . . and so sell it (the plunder) in bulk to the Jews, whom they have lately admitted to set up their banks and magazines of Trade amongst us contrary to an Act of Parliament for their banishment.'" See H.S.Q. Henriques, "The Jews and the English Law. IV," *The Jewish Quarterly Review* 14:4 (July 1902): 688.

4. David Katz questionably characterizes the petition as an "irrational" example of "the fantastic elements in the debate over the readmission of the Jews into Eng-land." See David S. Katz, "Edmund Gayton's Anti-Jewish Poem Addressed to Menasseh Ben Israel, 1656," *The Jewish Quarterly Review*, New Series 71:4 (April 1981): 242. For a more subdued description, see Nathan Osterman, "The Con-troversy over the Proposed Readmission of the Jews to England (1655)," *Jewish Social Studies* 3:3 (July 1941): 305.

5. For the most comprehensive analysis of Judeo-centric thought on English dis-course in the modern era, see the series of articles by Nabil Matar: "The Idea of the Restoration of the Jews in English Protestant Thought," as detailed in the bibliography.

6. Christopher Hill, "Till the Conversion of the Jews," in *The Collected Essays of Christopher Hill, Vol. 2: Religion and Politics in Seventeenth-Century England* (Am-herst: University of Massachusetts Press, 1985–1986), 273.

7. Christopher Hill, "Censorship and English Literature," in *The Collected Essays of Christopher Hill, Vol. 1: Writing and Revolution in Seventeenth-Century England* (Amherst: University of Massachusetts Press, 1985), 40.

8. See *Brightmans Predictions and Prophecies Written 46 yeares since* (London: n.p., 1641); and *Brightmans Iudgement, or prophecies what shall befall Germany, Scotland, Holland, and the Churches adhering to them. . . .* (London: R.H., 1641). These anon-ymous pamphlets were themselves printed in numerous versions and iterations.

9. Thomas Brightman, *A Commentary on the Canticles or the Song of Salomon. . . .* (London: Printed by John Field for Henry Overton, 1644), and Thomas Brightman,

The Revelation of St. Iohn Illustrated with an Analysis & Scholions, fourth ed. (London: Samuel Cartwright, 1644).

10. Sarah Hutton, "The Appropriation of Joseph Mede: Millenarianism in the 1640s," in *Millenarianism and Messianism in Early Modern European Culture: The Millenarian Turn*, ed. J.E. Force and R.H. Popkin (Netherlands: Kluwer, 2001), 5.

11. Richard Bernard, *A Key of knowledge For the opening of the secret mysteries of St Iohns mysticall Revelation* (London: Felix Kyngston, 1617), 336, 338, 339.

12. Hill, "Till the Conversion of the Jews," 274.

13. Joseph Mede, *The Works of the Pious and Profoundly-Learned Joseph Mede, B.D.*, ed. John Worthington (London: James Flesher for Richard Royston, 1664).

14. Hutton, "The Appropriation of Joseph Mede," 8, 9, 11.

15. On the Fifth-Monarchists, see, for instance, Philip G. Rogers, *The Fifth Monarchy Men* (New York: Oxford University Press, 1966); Bernard S. Capp, *The Fifth Monarchy Men: A Study in Seventeenth-Century English Millenarianism* (London: Faber, 1972); and Louise Fargo Brown, *The Political Activities of the Baptists and Fifth Monarchy Men in England during the Interregnum* (Washington, D.C.: American Historical Association; London: Oxford University Press, 1913).

16. Robert Maton, *Israel's Redemption or the Propheticall History of our Saviours Kingdome on Earth* (London: R. Cotes and Daniel Frere, 1642), A5, 5, 6. Maton extends this introductory discourse with a fascinating theology of Jewish-Christian purpose: "The truth is, both Jew and Gentile are sick in the same disease; as well the one, as the other would faine ingrosse the benefits of the Messiah severally to himselfe; whereas they belong indeed first and chiefely to the Jew; but onley, to neither. And never will the happinesse of either receive perfection (never shall they have full possession of the gifts and grace which Christ hath purchased for them) till both are folded together, till the time come, that One fold shall receive them, and One Shepherd feed them" (A5). This notion of rightly dividing God's word, drawn from 2 Timothy 2:15, is used to same Judeo-centric effect by Cyrus Scofield as the hermeneutical key for the *Scofield Reference Bible*, first published in 1909.

17. Westminster Assembly (1643–1652), *The Humble Advice of the Assembly of Divines now by Authority of Parliament Sitting at Westminster, Concerning a Larger Catechism Presented by Them Lately to Both Houses of Parliament* (London and Edinburgh: Evan Tyler, 1647), 53.

18. John Owen and Philip Nye, *A Declaration of the Faith and Order Owned and Practised in the Congregational Churches in England, Agreed Upon and Consented Unto by their Elders and Messengers in their Meeting at the Savoy, October 12, 1658* (London: J.P., 1659), XXVI:4–5, pp. 28–29.

19. *A Directory for the Publique Worship of God, Throughout the Three Kingdoms of England, Scotland, and Ireland; Together with an Ordinance of Parliament for the taking away of the Book of Common-Prayer* (London: Printed for Evan Tyler, Alexander Fifield, Ralph Smith, and John Field, 1644), 20–21.

20. Richard Hooker, *Of the Lawes of Ecclesiasticall Politie* (London: John Windet, 1593).

21. Sir Edwin Sandys, *A Relation of the State of Religion* (London: Val. Sims for Simon Waterson, 1605); George Sandys, *A relation of a iourney begun an: Dom: 1610 Foure bookes. Containing a description of the Turkish Empire, of AEgypt, of the Holy Land, of the remote parts of Italy, and ilands adjoyning* (London: Richard Field for W: Barrett, 1615); Richard Hakluyt, *The Principall Navigations, Voiages and Discoveries of the English nation made by Sea or ouer Land* (London: George Bishop and Ralph Newberie, 1589); and Thomas Coryate, *Coryats crudities hastily gobled up in five moneths travels* (London: William Stansby, 1611).

22. Theodore K. Rabb, "The Stirrings of the 1590s and the Return of the Jews to England" (delivered May 12, 1976) *Transactions of the Jewish Historical Society of England* 26 (1974–1978): 26, 29, 32–33 n.3, 32.

23. Francis Cheynell, *An Account Given to the Parliament by the Ministers Sent by Them to Oxford* (London: Printed by F.K. for Samuell Gellibrand, 1647), 13, 35.

24. Roger Williams, *The Bloudy Tenent, of Persecution, for cause of Conscience* (London, n.p., 1644), A3.

25. Ibid.

26. Matar, "The Idea of the Restoration of the Jews in English Protestant Thought: From the Reformation until 1660," 28.

27. Hugh Peters, *A word for the Armie. And two words to the kingdome: To Cleare the One, And Cure the Other* (London: M. Simmons and Giles Calvert, 1647), 11.

28. Edward Nicholas [Menasseh ben-Israel?], *An Apology for the Honorable Nation of the Jews, And all the Sons of Israel* (London: Printed by John Field, 1648/9). Like the Cartwright petition, the *Apology* is dated as 1648. The copy in the British Library includes an old, hand-written notation on the title-page, specifying the publishing date as February 21, presumably to demarcate between Old Style and New Style dating.

29. Ibid., 4, 5, 6.

30. Ibid., 11, 8, 8–9, 6, 7. The use throughout the *Apology* of "reduction" to describe the Jews' coming immigration to Palestine is precise. The *Oxford English Dictionary* defines "reduction" as "the action of bringing back a person, thing, institution, etc., to a place previously occupied; return, retrieval." *Oxford English Dictionary*, 3d ed. (Draft Revision, March 2010), s. v. "reduction, *n.*, I.3.a."

31. Ibid., 7, 8.

32. Ibid., 11, 12, 14, 15.

33. See Nahum Sokolow, *History of Zionism, 1600–1918*, vol. 2 (London: Longmans, Green, 1919), 182, referencing Israel Solomons, "Edward Nicholas," *Jewish Chronicle*, February 9, 1906. This attribution has gained acceptance. See Paul Johnson, *A History of the Jews* (New York: Harper & Row, 1987), 276.

34. Eduardo Nicholas [Menasseh ben-Israel?], *Apologia por la noble nacion de los Iudios y hijos de Israel* (Londres: E impresa en casa de Juan Field, 1649). The copy

of the *Apology*'s Spanish translation housed in the Yale University Library bears an undated inscription in Latin noting authorship by "Menaßie ben Israel."

35. Manasseh ben-Israel, *The Hope of Israel*, trans. Moses Wall (London: R.I. for Hannah Allen, 1650).

36. Edward Winslow, *The Glorious Progress of the Gospel amongst the Indians in New England* (London: Hannah Allen, 1649), 4.

37. Thomas Thorowgood, *Iewes in America, or, Probabilities that the Americans are of that Race; With the Removall of some contrary reasonings, and earnest desires for effectuall endeavours to make them Christian* (London: W.H., 1650).

38. Zvi Ben-Dor Benite, *The Ten Lost Tribes: A World History* (New York: Oxford University Press, 2009), 174. Special thanks to Santiago Slabodsky for pointing me to this resource.

39. Benite, 180.

40. See, for instance, the anonymous tract, *The Great Deliverance of The Whole House of Israel: What it truly is, by whom it shall be performed, and in what Year, Declared plainly by the word of God: In Answer to a Book called The Hope of Israel, Written by a Learned Jew of Amsterdam, Named Menasseh Ben Israel* (London: M.S., 1652): "Now let the Translator of Ben Israels hope, know, that God doth not promise mountains and performe mole-hills, nor promise eternall things, and performe with temporals, but that God is true of his word. And let him know that he himself, and all the rest of his Millenarian brethren, and Jew restorers for a thousand years, doe erre, not understanding the Scriputres" (55).

41. Moses Wall, "Considerations Upon the Point of the Conversion of the Jewes," in Manasseh ben-Israel, *The Hope of Israel*, trans. Moses Wall, second ed. (London: R. Ibbitson and Livewell Chapman, 1651), B1.

42. Ibid., 46, 47, 48.

43. Ibid., 49–54.

44. Matar, "The Idea of the Restoration of the Jews in English Protestant Thought," 34. Matar mistakenly describes Wall's purpose as "evangelical and missionary."

45. Toon, 122. Benite, 176. Many Jews have infused the modern State of Israel with messianic significance. See, for instance, the reconciliation ancient and modern ideas in Levinas's discussion of "non-apocalyptic messianism" in which "[Jewish thought . . . moves beyond beautiful dreams in order to accomplish an ideal in real terms which are set out by a State." Emmanuel Levinas, "Zionisms: The State of Caesar and the State of David," in *The Levinas Reader*, ed. Sean Hand (Oxford: Blackwell, 1989), 271.

46. See Toon, "The Question of Jewish Immigration," 117; and Ernestine G.E. van der Wall, "A Philo-Semitic Millenarian on the Reconciliation of Jews and Christians: Henry Jessey and his 'The Glory and Salvation of Jehudah and Israel' (1650)," in *Skeptics, Millenarians and Jews*, ed. David S. Katz and Jonathan I. Israel (The Netherlands: Brill, 1990): 161–84.

47. Manasseh ben-Israel, *To His Highnesse the Lord Protector of the Common-wealth of England, Scotland, and Ireland: The Humble Addresses of Menasseh Ben Israel . . . in behalfe of the Jewish Nation* (London, 1655).

48. Toon, 123, following Henry Jessey, *A Narrative Of the late Proceeds at White-hall concerning the Jews Who had desired by R[abbi] Manasses an Agent for them that they might return into England and Worship the God of their Fathers here in the Synagogues* (London: L. Chapman, 1656). Jessey lists the theological arguments used to justify allowing Jews to have a public life in England: "First, Christian gentiles were debtors of the Jews and so should help them (Romans 15:27). Secondly, in the reigns of kings John, Henry III and Edward I, the English badly treated the Jews and God's judgment might fall upon the Commonwealth if this opportunity for helping them in 1655 was not taken. Thirdly, God has commanded His people to give hospitality to strangers (Exodus 22:21, 23:9). Fourthly, since England had in recent days experienced many spiritual and temporal mercies, all of which came from Christ, the nations should help those who were the descendents of Abraham and of the same race as Jesus Christ" (125).

49. Ariel Hessayon, review of *Judaism without Jews: Philosemitism and Christian Polemic in Early Modern England*, by Eliane Glaser, Reviews in History 798 (Institute of Historical Research, University of London), http://www.history.ac.uk/reviews/review/798 (accessed January 30, 2012).

50. Arthur H. Williamson, "Britain and the Beast: The Apocalypse and the Seventeenth-Century Debate about the Creation of the British State," in *Millenarianism and Messianism in Early Modern European Culture: The Millenarian Turn*, ed. J.E. Force and R.H. Popkin (Netherlands: Kluwer, 2001), 22.

51. Williamson, "Britain and the Beast," 18, 22.

52. Ibid., 24, 25.

53. Thomas Cooper, *The blessing of Japheth proving the gathering in of the Gentiles, and finall conversion of the Iewes. Expressed in divers profitable sermons* (London: Richard Redmer, 1615), A2–3.

54. Hill, "Till the Conversion of the Jews," 278, 278–79.

55. Thorowgood, B6.

56. For Isaac Newton's thoughts on eschatology and prophetic interpretation, see his posthumously published *Observations upon the Prophecies of Daniel, and the Apocalypse of St. John, in two Parts* (London: J. Darby and T. Browne, 1733). See also Joseph Priestley, *Letters to the Jews; Inviting Them to an Amicable Discussion of the Evidences of Christianity* (Birmingham, 1786) and, for the response, David Levi, *Letters to Dr. Priestley, in Answer to Those He Addressed to the Jews* (London, 1787).

57. Ernest Lee Tuveson, *Redeemer Nation: The Idea of America's Millennial Role* (Chicago: University of Chicago Press, 1968), 213.

58. William E. Blackstone, *Jesus Is Coming* (Chicago: Fleming H. Revell, 1908/1916), 235.

CHAPTER 6

1. George Marsden, *Jonathan Edwards: A Life* (New Haven: Yale University Press, 2004), 89.

2. Ironically, the message of Jesus, as it is put forth in the Gospel According to St. Matthew, seeks to complexify and deemphasize this very scriptural theme.

3. Mark A. Noll, *America's God: From Jonathan Edwards to Abraham Lincoln* (New York: Oxford University Press, 2002), 38.

4. John Winthrop, "A Model of Christian Charity," in *God's New Israel: Religious Interpretations of American History*, ed., Conrad Cherry, revised ed. (Chapel Hill: The University of North Carolina Press, 1998), 40–41.

5. See especially Perry Miller, *Errand into the Wilderness*, first ed. (Cambridge: Harvard University Press, 1956); and Sacvan Bercovitch, *The Puritan Origins of the American Self* (New Haven: Yale University Press, 1975), and Sacvan Bercovitch, *The American Jeremiad* (Madison: University of Wisconsin Press, 1978).

6. Robert Middlekauff, *The Mathers: Three Generations of Puritan Intellectuals, 1596–1728* (London: Oxford University Press, 1971), 32.

7. Martin Luther, "Preface to the Prophets" (1532/1545), in *LW* 35:265–66.

8. Noll, *America's God*, 32–33.

9. Theodore Dwight Bozeman, *To Live Ancient Lives: The Primitivist Dimension in Puritanism* (Chapel Hill: The University of North Carolina Press, 1988), 193, 194, 228, 222).

10. John Cotton, *The Churches Resurrection, or the Opening of the Fift and sixt verses of the 20th Chap. of the Revelation* (London: Timothy Smart, 1656), 87, 88, 90. See also 89, 91. For Cotton's other collected lectures on Revelation from the same period, see *The Churches Resurrection, or the Opening of the Fift and sixt verses of the 20th Chap. of the Revelation* (London: Henry Overton, 1642); and *The powring out of the seven vials: or An exposition, of the 16. chapter of the Revelation, with an application of it to our times* (London: Henry Overton, 1642).

11. Cotton, *An exposition upon . . . Revelation*, 259, 260, 261. Cotton identified the pope as "one of the heads and rulers of this Beast, but yet distinguished from the beast it selfe, and is not the same with the beast." The "first beast" of Revelation 13, therefore, is "the Roman Catholick visible Church" (7).

12. Bozeman, 229–30, n. 85.

13. John Cotton, *A Brief Exposition Of the whole Book of Canticles, or, Song of Solomon; Lively Describing the Estate of the Church in all the Ages thereof, both Jewish and Christian, to this day* (London: Philip Nevil, 1642), 10, 193–94, 195, 196. See Thomas Brightman, *A commentary on the Canticles or the Song of Salomon . . .* (London: John Field for Henry Overton, 1644), 1055.

14. Edward Winslow, ed., *The glorious progress of the Gospel, amongst the Indians in New England. Manifested by three letters, under the hand of that famous instrument of the Lord Mr. John Eliot, and another from Mr. Thomas Mayhew* (London: Hannah Allen, 1649), 4, 16.

15. *Strength out of Weakness, or A Glorious Manifestation Of the further Progresse of the Gospel amongst the Indians in New-England* (London: John Blague and Samuel Howes, 1652), 6.

16. Giles Fletcher, *Israel Redux: or, The Restauration of Israel, Exhibited in Two Short Treatises* (London: John Hancock, 1677), 62.

17. See Gershom Scholem, *Sabbatai Ṣevi: The mystical Messiah, 1626–1676* (Princeton: Princeton University Press, 1973); and, for contemporary commentary on Tzvi, both negative and positive, see David J. Halperin, *Sabbatai Zevi: Testimonies to a fallen Messiah* (Oxford: Littman Library of Jewish Civilization, 2007).

18. Nabil I. Matar, "Milton and the Idea of the Restoration of the Jews," *Studies in English Literature, 1500–1900* 27:1 (Winter, 1987), 115.

19. Carl F. Ehle, Jr., "Prolegomena to Christian Zionism in America: The Views of Increase Mather and William E. Blackstone Concerning the Doctrine of the Restoration of Israel" (Ph.D. diss., Institute of Hebrew Studies, New York University, October 1977), 80.

20. Increase Mather, *The Mystery of Israel's Salvation, Explained and Applied: or, A Discourse Concerning the General Conversion of the Israelitish Nation* (London: John Allen, 1669), 8–9.

21. Increase Mather, *A Dissertation Concerning the Future Conversion of the Jewish Nation* (London, 1709), 27.

22. Increase Mather, *Mystery of Israel's Salvation*, 24, 25, 34, 36.

23. Ibid., 43–44, 53–54.

24. Ibid., 54, 56–57, 65, 89, 105.

25. J. F. Maclear, "New England and the Fifth Monarchy: The Quest for the Millennium in Early American Puritanism," *The William and Mary Quarterly*, Third Series, 32:2 (April 1975): 259. Cf. Michael G. Hall, *The Last American Puritan: The Life of Increase Mather, 1639–1723* (Hanover, NH: University Press of New England/Wesleyan University Press, 1988), 78.

26. Thomas S. Kidd, *American Christians and Islam: Evangelical Culture and Muslims from the Colonial Period to the Age of Terrorism* (Princeton: Princeton University Press, 2008), 10.

27. Paul Coles, *The Ottoman Impact on Europe* (London: Thames & Hudson, 1968), 195.

28. Samuel Sewall, *Phaenomena quaedam Apocalyptica ad Aspectum Novi Orbis configurata, or, some few Lines towards a description of the New Heaven As It makes to those who stand upon the New Earth* (Boston: Bartholomew Green and John Allen, 1697), 25.

29. Mukhtar Ali Isani, "Cotton Mather and the Orient," *New England Quarterly* 43 (March 1970): 46, 58.

30. Cotton Mather, *A Pastoral Letter to the English Captives, in Africa, from New-England* (Boston: B. Green and J. Allen, 1698), 8.

31. Cotton Mather, *Decennium Luctuosum: An History of Remarkable Occurrences, In the Long War, which New-England hath had with the Indian Salvages. . . .* (Boston: Samuel Phillips, 1699), 231–32.

32. For collections of the narratives with strong analysis, see, for instance, Daniel J. Vitkus, ed., *Piracy, Slavery, and Redemption: Barbary Captivity Narratives from Early Modern England* (New York: Columbia University Press, 2001); Kathryn Zabelle Derounian-Stodola, ed., *Women's Indian Captivity Narratives* (New York: Penguin, 1998); and Alden T Vaughan; Edward W Clark, eds., *Puritans among the Indians: Accounts of Captivity and Redemption, 1676–1724* (Cambridge, MA: Belknap, 1981). For an analysis of the genre, see Pauline Turner Strong, *Captive Selves, Captivating Others: The Practice and Representation of Captivity across Colonial Borders in North America* (Boulder, CO: Westview, 1988).

33. Cotton Mather, *American Tears upon the Ruines of the Greek Churches* (Boston, 1701), 38, cited in Kidd, 1.

34. William Waller Hening, ed., *The Statutes at Large: Being a Collection of All the Laws of Virginia from the First Session of the Legislature in the Year 1619*, Vol. 3 (Philadelphia: Thomas Desilver, 1823), 449–50. The same law was affirmed again under George II in 1753. See Hening, ed., *The Statutes at Large*, Vol. 6 (Richmond: Franklin Press, 1819), 359.

35. Winthrop D. Jordan, *The White Man's Burden: Historical Origins of Racism in the United States* (New York: Oxford University Press, 1974), 51.

36. Peter Silver, *Our Savage Neighbors: How Indian War Transformed Early America* (New York: W.W. Norton, 2008), 114, 115.

37. See Nabil Matar, *Turks, Moors, and Englishmen in the Age of Discovery* (New York: Columbia University Press, 2000), and Reginald Horsman, *Race and Manifest Destiny: Origins of American Racial Anglo-Saxonism* (Cambridge: Harvard University Press, 1981).

38. Joseph Mede, *The Works of the Pious and Profoundly-Learned Joseph Mede* (London: Roger Norton and Richard Royston, 1672), 799, 800, 843, 800. See also Mede's short essay, "DE GOGO & MAGOGO in Apocalypsi Conjectura" in *Works*, 574–76.

39. Reiner Smolinski, "*Israel Redivivus*: The Eschatological Limits of Puritan Typology in New England," *The New England Quarterly* 63:3 (1990): 371. Smolinski has traced responses to Mede's conjectures. See "*Israel Redivivus*," Appendix 3.

40. Sewall, *Phaenomena*, 27, 38, 2.

41. Ibid., 39, 28. Although Sewall appeals to the possibility that Winthrop and ben-Israel could still be proven correct, theories of the Ten Tribes were losing their appeal.

42. Smolinski, "*Israel Redivivus*," 380.

43. Smolinski, "*Israel Redivivus*," 376, 378.

44. Reiner Smolinski, ed., *The Threefold Paradise of Cotton Mather: An Edition of "Triparadisus"* (Decatur: University of Georgia Press, 1993), 316.

45. Cotton Mather, *Diary*, 2:733, cited in Smolinski, "*Israel Redivivus*," 385.

46. Smolinski, "*Israel Redivivus*," 387.

47. Cotton Mather, *Terra Beata: A Brief Essay, on the Blessing of Abraham; Even the Grand Blessing of a glorious Redeemer, which, all the nations of the earth, are to ask

for, and hope for (Boston: J. Phillips, 1726), 35, 33; cited in Smolinski, "*Israel Redivivus*," 388.

48. Cotton Mather, *Theopolis Americana: An Essay on the Golden Street of the Holy City* (Boston: B. Green, 1710), 34; idem., "Problema Theologicum," ms., American Antiquarian Society, 1703, 68 (cited in Smolinski, *Triparadisus*, 42). Mather's concern in *Theophilus Americana* is more focused on proper conduct in the marketplace (where the golden street is located) than about any particular eschatological proposition. It can be read as an echo of Winthrop's "A Model of Christian Charity."

49. Stephen J. Stein, "A Notebook on the Apocalypse by Jonathan Edwards," *William and Mary Quarterly*, Third Series, 29:4 (October 1972): 634.

50. George Marsden, *Jonathan Edwards: A Life* (New Haven: Yale University Press, 2004), 88.

51. Jonathan Edwards, *Works of Jonathan Edwards, Volume 5, Apocalyptic Writings*, ed. Stephen J. Stein (New Haven, Yale University Press, 1977), 167. Hereafter, *WJE*.

52. Jonathan Edwards to Rev. William McCulloch, September 23, 1747, *WJE* 16: 239–40.

53. Jonathan Edwards, *The Suitableness of Union in Extraordinary Prayer for the Advancement of God's Church* (February 3, 1747), *WJE* 25:201, 202–203. See also *Apocalyptic Writings*, 314.

54. Jonathan Edwards to the Trustees of the College of New Jersey, October 19, 1757, *WJE* 16:727–28.

55. Jonathan Edwards, *A History of the Work of Redemption*, *WJE* 9:178–79, 469, 468, 469, 470.

56. Jonathan Edwards, "Blank Bible," note on Deut. 11:24, *WJE* 24:294 (cf. 304, 310).

57. Jonathan Edwards, "Blank Bible," note on Rom. 11:12, *WJE* 24:1028.

58. Jonathan Edwards, *Apocalyptic Writings*, *WJE* 5:135, 134.

59. Jonathan Edwards, *Apocalyptic Writings*, *WJE* 5:196, cf. 337, "which shall be as life from the dead to the Gentiles."

60. Marsden, *Jonathan Edwards*, 337.

61. Nathan O. Hatch, "The Origins of Civil Millennialism in America: New England Clergymen, War with France, and the Revolution," *The William and Mary Quarterly*, third series 31:3 (July 1974):408, 409. See also Nathan O. Hatch, *The Sacred Cause of Liberty: Republican Thought and the Millennium in Revolutionary New England* (New Haven: Yale University Press, 1977); and Nathan O. Hatch, *The Democratization of American Christianity* (New Haven: Yale University Press, 1989).

62. Ibid., "Origins of Civil Millennialism," 417, 419, 425.

63. Thomas Paine, *Common Sense*, in *Rights of Man; Common Sense; and Other Political Writings*, ed. MarkPhilip (Oxford: Oxford University Press, 1995), 14–15, 16. Philip describes Paine's reference to Muhammad as "obscure" and "for Paine, an uncharacteristically intolerant view of another religion." Neither observation is true.

64. Noll, *America's God*, 50.
65. Alexis de Tocqueville, *Democracy in America*, trans. Arthur Goldhammer (New York: Library of America, 2004), 338.
66. Cherry, *God's New Israel*, 19.
67. I disagree with Richard Cogley's assertion that a "The sequence or pattern of apocalyptic events . . . may be termed 'Judeo-centric' because it located the start of the millennium in Jerusalem and because it assigned the role of inaugurating the kingdom to the converted posterity of Jacob" (Richard W. Cogley, "The Fall of the Ottoman Empire and the Restoration of Israel in the 'Judeo-centric' Strand of Puritan Millenarianism," *Church History* 72:2 [June 2003]:304). Victoria Clark, more convincingly attributing the same source to Sabbatai Zvi, provides the unsubstantiated speculation that "The Lurianic kabbala may have sowed the first seeds of Christian Zionism in England" (Victoria Clark, *Allies for Armageddon: The Rise of Christian Zionism* [New Haven: Yale University Press, 2007], 36, 47).
68. Ralph Bauer, "Millennium's Darker Side: The Missionary Utopias of Franciscan New Spain and Puritan New England," in *Finding Colonial Americas: Essays Honoring J.A. Leo Lemay*, ed. Carla Mulford and David S. Shields (Cranbury, NJ: Associated University Presses, 2001), 44.
69. Hatch, "The Origins of Civil Millennialism in America," 409.
70. Ernest Lee Tuveson, *Redeemer Nation: The Idea of America's Millennial Role* (Chicago: University of Chicago Press, 1968), 18, 46.

CHAPTER 7

1. Johanna and Ebenezer Cartwright, *The Petition of the Jewes for the Repealing of the Act of Parliament for their banishment out of England. . . .* (London: George Roberts, 1649).
2. Ruth Bloch, *Visionary Republic: Millennial Themes in American Thought, 1756–1800* (Cambridge: Cambridge University Press, 1985), 231, 79, 105, 151. I join several others in critiquing Bloch's imprecise use of "millennial" to describe the patterns of thought she seeks to analyze. While millenarian commitments had long entered American discourse, much of what she records is best described by the broader term "apocalyptic."
3. Bloch, 169, 170, 171, 169. Bloch mistakenly says that Napoleon "marched into the Vatican in 1798" (170).
4. Bloch, 122, 148, 122–23, 145, 148, 151. The growth of Judeo-centric apocalyptic thought in Britain in the same period further complicates Bloch's presumption that concern for the eschatological place of Jews is fundamentally esoteric. On the exchange between Joseph Priestley and David Levi, for instance, see Jack Fruchtman, Jr., "David and Goliath: Jewish Conversion and Philo-Semitism in Late-Eighteenth-Century English Millenarian Thought," in *Millenarianism and*

Messianism in Early Modern European Culture: The Millenarian Turn, ed. J.E. Force and R.H. Popkin (Netherlands: Kluwer, 2001). See also Richard H. Popkin, "David Levi, Anglo-Jewish Theologian," *The Jewish Quarterly Review*, New Series 87:1/2 (July–Oct. 1996): 79–101.

5. Bloch, 231.

6. John Adams, to M.M. Noah, Esq. (March 15, 1819), cited in Moshe Davis, *With Eyes toward Zion: Scholars Colloquium on America-Holy Land Studies* (New York: Arno, 1977), 19. See Mordecai Manuel Noah, *Travels in England, France, Spain, and the Barbary States, in the years 1813–1814 and 15* (New York: Kirk and Mercein, 1819).

7. The letter is quoted in Nahum Sokolow, *History of Zionism: 1600–1918* in two vols. (London: Longmans, Green and Co., 1919), 1:80–90. Further excerpts of the call are in Appendix XL of the second volume (2:220). The letter to Jewish co-religionists is included in Appendix XLI (2:220–22). The most thorough effort to link Napoleon's "proclamation" to the letter cited by Sokolow Franz Kobler, *Napoleon and the Jews* (New York: Schocken, 1976). Other scholars doubt any connection between the letter and Napoleon's views and suggest that the Napoleon's "proclamation" may have never existed. See, for instance, the critical historiography of Jeremy D. Popkin, "Zionism and the Enlightenment: The 'Letter of a Jew to His Brethren,'" *Jewish Social Studies* 43:2 (Spring 1981), esp. p. 120, n. 19. Barbara Tuchman, who weaves the proclamation into her popular history of British interest in the Holy Land, notes that "the original of this Proclamation has never been found. Its wording remained unknown until a manuscript copy in German translation came to light in 1940" (Barbara Tuchman, *Bible and Sword: England and Palestine from the Bronze Age to Balfour*, reprint ed. [New York: Ballantine, 1984], 163). On the changing status of Jews in France during the late eighteenth and early nineteenth centuries, see S. Debré, "The Jews of France," *The Jewish Quarterly Review* 3:3 (April 1891): 367–435; and Shmuel Trigano, "The French Revolution and the Jews," *Modern Judaism* 10:2 (May 1990): 171–90. For the long-term effects of the revolutionary experience, see Jay R. Berkovitz, "The French Revolution and the Jews: Assessing the Cultural Impact," *AJS Review* 20:1 (1995): 25–86.

8. Bloch, 196. See also Joseph J. Shulim, "Napoleon I as the Jewish Messiah: Some Contemporary Conceptions in Virginia," *Jewish Social Studies* 7:3 (July 1945): 275–80.

9. On the Sanhedrin and responses to the idea in the Jewish and British Protestant communities, see Sokolow, *History of Zionism*, 1:80–90.

10. Stuart Semmel, *Napoleon and the British* (New Haven: Yale University Press, 2004), 84. The transfer of this identity helped loyalist Protestants resolve the cognitive dissonance resulting from Britain's military alliance with Catholic forces.

11. James Bicheno, *The Signs of the Times: In Three Parts*, rev. ed. (London: J. Adlard, 1808), 26–27.

12. Scult, *Millennial Expectations*, 85–86.

13. Thomas Witherby, *Observations on Mr. Bicheno's Book, Entitled The Restoration of the Jews the Crisis of All Nations* (London: S. Couchman, 1800), 153, cited in Semmel, *Napoleon and the British*, 84; Thomas Witherby, *An Attempt to Remove the Prejudices Concerning the Jewish Nation* (London: S. Couchman, 1804), 252, cited in Mel Scult, *Millennial Expectations and Jewish Liberties: A Study of the Efforts to Convert the Jews in Britain, Up to the Mid Nineteenth Century* (Leiden: Brill, 1978), 84.

14. Nabil Matar, "The Controversy over the Restoration of the Jews: From 1754 until the London Society for Promoting Christianity Among the Jews," *The Durham University Journal* 87 (1990):40.

15. George Stanley Faber, *A Dissertation on the Prophecies, that Have Been Fulfilled, are Now Fulfilling, or will Hereafter be Fulfilled, Relative to the Great Period of 1260 Years; The Papal and Mohammedan Apostacies; The Tyrannical Reign of Antichrist, or the Infidel Power; and the Restoration of the Jews*, Volume 1, first American ed. (Boston: Andrews and Cummings, 1808), 268, 247. This immensely influential book was reprinted in three volumes in 1828 as *The Sacred Calendar of Prophecy*, 3 vols. (London: C. & J. Rivington, 1828). See also Faber, *A General and Connected View of the Prophecies, Relative to the Conversion, Restoration, Union, and Future Glory of the Houses of Judah and Israel; the Progress, Overthrow, of the Antichristian Confederacy in the Land of Palestine; and the Ultimate General Diffusion of Christianity* (Boston: William Andrews, 1809), esp. 123, 249–50.

16. "Of the return of the Jews to their own land in the Millennium; being a brief answer to the difficulties suggested in a piece written by the late Dr. Edwards, and republished in the U.C. Mag. Vol. II. No. 10," *The Utica Christian Magazine* 3:1 (July 1815):37–38. The author continues: "God did not say, that those Jews who embraced christianity, should be kept distinct; but he has foretold the literal restoration of those Jews who until the time of the Millennium should remain in unbelief, and who have been known to the world as the literal seed of Abraham." The restoration of unbelieving Jews will "strikingly display that faithfulness of the God of Abraham."

17. Edward Bickersteth, *The Restoration of the Jews to Their Own Land: In Connection with Their Future Conversion and the Final Blessedness of Our Earth*, second ed. (London: Seeley and Burnside, 1841), 119. See also pp. 188, 205, 225. For the context of Bickersteth's writing on Jewish restoration, see T.R. Birks, *Memoir of the Rev. Edward Bickersteth: Late Rector of Watton, Herts*, 2 vols. (New York: Harper & Brothers, 1851), esp. 2:62, 136, 156, 169, 293.

18. John Cumming, *Voices of the Day* (Boston: John P. Jewett, 1858), 295. See also John Thomas, *The Coming Struggle Among the Nations of the Earth, Or, The Political Events of the Next Thirteen Years, Described in Accordance with Prophecies in Ezekiel, Daniel, and the Apocalypse* (Toronto: Thomas Maclear, 1853), 90, 92, 93.

19. Grant Underwood, *The Millenarian World of Early Mormonism* (Urbana: University of Illinois Press, 1993), 29–30, 34. Underwood underscores long-standing

LDS apologetics that revelations concerning American Indians as Israelites is not "merely another variation of the old 'lost tribes' theory." That "separate group" was "sequestered somewhere in the frozen 'north countries'" and should not "be confused with the 'Jewish' Indians" (66).

20. Ibid., 30.

21. Orson Hyde, *A Voice from Jerusalem* (Boston: Albert Morgan, 1842), 30, 17.

22. Gershon Greenberg, *The Holy Land in American Religious Thought, 1620–1948: The Symbiosis of American Religious Approaches to Scripture's Sacred Territory* (Lanham, MD: The University Press of America, 1994), 250, 229.

23. Underwood, 65, 67. As he says elsewhere, "it should be clearly understood that [the LDS] vision was of a dual reenactment and that they used many of the traditional passages in the usual way to refer to the restoration of the Jews alone" (35). The "traditional" and "usual" way for interpreting such passages had long been established through the popularization of the tradition of Judeo-centric prophecy interpretation outlined in this study. The LDS reading fit into this tradition; they simply found a more robust place for themselves there.

24. See Steven Epperson, "Dedicating and Consecrating the Land: Mormon Ritual Performance in Palestine," in *America and Zion: Essays and Papers in Memory of Moshe Davis*, ed. Eli Lederhendler and Jonathan D. Sarna (Detroit: Wayne State University Press, 2002): 91–116.

25. See Francis D. Nichol, *The Midnight Cry: A Defense of the Character and Conduct of William Miller and the Millerites, Who Mistakenly Believed that the Second Coming of Christ would Take Place in the Year 1844* (1944; repr. Brushton, NY: TEACH Services, 2000), 23–24.

26. For Newton's contribution to prophecy interpretation, see Isaac Newton, *Observations upon the Prophecies of Daniel, and the Apocalypse of St. John, in two Parts* (London: J. Darby and T. Browne, 1733). For Newton's motivations and influence, see Scott Mandelbrote, "'A Duty of the Greatest Moment': Isaac Newton and the Writing of Biblical Criticism," *The British Journal for the History of Science* 26:3 (September 1993): 281–302; Richard H. Popkin, "Newton and the Origins of Fundamentalism," in *The Scientific Enterprise*, ed. Edna Ullmann-Margalit (Dordrecht: Kluwer, 1992); and Popkin, "Newton and Fundamentalism, II," in *Essays on the Context, Nature, and Influence of Isaac Newton's Theology*, ed. James E. Force and Richard H. Popkin (Dordecht, The Netherlands: Kluwer, 1990).

27. Cited in Sylvester Bliss, *Memoirs of William Miller: Generally Known as a Lecturer on the Prophecies and the Second Coming of Christ* (Boston: Joshua V. Himes, 1853), 79.

28. Bliss, *Memoirs of William Miller*, 256.

29. Malcolm Bull, "The Seventh-Day Adventists: Heretics of American Civil Religion," *Sociological Analysis* 50: 2 (1989): 183, 184, 182–83. Citing J.N. Andrews, "Thoughts on Revelation XIII and XIV," in *Review and Herald* 1: 11 (1851): 81–86.

30. Bull, "The Seventh-Day Adventists," 182.

31. Bliss, *Memoirs*, 72.

32. Isaac Cummings Wellcome, *History of the Second Advent Message and Mission, Doctrine and People* (Boston: Advent Christian Publication Society, 1874), ld53, 165.

33. B.H. Roberts, ed., *History of the Church of Jesus Christ of Latter-day Saints*, Vol. 5 (Desert News: Salt Lake City, 1909), 337.

34. Grant Underwood, *The Millenarian World of Early Mormonism* (Urbana: University of Illinois Press, 1991), 121.

35. Ibid., 419, 422.

36. See Bliss, *Memoirs of William Miller*, 344–45, 357.

37. The Pew Forum on Religion and Public Life, "Spirit and Power: A 10-Country Survey of Pentecostals' (October 2006), 24, available at www.pewforum.org. Among Pentecostals, the object of the survey, the figure jumped to 90 percent.

38. Cotton Mather, *Diary*, 2:733, cited in Smolinski, "*Israel Redivivus,*' 385.

39. John N. Darby, "The Rapture of the Saints and the Character of the Jewish Remnant,' in *The Collected Works of J.N. Darby*, 34 vols., ed. William Kelly (Sunbury, PA: Believers Bookshelf), 11:157. Hereafter, *DCW* 1–34.

40. J.N. Darby, "A few brief remarks on "A Letter on Revelation 12," *DCW* 11:25, 26.

41. David W. Bebbington, *The Dominance of Evangelicalism: The Age of Spurgeon and Moody* (Downers Grove, IL: InterVarsity, 2005), 197, 192, 198.

42. The dispensationalist blend of entertainment and comfort is best seen in the Left Behind series. For helpful analyses of this multimedia phenomenon, see Amy Johnson Frykholm, *Rapture Culture: Left Behind in Evangelical America* (New York: Oxford University Press, 2004); Bruce David Forbes and Jeanne Halgren Kilde, eds., *Rapture, Revelation, and the End Times: Exploring the Left behind Series* (New York: Palgrave Macmillan, 2004); Glenn W. Shuck, *Marks of the Beast: The Left Behind Novels and the Struggle for Evangelical Identity* (New York: New York University Press, 2005); Michael Standaert, *Skipping towards Armageddon: The Politics and Propaganda of the Left Behind Novels and the LaHaye Empire* (Brooklyn, NY: Soft Skull Press, 2006).

43. Review of *Remarks on a Letter on Subjects connected with the Lord's Humanity*, by J.N. Darby, *The Quarterly Journal of Prophecy*, Vol. 1 (October 1848): 209.

44. Peter David Lee, "The Shaping of John Nelson Darby's Eschatology' (PhD diss., University of Wales, Lampeter, 2010), 5, 184.

45. Wellcome, *History*, 165.

46. John N. Darby, "Divine Mercy in the Church and towards Israel,' *DCW* 2:122, 136, 145.

47. Darby, "Studies on the Book of Daniel,' *DCW* 5:151.

48. Darby to J.A. Von Poseck, 1861, in *Letters of J.N.D.*, 3 vols. (Sunbury, PA: Believers Bookshelf, 1971), 3:334. Hereafter, *DL*.

49. Darby, "Notes on the Epistles to the Thessalonians,' *DCW* 27:304.

50. Stanley J. Grenz, *The Millennial Maze: Sorting Out Evangelical Options* (Downers Grove, IL: InterVarsity, 1992), 107.

51. Lee, "The Shaping of John Nelson Darby's Eschatology,' 176.

52. Darby, "The Hopes of the Church of God," *DCW* 2:344, 361.

53. Darby, "Reflections Upon the Prophetic Inquiry," *DCW* 2:26, 28.

54. Darby, "Notes and Commentaries: Joel," *DCW* 4:196.

55. Darby, "The Hopes of the Church of God," *DCW* 2:377, 378, 379, 380, 381.

56. Stephen Spector, *Evangelicals and Israel: The Story of American Christian Zionism* (New York: Oxford University Press, 2009), 21. Spector embeds in his end-notes a more nuanced view of dispensational approaches to Jewish-Christian relations (258, n42).

57. David Brog, *Standing with Israel: Why Christians Support the Jewish State* (Lake Mary, FL: FrontLine, 2006), 46, 63, 34.

58. For a good summary of French Protestant motivations to rescue Jews during the Holocaust, see Robert Marquand, "A Protestant town's "conspiracy of good' in Vichy France," *Christian Science Monitor*, May 14, 2008.

59. Lee, "The Shaping of John Nelson Darby's Eschatology," 101, citing Marilyn J. Salmon, *Preaching without Contempt: Overcoming Unintended anti-Judaism*, Fortress Resources for Preaching (Minneapolis: Fortress, 2006), 37. For another helpful discussion of supersessionism, see Ellen T. Charry, "Judaism," in *Global Dictionary of Theology: A Resource for the Worldwide Church*, ed. William A. Dyrness and Veli-Matti Kärkkäinen (Downers Grove, IL: IVP Academic, 2008), esp. sec. "Judaism on Christian terms."

60. Jules Isaac, *Jésus et Israël*, quoted in Marco Morselli, "Jules Isaac and the Origins of Nostra Aetate," in Nostra Aetate: *Origins, Promulgation, Impact on Jewish-Catholic Relations*, ed. Uri Bialer and Neville Lamdan (Berlin: LIT Verlag Münster, 2005), 24. See also Jules Isaac, *The Teaching of Contempt: Christian Roots of Anti-Semitism* (New York: Holt, Rinehart and Winston, 1964); and Andre Kaspi, "Jules Isaac and His Role in Jewish-Christian Relations," in *Jews, Catholics, and the Burden of History*, Studies in Contemporary Jewry 21, ed. Eli Lederhendler (New York: Oxford University Press, 2005), 12–20.

61. Darby, "The Hopes of the Church of God," *DCW* 2:378.

62. Darby, "Matthew's Gospel," *DCW* 24:183. See also Darby, "Enquiry as to the Antichrist of Prophecy," *DCW* 5:219.

63. Paul Richard Wilkinson, *For Zion's Sake: Christian Zionism and the Role of John Nelson Darby*, Studies in Evangelical History and Thought (Colorado Spring, CO: Paternoster, 2007), 115.

64. J.N. Darby, *Collectanea: Being Some of the Subjects Considered at Leamington on 3rd June and Four Following Days in the Year 1839* (Edinburgh: J.S. Robertson, 1882), n.p. For God's earthly people, the tribulation will not be the end of their judgment according to God's law: "the millennial dispensation, as regards the saints on earth, will be a dispensation of judgment. In one sense it was grace to the Jew, yea, even in paradise. There can be no dealing with the sinner except in grace; but the Jewish economy is not one of grace, but of the law. The law is of works, but grace is not' (Darby, "The Value of Scripture Knowledge," *DCW* 32:276).

65. Darby, "Notes on the Apocalypse gleaned at lectures in Geneva, 1842," *DCW* 5:96.
66. Darby, "An Examination of the statements made in the "Thoughts on the Apocalypse," by B. W. Newton," *DCW* 8:222, 223.
67. Darby, "Notes on the Apocalypse gleaned at lectures in Geneva, 1842," *DCW* 5:101.
68. Darby letter fragment, 1860, *DL* 1:129–30.
69. Darby, "Answer to a "Second Letter to the Brethren and Sisters who meet for communion in Ebrington Street," *DCW* 8:369.
70. David Horovitz, "Evangelicals Seeing the Error of "Replacement Theology," *Jerusalem Post*, March 20, 2006.
71. Brog, 44.
72. Fresh Air from WHYY, "Gershom Gorenberg on Christian Zionism" (September 18, 2006), available at www.npr.org. See also Gershom Gorenberg, "Unorthodox Alliance: Israeli and Jewish Interests Are Better Served by Keeping a Polite Distance from the Christian Right," *Washington Post*, October 11, 2002, A37.
73. Darby, "Reflections upon the Prophetic Inquiry and the views advanced in it," *DCW* 2: 17.
74. Darby, "On "Days' signifying "Years' in Prophetic Language," *DCW* 2:35. This principle had to be accommodated the year/day principle necessary for applying Daniel to modern applications of prophecy.
75. Darby to E. Maylan, March 24, 1848, *DL* 1:129–30.
76. Darby to the editor of *The Français*, 1878, *DL* 2:431, 439.
77. Darby, "The Hopes of the Church of God," *DCW* 2:377.
78. Since the instances are too numerous to cite, I will point to two of my own publications that propagate the perspective, which I now believe to be erroneous: Robert O. Smith, "Between Restoration & Liberation: Theopolitical Contributions & Responses to U.S. Foreign Policy in Israel/Palestine," *Journal of Church and State* 46:4 (Autumn 2004): 833–60; and "Toward a Lutheran Response to Christian Zionism," *dialog: A Journal of Theology* 48:3 (Fall 2009): 281–93.
79. Lee, "The Shaping of John Nelson Darby's Eschatology," 207, 184. Although neither Lee nor I attempt to dismiss Darby's contributions as some detractors attempt to do, this insight is helpful for determining Darby's relationship to contemporary Christian Zionism.
80. Timothy P. Weber, *Living in the Shadow of the Second Coming: American Premillennialism, 1875–1982*, enlarged ed. (Chicago: University of Chicago Press, 1987), 226. A 1983 survey of the Indiana chapter of the Moral Majority asked this overarching question: "How can we account for a movement of political reform among those whose doctrine implies that such reform is doomed to historical defeat?" The survey data provided a "hint that at least some Moral Majority members may have resolved their dissonance by reducing their commitment to pre-millennialism." But there are other options: "the most common route of

dissonance reduction seems to have been the bolstering of the importance of a different cognition: that Satan poses an active threat to the U.S.' See Clyde Wilcox, Sharon Linzey, and Ted G. Jelen, "Reluctant Warriors: Premillennialism and Politics in the Moral Majority," *Journal for the Scientific Study of Religion* 30:3 (Sept. 1991): 245, 246, 254.

81. Angela M. Lahr, *Millennial Dreams and Apocalyptic Nightmares: The Cold War Origins of Political Evangelicalism* (New York: Oxford University Press, 2007), 143–44.

82. James M. Gray, "Practical and Perplexing Questions Answered: Civic Righteousness," *The Christian Workers Magazine* 14:12 (August 1914), 799–800. Weber has pointed this quotation out in several of his books and articles.

83. Weber, *Living in the Shadow*, 226, 237.

CHAPTER 8

1. See David W. Bebbington, *The Dominance of Evangelicalism: The Age of Spurgeon and Moody, A History of Evangelicalism* (Downers Grove, IL: InterVarsity, 2005), esp. chap. 5; and *Evangelicalism in Modern Britain: A History from the 1730s to the 1980s* (New York: Routledge, 1989), esp. chap. 3.

2. For good studies of Blackstone from various perspectives, see Yaakov S. Ariel, *On Behalf of Israel: American Fundamentalist Attitudes toward Jews, Judaism, and Zionism, 1865–1945* (Brooklyn, N.Y.: Carlson, 1991); Carl F. Ehle, Jr., "Prolegomena to Christian Zionism in America: The Views of Increase Mather and William E. Blackstone Concerning the Doctrine of the Restoration of Israel" (Ph.D. diss., Institute of Hebrew Studies, New York University, October 1977); Jonathan David Moorhead, "Jesus is Coming: The Life and Work of William E. Blackstone (1841–1935)" (Ph.D. diss., Dallas Theological Seminary, 2008); Hilton Obenzinger, "In the Shadow of 'God's Sun-Dial': The Construction of American Christian Zionism and the Blackstone Memorial," in *Stanford Electronic Humanities Review* 5:1 (Feb. 1996); and Paul C. Merkley, *The Politics of Christian Zionism, 1891–1948* (Portland, OR: Frank Cass, 1998), esp. chap. 7.

3. See Boyd Hilton, *The Age of Atonement: The Influence of Evangelicalism on Social and Economic Thought, 1785–1865* (Oxford: Clarendon, 1986), esp. pp. 10–19.

4. Eitan Bar-Yosef, *The Holy Land in English Culture, 1799–1917: Palestine and the Question of Orientalism* (Oxford: Oxford University Press, 2005), 184, 188. Chap. 4, "Eccentric Zion," is an expanded version of Eitan Bar-Yosef, "Christian Zionism and Victorian Culture," *Israel Studies* 8:2 (2003): 18–44.

5. Donald M. Lewis, *The Origins of Christian Zionism: Lord Shaftesbury and Evangelical Support for a Jewish Homeland* (Cambridge: Cambridge University Press, 2010), 12, 102, 103, 107, 319.

6. The best history of the Jerusalem bishopric remains the documentary history compiled and edited by Hechler: William Henry Hechler, ed., *The Jerusalem Bishopric: Documents, with Translations* (London: Trübner & Co., 1883). On Hechler,

see Enzo Maaß, "Forgotten Prophet: William Henry Hechler and the Rise of Political Zionism," in *Nordisk Judaistik/Scandinavian Jewish Studies* 23: 2 (2002): 157–92.

7. Darby, letter to G.V. Wigram (received December 24, 1862), *DL* 1:336.

8. Darby, letter to Mr. Haldo (1866), *DL* 1:472. See also Darby, letter to Mr. Pollock (Toronto, May 27, 1863), *DL* 1:351.

9. Darby, letter (Boston, September 27, 1874), *DL* 2:304.

10. Darby, letter to Walter Wolston (1874), *DL* 2:257.

11. Ernest R. Sandeen, *The Roots of Fundamentalism: British & American Millenarianism, 1800–1930* (University of Chicago Press, 1970), 89, 87, 90.

12. Cyrus I. Scofield, ed., *The Scofield Reference Bible* (New York: Oxford University Press, 1909).

13. George M. Marsden, *Fundamentalism and American Culture*, second ed. (New York: Oxford University Press, 2006), 51, 62.

14. Marsden, *Fundamentalism and American Culture*, 51, 62, 71, 222, 233.

15. Blackstone's *Jesus Is Coming* went through several editions and expansions, often with the author listed simply as "W.E.B." Of particular note is the Yiddish translation published in 1927: William E. Blackstone, *Jesus Is Coming*, translated into Yiddish by Rev. P.M. Gorodishz (New York: Fleming H. Revell, 1927). Citations will be to William E. Blackstone, *Jesus Is Coming* (Chicago: Fleming H. Revell, 1908/1916), a presentation edition distributed by the Moody Bible Institute. Moorhead notes that "Blackstone's treatment of the Rapture in *Jesus Is Coming* was among the earlier in pretribulational historiography, establishing the book's significance in emerging fundamentalist culture" (51).

16. Blackstone, *Jesus Is Coming*, 209.

17. Hilton Obenzinger and Peter Grose (*Israel in the Mind of America* [New York: Knopf, 1983], 36) suggest that the signers of the memorial were motivated, in part, by a desire to limit Russian Jewish immigration to the United States. Ariel sharply disagrees (*On Behalf of Israel*, 73).

18. William E. Blackstone, "Memorial Presented to President Harrison on March 5, 1891," Billy Graham Center Archives, Wheaton College, Wheaton, IL (CN 540/Box 6/Folder 9 "Memorials"). The memorial is reproduced with all signatories in Aaron S. Klieman, ed., *Cultivating an Awareness: America and the Holy Land*, American Zionism: A Documentary History, Vol. 1 (New York: Garland, 1990), 212–25.

19. Blackstone's correspondence with Rb. Stephen Wise and Justice Brandeis is reproduced, in part, by Ehle, 294–302.

20. William E. Blackstone, "Memorial to President Woodrow Wilson," Billy Graham Center Archives, Wheaton College, Wheaton, IL (540.6.9 "Memorials"). Hereafter BGCA.

21. Yaakov Ariel, "A Neglected Chapter in the History of Christian Zionism in America: William E. Blackstone and the Petition of 1916," in *Jews and Messianism*

in the Modern Era: Metaphor and Meaning, ed. Jonathan Frankel, Studies in Contemporary Jewry, Vol. 7 (New York: Oxford University Press, 1991), 77.

22. *Jewish Messenger* (March 13, 1891), quoted in Yaakov Ariel, "An American Initiative for a Jewish State: William Blackstone and the Petition of 1891," *Studies in Zionism* 10:2 (1989): 135.

23. *Ha Pisga* 3 (May 8, 1891): 1, quoted in Ariel, *On Behalf of Israel*, 75. Moorhead, 159–70, compiles the specific responses to Blackstone's earlier memorial. On American Jewish attitudes toward Zionism in late nineteenth-century Chicago, with reference to Blackstone, see Anita Libman Lebeson, "Zionism Comes to Chicago," *Early History of Zionism in America*, Proceeding of the American Jewish Historical Society, ed. Isidore S. Meyer (1958; repr., New York: Arno Press, 1977), 155–90.

24. Cited in Paul C. Merkley, *Christian Attitudes towards the State of Israel* (Montreal: McGill-Queen's University Press, 2001), 204.

25. Yaakov Ariel, "A Neglected Chapter in the History of Christian Zionism in America: William E. Blackstone and the Petition of 1916," in *Jews and Messianism in the Modern Era: Metaphor and Meaning*, ed. Jonathan Frankel, Studies in Contemporary Jewry, Vol. 7 (New York: Oxford University Press, 1991), 75.

26. See, for instance, Edward Alexander and Paul Bogdanor, eds., *The Jewish Divide over Israel: Accusers and Defenders* (New Brunswick, N.J.: Transaction, 2006); Marc H. Ellis, *Judaism Does Not Equal Israel: The Rebirth of the Jewish Prophetic* (New York: New Press, 2009); Tony Kushner and Alisa Solomon, eds., *Wrestling with Zion: Progressive Jewish-American Responses to the Israeli-Palestinian Conflict* (New York: Grove, 2003); and Roselle Tekiner, Samir Abed Rabbo, and Norton Mezvinsky, eds., *Anti-Zionism: Analytical Reflections* (Brattleboro, VT: Amana, 1988).

27. Ariel, *On Behalf of Israel*, 94.

28. Cited in Gershon Greenberg, *The Holy Land in American Religious Thought, 1620–1948: The Symbiosis of American Religious Approaches to Scripture's Sacred Territory* (Lanham, MD: The University Press of America, 1994), 215.

29. Blackstone, *Jesus Is Coming*, 172–73, 203, 237, 238, 239, 240.

30. Ibid., 241.

31. Brookes (1830–1897) was a leading dispensationalist, editor of *The Truth*, and an organizer of the Niagara Bible Conferences. Moorhead, following his discussion of Blackstone's article "Plan of the Aions and 1897–8—'The Time of the End'—1972" (*Jewish Era: A Christian Quarterly* 6 [April 1897]: 34–40), notes that "it has been observed that Scoefield copied Blackstone's dispensations almost word-for-word." (93).

32. Darby, Letter to Major Lancey (Plymouth, May 1, 1848), *DL* 1:131–32.

33. William E. Blackstone, "The Number of the Years," *Jewish Era: A Christian Quarterly* 2 (Oct. 1893): 238; quoted by Moorhead, 49.

34. Moorhead, 48, 49.

35. See William E. Blackstone, "Signs of Christ's Speedy Coming," *Jewish Era: A Christian Quarterly* 6 (Oct. 1897): 112–19; content of this article was included and expanded in following editions of *Jesus Is Coming*.

36. Blackstone, *Jesus Is Coming*, 228, 236. Arno Gaebelein, who would rise to prominence among fundamentalist premillennialists, concluded that Zionism could not be an expression of divine activity. See *Hath God Cast Away His People?* (New York: Gospel Publishing House, 1905).

37. "Theologians: Barth in Retirement," *Time Magazine* (May 31, 1963). Blackstone to C. F. Meeker; November 24, 1931, cited in Moorhead, 93.

38. Thomas S. Kidd, *American Christians and Islam: Evangelical Culture and Muslims from the Colonial Period to the Age of Terrorism* (Princeton: Princeton University Press, 2008), xvii.

39. Blackstone, *Jesus Is Coming*, 110–11; "The Number of the Years," 238–39.

40. Blackstone, *Jesus Is Coming*, 235. Blackstone here uses a common misspelling of the Seraglio Point on which Topkapi Palace, the seat of the Ottoman Empire, is situated in Istanbul.

41. Obenzinger, "In the Shadow of God's Sun-Dial." See, for instance, Blackstone, *Jesus Is Coming*, 154, 232–33.

42. These observations and their significance for subsequent political applications of dispensational doctrine challenge both Yaakov Ariel's conclusion that "Blackstone, on the whole, was not an original thinker, but a propagator of ideas," whose "hermeneutical and eschatological schemes very much follow closely John N. Darby's" (Ariel, *On Behalf of Israel*, 60) and Moorhead's suggestion that Blackstone's "significance lies in the fact that he popularized the doctrine" of the Second Coming "through *Jesus Is Coming*." Although he acknowledges that Blackstone "deviated" from "premillennialists of the time . . . with some of his historicist views" (114), Moorhead, with Ariel's guidance, does not sufficiently recognize the political significance of these adaptations.

43. Timothy P. Weber, *On the Road to Armageddon: How Evangelicals Became Israel's Best Friend* (Grand Rapids: Baker Academic, 2004), 13.

44. "The World's Columbian Exposition: Memorial for International Arbitration" (1893), including signatures of world and church leaders, BGCA 540.7.1. See also "An Appeal for Universal Peace: The World's Fair Memorial for International Arbitration," *New York Times* (December 25, 1893), 9.

45. Blackstone to Benjamin Harrison and James G. Blaine (March 5, 1891), copy in BGCA 540.6.9.

46. William E. Blackstone, "Will the United States Intercede for the Jews?" *Our Day* 8 (October 1891), copy in BGCA 540.6.9.

47. Blackstone to Pres. Woodrow Wilson (July 14, 1915), BGCA 540.7.5.

48. Blackstone, to Pres. Woodrow Wilson (November 17, 1916), BGCA 504.7.5.

49. Blackstone, telegram to Sen. Warren G. Harding (December 30, 1920), BGCA 540.7.5.

50. Moorhead, 108.

51. Yaakov Ariel, "How Are Jews and Israel Portrayed in the Left Behind Series? A Historical Discussion of Jewish-Christian Relations," in *Rapture, Revelation and the End Times: Exploring the Left Behind Series*, ed. Bruce David Forbes and Jeanne Halgren Kilde (New York: Palgrave Macmillan, 2004), 137.

52. Merkley, *Christian Attitudes*, 200. As he says, "It is a fact of great significance that the television evangelists are, at the same time, strong on patriotic national assertion, suspicious of internationalism and especially of un-sponsored efforts, and faithful towards Israel."

53. Stuart Creighton Miller, *Benevolent Assimilation: The American Conquest of the Philippines, 1899–1903* (New Haven: Yale University Press, 1982), 1.

54. Ernest Lee Tuveson, *Redeemer Nation: The Idea of America's Millennial Role* (Chicago: University of Chicago Press, 1968), 91.

55. Herman Melville, *White-Jacket, Or The World in a Man-of-War*, Oxford World's Classics (1850; repr. New York: Oxford University Press, 2000), 153.

56. Tuveson, *Redeemer Nation*, 213.

57. Obenzinger, "In the Shadow of God's Sun-Dial."

58. Frederick Jackson Turner, "The Significance of the Frontier in American History," in *Rereading Frederick Jackson Turner: "The Significance of the Frontier in American History" and Other Essays*, ed. John Mack Faragher (New York: Henry Holt, 1994), 31.

59. See the first chapters of Shari M. Huhndorf, *Going Native: Indians in the American Cultural Imagination* (Ithaca, NY: Cornell University Press, 2001).

60. Ussama Makdisi, "Reclaiming the Land of the Bible: Missionaries, Secularism, and Evangelical Modernity," *American Historical Review* 102:3 (June 1997): 680–713.

61. See Hilton Obenzinger, *American Palestine: Melville, Twain and the Holy Land Mania* (Princeton: Princeton University Press, 1999) and W.J.T. Mitchell, "Holy Landscape: Israel, Palestine, and the American Wilderness," *Critical Inquiry* 26:2 (Winter 2000): 193–223. Cf. Stephanie Stidham Rogers, "American Protestant Pilgrimage: Nineteenth-Century Impressions of Palestine," *Koinonia* 15:1 (2003): 60–80.

62. A.E. Thompson, cited in Weber, *Living in the Shadow*, 130.

63. David Lloyd George, "Afterward" to Philip Guedalla, *Napoleon and Palestine* (London, 1925), 47–49, cited in Eitan Bar-Yosef, "Christian Zionism and Victorian Culture," *Israel Studies* 8:2 (2003): 18–44. Bar-Yosef supplies an important critique of whiggish histories of British Christian Zionism's contribution to British foreign policy vis-à-vis Israel/Palestine. See also Eitan Bar-Yosef, *The Holy Land in English Culture, 1799–1917: Palestine and the Question of Orientalism* (New York: Oxford University Press, 2005), esp. chap. 4. Irvine H. Anderson seeks to detail how American biblical education related to the Holy Land and "Hebrew history" shaped American foreign policy approaches: *Biblical Interpretation And Middle East Policy: The Promised Land, America, And Israel, 1917–2002* (Gainesville: University Press of Florida, 2005).

64. *Establishment of a National Home in Palestine: Hearings before the Committee on Foreign Affairs, House of Representatives, Sixty-Seventh Congress, Second Session, on H. Con. Res. 52 Expressing Satisfaction at the Re-Creation of Palestine as the National Home of the Jewish Race (April 18, 2019, 20 and 21, 1922)*, Subcommittee of the House Committee on Foreign Affairs (Washington, U.S. Government Printing Office, 1922), 19, 20. This resolution was jointly put forth by Sen. Henry Cabot Lodge (Mass.) and Rep. Hamilton Fish (NY).

65. Kathleen Christison, *Perceptions of Palestine: Their Influence on U.S. Middle East Policy* (Berkeley: University of California Press, 1999), 31–32.

66. Rueben Fink, *America and Palestine: The Attitude of Official America and the American People toward the Rebuilding of Palestine as a Free and Democratic Jewish Commonwealth* (New York: American Zionist Emergency Council, 1944), 43.

67. Angela M. Lahr, *Millennial Dreams and Apocalyptic Nightmares: The Cold War Origins of Political Evangelicalism* (New York: Oxford University Press, 2007), 4–5.

68. For recent research into Truman's role at this historical turning point and a generally positive reassessment of Truman's legacy, see Michael J. Devine, Robert P. Watson, and Robert J. Wolz, eds., *Israel and the Legacy of Harry S. Truman* (Kirksville, Mo.: Truman State University Press, 2008).

69. Peter Grose, *Israel in the Mind of America* (New York: Knopf, 1983), 283. This account is drawn from Moshe Davis, "Reflections on Harry S. Truman and the State of Israel," in *Truman and the American Commitment to Israel: A Thirtieth Anniversary Conference*, ed. Moshe Ma'oz and Allen Weinstein (Jerusalem: Magnes Press, 1982).

70. For the cultural implications of this choice, see Tom Segev, *Elvis in Jerusalem: Post-Zionism and the Americanization of Israel*, trans. Haim Watzman (New York: Henry Holt, 2002).

71. Paul S. Boyer, *When Time Shall Be No More: Prophecy Belief in Modern American Culture* (Cambridge: Belknap Press, 1992), 200.

72. Lahr, 151.

73. See Reinhold Niebuhr, *The Children of Light and the Children of Darkness: A Vindication of Democracy and a Critique of its Traditional Defence* (New York: Charles Scribner's Sons, 1944).

74. Reinhold Niebuhr in *The Nation* (February 21, 1933), 214, cited in Franklin Littell, "Reinhold Niebuhr and the Jewish People," *Holocaust and Genocide Studies* 6:1 (1991), 51.

75. Ibid., 54.

76. See Lewis A. Coser, *Refugee Scholars in America: Their Impact and their Experiences* (New Haven, Conn.: Yale University Press, 1984) and Paul Tillich, *Against the Third Reich: Paul Tillich's Wartime Radio Broadcasts into Nazi Germany*, ed. Ronald H. Stone and Matthew Lon Weaver (Louisville: Westminster John Knox Press, 1998).

77. Paul Tillich, "Is There a Judeo-Christian Tradition?" *Judaism* 1:2 (1952): 106–109. See also Arthur A. Cohen, *The Myth of the Judeo-Christian Tradition and Other Dissenting Essays* (New York: Harper & Row, 1970) and Mark Silk, "Notes on the Judeo-Christian Tradition in America," *American Quarterly* 36:1 (Spring 1984): 65–85.

78. Will Herberg, *Protestant, Catholic, Jew: An Essay in American Religious Sociology* (Garden City, N.Y.: Doubleday, 1955).

79. Michael Mok, "The War: Astounding 60 Hours," *Life Magazine* (June 16, 1967), 33.

80. "War Sweeps the Bible Lands; Frantic Nations Forget that the Prophetic Vision of World Peace is Messianic," *Christianity Today* 9 (June 23, 1967).

81. Marsden, *Fundamentalism and American Culture*, 118.

82. See C.I. Scofield, "The Grace of God," and Arno C. Gaebelein, "Fulfilled Prophecy a Potent Argument for the Bible," in *The Fundamentals: A Testimony to the Truth*, 12 vols. (Chicago: Testimony Publishing, 1920), Vol. 11:43–54, 55–86.

83. J. Gresham Machen, *Christianity and Liberalism* (1923; repr. Grand Rapids, MI: Eerdmans, 2009), 41.

84. Marsden, *Fundamentalism and American Culture*, 207. Betty DeBerg argues, for instance, that fundamentalism finds its sociological foundation in reaction to shifting gender roles in the late nineteenth and early twentieth centuries: Betty DeBerg, *Ungodly Women: Gender and the First Wave of American Fundamentalism* (Philadelphia: Fortress Press, 1987).

85. Richard Hofstadter, *The Paranoid Style in American Politics and Other Essays* (New York: Vintage, 1967).

86. Irving Kristol, "The Neoconservative Persuasion," *Weekly Standard*, August 25, 2003.

87. David Frum and Richard Perle, *An End to Evil: How to Win the War on Terror* (New York: Random House, 2003).

88. Marsden, *Fundamentalism and American Culture*, 211, 329n63.

89. Ibid., 232, 233.

90. Carl F.H. Henry, *The Uneasy Conscience of Modern Fundamentalism* (1947; repr. Grand Rapids, MI: Eerdmans, 2003), 47, 58, 59–60.

91. Marsden, *Fundamentalism and American Culture*, 235, 236, 247, 249–50.

CONCLUSION

1. Samuel Sewall, *Phaenomena quaedam Apocalyptica ad Aspectum Novi Orbis configurata, or, some few Lines towards a description of the New Heaven As It makes to those who stand upon the New Earth* (Boston: Bartholomew Green and John Allen, 1697), 39.

2. Johanna and Ebenezer Cartwright, *The Petition of the Jewes for the Repealing of the Act of Parliament for their banishment out of England. . . .* (London: George Roberts, 1649).

3. Dwight D. Eisenhower, "Farewell Address," in *Our Nation's Archive: The History of the United States in Documents* (New York: Black Dog & Leventhal, 1999), 713–14.

4. David D. Kirkpatrick, "For Evangelicals, Supporting Israel Is 'God's Foreign Policy,'" *New York Times*, November 14, 2006.

5. John Hagee, *Beginning of the End: The Assassination of Yitzhak Rabin and the Coming Antichrist* (Nashville, TN: Thomas Nelson, 1996), 30.

6. Mark A. Noll, *The Scandal of the Evangelical Mind* (Grand Rapids: Eerdmans, 1994), 130, 132, 47, 123.

7. Douglas Little, *American Orientalism: The United States and the Middle East since 1945* (Chapel Hill: University of North Carolina Press, 2002), 87, 270.

8. Caspar W. Weinberger and Ariel Sharon, signers, "Memorandum of Understanding between Israel and the United States on Strategic Cooperation, Washington, November 30, 1981," in *The Major International Treaties of the Twentieth Century: A History and Guide with Texts, Vol. 1*, ed. John Ashley Soames Grenville and Bernard Wasserstein (London: Routledge, 2001), 384.

9. Thomas S. Kidd, *American Christians and Islam: Evangelical Culture and Muslims from the Colonial Period to the Age of Terrorism* (Princeton: Princeton University Press, 2008), xvii.

10. See Francis Fukuyama, "The End of History?" *The National Interest* 16 (Summer 1989): 3–18; and "A Reply to My Critics," *The National Interest* 18 (Winter 1989): 21–28; as well as *The End of History and the Last Man* (New York: Free Press, 1992).

11. See Samuel P. Huntington, "The Clash of Civilizations?" *Foreign Affairs* (Summer 1993): 22–49. See Huntington's further development of the thesis in Samuel P. Huntington, *The Clash of Civilizations and the Remaking of World Order* (New York: Simon & Schuster, 1998); and Bernard Lewis, "The Roots of Muslim Rage," *Atlantic Monthly* (September 1990): 47–60.

12. For efforts to expose the historical and political forces that exclude Islam from the "Judeo-Christian tradition," see Fuad Shaban, *For Zion's Sake: The Judeo-Christian Tradition in American Culture* (London: Pluto, 2005); and Richard W. Bulliet, *The Case for Islamo-Christian Civilization* (New York: Columbia University Press, 2004). For the contemporary domestic outworking of this ideological exclusion, see Steven Salaita, *Anti-Arab Racism in the USA: Where it Comes from and What it Means for Politics Today* (London: Pluto, 2006).

13. Nimrod Novik, *The United States and Israel: Domestic Determinants of a Changing US Commitment* (Boulder, CO: Westview, 1986), 71.

14. See Hal Lindsey, *The Everlasting Hatred: The Roots of Jihad* (Murrieta, CA: Oracle House, 2002).

15. See Tom Doyle, *Two Nations Under God: Why You Should Care about Israel*, 2nd ed. (Nashville, TN: B&H, 2008).

16. John Hagee, *Beginning of the End: The Assassination of Yitzhak Rabin and the Coming Antichrist* (Nashville: Thomas Nelson, 1996), 28.

17. The theme frames chap. 5 of *Beginning of the End* (1996), reissued with very little modification in *Can America Survive?* (2010), chap. 9.

18. John Hagee, *Jerusalem Countdown: A Warning to the World* (Lake Mary, FL: Front Line, 2006), 108.

19. As Hagee says in *Beginning of the End*, "we will be watching from the balconies of heaven by the time he [the Antichrist] is revealed" (135).

20. Hagee, *Jerusalem Countdown*, 193, 201, 194.

21. Hagee, *In Defense of Israel*, 149, 150, 162.

22. Ernest Lee Tuveson, *Redeemer Nation: The Idea of America's Millennial Role* (Chicago: University of Chicago Press, 1968), 50.

23. Quoted by Malcolm Foster, "Christian Zionists Feel the Heat for Fighting Peace: Extremists Wield Considerable Power within Republican Party," *The Daily Star* (Beirut), July 26, 2003, 3.

24. Peter Grose, *Israel in the Mind of America* (New York: Knopf, 1983), 316.

25. Thomas Morton of Berwick, *A Treatise of the Threefolde state of man* (London: R. Robinson for Robert Dexter and Raph Jackeson, 1596), 336.

Bibliography

PRIMARY SOURCES

Adams, Thomas. *The Blacke Devill or The Apostate Together With The Wolfe Worrying the Lambes. And The Spiritual Navigator, Bound For the Holy Land. In three Sermons*. London: William Iaggard, 1615.

Bale, John. *The Actes of Englysh votaryes comprehendynge their unchast practyses and examples by all ages, from the worldes begynnynge to thys present yeare, collected out of their owne legendes and chronicles*. Antwerp: S. Mierdman, 1546.

Bale, John. *The Image Of bothe churches after the moste wonderfull and heavley Revelacion of Sainct John the Evangelist, containing a very frutefull exposicion or paraphrase upon the same. Where it is conferred with the other scriptures, and most auctorised historyes*. Antwerp: S. Mierdman, 1545.

Bale, John. *The Image of bothe Churches, after the most wonderfull and heavenly Revelation of sainct Iohn the Euangelist, contayning a very fruitfull exposition or Paraphrase vpon the same*. 2nd ed. London: Thomas East, 1570.

Ben-Israel, Menasseh. *The Hope of Israel*. Translated by Moses Wall. London: Hannah Allen, 1650.

Ben-Israel, Menasseh. *The Great Deliverance of The Whole House of Israel: What it truly is, by whom it shall be performed, and in what Year, Declared plainly by the word of God: In Answer to a Book called The Hope of Israel, Written by a Learned Jew of Amsterdam, Named Menasseh Ben Israel*. London: M.S., 1652.

Ben-Israel, Menasseh. *To His Highnesse the Lord Protector of the Common-wealth of England, Scotlan, and Ireland: The Humble Addresses of Menasseh Ben Israel . . . in behalfe of the Jewish Nation*. London: n.p., 1655.

Bernard, Richard. *A Key of knowledge For the opening of the secret mysteries of St Iohns mysticall Revelation*. London: Felix Kyngston, 1617.

Bèza, Theodore, ed. *The Newe Testament of Our Lorde Iesus Christ*. London: Christopher Barker, Printer to the Queenes Majestie, 1578.

The Bible and Holy Scriptures Conteyned in the Olde and Newe Testament, Translated According to the Ebrue and Greke, and conferred With the best translations in divers languges, With moste profitable annotations vpon all the hard places, and other things of great importance as may appeare in the epistle to the reader. Geneva: Rouland Hall, 1560.

Bicheno, James. *The Signs of the Times: In Three Parts.* Revised ed. London: J. Adlard, 1808.

Bickersteth, Edward. *The Restoration of the Jews to Their Own Land: In Connection with Their Future Conversion and the Final Blessedness of Our Earth.* 2nd ed. London: Seeley and Burnside, 1841.

Birks, T.R. *Memoir of the Rev. Edward Bickersteth: Late Rector of Watton, Herts.* Two vols. New York: Harper & Brothers, 1851.

Blackstone, William E. Papers. Billy Graham Center Archives, Wheaton College, Wheaton, IL.

Blackstone, William E. *Jesus Is Coming.* 3rd ed. Chicago: Fleming H. Revell, 1916.

Bliss, Sylvester. *Memoirs of William Miller: Generally Known as a Lecturer on the Prophecies and the Second Coming of Christ.* Boston: Joshua V. Himes, 1853.

Boys, John. *The Autumne Part from the Twelfth Sunday after Trinitie, to the last in the whole yeere.* London: Melchisedech Bradwood and William Aspley, 1613.

Boys, John. *An Exposition of the Festivall Epistles and Gospels used in our English Liturgie Together with a reason why the church did chuse the same.* London: Eduuard Griffin for William Aspley, 1615.

Boys, John. *The Third Part from S. Iohn Baptists Nativitie to the last Holy day in the whole yeare.* London: William Aspley, 1615.

Bownd, Nicolas. *The Doctrine of the Sabbath, Plainely layde forth, and soundly proved by testimonies both of holy Scripture, and also of olde and new ecclesiasticall writers.* London: John Porter and Thomas Man, 1595.

Brightman, Thomas. *Apocalypsis apocalypseos: Id est, Apocalypsis D. Ioannis analysi et scholiis illustrata: ubi ex scriptura sensus, rerumque prędictarum ex historijs eventus discutiuntur. Huic synopsis prǽfigitur universalis: & refutatio Rob. Bellarmini de Antichristo libro tertio de Romano Pontifice, ad finem capitis decimi septimi inferitur.* Francofurti: Prostat apud viduam Levini Hulsij, 1609.

Brightman, Thomas. *A Commentary on the Canticles or the Song of Salomon: Wherein the text is Analized, the Native signification of the Words Declared, the Allegories Explained, and the Order of the times whereunto they relate Observed.* London: John Field for Henry Overton, 1644.

Brightman, Thomas. *A Most Comfortable Exposition of The last and most difficult part of the prophecie of Daniel from the 26 verse of the 11 chap, to the end of the 12 chapter: Wherin the restoring of the Iewes and their callinge to the faith of Christ after the utter overthrow of their three last enemies, is set forth in livelie coulours.* Amsterdam: G. Thorp, 1635.

Brightman, Thomas. *A Revelation of the Apocalyps, that is, The Apocalyps of S. Iohn, illustrated with an Analysis & Scolions: Where the sense is opened by the scripture, &*

the vents of things foretold, shewed by Histories. 1st English ed. Amsterdam: Iudocus Hondius & Hendrick Laurenss, 1611.

Brightman, Thomas. *The Revelation of St. Iohn Illustrated with an Analysis & Scholions.* 3rd ed. Leyden: John Class [i.e. J. Claesson van Dorpe], 1616.

Brightman, Thomas. *The Revelation of St. Iohn Illustrated with an Analysis & Scholions.* 4th ed. London: Samuel Cartwright, 1644.

Brightman, Thomas. *The Revelation of Saint Iohn, Illustrated with Analysis and Scholions.* 5th ed. Amsterdam: Thomas Stafford, 1644.

Brightmans Iudgement, or prophecies what shall befall Germany, Scotland, Holland, and the Churches adhering to them, Likewise what shall befall England, and the Hierarchy therein. Collected out of his exposition on the Revelations, Printed above forty yeares since. . . . Collected for the good of those who want time or coine, to purchase so large a volume. London: R. Harford, 1641.

Brightmans Predictions and Prophecies Written 46 yeares since: concerning the three Churches of Germanie, England, and Scotland: Fore-telling the miserie of Germanie, the fall of the pride of Bishops in England by the assistance of the Scottish Kirk: all which should happen, as he foretold, between the yeares of 36 and 41, &c. London, n.p., 1641.

Bulkeley, Peter. *The Gospel-Covenant; or The Covenant of Grace opened . . . Preached in Concord in New-England.* London: Benjamin Allen, 1646.

Burton, Henry. *Israels fast: Or, a Meditation upon the Seuenth Chapter of Joshuah; A Faire Precedent for these Times.* London: H.B. [Thomas Cotes and Michael Sparke], 1628.

Burton, Henry. *The Seven Vials or A briefe and plaine Exposition upon the 15: and 16: Chapters of the Revelation, very pertinent and profitable for the Church of God in these last times.* London: William Jones, 1628.

Burton, William. *Dauids Evidence; or, The assurance of Gods Love Declared in Seuen Sermons.* [London: R. Field for T. Cook, 1592].

Calvin, John. *A Harmonie upon the Three Euangelists, Matthew, Mark and Luke, with the Commentarie of M. Iohn Calvine . . . Whereunto is also added a commentarie upon the Euangelist S. Iohn, by the same authour.* Translated by Eusebius Pagit. London: Thomas Dawson, 1584.

Calvin, John. *Semons of M. Iohn Calvine upon the Epistle of Saincte Paule to the Galathians.* Translated by Arthur Golding. London: Lucas Harison and George Bishop, 1574.

Calvin, John. *The Sermons of M. Iohn Calvin upon the Fifth Booke of Moses called Deuteronomie faithfully gathered word for word as he preached them in open pulpet; Together with a preface of the Ministers of the Church of Geneva, and an admonishment made by the Deacons there.* Translated by Arthur Golding. London: Henry Middleton and George Bishop, 1583.

Canne, John. *A Voice from the Temple to the Higher Powers.* London: Matthew Simmons, 1653.

Cartwright, Johanna and Ebenezer. *The Petition of the Jewes For the Repealing of the Act of Parliament for their banishment out of England, Presented to his Excellency and the generall Councell of Officers on Fryday Jan. 5, 1648, With their favourable acceptance thereof.* London: George Roberts, 1649.

Cheynell, Francis. *An Account Given to the Parliament by the Ministers sent by them to Oxford.* London: Samuell Gellibrand, 1647.

Clapham, Henoch. *A Chronological Discourse touching, 1 The Church. 2 Christ. 3 Anti-Christ. 4 Gog & Magog. &c.* London: William White, 1609.

Columbus, Christopher. *The Journal of Christopher Columbus During His First Voyage, 1492–93.* Translated by Clements R. Markham. London: Hakluyt Society, 1893.

Cooper, Thomas. *The Blessing of Japheth, Prouing The Gathering in of the Gentiles, and Finall Conuersion of the Iewes.* London: T. Creede and Richard Redmer, 1615.

Coryate, Thomas. *Coryats Crudities Hastily gobled up in five Moneths travells in France, Sauoy, Italy, Rhetia comonly called the Grisons country, Helvetia aliàs Switzerland, some parts of high Germany, and the Netherlands.* London: William Stansby, 1611.

Cotton, John. *A Brief Exposition Of the whole Book of Canticles, or, Song of Solomon; Lively Describing the Estate of the Church in all the Ages thereof, both Jewish and Christian, to this day.* London: Philip Nevil, 1642.

Cotton, John. *The Churches Resurrection, or the Opening of the Fift and sixt verses of the 20th Chap. of the Revelation.* London: Henry Overton, 1642.

Cotton, John. *An Exposition upon The Thirteenth Chapter of the Revelation.* London: Timothy Smart, 1656.

Cumming, John. *Voices of the Day.* Boston: John P. Jewett, 1858.

Darby, John Nelson. *The Collected Writings of J.N. Darby.* 34 vols. Edited by William Kelly. London: G. Morrish, 1867–1900.

Darby, John Nelson. *Collectanea: Being Some of the Subjects Considered at Leamington on 3rd June and Four Following Days in the Year 1839.* Edinburgh: J.S. Robertson, 1882.

Darby, John Nelson. *Letters of J.N.D.* 3 vols. London: G. Morrish, 1914–1915.

Dent, Arthur. *The Ruine of Rome: or, An exposition vpon the whole Reuelation.* London: Simon Waterson and Cutbert Burby, 1603.

A Directory for the Publique Worship of God, Throughout the Three Kingdoms of England, Scotland, and Ireland; Together with an Ordinance of Parliament for the taking away of the Book of Common-Prayer. London: Printed for Evan Tyler, Alexander Fifield, Ralph Smith, and John Field, 1644.

Dove, John. *A Confutation of Atheisme.* London: Henry Rockett, 1605.

Doyle, Toml. *Two Nations Under God: Why You Should Care about Israel.* 2nd ed. Nashville, TN: B&H, 2008.

Draxe, Thomas. *An Alarum to the Last Iudgement. Or An exact discourse of the second comming of Christ and of the generall and remarkeable Signes and*

Fore-runners of it past, present, and to come. London: Nicholas Okes and Matthew Law, 1615.

Draxe, Thomas. *The Churches Securitie, Togither with the Antidote or preservative of ever waking faith.* London: George Eld and John Wright, 1608.

Draxe, Thomas. *The Earnest of Our Inheritance Together with a Description of the New Heaven and the New earth, and a demonstration of the glorious Resurrection of the bodie in the same substance.* London: Felix Kingston and George Norton, 1613.

Draxe, Thomas. "The Generall signes and forerunners of Christs comming to judgement, soundly and sincerely collected out of holy Scripture, and serving as well to awaken the drowsie and slumbering Protestant as to comfort and revive the Godlyand afflicted Christian," in *The Churches Securitie.* London: George Eld and John Wright, 1608.

Draxe, Thomas. *The Worldes Resurrection, or The generall calling of the Iewes, A familiar commentary upon the eleventh Chapter of Saint Paul to the Romaines, according to the sence of Scripture, and the consent of the most judicious interpreters.* London: G. Eld and John Wright, 1608.

Edwards, Jonathan. *Works of Jonathan Edwards.* 26 vols. New Haven, CT: Yale University Press, 1957–2008.

Edwards, Jonathan. *Works of Jonathan Edwards Online.* Vols. 27–73. New Haven, CT: Yale University Press, 1957–2008.

Eisenhower, Dwight D. "Farewell Address," in *Our Nation's Archive: The History of the United States in Documents.* New York: Black Dog & Leventhal, 1999.

Evans, Michael D. *Beyond Iraq—The Next Move: Ancient Prophecy and Modern Day Conspiracy Collide.* Lakeland, FL: White Stone, 2003.

Evans, Michael D. *Israel: America's Key to Survival.* Plainfield, IL: Logos International, 1983.

Faber, George Stanley. *A Dissertation on the Prophecies, that Have Been Fulfilled, are Now Fulfilling, or will Hereafter be Fulfilled, Relative to the Great Period of 1260 Years; The Papal and Mohammedan Apostacies; The Tyrannical Reign of Antichrist, or the Infidel Power; and the Restoration of the Jews.* 2 vols. Boston: Andrews and Cummings, 1808.

Faber, George Stanley. *A General and Connected View of the Prophecies, Relative to the Conversion, Restoration, Union, and Future Glory of the Houses of Judah and Israel; the Progress, Overthrow, of the Antichristian Confederacy in the Land of Palestine; and the Ultimate General Diffusion of Christianity.* Boston: William Andrews, 1809.

Faber, George Stanley. *The Sacred Calendar of Prophecy.* 3 vols. London: C. & J. Rivington, 1828

Finch, Henry. *An Exposition of the Song of Solomon: called Canticles, Together with Profitable Observations, collected out of the same.* London: William Gouge, 1615.

Finch, Henry. *The Worlds Great Restauration, or The Calling of the Iewes, and (with them) of all the Nations and Kindomes of the earth, to the faith of Christ.* London: William Gouge, 1621.

Fletcher, Giles. *Israel Redux: or, The Restauration of Israel, Exhibited in Two Short Treatises.* London: John Hancock, 1677.

Forbes, Patrick. *An Exquisite Commentarie upon the Revelation of Saint Iohn.* London: W. Hall and Francis Burton, 1613.

Fowler, John, Clement Saunders, and Robert Bulwarde. *A Shield of Defence against the Arrowes of Schisme Shot abroad by Iean de L'escluse in his advertisment against Mr. Brightman.* Amsterdam: Henry Laurenson, 1612.

Foxe, John. *Actes and Monuments of these latter and perillous dayes touching matters of the Church, wherein ar comprehended and decribed the great persecutions [and] horrible troubles, that haue bene wrought and practised by the Romishe prelates, speciallye in this Realme of England and Scotlande, from the yeare of our Lorde a thousande, vnto the tyme nowe present.* London: John Day, 1563.

Foxe, John. *A Sermon preached at the Christening of a certaine Iew at London, by Iohn Foxe. Containing an exposition of the xi. Chapter of S. Paul to the Romanes.* Translated by James Bell. London: Christopher Barker, 1578.

Frum, David, and Richard Perle. *An End to Evil: How to Win the War on Terror.* New York: Random House, 2003.

Fulke, William. *A Defense of the sincere and true Translations of the Holie Scriptures into the English tong[ue] against the manifolde cauils, friuolous quarels, and impudent slaunders of Gregorie Martin, one of the readers of popish diuinitie in the trayterous Seminarie of Rhemes.* London: Henrie Bynneman, 1583.

Gaebelein, Arno C. "Fulfilled Prophecy a Potent Argument for the Bible." In *The Fundamentals: A Testimony to the Truth*, Vol. 11. Edited by R.A. Torrey and A.C. Dixon. Chicago: Testimony Publishing, 1920.

Gaebelein, Arno C. *Hath God Cast Away His People?* New York: Gospel Publishing House, 1905.

Gelernter, David. *Americanism: The Fourth Great Western Religion.* New York: Doubleday, 2007.

Goodwin, Thomas. "An Exposition of the Book of Revelation." *The Works of Thomas Goodwin.* Vol. 3. Edited by Thomas Smith. Edinburgh: J. Nichol, 1861–1866.

Gray, James M. "Practical and Perplexing Questions Answered: Civic Righteousness." *The Christian Workers Magazine* 14:12 (August 1914): 799–800.

Greene, Robert. *The Life and Complete Works in Prose and Verse of Robert Greene.* 15 vols. Edited by Alexander Balloch Grosart. London: Huth Library, Printed for private circulation only, 1881–86.

Hagee, John. *Attack on America: New York, Jerusalem, and the Role of Terrorism in the Last Days.* Nashville: Thomas Nelson, 2001.

Hagee, John. *The Battle for Jerusalem.* Nashville: Thomas Nelson, 2001.

Hagee, John. *Beginning of the End: The Assassination of Yitzhak Rabin and the Coming Antichrist.* Nashville: Thomas Nelson, 1996.

Hagee, John. *Can American Survive? Ten Prophetic Signs that We are the Terminal Generation* (New York: Howard), 2010.

Hagee, John. *Day of Deception: Separating Truth from Falsehood in These Last Days.* Nashville: Thomas Nelson, 1997.

Hagee, John. *In Defense of Israel: The Bible's Mandate for Supporting the Jewish State.* First ed. Lake Mary, FL: Front Line, 2007.

Hakluyt, Richard. *The Principall Navigations, Voiages and Discoveries of the English nation made by Sea or ouer Land, to the most remote and farthest distant Quarters of the earth at any time within the compasse of these 1500. yeeres.* London: George Bishop and Ralph Newberie, 1589.

Hening, William Waller, ed. *The Statutes at Large: Being a Collection of All the Laws of Virginia from the First Session of the Legislature in the Year 1619.* Vol. 3. Philadelphia: Thomas Desilver, 1823.

Henry, Carl F.H. *The Uneasy Conscience of Modern Fundamentalism.* 1947. Reprint, Grand Rapids, MI: Eerdmans, 2003.

Hooker, Richard. *Of the Lawes of Ecclesiasticall Politie.* London: John Windet, 1593.

Hyde, Orson. *A Voice from Jerusalem.* Boston: Albert Morgan, 1842.

Jessey, Henry. *A Narrative Of the late Proceeds at White-hall concerning the Jews Who had desired by R[abbi] Manasses an Agent for them that they might return into England and Worship the God of their Fathers here in the Synagogues.* London: L. Chapman, 1656.

Kett, Francis. *An Epistle Sent to Divers Papistes in England proving the Pope to bee the Beast in the 13 of the Reuelations, and to be the man exalted in the Temple of God, as God, Thess. 2.2.* London: Henry Marsh, 1585.

Kett, Francis. *The Glorious and beautifull garland of mans glorification, Containing the godlye misterie of heauenly Ierusalem, the helmet of our saluation. The comming of Christ in the fleshe for our glorie, and his glorious com[m]ing in the end of the world to crowne men with crownes of eternall glorie.* London: Roger Ward, 1585.

LaHaye, Tim, and Jerry Jenkins. *Left Behind: A Novel of Earth's Last Days.* Wheaton, IL: Tyndale, 1995.

LaHaye, Tim, and Jerry Jenkins. *Tribulation Force: The Continuing Drama of Those Left Behind.* Wheaton, IL: Tyndale, 1995.

L'Écluse, Jean de. *An Advertisement to Everie Godly Reader of Mr. Thomas Brightman his book, namely, A revelation of the Apocalyps. In which advertisement is shewed how corruptly he teacheth, that notwithstanding all the sinns & abhominations that are in the Church of England, and by him shewed, yet that it is blasphemous to separate from it.* [Amsterdam: G. Thorp,] 1612.

Lindsey, Hal. *The 1980s: Countdown to Armageddon.* New York: Bantam, 1981.

Lindsey, Hal. *The Everlasting Hatred: The Roots of Jihad.* Murrieta, CA: Oracle House, 2002.

Lindsey, Hal, with Carole C. Carlson. *The Late, Great Planet Earth.* Grand Rapids: Zondervan, 1970.

Luther, Martin. *Luther's Works.* American Edition. 55 vols. Edited by Jaroslav Pelikan and Helmut T. Lehmann. Philadelphia: Muehlenberg and Fortress, and St. Louis: Concordia, 1955–86.

Luther, Martin. *D. Martin Luthers Werke: Kritische Gesamtausgabe.* Weimar: H. Bohlau, 1883.

Lutheran Church. *The Book of Concord: The Confessions of the Evangelical Lutheran Church.* Edited by Robert Kolb and Timothy J. Wengert. Minneapolis: Fortress, 2000.

Machen, J. Gresham. *Christianity and Liberalism. 1923.* Reprint, Grand Rapids, MI: Eerdmans, 2009.

Mather, Cotton. *Decennium Luctuosum: An History of Remarkable Occurrences, In the Long War, which New-England hath had with the Indian Salvages, From the Year 1688 to the Year 1698.* Boston: Samuel Phillips, 1699.

Mather, Cotton. *A Pastoral Letter to the English Captives, in Africa, from New-England.* Boston: B. Green and J. Allen, 1698.

Mather, Cotton. *Theopolis Americana: An Essay on the Golden Street of the Holy City.* Boston: B. Green, 1710.

Mather, Cotton. *"Triparadisus."* Unpublised manuscript. Edited by Reiner Smolinski. Decatur: University of Georgia Press, 1993.

Mather, Increase. *A Dissertation Concerning the Future Conversion of the Jewish Nation.* London: R. Tookey, 1709.

Mather, Increase. *The Mystery of Israel's Salvation, Explained and Applied: or, A Discourse Concerning the General Conversion of the Israelitish Nation.* London: John Allen, 1669.

Maton, Robert. *Israel's Redemption or the Propheticall History of our Saviours Kingdome on Earth; That is, Of the Church Catholicke, and Triumphant. With a discourse of Gog and Magog, or The Battle of the Great Day of God Almightie.* London: R. Cotes and Daniel Frere, 1642.

Mede, Joseph. *The Apostasy of the Latter Times; In which (according to divine prediction) the world should wonder after the Beast, the Mystery of Iniquity should so farre prevaile over the Mystery of Godlinesse, whorish Babylon over the virgin-Church of Christ . . . Or, The Gentiles Theology of Daemons, i.e. inferiour divine powers: Supposed to be mediators between God and man.* London: Samuel Man, 1641.

Mede, Joseph. *Clavis apocalyptica ex innatis et insitis visionum characteribus eruta et demonstrata. Ad eorum usum quibus deus amorem studiúmq[ue] indiderit prophetiam illam admirandam cognoscendi scrutandíque.* 1st ed. Cantabrigiae [Cambridge]: T. and J. Buck, 1627.

Mede, Joseph. *Clavis apocalyptica ex innatis et insitis visionum characteribus eruta et demonstrata. Ad eorum usum quibus deus amorem studiúmq[ue] indiderit prophetiam illam admirandam cognoscendi scrutandíque.* 2nd ed. Cantabrigiae [Cambridge]: Thom. Buck, 1632.

Mede, Joseph. *The key of the Revelation, searched and demonstrated out of the Naturall and proper Charecters of the Visions; With a Coment thereupon, according to the Rule of the same Key, published in Latine.* Translated by Richard More. 1st English ed. London: Phil Stephens, 1643.

Mede, Joseph. *Paraleipomena: Remaines on some Passages in the Revelation, Whereunto are added Severall Discourses concerning The Holinesse of Churches.* London: John Clarke, 1650.

Mede, Joseph. *A Translation of Mede's Clavis Apocalyptica.* Translated by Robert Bransby Cooper. London: Rivington, 1833.

Mede, Joseph. *The Works of the Pious and Profoundly-Learned Joseph Mede, B.D.* Edited by John Worthington. London: James Flesher for Richard Royston, 1664.

Merbecke, John. *A Booke of Notes and Common places, with their expositions, collected and gathered out of the Workes of divers singular Writers, and brought Alphabetically into order; A worke both profitable and also necessarie, to those that desire the true understanding & meaning of holy Scripture.* London: Thomas East, 1581.

Mok, Michael. "The War: Astounding 60 Hours." *Life Magazine* (16 June 1967): 33.

Morton, Thomas, of Berwick. *A Treatise of the Threefolde state of man.* London: Robert Dexter and Raph Jackeson, 1596.

Napier, John. *A Plaine Discouery of the whole Reuelation of Saint Iohn, set downe in two treatises: The one searching and proving the true interpretation thereof: The other applying the same paraphrastically and historically to the text.* Edinburgh: Robert Walde-Grave, 1593.

Newton, Isaac. *Observations upon the Prophecies of Daniel, and the Apocalypse of St. John, in two Parts.* London: J. Darby and T. Browne, 1733.

Nichol, Francis D. *The Midnight Cry: A Defense of the Character and Conduct of William Miller and the Millerites, Who Mistakenly Believed that the Second Coming of Christ would Take Place in the Year 1844.* 1944. Reprint, Brushton, NY: TEACH Services, 2000.

Nicholas, Edward [Menasseh ben-Israel?]. *An Apology for the Honorable Nation of the Jews, And all the Sons of Israel.* London: John Field, 1648/9.

Nicholas, Edward. *Apologia por La noble nacion de los Iudios y hijos de Israel* (Londres: E impresa en casa de Juan Field, 1649).

Noah, Mordecai Manuel. *Travels in England, France, Spain, and the Barbary States, in the years 1813–1814 and 15.* New York: Kirk and Mercein, 1819.

Owen, John, and Philip Nye. *A Declaration of the Faith and Order Owned and Practised in the Congregational Churches in England, Agreed Upon and Consented Unto by their Elders and Messengers in their Meeting at the Savoy, October 12, 1658.* London: J.P., 1659.

Paine, Thomas. *Common Sense,* in *Rights of Man; Common Sense; and Other Political Writings.* Edited by Mark Philip. 1776. Reprint, Oxford: Oxford University Press, 1995.

Peters, Hugh. *A word for the Armie. And two words to the kingdome: To Cleare the One, And Cure the Other.* London: M. Simmons and Giles Calvert, 1647.

Peyton, Edward. *The Divine Catastrophe of The Kingly Family of the House of Stuarts, or, A Short History of the Rise, Reign, and Ruine Thereof.* London: Giles Calvert, 1652.

Purchas, Samuel. *Purchas his Pilgrimage, or Relations of the World and the Religions Observed in All Ages and places discovered, from the Creation unto this Present.* London: Henrie Fetherstone, 1613.

Quarterly Journal of Prophecy. Review of *Remarks on a Letter on Subjects connected with the Lord's Humanity*, by J.N. Darby. *The Quarterly Journal of Prophecy* 1 (October 1848): 209.

Sandys, Sir Edwin. *A Relation of the State of Religion: and with what Hopes and Pollicies it hath beene framed, and is maintained in the severall States of these Westerne partes of the world.* London: Simon Waterson, 1605.

Sandys, George. *A Relation of a Journey begun An. Dom. 1610; Foure bookes, Containing a description of the Turkish Empire, of AEgypt, of the Holy Land, of the remote parts of Italy, and ilands adjoyning.* London: Richard Field for W: Barrett, 1615.

Scofield, Cyrus I. "The Grace of God." In *The Fundamentals: A Testimony to the Truth*, Vol. 11. Edited by R.A. Torrey and A.C. Dixon. Chicago: Testimony Publishing, 1920.

Scofield, Cyrus I., ed. *The Scofield Reference Bible: The Holy Bible Containing the Old and New Testaments, Authorized Version, with a New System of Connected Topical References to All the Greater Themes of Scripture, with Annotations, Revised Marginal Renderings, Summaries, Definitions, and Index, to which are added Helps at Hard Places, Explanations of Seeming Discrepancies, and a New System of Paragraphs.* New York: Oxford University Press, 1909.

Sewall, Samuel. *Phaenomena quaedam Apocalyptica ad Aspectum Novi Orbis configurata, or, some few Lines towards a description of the New Heaven As It makes to those who stand upon the New Earth.* Boston: Bartholomew Green and John Allen, 1697.

Strength out of Weakness, or A Glorious Manifestation Of the further Progresse of the Gospel amongst the Indians in New-England. London: John Blague and Samuel Howes, 1652.

Thomas, John. *The Coming Struggle Among the Nations of the Earth, Or, The Political Events of the Next Thirteen Years, Described in Accordance with Prophecies in Ezekiel, Daniel, and the Apocalypse.* Toronto: Thomas Maclear, 1853.

Thorowgood, Thomas. *Iewes in America, or, Probabilities that the Americans are of that Race; With the Removall of some contrary reasonings, and earnest desires for effectuall endeavours to make them Christian.* London: W.H., 1650.

Tillich, Paul. "Is There a Judeo-Christian Tradition?" *Judaism* 1:2 (1952): 106–9.

Tillich, Paul. *Against the Third Reich: Paul Tillich's Wartime Radio Broadcasts into Nazi Germany.* Edited by Ronald H. Stone and Matthew Lon Weaver. Louisville: Westminster John Knox Press, 1998.

De Tocqueville, Alexis. *Democracy in America. Translated by Arthur Goldhammer. 1835/1840.* Reprinted, New York: Library of America, 2004.

Turner, Frederick Jackson. "The Significance of the Frontier in American History." In *Rereading Frederick Jackson Turner*, edited by John Mack Faragher. New York: Henry Holt, 1994.

U.S. Congress. House. *Establishment of a National Home in Palestine: Hearings before the Committee on Foreign Affairs, House of Representatives, Sixty-Seventh Congress, Second Session, on H. Con. Res. 52 Expressing Satisfaction at the Re-Creation of Palestine as the National Home of the Jewish Race (April 18, 19, 20 and 21, 1922)*, Subcommittee of the House Committee on Foreign Affairs. Washington, U.S. Government Printing Office, 1922.

Utica Christian Magazine. "Of the return of the Jews to their own land in the Millennium; being a brief answer to the difficulties suggested in a piece written by the late Dr. Edwards, and republished in the U.C. Mag. Vol. II. No. 10." *The Utica Christian Magazine* 3:1 (July 1815): 37–38.

Wall, Moses. "Considerations Upon the Point of the Conversion of the Jewes." In Manasseh ben-Israel. *The Hope of Israel*. Translated by Moses Wall. 2nd ed. London: R. Ibbitson and Livewell Chapman, 1651.

Weinberger, Caspar W., and Ariel Sharon. "Memorandum of Understanding between Israel and the United States on Strategic Cooperation, Washington, 30 November 1981." In *The Major International Treaties of the Twentieth Century: A History and Guide with Texts, Vol. 1*. Edited by John Ashley Soames Grenville and Bernard Wasserstein. London: Routledge, 2001.

Wellcome, Isaac Cummings. *History of the Second Advent Message and Mission, Doctrine and People*. Boston: Advent Christian Publication Society, 1874.

Westminster Assembly (1643–1652). *The Humble Advice of the Assembly of Divines now by Authority of Parliament Sitting at Westminster, Concerning a Larger Catechism Presented by Them Lately to Both Houses of Parliament*. London and Edinburgh: Evan Tyler, 1647.

Whittingham, William, Théodore de Bèze, and John Calvin, eds. *The Newe Testament of Our Lord Jesus Christ: Conferred diligently with the Greke, and best approved translations*. Geneva: Conrad Badius, 1557.

Willet, Andrew. *Ecclesia Triumphans; that is, The Joy of the English Church, for the Happie Coronation of the most vertuous and pious Prince, James by the grace of God, King of England, Scotland, France, and Ireland*. (Cambridge: John Legat, 1603).

Willet, Andrew. *Hexapla: that is, A Six-Fold Commentarie upon the most Divine Epistle of the holy Apostle S. Paul to the Romanes*. Cambridge: Cantrell Legge, 1611.

Willet, Andrew. *Synopsis Papismi, that is, A Generall Viewe of Papistry; wherein the whole mysterie of iniquitie, and summe of Antichristian doctrine is set downe, which is maintained this day by the Synagogue of Rome, against the Church of Christ*. 1st ed. London: Thomas Man, 1592.

Williams, Roger. *The Bloudy Tenent, of Persecution, for cause of Conscience, discussed, in A Conference betweene Truth and Peace*. London, n.p., 1644.

Wilson, Thomas. *A Christian Dictionarie Opening the signification of the chiefe words dispersed generally through Holie Scriptures of the Old and New Testament, tending to increase Christian knowledge; Whereunto is annexed, a perticular Dictionary for the Revelation of S. Iohn, For the Canticles or Song of Salomon, For the Epistle to the Hebrues.* London: William Iaggard, 1612.

Winslow, Edward, ed. *The Glorious Progress of the Gospel amongst the Indians in New England Manifested by three Letters under the Hand of that famous instrument of the Lord, Mr. John Eliot, and another from Mr. Thomas Mayhew . . . both Preachers of the Word, as well to the English as Indians in New England.* London: Hannah Allen, 1649.

Winthrop, John. "A Model of Christian Charity." In *God's New Israel: Religious Interpretations of American History.* Edited by Conrad Cherry. 2nd ed. Chapel Hill: The University of North Carolina Press, 1998.

Witherby, Thomas. *An Attempt to Remove the Prejudices Concerning the Jewish Nation.* London: S. Couchman, 1804.

Witherby, Thomas. *Observations on Mr. Bicheno's Book, Entitled The Restoration of the Jews the Crisis of All Nations.* London: S. Couchman, 1800.

SECONDARY SOURCES
Books

Alexander, Edward, and Paul Bogdanor, eds. *The Jewish Divide over Israel: Accusers and Defenders.* New Brunswick, N.J.: Transaction, 2006.

Alter, Robert, and Frank Kermode, eds. *The Literary Guide to the Bible.* Cambridge, MA: Belknap / Harvard, 1987.

Anderson, Benedict. *Imagined Communities: Reflections on the Origin and Spread of Nationalism.* 2nd ed. London: Verso, 1991.

Anderson, Irvine H. *Biblical Interpretation and Middle East Policy: The Promised Land, America, and Israel, 1917–2002.* Gainesville: University Press of Florida, 2005.

Ariel, Yaakov S. *Evangelizing the Chosen People: Missions to the Jews in America, 1880–2000.* Chapel Hill: University of North Carolina Press, 2000.

Ariel, Yaakov S. *On Behalf of Israel: American Fundamentalist Attitudes toward Jews, Judaism, and Zionism, 1865–1945.* Brooklyn, NY: Carlson, 1991.

Ariel, Yaakov S. *Philosemites or Antisemites? Evangelical Christian Attitudes toward Jews, Judaism, and the State of Israel.* Analysis of Current Trends in Antisemitism 20. Jerusalem: Vidal Sassoon International Center for the Study of Antisemitism, 2002.

Armour, Rollin, Sr. *Islam, Christianity, and the West: A Troubled History.* Maryknoll: Orbis, 2002.

Ashton, Robert. *Counter-Revolution: The Second Civil War and its Origins, 1646–8.* New Haven: Yale University Press, 1994.

Ateek, Naim Stifan, Cedar Duaybis, and Maurine Tobin, eds. *Challenging Christian Zionism: Theology, Politics and the Israel-Palestine Conflict*. London: Melisende, 2005.

Bailey, Betty Jane, and J. Martin Bailey. *Who Are the Christians in the Middle East?* Grand Rapids: Eerdmans, 2003.

Baker, James A., and Lee H. Hamilton, eds. *The Iraq Study Group Report: The Way Forward—A New Approach*. New York: Vintage Books, 2006.

Bar-Yosef, Eitan. *The Holy Land in English Culture, 1799–1917: Palestine and the Question of Orientalism*. Oxford: Oxford University Press, 2005.

Benite, Zvi Ben-Dor. *The Ten Lost Tribes: A World History*. New York: Oxford University Press, 2009.

Barnes, Robin Bruce. *Prophecy and Gnosis: Apocalypticism in the Wake of the Lutheran Reformation*. Stanford: Stanford University Press, 1988.

Bauckham, Richard. *Tudor Apocalypse: Sixteenth Century Apocalypticism, Millenarianism and the English Reformation: From John Bale to John Foxe and Thomas Brightman*. Oxford: Sutton Courtenay Press, 1978.

Bebbington, David W. *Evangelicalism in Modern Britain: A History from the 1730s to the 1980s*. New York: Routledge, 1989.

Bebbington, David W. *The Dominance of Evangelicalism: The Age of Spurgeon and Moody*. Downers Grove, IL: InterVarsity, 2005.

Bercovitch, Sacvan. *The American Jeremiad*. Madison: University of Wisconsin Press, 1978.

Bercovitch, Sacvan. *The Puritan Origins of the American Self*. New Haven: Yale University Press, 1975.

Birch, Thomas, and Robert Folkestone Williams. *The Court and Times of James the First: Illustrated by Authentic and Confidential Letters, from Various Public and Private Collectionsv*. 2 vols. London: Henry Colburn, 1848.

Bloch, Ruth. *Visionary Republic: Millennial Themes in American Thought, 1756–1800*. Cambridge: Cambridge University Press, 1985.

Blumenthal, Max. *Republican Gomorrah: Inside the Movement that Shattered the Party*. New York: Nation, 2009.

Bodansky, Yossef. *The High Cost of Peace: How Washington's Middle East Policy Left America Vulnerable to Terrorism*. New York: Forum, 2002.

Boyer, Paul S. *When Time Shall Be No More: Prophecy Belief in Modern American Culture*. Cambridge, Mass.: Belknap Press of Harvard University Press, 1992.

Bozeman, Theodore Dwight. *To Live Ancient Lives: The Primitivist Dimension in Puritanism*. Chapel Hill: The University of North Carolina Press, 1988.

Brog, David. *Standing with Israel: Why Christians Support the Jewish State*. Lake Mary, FL: FrontLine, 2006.

Brown, Louise Fargo. *The Political Activities of the Baptists and Fifth Monarchy Men in England during the Interregnum*. Washington, D.C.: American Historical Association, 1913.

Bulliet, Richard W. *The Case for Islamo-Christian Civilization*. New York: Columbia University Press, 2004.

Burge, Gary M. *Whose Land? Whose Promise? What Christians Are Not Being Told about Israel and the Palestinians*. Cleveland: Pilgrim Press, 2003.

Butterfield, Herbert. *The Whig Interpretation of History*. 1931. *Reprinted*, New York: W.W. Norton, 1965.

Capp, Bernard S. *The Fifth Monarchy Men: A Study in Seventeenth-Century English Millenarianism*. London: Faber, 1972.

Case, Shirley Jackson. *The Millennial Hope: A Phase of War-Time Thinking*. Chicago: University of Chicago Press, 1918.

Chafets, Ze'ev. *A Match Made in Heaven: American Jews, Christian Zionists, and One Man's Exploration of the Weird and Wonderful Judeo-Evangelical Alliance*. New York: HarperCollins, 2007.

Chapman, Colin. *Whose Promised Land? The Continuing Crisis over Israel and Palestine*. 4th ed. Grand Rapids: Baker, 2002.

Christison, Kathleen. *Perceptions of Palestine: Their Influence on U.S. Middle East Policy*. Berkeley: University of California Press, 1999.

Cohen, Arthur A. *The Myth of the Judeo-Christian Tradition and Other Dissenting Essays*. New York: Harper & Row, 1970.

Cohn-Sherbok, Dan. *The Politics of Apocalypse: The History and Influence of Christian Zionism*. Oxford: Oneworld, 2006.

Coles, Paul. *The Ottoman Impact on Europe*. London: Thames & Hudson, 1968.

Coser, Lewis A. *Refugee Scholars in America: Their Impact and their Experiences*. New Haven, Conn.: Yale University Press, 1984.

Cox, Harvey. *Common Prayers: Faith, Family, and a Christian's Journey through the Jewish Year*. New York: Houghton Mifflin, 2001.

Clark, Victoria. *Allies for Armageddon: The Rise of Christian Zionism*. New Haven: Yale University Press, 2007.

Culver, Douglas J. *Albion and Ariel: British Puritanism and the Birth of Political Zionism*. New York: Peter Lang, 1995.

Cummings, Brian. *The Literary Culture of the Reformation: Grammar and Grace*. Oxford: Oxford University Press, 2007.

Dallmayr, Fred R., and Abbas Manoochehri, eds. *Civilizational Dialogue and Political Thought: Tehran Papers*. Lanham, MD: Lexington, 2007.

Daniel, Norman. *Islam and the West: The Making of an Image*. Revised ed. Oxford: OneWorld, 1993.

Davis, Moshe. *With Eyes toward Zion: Scholars Colloquium on America-Holy Land Studies*. New York: Arno, 1977.

Dawson, Michael. *Behind the Mule: Race and Class in African-American Politics*. Princeton: Princeton University Press, 1994.

DeBerg, Betty. *Ungodly Women: Gender and the First Wave of American Fundamentalism*. Philadelphia: Fortress Press, 1987.

Derounian-Stodola, Kathryn Zabelle, ed. *Women's Indian Captivity Narratives*. New York: Penguin, 1998.

Devine, Michael J., Robert P. Watson, and Robert J. Wolz, eds. *Israel and the Legacy of Harry S. Truman*. Kirksville, Mo.: Truman State University Press, 2008.

Ehle, Carl F., Jr. "Prolegomena to Christian Zionism in America: The Views of Increase Mather and William E. Blackstone Concerning the Doctrine of the Restoration of Israel." Ph.D. diss., New York University, 1977.

Ellis, Marc H. *Judaism Does Not Equal Israel: The Rebirth of the Jewish Prophetic*. New York: New Press, 2009.

Fink, Rueben. *America and Palestine: The Attitude of Official America and the American People toward the Rebuilding of Palestine as a Free and Democratic Jewish Commonwealth*. New York: American Zionist Emergency Council, 1944.

Finke, Roger, and Rodney Stark. *The Churching of America—1776–1990: Winners and Losers in Our Religious Economy*. New Brunswick: Rutgers University Press, 1992.

Fraser, Antonia. *Faith and Treason: The Story of the Gunpowder Plot*. New York: Random House, 1997.

Forbes, Bruce David, and Jeanne Halgren Kilde, eds. *Rapture, Revelation, and the End Times: Exploring the Left behind Series*. New York: Palgrave Macmillan, 2004.

Frykholm, Amy Johnson. *Rapture Culture: Left Behind in Evangelical America*. New York: Oxford University Press, 2004.

Fukuyama, Francis. *The End of History and the Last Man*. New York: Free Press, 1992.

Gadamer, Hans-Georg. *Truth and Method*. 2nd rev. ed. Translated by Joel Weinsheimer and Donald G. Marshall. New York: Continuum, 2002.

Gold, Dore. *Tower of Babble: How the United Nations has Fueled Global Chaos*. New York: Crown Forum, 2004.

Goldberg, Michelle. *Kingdom Coming: The Rise of Christian Nationalism*. New York: W.W. Norton, 2006.

Goldman, Shalom. *God's Sacred Tongue: Hebrew & the American Imagination*. Chapel Hill: University of North Carolina Press, 2004.

Goldman, Shalom. *Zeal for Zion: Christians, Jews, & the Idea of the Promised Land*. Chapel Hill: University of North Carolina Press, 2009.

Gorenberg, Gershom. *The End of Days: Fundamentalism and the Struggle for the Temple Mount*. New York: Free Press, 2000.

Glassman, David. *Anti-Semitic Stereotypes Without Jews: Images of the Jews in England 1290–1700*. Detroit: Wayne State University Press, 1975.

Glock, Charles Y., and Rodney Stark. *Christian Beliefs and Anti-Semitism*. New York: Harper & Row, 1966.

Goldhagen, Daniel Jonah. *Hitler's Willing Executioners: Ordinary Germans and the Holocaust*. New York: Vintage, 1997.

Grafton, David D. *Piety, Politics and Power: Lutherans Encountering Islam in the Middle East*. Eugene, Ore.: Pickwick, 2009.

Green, John C., James L. Guth, Corwin E. Smidt, and Lyman A. Kellstedt, eds. *Religion and the Culture Wars: Dispatches from the Front*. Lanham, MD.: Rowman & Littlefield, 1996.

Greenberg, Gershon. *The Holy Land in American Religious Thought, 1620–1948: The Symbiosis of American Religious Approaches to Scripture's Sacred Territory*. Lanham, MD: The University Press of America, 1994.

Grenz, Stanley J. *The Millennial Maze: Sorting Out Evangelical Options*. Downers Grove, Ill.: InterVarsity Press, 1992.

Grose, Peter. *Israel in the Mind of America*. New York: Knopf, 1983.

Haigh, Christopher. *English Reformations: Religion, Politics and Society under the Tudors*. Oxford: Oxford University Press, 1993.

Hall, Michael G. *The Last American Puritan: The Life of Increase Mather, 1639–1723*. Hanover, NH: University Press of New England / Wesleyan University Press, 1988.

Haller, William. *Foxe's Book of Martyrs and the Elect Nation*. London: J. Cape, 1963.

Halperin, David J. *Sabbatai Zevi: Testimonies to a Fallen Messiah*. Oxford: Littman Library of Jewish Civilization, 2007.

Halpern, Ben. *The Idea of the Jewish State*. Cambridge: Harvard University Press, 1961.

Halsell, Grace. *Prophecy and Politics: Militant Evangelists on the Road to Nuclear War*. Westport, CT: Lawrence Hill, 1986.

Hatch, Nathan O. *The Democratization of American Christianity*. New Haven: Yale University Press, 1989.

Hatch, Nathan O. *The Sacred Cause of Liberty: Republican Thought and the Millennium in Revolutionary New England*. New Haven: Yale University Press, 1977.

Haynes, Stephen R. *Reluctant Witnesses: Jews and the Christian Imagination*. Louisville: Westminster John Knox Press, 1995.

Hechler, William Henry, ed. *The Jerusalem Bishopric: Documents, with Translations*. London: Trübner & Co., 1883.

Herberg, Will. *Protestant-Catholic-Jew: An Essay in American Religious Sociology*. Garden City, N.Y.: Doubleday, 1955.

Hill, Christopher. *The Collected Essays of Christopher Hill, Vol. 2: Religion and Politics in Seventeenth-Century England*. Amherst: University of Massachusetts Press, 1985–1986.

Hillerbrand, Hans J. *The Division of Christendom: Christianity in the Sixteenth Century*. Louisville, KY: Westminster John Knox, 2007.

Hilton, Boyd. *The Age of Atonement: The Influence of Evangelicalism on Social and Economic Thought, 1785–1865*. Oxford: Clarendon, 1986.

Hofstadter, Richard. *The Paranoid Style in American Politics and Other Essays*. New York: Vintage, 1967.

Horsman, Reginald. *Race and Manifest Destiny: Origins of American Racial Anglo-Saxonism.* Cambridge: Harvard University Press, 1981.

Huhndorf, Shari M. *Going Native: Indians in the American Cultural Imagination.* Ithaca, NY: Cornell University Press, 2001.

Hunt, Michael H. *Ideology and U.S. Foreign Policy.* New Haven: Yale University Press, 1987.

Hunter, James Davison. *Culture Wars: The Struggle to Define America.* New York: Basic Books, 1992.

Huntington, Samuel P. *The Clash of Civilizations and the Remaking of World Order.* New York: Simon & Schuster, 1998.

Isaac, Jules. *The Teaching of Contempt: Christian Roots of Anti-Semitism.* New York: Holt, Rinehart and Winston, 1964.

Johnson, Paul. *A History of the Jews.* New York: Harper & Row, 1987.

Jordan, Winthrop D. *The White Man's Burden: Historical Origins of Racism in the United States.* New York: Oxford University Press, 1974.

Jue, Jeffrey K. *Heaven upon Earth: Joseph Mede (1586–1638) and the Legacy of Millenarianism.* Archives internationales d'histoire des idées, 194. Dordrecht, The Netherlands: Springer, 2006.

Kadir, Djelal. *Columbus and the Ends of the Earth: Europe's Prophetic Rhetoric as Conquering Ideology.* Berkeley: University of California Press, 1992.

Kean, Thomas H., and Lee H. Hamilton, co-chairs. *The 9/11 Commission Report: Final Report of the National Commission on Terrorist Attacks upon the United States.* New York: W.W. Norton, 2004.

Kennedy, Sheila Suess. *God and Country: America in Red and Blue.* Waco, TX: Baylor University Press, 2007.

Kidd, Thomas S. *American Christians and Islam: Evangelical Culture and Muslims from the Colonial Period to the Age of Terrorism.* Princeton: Princeton University Press, 2008.

Kiracofe, Clifford A. *Dark Crusade: Christian Zionism and U.S. Foreign Policy.* New York: I.B. Tauris, 2009.

Klieman, Aaron S., ed. *Cultivating an Awareness: America and the Holy Land,* American Zionism: A Documentary History, Vol. 1. New York: Garland, 1990.

Kobler, Franz. *Napoleon and the Jews.* New York: Schocken, 1976.

Koester, Craig R. *Revelation and the End of All Things.* Grand Rapids: Eerdmans, 2001.

Kushner, Tony, and Alisa Solomon, eds. *Wrestling with Zion: Progressive Jewish-American Responses to the Israeli-Palestinian Conflict.* New York: Grove, 2003.

Lahr, Angela M. *Millennial Dreams and Apocalyptic Nightmares: The Cold War Origins of Political Evangelicalism.* New York: Oxford University Press, 2007.

Larson, Edward J. *Summer for the Gods: The Scopes Trial and America's Continuing Debate over Science and Religion.* New York: Basic Books, 1997.

Lee, Peter David. "The Shaping of John Nelson Darby's Eschatology." PhD diss., University of Wales, Lampeter, 2010.

Levy, F.J. *Tudor Historical Thought. 1967.* Reprinted, Toronto: University of Toronto Press, 2004.

Lewis, Donald M. *The Origins of Christian Zionism: Lord Shaftesbury and Evangelical Support for a Jewish Homeland.* Cambridge: Cambridge University Press, 2010.

Little, Douglas. *American Orientalism: The United States and the Middle East since 1945.* Chapel Hill: University of North Carolina Press, 2002.

Marsden, George M. *Fundamentalism and American Culture.* 2nd ed. New York: Oxford University Press, 2006.

Marsden, George M. *Jonathan Edwards: A Life.* New Haven: Yale University Press, 2004.

Matar, Nabil. *Islam in Britain, 1558–1685.* Cambridge: Cambridge University Press, 1998.

Matar, Nabil. *Turks, Moors, and Englishmen in the Age of Discovery.* New York: Columbia University Press, 2000.

Mead, Walter Russell. *God and Gold: Britain, America, and the Making of the Modern World.* New York: Knopf, 2007.

Mearsheimer, John J., and Stephen M. Walt. *The Israel Lobby and U.S. Foreign Policy.* New York: Farrar, Straus and Giroux, 2007.

Melville, Herman. *White-Jacket, Or The World in a Man-of-War. 1850.* Oxford World's Classics. Reprinted, New York: Oxford University Press, 2000.

Merkley, Paul C. *American Presidents, Religion, and Israel: The Heirs of Cyrus.* Westport, CT: Praeger, 2004.

Merkley, Paul C. *Christian Attitudes towards the State of Israel.* Montreal: McGill-Queens University Press, 2001.

Merkley, Paul C. *The Politics of Christian Zionism, 1891–1948.* Portland, OR: Frank Cass, 1998.

Middlekauff, Robert. *The Mathers: Three Generations of Puritan Intellectuals, 1596–1728.* London: Oxford University Press, 1971.

Miller, Perry. *Errand into the Wilderness.* 1st ed. Cambridge: Harvard University Press, 1956.

Miller, Stuart Creighton. *Benevolent Assimilation: The American Conquest of the Philippines, 1899–1903.* New Haven: Yale University Press, 1982.

Moorhead, Jonathan David. "Jesus is Coming: The Life and Work of William E. Blackstone (1841–1935)." PhD diss., Dallas Theological Seminary, 2008.

Murphy, Andrew R. *Prodigal Nation: Moral Decline and Divine Punishment from New England to 9/11.* New York: Oxford University Press, 2009.

Noll, Mark A. *America's God: From Jonathan Edwards to Abraham Lincoln.* New York: Oxford University Press, 2002.

Noll, Mark A. *The Scandal of the Evangelical Mind.* Grand Rapids, MI: W.B. Eerdmans, 1994.

Novik, Nimrod. *The United States and Israel: Domestic Determinants of a Changing US Commitment.* Boulder, CO: Westview, 1986.

Oldys, William, and Thomas Park, eds. *The Harleian Miscellany: A Collection of scarce, curious, and entertaining pamphlets and tracts, as well in manuscript as in print. Selected from the library of Edward Harley, second Earl of Oxford.* 7 vols. London: White and Cochrane, and John Murray, 1811.

Oren, Michael B. *Power, Faith, and Fantasy: America in the Middle East: 1776 to the Present.* New York: W.W. Norton, 2007.

Pelikan, Jaroslav. *The Reformation of the Bible, The Bible of the Reformation.* New Haven: Yale University Press, 1996.

Posner, Sarah. *God's Profits: Faith, Fraud, and the Republican Crusade for Values Voters.* Sausalito, CA: Polipoint, 2008.

Qureshi, Emran, and Michael A. Sells, eds. *The New Crusades: Constructing the Muslim Enemy.* New York: Columbia University Press, 2003.

Raheb, Mitri. *I am a Palestinian Christian.* Minneapolis: Fortress, 2005.

Rogers, Philip G. *The Fifth Monarchy Men.* New York: Oxford University Press, 1966.

Rossing, Barbara R. *The Rapture Exposed: The Message of Hope in the Book of Revelation.* Boulder, Colo.: Westview, 2004.

Ryrie, Charles C. *Dispensationalism.* 2nd ed. Chicago: Moody, 2007.

Salaita, Steven. *Anti-Arab Racism in the USA: Where it Comes from and What it Means for Politics Today.* London: Pluto, 2006.

Sandeen, Ernest R. *The Roots of Fundamentalism: British & American Millenarianism, 1800–1930.* Chicago: University of Chicago Press, 1970.

Scholem, Gershom. *Sabbatai Sevi: The mystical Messiah, 1626–1676.* Princeton: Princeton University Press, 1973.

Scult, Mel. *Millennial Expectations and Jewish Liberties: A Study of the Efforts to Convert the Jews in Britain, Up to the Mid Nineteenth Century.* Leiden: Brill, 1978.

Segev, Tom. *Elvis in Jerusalem: Post-Zionism and the Americanization of Israel.* Translated by Haim Watzmann. New York: Owl Books, 2003.

Semmel, Stuart. *Napoleon and the British.* New Haven: Yale University Press, 2004.

Sennott, Charles M. *The Body and the Blood: The Holy Land's Christians at the Turn of a New Millennium.* New York: Public Affairs, 2001.

Setton, Kenneth M. *Western Hostility to Islam and Prophecies of Turkish Doom.* Philadelphia: American Philosophical Association, 1992.

Shaban, Fuad. *For Zion's Sake: The Judeo-Christian Tradition in American Culture.* London: Pluto, 2005.

Shuck, Glenn W. *Marks of the Beast: The Left Behind Novels and the Struggle for Evangelical Identity.* New York: New York University Press, 2005.

Silk, Mark. "Notes on the Judeo-Christian Tradition in America." *American Quarterly* 36:1 (Spring 1984): 65–85.

Silver, Peter. *Our Savage Neighbors: How Indian War Transformed Early America.* New York: W.W. Norton, 2008.

Sizer, Stephen. *Christian Zionism: Road-Map to Armageddon?* Leicester: InterVarsity Press, 2004.

Sizer, Stephen. *Zion's Christian Soldiers? The Bible, Israel and the Church.* Downers Grove, IL: InterVarsity, 2007.

Smith, Charles. *Palestine and the Arab-Israeli Conflict: A History with Documents.* 4th ed. Boston: Bedford/St. Martin's, 2001.

Smith, Robert C., and Richard Seltzer. *Contemporary Controversies and the American Racial Divide.* Lanham, MD: Rowman and Littlefield, 2000.

Smolinski, Reiner, ed. *The Threefold Paradise of Cotton Mather: An Edition of "Triparadisus."* Decatur: University of Georgia Press, 1993.

Sokolow, Nahum. *History of Zionism, 1600–1918.* 2 vols. London: Longmans, Green, and Co., 1919.

Southern, R.W. *Western Views of Islam in the Middle Ages.* Cambridge: Harvard University Press, 1962.

Spector, Stephen. *Evangelicals and Israel: The Story of American Christian Zionism.* New York: Oxford University Press, 2009.

Standaert, Michael. *Skipping towards Armageddon: The Politics and Propaganda of the Left Behind Novels and the LaHaye Empire.* Brooklyn, NY: Soft Skull, 2006.

Stark, Rodney, and Charles Y. Glock. *American Piety: The Nature of Religious Commitment.* Berkeley: University of California Press, 1968.

Sullivan, Shannon. *Revealing Whiteness: The Unconscious Habits of Racial Privilege.* Bloomington: Indiana University Press, 2006.

Strong, Pauline Turner. *Captive Selves, Captivating Others: The Practice and Representation of Captivity across Colonial Borders in North America.* Boulder, CO: Westview, 1988.

Tekiner, Roselle, Samir Abed Rabbo, and Norton Mezvinsky, eds. *Anti-Zionism: Analytical Reflections.* Brattleboro, VT: Amana, 1988.

Tolan, John V. *Saracens: Islam in the Medieval European Imagination.* New York: Columbia University Press, 2002.

Tuchman, Barbara W. *Bible and Sword: England and Palestine from the Bronze Age to Balfour.* 1956. Reprinted, New York: Ballantine, 1984.

Tuveson, Ernest Lee. *Redeemer Nation: The Idea of America's Millennial Role.* Chicago: University of Chicago Press, 1968.

Underwood, Grant. *The Millenarian World of Early Mormonism.* Urbana: University of Illinois Press, 1993.

Unger, Craig. *The Fall of the House of Bush: The Untold Story of How a Band of True Believers Seized the Executive Branch, Started the Iraq War, and Still Imperils America's Future.* New York: Simon & Schuster, 2007.

Vaughan, Alden T., and Edward W. Clark, eds. *Puritans among the Indians: Accounts of Captivity and Redemption, 1676–1724.* Cambridge, MA: Belknap, 1981.

Vitkus, Daniel J., ed. *Piracy, Slavery, and Redemption: Barbary Captivity Narratives from Early Modern England.* New York: Columbia University Press, 2001.

Wagner, Donald E. *Anxious for Armageddon: A Call to Partnership for Middle Eastern and Western Christians*. Scottdale, PA: Herald, 1995.

Wald, Kenneth D. *Religion and the Politics of the United States*. 4th ed. Lanham, MD: Rowman & Littlefield, 2003.

Walker, Williston, Richard A. Norris, David W. Lotz, and Robert T. Handy. *A History of the Christian Church*. 4th ed. New York: Scribner, 1985.

Walton, Hanes. *Invisible Politics: Black Political Behavior*. SUNY Series in Afro-American Society. Albany: State University of New York Press, 1985.

Weber, Timothy P. *Living in the Shadow of the Second Coming: American Premillennialism, 1875–1982*. 2nd ed. Chicago: University of Chicago Press, 1987.

Weber, Timothy P. *On the Road to Armageddon: How Evangelicals Became Israel's Best Friend*. Grand Rapids: Baker Academic, 2004.

Wilkinson, Paul Richard. *For Zion's Sake: Christian Zionism and the Role of John Nelson Darby*. Studies in Evangelical History and Thought. Milton Keynes: Paternoster, 2007.

Williamson, Hugh Ross. *The Gunpowder Plot*. New York: Macmillan, 1952.

Zakai, Avihu. *Exile and Kingdom: History and Apocalypse in the Puritan Migration to America*. Cambridge Studies in Early Modern and British History. Cambridge: Cambridge University Press, 1992.

Zebiri, Kate. *Muslims and Christians Face to Face*. Oxford: Oneworld, 1997.

ARTICLES AND CHAPTERS IN BOOKS

Achinstein, Sharon. "John Foxe and the Jews." *Renaissance Quarterly* 54:1 (Spring 2001): 86–120.

Ariel, Yaakov. "An American Initiative for a Jewish State: William Blackstone and the Petition of 1891." *Studies in Zionism* 10:2(1989): 125–37.

Ariel, Yaakov. "A Neglected Chapter in the History of Christian Zionism in America: William E. Blackstone and the Petition of 1916." In *Jews and Messianism in the Modern Era: Metaphor and Meaning*, edited by Jonathan Frankel. Studies in Contemporary Jewry 7. New York: Oxford University Press, 1991.

Ariel, Yaakov. "How Are Jews and Israel Portrayed in the Left Behind Series? A Historical Discussion of Jewish-Christian Relations." In *Rapture, Revelation and the End Times: Exploring the Left Behind Series*, edited by Bruce David Forbes and Jeanne Halgren Kilde. New York: Palgrave Macmillan, 2004.

Awad, Alex. "Christian Zionism: Their Theology, Our Nightmare!" In *Christian Zionism and Peace in the Holy Land*, Mennonite Central Committee Peace Office Newsletter 35:3 (July–September 2005: 2–4.

Ball, Bryan W. "Mede, Joseph (1586–1638)." In *Oxford Dictionary of National Biography*, edited by H.C.G. Matthew and Brian Harrison (Oxford: Oxford University Press, 2004); online edition, edited by Lawrence Goldman, January 2008, http://www.oxforddnb.com/view/article/18465 (accessed April 20, 2009).

Bar-Yosef, Eitan. "Christian Zionism and Victorian Culture." *Israel Studies* 8:2(2003): 18–44.

Beinart, Peter. "The Failure of the American Jewish Establishment." *New York Review of Books*, June 10, 2010.

Beinin, Joel. "The Israelization of American Middle East Policy Discourse." *Social Text*, 21:2 75 (Summer 2003): 125–139.

Bellah, Robert N. "Civil Religion in America." *Dædalus, Journal of the American Academy of Arts and Sciences* 96:1 (Winter 1967): 1–21.

Berkovitz, Jay R. "The French Revolution and the Jews: Assessing the Cultural Impact." *AJS Review* 20:1(1995): 25–86.

Bertlet, Chip. "The New Political Right in the United States: Reaction, Rollback, and Resentment." In *Confronting the New Conservatism: The Rise of the Right in America*, edited by Michael Thompson. New York: New York University Press, 2007.

Boyer, Paul S. "John Darby Meets Saddam Hussein: Foreign Policy and Bible Prophecy." *The Chronicle of Higher Education* 49:23 (14 February 2003, supplement), B10–B11.

Breger, Marshall J. "The Chosen Lobby." Review of *Jewish Power: Inside the American Jewish Establishment* by J.J. Goldberg, in *Commentary* 103:2 (Feb. 1997): 69.

Bull, Malcolm. "The Seventh-Day Adventists: Heretics of American Civil Religion." *Sociological Analysis* 50:2(1989): 177–87.

Charry, Ellen T. "Judaism." In *Global Dictionary of Theology: A Resource for the Worldwide Church*, edited by William A. Dyrness and Veli-Matti Kärkkäinen. Downers Grove, IL: IVP Academic, 2008.

Clouse, Robert. "The Apocalyptic Interpretation of Thomas Brightman and Joseph Mede." *Bulletin of the Evangelical Theological Society* 11:4 (Fall 1968): 181–93.

Cogley, Richard W. "The Fall of the Ottoman Empire and the Restoration of Israel in the 'Judeo-centric' Strand of Puritan Millenarianism." *Church History* 72:2 (June 2003): 304–32.

Cogley, Richard W. "John Eliot and the Millennium." *Religion and American Culture* 1:2 (Summer 1991): 227–50.

Cogley, Richard W. "'The Most Vile and Barbarous Nation of All the World': Giles Fletcher the Elder's 'The Tartars or, Ten Tribes' (Ca. 1610)." *Renaissance Quarterly* 58:3 (Fall 2005): 781–814.

Cogley, Richard W. "'Some Other Kinde of Being and Condition': The Controversy in Mid-Seventeenth-Century England over the Peopling of Ancient America," *Journal of the History of Ideas* 68:1 (January 2007): 35–56.

Collins, Adela Yarbro. "The Apocalypse (Revelation)." In *The New Jerome Biblical Commentary*, edited by Raymond E. Brown, Joseph A. Fitzmyer, and Roland E. Murphy. Englewood Cliffs, NJ: Prentice Hall, 1990.

Davis, Moshe. "Reflections on Harry S. Truman and the State of Israel." In *Truman and the American Commitment to Israel: A Thirtieth Anniversary Conference*. Edited by Moshe Ma'oz and Allen Weinstein. Jerusalem: Magnes Press, 1982.

Debré, S. "The Jews of France." *Jewish Quarterly Review* 3:3 (April 1891): 367–435.

Ehlers, Benjamin A. "Luther and English Apocalypticism: The Role of Luther in Three Seventeenth-Century Commentaries on the Book of Revelation." *Essays in History* 34 (1992), under http://etext.virginia.edu/journals/EH/EH34/ehlers34.html (accessed 5 Oct. 2008).

Epperson, Steven. "Dedicating and Consecrating the Land: Mormon Ritual Performance in Palestine," in *America and Zion: Essays and Papers in Memory of Moshe Davis*, ed. Eli Lederhendler and Jonathan D. Sarna (Detroit: Wayne State University Press, 2002): 91–116.

Erskine, Hazel. "The Polls: Western Partisanship in the Middle East." *The Public Opinion Quarterly* 33:4 (Winter 1969–1970): 627–40.

Finestein, Israel. "An Approach to a New Emphasis." In *Zionism in Transition*, edited by Moshe Davis. New York: Arno Press, 1980.

Fruchtman, Jack, Jr. "David and Goliath: Jewish Conversion and Philo-Semitism in Late-Eighteenth-Century English Millenarian Thought." In *Millenarianism and Messianism in Early Modern European Culture: The Millenarian Turn*, edited by J.E. Force and R.H. Popkin. Netherlands: Kluwer, 2001.

Frykholm, Amy. "Calculated Blessings: A Visit to John Hagee's Church." *The Christian Century* 125:20 (October 7, 2008): 35–7.

Fukuyama, Francis. "A Reply to My Critics." *The National Interest* 18 (Winter 1989): 21–28.

Fukuyama, Francis. "The End of History?" *The National Interest* 16 (Summer 1989): 3–18.

Gifford, Paul. "The Complex Provenance of Some Elements of African Pentecostal Theology." In *Between Babel and Pentecost: Transnational Pentecostalism in Africa and Latin America*, edited by André Corten and Ruth Marshall-Fratani. Bloomington: Indiana University Press, 2001.

Goldman, Shalom. "Christians and Zionism." *American Jewish History* 93:2 (June 2007): 245–60.

Green, John C. *The American Religious Landscape and Political Attitudes: A Baseline for 2004*. Under http://www.uakron.edu/bliss/docs/Religious_Landscape_2004.pdf (accessed February 16, 2009).

Griffin, Kenyon N., John C. Martin, and Oliver Walter. "Religious Roots and Rural Americans' Support for Israel during the October War." *Journal of Palestine Studies* 6:1 (Autumn 1976): 104–14.

Guth, James L., Cleveland R. Fraser, John C. Green, Lyman A. Kellstedt, and Corwin E. Smidt. "Religion and Foreign Policy Attitudes: The Case of Christian Zionism." In *Religion and the Culture Wars: Dispatches from the Front*, edited by John C. Green, James L. Guth, Corwin E. Smidt, and Lyman A. Kellstedt. Lanham, Md.: Rowman & Littlefield, 1996.

Guth, James L., John C. Green, Lyman A. Kellstedt, and Corwin E. Smidt. "Faith and Foreign Policy: A View from the Pews." *The Review of Faith and International Affairs* 3:2 (Fall 2005): 3–10.

Hafften, Ann E. "Challenge the Implications of 'Christian Zionism." *Journal of Lutheran Ethics* 5:5 (May 2005), under www.elca.org/jle.

Haija, Rammy M. "The Armageddon Lobby: Dispensationalist Christian Zionism and the Shaping of US Policy towards Israel-Palestine." *Holy Land Studies* 5 1(2006): 75–95.

Hatch, Nathan O. "The Origins of Civil Millennialism in America: New England Clergymen, War with France, and the Revolution." *The William and Mary Quarterly* 31:3 (July 1974): 407–30.

Henrich, Sarah, and James L. Boyce. "Martin Luther—Translations of Two Prefaces on Islam: Preface to the *Libellus de ritu et moribus Turcorum* (1530), and Preface to Bibliander's Edition of the Qur'ān (1543)." *Word & World* 16:2 (Spring 1996): 250–66.

Heal, Felicity. "Appropriating History: Catholic and Protestant Polemics and the National Past." *The Huntington Library Quarterly* 68:1/2, The Uses of History in Early Modern England (2005): 109–32.

Henriques, H. S. Q. "The Jews and the English Law. IV." *The Jewish Quarterly Review* 14:4 (July 1902): 653–97.

Henry, Patrick. "'And I Don't Care What It Is': The Tradition-History of a Civil Religion Proof-Text." *Journal of the American Academy of Religion* 49:1(1981): 35–49.

Hessayon, Ariel. Review of *Judaism without Jews: Philosemitism and Christian Polemic in Early Modern England*, by Eliane Glaser, *Reviews in History* 798, under http://www.history.ac.uk/reviews/review/798 (accessed 23 April 2010).

Hornstra, Wilrens L. "Western Restorationism and Christian Zionism: Germany as a Case Study." In *Christian Perspectives on the Israeli-Palestinian Conflict*, edited by Wesley H. Brown and Peter F. Penner. Schwarzenfeld, Germany: Neufeld Verlag, 2008.

Hubers, John. "Palestinians, Christian Zionists and the Good News Gospel." *Journal of Lutheran Ethics* 7:5 (May 2007), under www.elca.org/jle.

Hubers, John. "It is a Strange Thing: The Millennial Blindness of Christopher Columbus." *Missiology* 37:3 (July 2009): 333–53.

Hunt, Michael H. "Ideology," in "A Roundtable: Explaining the History of American Foreign Relations." *Journal of American History* 77 (June 1990): 108–15.

Huntington, Samuel P. "The Clash of Civilizations?" *Foreign Affairs* 72 :3 (Summer 1993): 22–49.

Hutton, Sarah. "The Appropriation of Joseph Mede: Millenarianism in the 1640s." In *Millenarianism and Messianism in Early Modern European Culture: The Millenarian Turn*, edited by J.E. Force and R.H. Popkin. Netherlands: Kluwer, 2001.

Isani, Mukhtar Ali. "Cotton Mather and the Orient." *New England Quarterly* 43 (March 1970): 46–58.

Isani, Mukhtar Ali. "The Growth of Sewall's 'Phaenomena Quaedam Apocalyptica.'" *Early American Literature* 7:1 (Spring 1972): 64–75.

Jowitt, Claire. "'The Consolation of Israel': Representations of Jewishness in the Writings of Gerrard Winstanley and William Everard." In *Winstanley and the Diggers, 1649–1999*, edited by Andrew Bradstock. London: Frank Cass, 2000.

Kaspi, Andre. "Jules Isaac and His Role in Jewish-Christian Relations." In *Jews, Catholics, and the Burden of History*, Studies in Contemporary Jewry 21, edited by Eli Lederhendler. New York: Oxford University Press, 2005.

Katz, David S. "Edmund Gayton's Anti-Jewish Poem Addressed to Menasseh Ben Israel, 1656," *The Jewish Quarterly Review*, New Series 71:4 (April 1981): 239–50.

Kidd, Colin. *The Forging of Races: Race and Scripture in the Protestant Atlantic World, 1600–2000*. Cambridge: Cambridge University Press, 2000.

Kiracofe, Clifford A., Jr. "Christian Zionism: A Foreign Policy Challenge." Unpublished paper delivered at the Palestine Center (Washington, D.C.), November 21, 2003.

Klieman, Aaron S., ed. *Cultivating an Awareness: America and the Holy Land*, American Zionism: A Documentary History, Vol. 1. New York: Garland, 1990.

Kohut, Andrew, John C. Green, Scott Keeter, and Robert C. Toth. *The Diminishing Divide: Religion's Changing Role in American Politics*. Washington, DC: Brookings Institution Press, 2000.

Lebeson, Anita Libman. "Zionism Comes to Chicago." In *Early History of Zionism in America*, Proceeding of the American Jewish Historical Society, edited by Isidore S. Meyer. 1958. Reprinted, New York: Arno Press, 1977.

Lewis, Bernard. "Rethinking the Middle East." *Foreign Affairs* 71:3 (Fall 1992): 99–119.

Lewis, Bernard. "The Roots of Muslim Rage." *Atlantic Monthly* 266:3 (September 1990): 47–60.

Littell, Franklin. "Reinhold Niebuhr and the Jewish People." *Holocaust and Genocide Studies* 6:1 (1991): 45–61.

Mandelbrote, Scott. "'A Duty of the Greatest Moment': Isaac Newton and the Writing of Biblical Criticism." *The British Journal for the History of Science* 26:3 (September 1993): 281–302.

Maaß, Enzo. "Forgotten Prophet: William Henry Hechler and the Rise of Political Zionism." *Nordisk Judaistik / Scandinavian Jewish Studies* 23:2(2002): 157–92.

Makdisi, Ussama. "Reclaiming the Land of the Bible: Missionaries, Secularism, and Evangelical Modernity." *American Historical Review* 102:3 (June 1997): 680–713.

Marsden, George. "Defining Fundamentalism." *Christian Scholar's Review* 1:2 (Winter 1971): 141–51.

Matar, Nabil. "The Idea of the Restoration of the Jews in English Protestant Thought: From the Reformation until 1660." *The Durham University Journal* 78 (December 1985): 23–36.

Matar, Nabil. "The Idea of the Restoration of the Jews in English Protestant Thought, 1661–1701." *Harvard Theological Review* 78:1–2 (1985): 115–48.

Matar, Nabil. "The Controversy over the Restoration of the Jews in English Protestant Thought: 1701–1753." *The Durham University Journal* 80 (1988): 241–56.

Matar, Nabil. "The Controversy over the Restoration of the Jews: From 1754 until the London Society for Promoting Christianity Among the Jews." *The Durham University Journal* 87 (1990): 29–44.

Matar, Nabil. "Milton and the Idea of the Restoration of the Jews." *Studies in English Literature, 1500–1900* 27:1 (Winter, 1987): 109–24.

McKenzie, Brian D. "Polling Data and Black Religious Opinion on Middle East Concerns." *The Review of Faith & International Affairs* 6:1 (Spring 2008): 27–36

McLaren, Anne. "Gender, Religion, and Early Modern Nationalism: Elizabeth I, Mary Queen of Scots, and the Genesis of English Anti-Catholicism." *American Historical Review* 107:3 (June 2002): 739–67.

Maclear, J. F. "New England and the Fifth Monarchy: The Quest for the Millennium in Early American Puritanism." *The William and Mary Quarterly* 32:2 (April 1975): 223–60.

Mead, Walter Russell. "God's Country?" *Foreign Affairs* 85:5 (Sept./Oct. 2006): 24–43.

Mead, Walter Russell. "The New Israel and the Old." *Foreign Affairs* 84:4 (July/Aug. 2008): 28–46.

Mearsheimer, John, and Stephen Walt. "The Israel Lobby." *London Review of Books* (March 23, 2006): 3–12.

Metzger, Bruce M. "The Geneva Bible of 1560." *Theology Today* 17:3 (Oct. 1960): 339–52.

Mitchell, W.J.T. "Holy Landscape: Israel, Palestine, and the American Wilderness." *Critical Inquiry* 26:2 (Winter 2000): 193–223.

Moore, LeRoy, Jr. "Another Look at Fundamentalism: A Response to Ernest R. Sandeen." *Church History* 37:2 (June 1968): 195–202.

Morselli, Marco. "Jules Isaac and the Origins of *Nostra Aetate*," in Nostra Aetate: *Origins, Promulgation, Impact on Jewish-Catholic Relations*, edited by Uri Bialer and Neville Lamdan. Berlin: LIT Verlag Münster, 2005.

Moruzzi, Norma Claire. "Strange Bedfellows: The Question of Lawrence Oliphant's Christian Zionism," *Modern Judaism* 26:1 (February 2006): 55–73.

Mueller, Janel. "The Mastery of Decorum: Politics as Poetry in Milton's Sonnets." *Critical Inquiry* 13:3, Politics and Poetic Value (Spring 1987): 475–508.

Niebuhr, H. Richard. "Fundamentalism." In *Encyclopaedia of Social Sciences*, edited by Edwin Robert Anderson Seligman and Alvin Saunders Johnson. New York: Macmillan, 1937.

Obenzinger, Hilton. "In the Shadow of 'God's Sun-Dial': The Construction of American Christian Zionism and the Blackstone Memorial." *Stanford Electronic Humanities Review* 5:1 (Feb. 1996), under http://www.stanford.edu/group/SHR/5-1/text/obenzinger.html (accessed September 25, 2012).

Osterman, Nathan. "The Controversy over the Proposed Readmission of the Jews to England (1655)." *Jewish Social Studies* 3:3 (July 1941): 301–28.

Parker, Geoffrey. "The Place of Tudor England in the Messianic Vision of Philip II of Spain: The Prothero Lecture." *Transactions of the Royal Historical Society*, Sixth Series 12 (2002): 167–221.

Popkin, Jeremy D. "Zionism and the Enlightenment: The 'Letter of a Jew to His Brethren,'" *Jewish Social Studies* 43:2 (Spring 1981): 113–20.

Popkin, Richard H. "David Levi, Anglo-Jewish Theologian." *The Jewish Quarterly Review, New Series* 87:1/2 (July–Oct. 1996): 79–101.

Popkin, Richard H. "Newton and the Origins of Fundamentalism." In *The Scientific Enterprise*, edited by Edna Ullmann-Margalit. Dordrecht: Kluwer, 1992.

Popkin, Richard H. "Newton and Fundamentalism, II." In *Essays on the Context, Nature, and Influence of Isaac Newton's Theology*, edited by James E. Force and Richard H. Popkin. Dordecht, The Netherlands: Kluwer, 1990.

Prest, Wilfred R. "The Dialectical Origins of Finch's Law." *The Cambridge Law Journal* 36:2 (Nov. 1977): 326–52.

Prest, Wilfred R. "The Published Writings of Sir Henry Finch." *Notes and Queries* CCXXII (Dec. 1977): 501–3.

Rabb, Theodore K. "The Stirrings of the 1590s and the Return of the Jews to England." *Transactions of the Jewish Historical Society of England* 26 (1974–1978): 26–36.

Rogers, Stephanie Stidham. "American Protestant Pilgrimage: Nineteenth-Century Impressions of Palestine." *Koinonia* 15:1(2003): 60–80.

Ruether, Rosemary Radford. "Christian Zionism is a Heresy." *Journal of Theology for Southern Africa* 69 (December 1989): 60–64.

Sandeen, Ernest R. "Defining Fundamentalism: A Reply to Professor Marsden." *Christian Scholar's Review* 1:3 (Spring 1971): 227–33.

Sandeen, Ernest R. "Toward a Historical Interpretation of the Origins of Fundamentalism." *Church History* 36:1 (March 1967): 66–83.

Schoeni, Marc. "The Roots of Christian Zionism." *Theological Review* 26:1(2005): 3–38.

Shulim, Joseph J. "Napoleon I as the Jewish Messiah: Some Contemporary Conceptions in Virginia." *Jewish Social Studies* 7:3 (July 1945): 275–80.

Silk, Mark. "Notes on the Judeo-Christian Tradition in America." *American Quarterly* 36:1 (Spring 1984): 65–85.

Skillen, James W. "Evangelicals and American Exceptionalism." *The Review of Faith & International Affairs* 4:3 (Winter 2006): 45–46.

Smith, R. Drew. "Black Denominational Responses to U.S.-Middle East Policy since 9/11." *The Review of Faith & International Affairs* 6:1 (Spring 2008): 1–3.

Smith, Robert O. "Between Restoration & Liberation: Theopolitical Contributions & Responses to U.S. Foreign Policy in Israel/Palestine." *Journal of Church and State* 46:4 (Autumn 2004): 833–60.

Smith, Robert O. "Luther, the Turks and Islam." *Currents in Theology & Mission* 34:5 (October 2007): 351–64.

Smith, Robert O. "Toward a Lutheran Response to Christian Zionism." *dialog: A Journal of Theology* 48:3 (Fall 2009): 281–93.

Smolinski, Reiner. "Caveat Emptor: Pre- and Postmillennialism in the Late Reformation Period." In *Millenarianism and Messianism in Early Modern European Culture: Volume III, The Millenarian Turn: Millenarian Contexts of Science, Politics and Everyday Anglo-American Life in the Seventeenth and Eighteenth Centuries*, edited by James E. Force and Richard H. Popkin (Dordecht: Kluwer, 2001).

Smolinski, Reiner. "*Israel Redivivus*: The Eschatological Limits of Puritan Typology in New England." *The New England Quarterly* 63:3(1990): 357–95.

Snobelen, Stephen. "'The Mystery of this Restitution of All Things': Isaac Newton and the Return of the Jews." In *Millenarianism and Messianism in Early Modern European Culture: The Millenarian Turn*, edited by J.E. Force and R.H. Popkin (Netharlands: Kluwer, 2001).

Stark, Rodney. "Bringing Theory Back In." In *Rational Choice Theory and Religion: Summary and Assessment*, edited by Lawrence E. Young. New York: Routledge, 1997.

Stein, Stephen J. "A Notebook on the Apocalypse by Jonathan Edwards." *William and Mary Quarterly*, 29:4 (October 1972): 623–34.

Stockton, Ronald R. "Christian Zionism: Prophecy and Public Opinion." *Middle East Journal* 41:2 (Spring 1987): 234–53.

Sweet, Leonard I. "Christopher Columbus and the Millennial Vision of the New World." *The Catholic Historical Review* 72:3 (July 1986): 369–82.

Tillich, Paul "Is There a Judeo-Christian Tradition?" *Judaism* 1:2(1952): 106–9.

Toon, Peter. "The Question of Jewish Immigration." In *Puritans, the Millennium and the Future of Israel: Puritan Eschatology, 1600 to 1660: A Collection of Essays*, edited by Peter Toon. Cambridge: James Clarke, 1970.

Trigano, Shmuel. "The French Revolution and the Jews." *Modern Judaism* 10:2 (May 1990): 171–90.

Van der Wall, Ernestine G.E. "A Philo-Semitic Millenarian on the Reconciliation of Jews and Christians: Henry Jessey and his 'The Glory and Salvation of Jehudah and Israel' (1650)." In *Skeptics, Millenarians and Jews*, edited by David S. Katz and Jonathan I. Israel. The Netherlands: Brill, 1990.

West, Delno C. "Medieval Ideas of Apocalyptic Mission and the Early Franciscans in Mexico and the Americas." *The Americas* 45:3 (Jan. 1989): 293–313.

Westfall, Richard S. "Isaac Newton." In *Science and Religion: A Historical Introduction*, edited by Gary B. Ferngren. Baltimore, MD: Johns Hopkins University Press, 2002.

Williamson, Arthur H. "'A Pil for Pork-Eaters': Ethnic Identity, Apocalyptic Promise and the Strange Creation of the Judeo-Scots." In *The Expulsion of the Jews: 1492 and After*, edited by R.B. Waddington and A.H. Williamson. New York: Garland, 1994.

Williamson, Arthur H. "Britain and the Beast: The Apocalypse and the Seventeenth-Century Debate about the Creation of the British State." In *Millenarianism and Messianism in Early Modern European Culture: The Millenarian Turn*, edited by J.E. Force and R.H. Popkin. Netherlands: Kluwer, 2001.

Williamson, Arthur H. "Latter-Day Judah, Latter-Israel: The Millennium, the Jews, and the British Future." In *Chiliasmus in Deutschland und England im 17. Jahrhundert*, edited by Klaus Deppermann, et al. Göttingen: Vanderhoeck & Ruprecht, 1988.

Wilcox, Clyde, Sharon Linzey, and Ted G. Jelen. "Reluctant Warriors: Premillennialism and Politics in the Moral Majority." *Journal for the Scientific Study of Religion* 30:3 (Sept. 1991): 245–58.

Younan, Munib. "An Ethical Critique of Christian Zionism." *Journal of Lutheran Ethics* 7:5 (May 2007), under www.elca.org/jle.

Zebiri, Kate. "Muslim Perceptions of Christianity and the West." In *Islamic Interpretations of Christianity*, edited by Lloyd V.J. Ridgeon. New York: St. Martin's Press, 2000.

Index

Adams, John, 144
America. *See* United States of America
American Board of Commissioners for
  Foreign Mission (ABCFM), 177
American Indians
  in American racial thought,
    127–9, 132
  as Lost Tribes of Israel, 108, 123,
    138, 147
  Mede on, 129–30
  Latter-Day Saints on, 147, 148
  and Palestinians, 178–9
  U.S. policy toward, 43, 128
  See also French and Indian Wars
American Israel Public Affairs
  Committee (AIPAC), 1
Americanism, 2, 9, 139
  See also Nationalism
Antichrist
  Blackstone on, 172, 173
  Catholicism as, 12, 56, 63, 70, 73, 82,
    121, 134
  and Christian eschatology, 12, 23, 90,
    92, 101, 114, 145, 179
  Darby on, 154
  John Calvin on, 53–54
  Martin Luther on, 49–50, 52–53
  Melanchthon on, 53

Napoleon as, 144–5
Pope as, 6, 49, 53, 65, 101
Pope and Turk as two heads of,
  49–50, 53–54, 55, 57, 127
United States as, 150
See also Turko-Catholic threat
Anti-Defamation League (ADL), 14,
  19, 31
Armey, Richard (Dick), 1, 8

Bacon, Francis, 83, 182
Bale, John, 55–59, 61–63, 64, 66,
  72, 79, 92, 96, 115, 120, 187,
  213 n.58
  and the Catholic Church,
    56–57, 63
  and English nationalism, 61–63
  and Judeo-centrism, 57–58, 63, 64
  See also John Foxe
Balfour Declaration (1917), 3, 4, 177,
  178, 192
Balfour, Lord Arthur, 114
Barak, Ehud, 12
Barbary Pirates, 17, 127–8, 144, 172
Barth, Karl, 171
Bauer, Gary, 1, 31, 38
Bernard, Richard, 98
Bèza, Theodore, 55, 79